MAMMALIAN
REPRODUCTIVE
BIOLOGY

MAMMALIAN REPRODUCTIVE BIOLOGY

—

F. H. Bronson

The University of Chicago Press
Chicago and London

F. H. Bronson is professor of zoology and director of the
Institute of Reproductive Biology at the University of Texas,
Austin.

The University of Chicago Press, Chicago 60637
The University of Chicago Press, Ltd., London
© 1989 by The University of Chicago
All rights reserved. Published 1989
Printed in the United States of America

98 97 96 95 94 93 92 91 90 89 54321

Library of Congress Cataloging-in-Publication Data
Bronson, F. H.
    Mammalian reproductive biology / F. H. Bronson.
        p.   cm.
    Bibliography: p.
    Includes index.
    ISBN 0-226-07558-3 (alk. paper).—ISBN 0-226-07559-1 (pbk. :
alk. paper)
    1. Mammals—Reproduction.   I. Title.
QL739.2.B76   1989
599'.016—dc20   89-5033
                                                                    CIP

Contents

Order Chiroptera
Order Primates
Order Cetacea
Order Artiodactyla
Conclusions

Preface

The concern of this book is with the way a mammal's reproduction is regulated by its environment. A full appreciation of this phenomenon requires an honest blending of ecological and physiological principles with no overwhelming bias in either direction. Broad interdisciplinary efforts generate two kinds of problems. First, of necessity, each of the disciplines to be blended must be treated somewhat superficially. Thus, mainstream physiologists and mainstream ecologists both may wonder why their particular interests have been treated more lightly here than they might prefer. The reason is obvious, of course, if they think about it. Second, dealing with more than one discipline greatly expands the relevant literature. There is a truly immense literature now in both reproductive physiology and reproductive ecology. The literature of these two areas prior to mid-1987 is reasonably well represented in this book. References noted after that time were collected hit or miss.

Finally, some acknowledgments are in order. The major thrust of this book has been to provide a conceptual framework within which our knowledge about mammalian reproductive biology can be organized. One does not arrive at one's broad concepts in isolation. A large number of graduate students, postdoctoral fellows, colleagues, and early mentors have influenced the way I view reproductive biology. These include Jack Christian, Art Coquelin, Dave Davis, Claude Desjardins, Paul Heideman, Judy Manning, Fred Marsteller, Joel Maruniak, Mike Menaker, Glenn Perrigo, Emilie Rissman, Milt Stetson, Fred vom Saal, Mal Whitsett, and Wes Whitten. As importantly, on a more technical level, three people have greatly aided my scientific effort over the past several years, and I owe them much: Shirley Beckwith, Kimberly Hoskins, and Reese Vaughn.

1

Mammals: Strategies and Perspectives

About 250 million years ago, one or more identifiable mammalian forms emerged from the therapsid reptiles. At this time, the world's land masses were connected to form the single continent Pangaea. The dominant vertebrates were fish and reptiles; the age of the amphibians had already passed. We know little about these early mammals. The few for which fossil evidence exists were only about 10 cm in length and weighed perhaps 20g or 30g. In general body form they resembled our modern shrews. These archaic mammals had a particularly large olfactory apparatus, suggesting a strong dependence on the sense of smell and possibly a nocturnal habit. They may or may not have been egg layers like their reptilian ancestors.

By 200 million years ago, Pangaea was breaking up to form Laurasia and Gondwanaland. The dominant terrestrial life forms were the dinosaurs. The radiation of birds began in earnest about this time, and according to Eisenberg (1981) the three major groups of modern mammals with their three different modes of reproduction were already present in recognizable form. These are the egg-laying prototherians, the marsupials, and the eutherians.

The reproductive characteristics of the marsupials and eutherians include a period of development in the uterus and, after birth, lactational nurturing by the mother until some degree of independence is attained. The marsupials differ from the eutherians in many ways, but most obvious is the marsupial's abbreviated period of gestation and, correlatively, minimal placentation.

Diversification of the marsupials and eutherians accelerated when Laurasia and Gondwanaland began to break up about 135 million years ago. This fragmented and isolated the existing stocks of mammals. All our modern orders of mammals were established during or before this time.

About 65 million years ago, the marsupials and eutherians experienced almost explosive radiation. This was correlated with the decline of the reptiles, but the relation between these two events remains uncertain. Within a few tens of millions of years our modern families and genera of mammals were all established.

Mammalian diversification and speciation proceeded rapidly until the current niches in the habitable parts of the world were filled, after which these processes slowed precipitously. Most of our modern species of mammals have existed in readily recognizable forms for 1 or 2 million years now. The geographic populations composing a species have a much more ephemeral history.

From a purely taxonomic perspective, the result of this 250-million-year course of events is today's fascinating assemblage of mammals. There are innumerable populations of these animals grouped by taxonomists, mostly on morphological grounds, into somewhat over four thousand species. Only remnants remain of the prototherians: three species of monotremes living in Australia. About 6 percent of today's mammalian species are marsupials. Most of these are confined to Australia, its surrounding islands, and South America. The other 94 percent are eutherians that enjoy a worldwide distribution.

According to Vaughan (1978), over 40 percent of today's mammalian species are rodents, and over 20 percent are bats. Thus, almost two-thirds of today's mammals are one of these two kinds. In descending order of numerical importance, the insectivores come next, followed by the carnivores, the even-toed ungulates, the primates, and the rabbits and hares of the order Lagomorpha. The marsupials and these seven orders of eutherians account for about 96 percent of all living mammals.

Strategies

Taxonomic classification based on morphology becomes a truly dynamic subject when it is combined with a concern for similarities and dissimilarities between life-history strategies (Stearns 1976). There are aquatic, fossorial, terrestrial, arboreal, and flying mammals and every conceivable gradation in between. In these different modes of existence, mammals may specialize in finding and consuming foods as diverse as plankton, crustaceans, insects, mollusks, all kinds of vertebrate flesh, and a variety of plant parts, including leaves, tubers, fruits, nectar, pollen, gum, and flowers. Alternatively, they may be true omnivores. There are short-lived and long-lived mammals. Just in terms of body size, at one extreme are the great baleen whales that graze on plankton, while at the other extreme are some of the insectivores and insectivorous bats that weigh only a few grams.

By one classification these many variations combine to yield over fifty different mammalian niches (Eisenberg 1981). These niches, in turn, are found in almost every conceivable habitat from the equator to the polar regions. Each niche in each habitat presents a different set of physical and biological challenges that must be surmounted. When viewed on a global scale then, the rich diversity of life-history strategies to be found in mammals is readily apparent. Likewise, the reproductive strategies of mammals are intriguingly diverse (e.g., May and Rubenstein 1984).

The age at which a female mammal experiences the pubertal ovulation can vary from less than 2 weeks to well over a decade. Ovulation may or may not be a cyclical event in mammals. When it is cyclical, this cycle can vary from a few days to well over a month. In the absence of pregnancy, these cycles can reoccur every few days or only once a year. Sometimes they are regulated seasonally, and sometimes not. Sometimes males remain reproductively capable throughout the year, while females do not. Sometimes seasonal reproduction is enforced by photoperiodic cuing; sometimes it is not. Ovulation can be induced or spontaneous, and copulation may or may not be dependent on preconditioning by the gonadal steroids.

The mating systems of mammals range from lifelong monogamy, through a stereotyped polygyny or polyandry that lasts for one or more breeding seasons, to chance meetings between two individuals during which copulation occurs. Gestation can vary from less than 2 weeks to almost 2 years. Some species employ embryonic diapause to lengthen gestation; others do not. Sometimes there is a postpartum estrus, and sometimes not. Some mammalian offspring are born totally helpless and weighing only a few milligrams, while others are born in a highly precocial state and weighing hundreds of kilograms. Sometimes fathers help in caring for the newborn; often it is left just to the mother. Sometimes older siblings help, sometimes not.

Is there such a thing as a typical mammal or a typical mammalian reproductive strategy? Only if *typical* means *most common*. In that sense, the "median mammal" probably would be a terrestrial rodent that is heavily preyed on by other vertebrates. As a consequence, its life expectancy would be measured in months, and it would have undergone intense selection to maximize its reproductive potential.

Our hypothetical rodent would mature quickly, and thereafter it would rapidly and repeatedly produce large litters of young unless prevented from doing so by adverse environmental conditions. It would be a spontaneous ovulator. It would be somewhat larger than the domestic rat (Eisenberg 1978), and it would spent most of its time finding and consuming plant parts, but it would eat insects when available. Finally, it would live in the tropics. Four to five times as many species of mammals exist in the tropics as are found throughout the rest of the world.

Perspectives

The concept of a median mammal is interesting, but probably of little value. Indeed, it is probably a harmful concept because it obscures the wonderful diversity that exists in this class of animals. The same can be said about the people who study mammalian reproduction. The concept of a "median reproductive biologist" has as little value as the concept of a median mammal. Scientists interested in mammalian reproduction differ markedly in their backgrounds, their methods, and their motivations for studying this subject.

To some scientists the concept of a reproductive strategy is foreign; to others it is the only facet of reproduction worthy of concern. To some the term *reproduction* translates only as the concentration of a hormone in the blood, or as the concentration of a hormone receptor in a cell, or in the way a neuronal network is organized developmentally to allow either the secretion of gonadotropin or complex sexual behavior. To other scientists the term *reproduction* is simply a number that must balance a population's rate of mortality.

Most of what we know about mammalian reproduction stems from the efforts of ecologists and endocrine physiologists. The field of mammalian reproductive endocrinology began in earnest early in this century, when anatomists first began to query the function of the pituitary and gonads. With the realization that the reproductive organs were actually under neural control, reproductive endocrinology became progressively more oriented toward regulatory pathways in the brain. With the passage of time, this subdiscipline also became first more biochemically oriented and later more molecularly oriented.

Our knowledge about the physiology of reproduction is now almost staggering in its magnitude and elegance of detail (see Knobil and Neill 1988). The major driving force for the collection of this knowledge, however, always has been the need for information that can be applied clinically to humans or to animals that are of agricultural import. This has given this field a uniquely practical bias unlike that associated with the study of any other group of organisms.

Mainstream mammalian reproductive physiologists tend to specialize. They usually focus on a limited dimension of the reproductive process of one sex, and they usually use only one domesticated stock of mammal as their model for understanding this dimension. They are guided traditionally by the absolute need for rigorous experimental proof. This is one of the great strengths of this discipline, but, correlatively, reproductive physiologists are sometimes impatient with broad biological concerns for which such proof is difficult or impossible to obtain.

Ecologists have been working for about the same number of decades to develop an equally impressive, but different, body of knowledge about the reproduction of wild mammals living in wild habitats. The classic mammalogists of the middle decades of this century produced a multitude of papers dealing with the natural history of individual populations of mammals. Included in most of these papers was information about whatever reproductive characteristics could be measured under field conditions and about correlations between changes in these characteristics and whatever environmental variation could be assessed. Thus, along with the need to improve livestock production, and the trailblazing efforts of a few physiologists, arose our modern concern for the regulation of reproduction by ambient cues.

The ecologists' focus traditionally is on wild populations in wild habitats. This often necessitates the acceptance of correlational evidence as adequate, something that is anathema to the traditional physiologist. The overwhelming strength of mammalian ecology is its capacity to visualize the way diverse forces interact on a grand evolutionary scale and thus to provide a meaningful framework for organizing all kinds of information, physiological and otherwise. Its weakness is an impatience with mechanical concerns.

The study of mammalian ecology has changed dramatically in the last two decades. It has matured and become integrated with the larger and more theoretically oriented field of population biology. It has also become more experimental and more sophisticated. We have witnessed many attempts now to manipulate natural populations of mammals experimentally and many other attempts to study mammals in seminatural confines where one can better isolate the natural forces that influence them. Often such efforts are made to test complex hypotheses that are globally important in biology, and many of these hypotheses relate specifically to reproductive performance. Still missing in most cases, however, is genuine concern for the physiological bases of the phenomena that are being observed.

A third group of researchers deserves mention here because they also have contributed much to our knowledge of mammalian reproduction. These are behaviorists, mostly trained in psychology or anthropology rather than ethology. In regard to the former, a concentrated interest in the endocrine and neural substrates underlying sexual behavior began to appear in the literature in the 1940s. Originally dominated by laboratory studies with the domestic rat, this well-populated field has evolved in the last two decades to include a concern for many other mammals and many other dimensions of the relation between hormones and behavior. With regard to anthropologists, our knowledge of primate reproductive strategies in the wild would be almost nonexistent without the efforts of these workers.

While ecologists, physiologists, and behaviorists each have contributed much to our knowledge of reproduction, these disciplines remain poorly integrated in their perspectives of it. This is reflected repeatedly in the many reviews that appear each year on this subject. Each tends to focus on a limited dimension of the process of reproduction without much concern for other perspectives. Lost in this process is a richness of principles that emerges when one takes a more integrative approach. There really are some universally important principles associated with mammalian reproduction, and it behooves all of us to be aware of these "great truths." The general objective of this book is to develop a broader and more integrative view of mammalian reproduction, thereby revealing some of these important principles.

The specific concerns of this book will include natural selection, genes, reproductive strategies, the actions of domestication, diet, a mammal's physical environment, social cues, neural pathways, the organization of the reproduction system, endocrine functions and interactions, gamete production, behavior, and variation. All these concerns are linked in their relation to reproduction, and the objective here is to focus on these linkages.

Obviously, a central theme is necessary to organize such a broad spread of interests. To satisfy this need, the core concern here will be with the interface between the mammal's reproductive substrate and its environment. If one defines a mammal's environment broadly to include social as well as physical and dietary factors, and if one visualizes this interface as extending through time both within and between generations, it provides an excellent framework for integrating many of the diverse concerns noted above. In general, then, the perspective here will be that of the physiological ecologist or that of the ecologically oriented physiologist.

2

Environmental Regulation:
Some General Principles

The diverse environmental factors that can influence a mammal's reproductive performance can be classified as either dietary, physical, or social in origin. How the mammal actually reacts to these factors depends on a horde of variables, including its species, its sex, its own unique genetic makeup, and its reproductive state at the moment of concern.

To establish some general principles about environmental regulation, we will focus here on just one reproductive event—the onset of fertility. This is an event of major importance for the well-being of a mammalian population (Cole 1954), and it is an event that has attracted much attention in reproductive physiology (Donovan and van der Werff ten Bosch 1965; Foxcroft 1978; Ramaley 1979; Levasseur and Thibault 1980; Foster 1980; Reiter and Grumbach 1982; Ojeda, Aguado, and Smith 1983; Bronson and Rissman 1986).

By way of background then, several facts about puberty are obvious. For one, the average age at which this event occurs often differs between the two sexes, and it may vary greatly between populations, even of the same species. Furthermore, it can vary markedly between individuals, even when these individuals are of the same sex and even when they belong to the same population. It is self-evident that genic action underlies all facets of pubertal development, at least at some level, and that genetic differences must account for some proportion of the variation in timing that exists among individuals, sexes, and populations. It is also well established that a variety of environmental factors can influence reproductive development, and thus some proportion of the total variation must reflect these influences as well. The first problem at hand then is to organize our knowledge about genes and environmental factors within the frame-

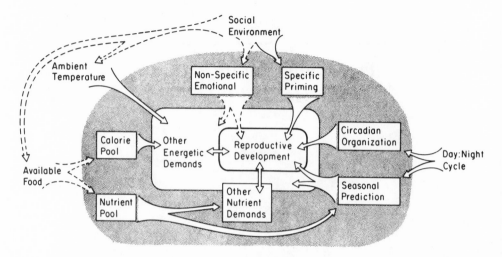

Figure 2.1. The environmental regulation of reproductive development in mammals. The environmental factors known to be of major importance are shown outside the stippled area, while their internal interactions are shown inside the stippled area. As will be discussed shortly in relation to figure 2.3, obviously "adaptive" pathways are shown as solid lines; those readily influenced by chance experiences are represented by dashed lines. Adapted from Bronson (1985).

work of a scheme that deals with their interaction. We will start by considering environmental input, as it affects individuals.

Environmental Regulation of Fertility Onset

Figure 2.1 illustrates the kinds of environmental factors that are known to influence reproductive development in mammals and thus the age at which they become fertile (see Sadleir 1969; Bronson and Rissman 1986). Not all mammals are subject to regulation by all these factors, but many are.

Most basic here is the amount and quality of available food, whether it is obtained in the form of milk from the mother or by the weaned juvenile while it is foraging. Food availability, ambient temperature, and, to a lesser extent, humidity interact to determine an individual's rate of growth, and thus indirectly these factors determine its rate of reproductive development. Reproductive and nonreproductive development must be synchronized. Internally, we can functionally divide assimilated food into its energetic and nutritional components (the latter including water), something that will be explored in considerable detail in a later chapter.

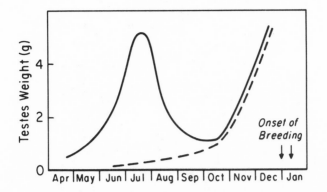

Figure 2.2. Change in the weight of the testes in a wild population of European hares (*Lepus europaeus*) in Scotland. The solid line indicates the average testes weight of males born early in the breeding season, while the dashed line represents the average testes weight of males born late in the breeding season. The latter delay reproductive development until the next breeding season. Redrawn from Lincoln and MacKinnon (1976).

Many mammals live in environments that change seasonally. In such situations, it is often advantageous to reproduce during only part of the year and, correlatively, sometimes to delay the onset of fertility until the following breeding season (e.g., fig. 2.2). Some mammals do so strictly in response to dietary and climatic conditions; others opt to use a reliable predictor of the expected seasonal changes in these conditions. Photoperiod is often used in this manner, at least in the temperate zone, but at least one secondary plant compound obtained while foraging can serve the same function on a more short-term basis. Photoperiod also entrains the circadian organization that permeates most reproductive processes in mammals, pubertal and otherwise.

The social environment influences reproductive development in many ways. An individual's mother is its source of food and warmth prior to weaning. Also prior to weaning, the young mammal's siblings, if there are any, provide insulation, and, simultaneously, they compete with it for warmth and food. These factors act indirectly on pubertal development by affecting growth. After weaning, the young mammal's social environment can be an important source of more directly acting pheromonal and tactile cues that regulate (i.e., prime) specific reproductive processes such as the first ovulation. Finally, many social situations provoke complex emotional states like arousal or stress. These can influence reproductive development in an indirect manner.

All the factors shown in figure 2.1 will be discussed in great

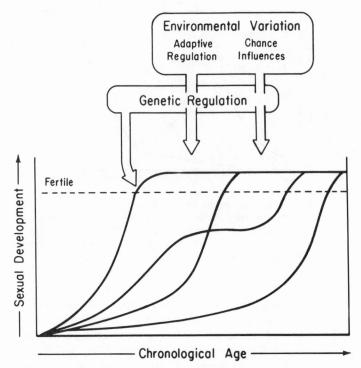

Figure 2.3. A theoretical scheme dealing with the ways that genes and environmental variation interact to influence reproductive development. The lower part of this figure suggests great *potential* variation in the rate at which a mammal matures reproductively. Four possible patterns of development are shown. One of these patterns, the earliest possible rate of reproductive development, is conceptualized as being rigidly limited by an individual's genes. The other patterns result from environmental interventions. These interventions are conceptualized here as being of two kinds, both operating through each individual's own unique genetic makeup, however (see text). Adapted from Bronson and Rissman (1986).

detail later. For now it is sufficient simply to introduce and enumerate these factors and thus to indicate generally the large array of environmental influences that can potentially alter a young mammal's rate of reproductive development.

Genes and Environmental Factors

The end product of natural selection is a complement of alleles. How can one visualize the way these alleles interact with environmental factors to regulate fertility onset in an individual mammal? The scheme proposed in figure 2.3 suggests that each individual inherits the potential for experiencing many different temporal patterns of reproductive development (see Donovan and van der Werff ten Bosch 1965). The fastest development of the reproductive axis itself, and hence the earliest possible onset of fertility, must be limited rigidly by genes and probably in relation to some dimension of somatic development rather than chronological age per se. The genetic limitations on the earliest possible development of each of the component parts of this axis, and their immediate neural and endocrine controls, must constitute the most direct action of genes on the timing of puberty.

As conceptualized in figure 2.3, however, the genetically limited, earliest possible onset of fertility is usually only a theoretical construct. Except under rare, utopian conditions that will be noted later, most individuals do not achieve their fastest possible rate of reproductive maturation. Varying degrees of delay occur because of environmental intervention. These interventions can exert their impact either pre- or postnatally, and they need not be deceleratory in nature. Acceleratory interventions can occur, and they can antagonize deceleratory actions, but they can never overcome the earliest limits dictated by an individual's genes.

As suggested in figure 2.3, the interactions between genes and environmental factors that are important for fertility onset can be functionally dichotomized. First, natural selection can provide specific pathways by way of which discrete environmental cues can act to regulate pubertal processes for obviously adaptive purposes. Seasonal regulation via photoperiod and more acute regulation via specific pheromonal and tactile cues are good examples of this need. Both types of regulation involve complex signaling systems that link specific external cues with specific neuroendocrine responses to fulfill needs placed on the mammal by its physical, dietary, or social environment. These are genetically programmed pathways that require triggering by specific environmental cues.

Second, most of the genes of concern here probably will act still more indirectly, manifesting themselves only as broad potentials that are subject to the whim of chance environmental forces. These will be genes that have been fixed for purposes not related directly to fertility onset but that allow secondary regulation of reproductive development anyhow. As an example, the position of a rodent fetus in the uterus, relative to neighboring male fetuses, allows a greater or lesser degree of masculinization and thus indirectly influences the timing of puberty (e.g., vom Saal, Pryor, and Bronson 1981). Position in the uterus is a randomly determined process, and the evolutionary concerns here relate to the need of these short-lived individuals to produce large numbers of offspring rather than to the specific control of either masculinization or the timing of fertility onset.

The relation between body growth and fertility onset is particularly interesting in regard to the scheme shown in figure 2.3 since in females it reflects both adaptive and chance forces at work. As will be discussed in detail later, it is adaptive for a female not to ovulate until she has achieved a particular body size, but her size in relation to her age is the end result of a horde of chance experiences occurring throughout her prepubertal existence.

Individual mothers vary in the quality of their maternal behavior, for example, and they vary in their ability to provide excess quantities of milk even under the constant conditions of the laboratory. Experimentally, such variation has been traced in laboratory rats (*Rattus norvegicus*) directly to the lactating female's genes, to her neonatal experiences, to her prior maternal experiences, and to her present emotional state (e.g., Denenberg, Ottinger, and Stephens 1962; Morton, Denenberg, and Zarrow 1963; for an example of such effects in another rodent, see also Clark and Galef 1981).

The various experiential factors interact with each other and with the mother's genes to determine the quality of her maternal care (see Daly 1973). In the wild, the result is further influenced by the climatic and dietary challenges that the lactating female faces both in the nest and while foraging for food. The result of all this can be great variation that is randomly felt at the level of the individual offspring.

Also prior to weaning, if the mammal of concern produces its offspring in litters rather than by individual births, some litters are larger than others, and some individuals in a litter may achieve an early advantage in their competition for milk and warmth (Leon and Woodside 1983). Their faster growth rate allows them physically to dominate their littermates, thereby exaggerating such differences. The result is still more variation in the growth rate of individuals— up to 25 percent as assessed at weaning in inbred laboratory mice (*Mus domesticus*), even in the constant confines of the laboratory (F. H. Bronson, unpublished data). After weaning, the nature of the dietary challenges facing the young mammal can vary immensely from individual to individual, depending on the characteristics of the habitats in which they live. Food is distributed in patches in most habitats. Some individuals find and exploit rich patches; others are not so lucky.

In general then, the developing mammal is subject to many potential sources of variation, starting while it is in the uterus and continuing throughout its life. These sources of variation are randomly applied to individuals. Cumulatively, they influence the rate of growth of these individuals, and hence, indirectly, they all cumulate to influence the rate of reproductive development.

In summary, the scheme shown in figure 2.3 suggests that all facets of pubertal development are controlled by genes and that the genes of concern can act at one of at least three levels of directness. The result is a genetically programmed yet environmentally susceptible and thus stochastic process whose limits vary from individual to individual. It is important to note, however, that this scheme finds neither support nor lack of it in the genetic literature.

It is unfortunate that classical geneticists have not concerned themselves with the developmental pathways used by genes to regulate puberty. The geneticists' concern with reproductive development usually has been with the heritability of a single trait—the time of fertility onset—and, for economic purposes, how to alter this trait by selection. Heritability is estimated by determining the relative amount of additive versus nonadditive variance in a population. The former is that fraction of the total variance that is amenable to change by selection, and the latter includes all the remaining variance, whether genetic or environmental. This dichotomy obviously is poorly related to the actions of genes that are postulated in figure 2.3.

In the absence of a better way, the scheme proposed here seems like a reasonable way of viewing the question of how genes regulate reproductive development in individual mammals.

Sex Differences

Evolutionary biologists often view the two sexes as if they were different species entirely (e.g., Trivers 1972; Jewell 1976). We expect pubertal strategies to differ routinely between the sexes, even within the same population, simply because the evolutionary forces that act on this stage of development differ in relation to sex. These forces are best visualized for the female as an interaction between three basic influences.

First, there will be a drive by natural selection to accelerate the onset of fertility, thereby increasing the probability that the female's alleles will be passed on before death intervenes. This must be a particularly potent factor in smaller mammals, most of whom have short life expectancies. Antagonizing this influence will be another drive ensuring that reproduction will not occur before all supporting physiological systems have developed adequately. A third important drive should ensure that reproduction will occur only in harmony with extant environmental conditions. The female's survival could be jeopardized, and her reproductive effort wasted, if she were to achieve fertility and risk pregnancy and lactation either before she was ready physiologically or when there was no chance of success because of adverse environmental conditions.

While females compete with each other for the food and nesting

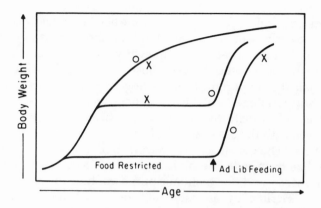

Figure 2.4. Age and body weight at which male (X) and female (O) rodents achieve fertility when their body growth is either allowed to proceed uninterrupted or stopped at one of two body weights. In the latter case, the animals are maintained at one of these two body weights by restricting their food intake until much later when ad lib feeding is resumed (arrow) and the animals experience "catch-up" growth. The generalized results shown here are modeled after data obtained in laboratory rats and mice by Hamilton and Bronson (1985, 1986). Reprinted from Bronson and Rissman (1986).

resources necessary to sustain pregnancy and lactation, males compete with each other mostly just for mates. Sometimes males compete for breeding territories, but in general they are not as resource oriented in their competition as females. The drive to accelerate puberty will be antagonized in males by the need to gain social experience and body size.

Reproductive success for the typical male mammal, who is polygynous, is determined by his ability to dominate other individuals physically as much as it is by his ability to produce sperm and seminal fluids. Most red deer (*Cervus elaphus*) bucks in Scotland, for example, are physiologically capable of mating when a year and a half old, but few do so until about 5 years of age, after they have achieved both the body size and the experience necessary to dominate other males and establish a harem (Lincoln 1971; Clutton-Brock, Guinness, and Albon 1982). This same phenomenon has been documented repeatedly now in many marine mammals that mate and give birth on shore (e.g., Cox and LeBoeuf 1977).

Different strategies for the two sexes are easily seen in figure 2.4, which examines the relation between food availability, body growth, and reproductive development as determined in the laboratory for domestic stocks of house mice and Norway rats. Under the utopian conditions of the laboratory, both sexes of these small mammals achieve functional fertility at about the same age, males perhaps a little later. In the experimental paradigm shown in figure 2.4, however, rats or mice are allowed to grow normally only until a particular stage of development, at which time further growth is inhibited by restricting the amount of food available to them. Sometime later, when the animals are again allowed unlimited access to food, they experience rapid "catch-up" growth (e.g., Widdowson, Mavor, and McCance 1964; Williams, Tanner, and Hughes 1974).

Both sexes cease reproductive development if growth is stopped early during somatic development. When ad lib feeding is resumed, females achieve their first ovulation in a few days, but males require much longer to achieve functional reproductive maturity. When maintained at a somewhat higher body weight, females again cease reproductive development, but males maintained at this weight become sexually mature despite their lack of further growth (Jean-Faucher et al. 1982; Hamilton and Bronson 1985, 1986).

Presumably, figure 2.4 reflects the way the two sexes of the wild ancestors of these domesticated rodents resolved a particular set of problems encountered during their evolution. That is, this figure appears to show two different strategies for balancing the length of the gametic cycle against two other factors: short life expectancy and the difference in investment required for successful reproduction on the part of the two sexes. Many small mammals in the wild face quite short life expectancies (e.g., weeks or a few months). Furthermore, they must be prepared to abandon body growth during dispersal from their natal environs, a hazardous phenomenon quite common in small mammals (Lidicker 1975).

Females, with their much shorter gametic cycles, can proceed rapidly through the final stages of reproductive development when a new home with resources sufficient to support pregnancy and lactation has been found. The spermatogenic cycle of a male is several weeks in length, however, and to initiate it only after a new home has been found would be tantamount to genetic suicide. Many individuals would exceed their life expectancy before becoming fertile. Thus, natural selection has yielded different strategies for the two sexes. In these rodents, the final stages of reproductive development proceed largely independently of growth in the male, but they are dependent on growth in the female.

While this particular sex-related difference in strategies probably is common among small, short-lived mammals, it certainly is not universal either in such animals or in mammals as a whole. As noted in the preceding chapter, the class Mammalia is a collection of greatly diverse populations, and these populations face a huge diversity of environmental challenges. Different challenges often call for different sex-related strategies.

The pubertal strategy of the red kangaroo (*Megalis rufa*), for example, is somewhat the reverse of that seen in figure 2.4. This marsupial is well adapted to the semiarid regions of Australia. According to Frith and Sharman (1964), females in New South Wales achieve their first ovulation several months before males become fertile, at least on the average. Both sexes achieve fertility earlier when living in regions characterized by good rainfall and abundant food and later in poorer regions, but the difference between males and females apparently remains more or less constant. Why it is advantageous for females of this particular species to precede males in achieving fertility in this locale is unknown (for other such examples, see Georgiadis 1985).

Population Differences

The cui (*Galea musteloides*) is a hystricomorph rodent living in South America. It is related to the guinea pig. Some young cuis can ovulate, mate, and become pregnant when only 9 days old (Weir 1970). In contrast, many larger mammals require years to mature. The human requires over a decade. Often such variation is conceptualized simply by labeling the cui an r-strategist and the human a K-strategist (Pianka 1976): r and K are mathematical components of the logistic growth curve, referring to the population's potential rate of growth and the carrying capacity of the habitat, respectively.

K-strategists view their environment as stable and highly predictable, while r-strategists view their surroundings as unstable and unpredictable. K-strategists, being selected for competitive ability in a saturated environment, tend to be large, long-lived animals that can afford to have long, well-spaced, reproductive cycles, during which only a few young are produced. These young are born in an altricial state, and they require a long time to mature and become fertile. In contrast, r-strategists tend to be small, short-lived animals that rapidly and repeatedly produce large litters of precocial young who can quickly mature and achieve fertility.

The r versus K dichotomy is an interesting and useful conceptualization of mammalian reproductive strategies, but one must acknowledge its limitations. First, these are relative terms. That is, a particular mammal is an r- or a K-strategist only relative to another mammal, not in an absolute sense. Members of the order Carnivora have modest life spans. They are r-strategists relative to humans, but they are K-strategists relative to cuis. Second, there is far too much variation in the class Mammalia to dichotomize it in any really meaningful way, and this is particularly true for the age of fertility onset. Trying to divide the pubertal strategies of mammals into only two camps obscures a great deal of fascinating diversity.

Some of this diversity can be seen in figure 2.5. This figure compares the time at which the first and last female in a population achieve fertility in relation to average life expectancy. At one extreme is a population of deermice (*Peromyscus maniculatus*) living in the seasonally harsh climate of Michigan. These small mammals have a mean life expectancy at birth of only 18 weeks (Howard 1949). This short life expectancy is balanced by a potential for rapid reproductive development, followed by the continual production of large numbers of young.

Females in this particular population of deermice experience their first ovulation anywhere from 5 to 25 weeks of age, depending in part on whether they are born early or late in the 7-month breeding season. Females born early in the breeding season proceed rapidly with their sexual development. They achieve maturity and reproduce during the same breeding season in which they were born. Most die before the following breeding season. Most females born late in the breeding season, when winter is approaching, cease reproductive development at a prepubertal stage and overwinter in that condition. The survivors of this late-born cohort compose most of the breeding population the following spring.

In terms of absolute time then, the deermice in this Michigan population achieve puberty rapidly—in 1–6 months. When viewed in terms of life span, however, the average female deermouse in Michigan actually passes through its pubertal transition relatively late in life. In fact, it probably dies before becoming fertile.

Deermice are broadly distributed on the North American continent, and not all populations of this species exhibit the same pubertal strategy. In marked contrast to the Michigan population is another population of the same species living 1,600 miles to the northwest near Great Slave Lake in the Northwest Territories. Here winter is so prolonged that the dietary and climatic window during which reproduction is possible is only 2 or 3 months in length. All the deermice born in this population delay maturation until the following year, when the few survivors achieve puberty and breed more or less simultaneously (Fuller 1969). Since most adults fail to survive their second winter, the phenomenon of seasonal breeding in this population is almost exclusively the result of the seasonal regulation of puberty. Again, however, the average female dies before achieving the onset of fertility.

The same high degree of synchrony seen in deermice living near Great Slave Lake can be found in humans in the United States and in domestic rats in the laboratory (fig. 2.5), but in all three cases for entirely different reasons. The cultural evolution of humans promotes living indoors in environments that are relatively constant, in terms

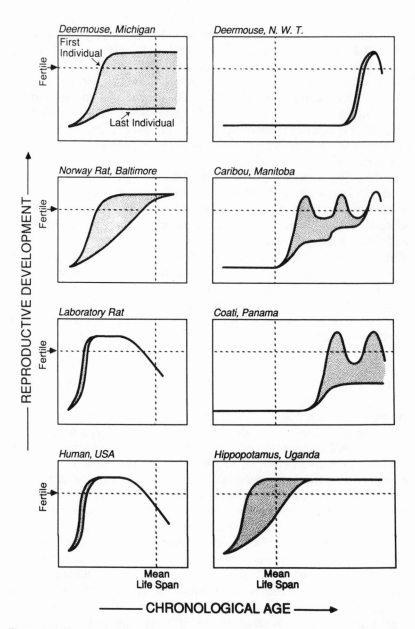

Figure 2.5. Variation in the age at which the first and last females in each of eight populations achieve fertility in relation to the mean life span of the population. Modeled after data extracted from Dauphine (1976), Davis (1953), Fuller (1969), Howard (1949), Laws and Clough (1966), Russell (1982), and Tanner (1962).

of both diet and climate. Our low reproductive rate is sufficient to balance an average life span that is measured in decades. This allows prolonged parental care, which in turn allows a greatly delayed and prolonged puberty as measured in absolute time.

Even under optimal conditions, the human female does not begin to ovulate until between the ages of 11 and 14 years (Tanner 1962), after which she still experiences a period of adolescent sterility during which ovulation can be infrequent (see Ford and Beach 1952; Short 1976). Even so, when viewed relative to life span, the pubertal transition of human females actually is completed quite early in life and with relatively little variation between individuals. Indeed, so early in life do we achieve puberty that we can "afford" evolutionarily to undergo reproductive senescence later in life.

The domestic rat lives in a utopian laboratory environment where a period of only a few days separates the time at which the first and last females in a cohort experience their pubertal ovulations. In the absence of predation, the life expectancy at birth of these pampered animals is well beyond 2 years. Thus, rats in the laboratory also have time to become reproductively senescent. The result is the same relation between onset of fertility and life span that exists in the human; only the absolute time parameter is different.

The wild counterpart of the domestic rat, the Norway rat (*Rattus norvegicus*), usually is found in the relatively constant environments of man's residences, farm outbuildings, and commercial establishments. In Baltimore, most of these animals achieve puberty and reproduce successfully before they die because there are few seasonal limits on their maturation and because they have an average life span of several months (Davis 1953). Considerable variation still can be seen in the timing of puberty among individual rats, however, because of the randomly acting factors noted earlier.

Again emphasizing that there is nothing sacrosanct about the taxon called a species, Norway rats living in a garbage dump outside Nome, Alaska, are decidedly seasonal in their breeding (Schiller 1956). Consequently, the pattern of variation in fertility onset in relation to life span in this population actually resembles that shown by deermice living in Michigan rather than that shown by their own species in Baltimore.

An interesting variation in pubertal strategies was recorded by Dauphine (1976) in a population of barren ground caribou (*Rangifer tarandus*) living in the Northwest Territories and northern Manitoba. These large animals live in a seasonally harsh climate, where they show only a short, sharp breeding season, followed each year by the birth of single calves. Only one in four of these young calves survives to the next breeding season, however. Of the few that do survive, most achieve their pubertal ovulation and become pregnant during their third year of life, a few during the second and fourth years. After maturity, they experience what can be visualized as a seasonally recurring puberty (see Karsch and Foster 1981). Survival is much improved once these caribou reach their second year, and thus the continual year-after-year production of single calves by a few surviving individuals allows the population to withstand the high mortality they experience early in life. Many marine mammals exhibit this same kind of strategy (e.g., Nazarenko 1975).

A somewhat similar strategy found in a mammal having a shorter maximum life span was seen in the coati (*Nasua narica*) population studied in Panama by Russell (1982). Like many tropical mammals, these coati experience seasonal changes in food availability (fruits and small animals) because of seasonal variation in rainfall. Furthermore, the amount of rainfall can vary somewhat from year to year, thereby resulting in a poor food supply in some years. When this happens, young coati do not mature reproductively, and even the adults fail to reproduce. This would seem to be a tenuous existence for animals with a relatively modest life span, but their continuing existence is testimony to the soundness of this strategy.

Still in relation to figure 2.5, the population of hippopotami (*Hippopotamus amphibius*) studied by Laws and Clough (1966) near the equator in Uganda is not subject to great seasonal variation. Thus, the individuals in this population can and do breed at any time of the year. They are relatively long lived; an occasional animal exceeds 40 years of age. The mortality they suffer is distributed much more evenly over these years than it is in caribou. The average age of fertility onset in this hippopotamus population is about 9 years, but there are several years of variation on either side of this mean. The resulting pattern of fertility onset in relation to life span is superficially like that of the Baltimore rat population, only shifted to a later part of the life cycle and with a different scale of time. The cause of the large variation in the time of fertility onset in this hippopotamus population is not known.

In general then, figure 2.5 illustrates several different strategies for timing the onset of fertility in females in relation to average life span. Considering the great variety of niches and habitats exploited by mammals, the variation suggested in this figure indeed must be only a very small fraction of that which actually exists in this class of animals. Certainly, in most populations there will also be sex-related differences in pubertal strategies. Furthermore, as will be discussed later, in some cases the unit of interest in mammals is a subset of animals in a population rather than the population or the species. In other words, even a single population can contain multiple strategies for regulating fertility onset.

Before leaving population-level considerations, one more facet of this subject deserves comment. It is self-evident that the time of fertility onset must be well correlated with all the other elements in a mammal's reproductive and life-history strategies. When viewing mammals as a whole, however, the two factors that seem best correlated with the timing of fertility onset are life span and body size. These two factors of course are often well correlated with each other, particularly if one ignores the bats and some of the hibernators in some of the other orders.

It is easy to measure the body size of a wild mammal but hard to measure its life expectancy. In part for that reason, and in part simply because of the obvious constraints placed on the rate of reproductive development by body size, there is a rich literature relating body size and fertility onset in mammals. An entrée into this literature can be gained by reading Stearns (1983), Caughley and Krebs (1983), Western (1983), May and Rubenstein (1984), and Reiss (1985).

The emphasis in this chapter has been placed on life span rather than body size—both because it is a more unique approach (see Begon 1985; Harvey and Zammuto 1985) and because it seems more reasonable biologically. The one thing that the process of reproduction must accomplish at the population level is to balance mortality. Otherwise, the population becomes extinct. Thus, this is not an argument against a concern for body size, only an argument for a variable that is equally or probably more important, even if difficult to measure.

Natural Selection versus Domestication

The major thrust of this book is to explore the way a mammal's external environment regulates its reproductive substrate. The fascinating results of this kind of regulation are best seen in wild mammals living in wild habitats, but its physiological details have been explored mostly by studying domestic stocks in carefully controlled environments. Indeed, almost everything that we know about the physiological mechanisms underlying reproductive development has been learned from experiments done with a very few highly domesticated stocks, mostly rodents and livestock. It is reasonable, then, to contrast in some detail the actions of domestication and natural selection in order to ask how well the body of knowledge generated so far by physiologists is representative of the wild ancestors of these animals and of mammals generally.

In one way, the actions of domestication and natural selection

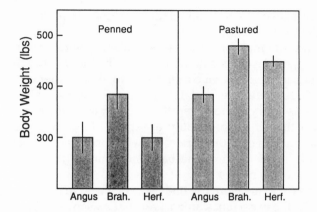

Figure 2.6. Mean body weight (±SE) at which heifers of three breeds of cattle achieved sexual maturity when housed either in pens where they were fed ad lib quantities of a nutritional diet or in pastures where food supplementation was necessary. Two species are represented here: *Bos indicus* (Brah.) and *Bos taurus* (Angus and Herf.). Data redrawn from Stewart, Long, and Cartwright (1980).

are similar: both produce population-to-population variation while decreasing but not eliminating individual variation. This is easily seen in today's various breeds of livestock. Cattle, for example, were domesticated over 9,000 years ago (Zeuner 1963). Most of our modern breeds, classified taxonomically as *Bos taurus*, trace their ancestry back to the aurochs (*Bos primagenius*), which at one time ranged widely in Europe and the Near East but which became extinct about 300 years ago. Another species, *Bos indicus*, which includes today's Brahman breeds, has a less certain ancestry.

During these several thousand years of domestication, cattle have been subjected to both intentional and unintentional selection for a variety of traits that yield economic benefits, including maximum reproduction. Since cattle have been transported and retransported widely around the world by humans, selection for these traits has been pursued under a wide variety of environmental conditions. As might be expected then, when several breeds are compared in any one locality, there usually is some difference in the age or body weight at which the average individual attains puberty (e.g., fig. 2.6; see also Joubert 1963). All genetic variation has not been removed from today's breeds of cattle, however. Usually, enough is left to allow intentional, directed selection for still more rapid growth and reproductive development (e.g., Long 1980).

As another example, laboratory rats have been domesticated for only about 200 years, but this still represents a large number of generations. Some stocks of laboratory mice trace their wild ancestry further back in time, but others have been domesticated for much less than 200 years. Both stocks of domestic rodents have been selected for a wide variety of reasons, but always indoors in environmental conditions that do not vary greatly from one part of the world to another. Even so, marked differences in the timing of fertility onset often are found when strains of these rodents are compared under any one set of environmental conditions (e.g., Schuler and Borodin 1976; Gates and Bozarth 1978), and, again, selection for accelerated puberty usually is successful (Bakker, Nagai, and Eisen 1977; Falconer 1984).

While similar in some ways, the results of natural selection and domestication also differ markedly. A typical action of domestication is to accelerate fertility onset, often dramatically. Domestication probably has exerted this action in one or all of three ways. First, the earliest possible genetic limits on the development of the reproductive axis itself may or may not have been advanced in some of our domestic stocks. No one knows for sure. Second, on firmer ground, the age of fertility onset often has been advanced by selection for greater body size. Third, some of the pathways used by decelerating dietary, physical, and social influences have been masked to some degree during domestication. The result of all this typically is an animal that reaches fertility much sooner than its wild ancestors and one that is less responsive to inhibitory environmental influences.

A classic exploration of the genetic correlates of domestication was done some time ago by King and his coworkers (e.g., King 1939). These researchers tried to recreate the domestication process by breeding wild-caught Norway rats in the laboratory for many generations. One of the most dramatic results of this endeavor concerned the inability of most wild rats to reproduce in a laboratory setting. Almost three-quarters of the wild-caught rats never produced offspring. Thus, King's breeding colony actually was founded by only one-quarter of the wild-caught animals.

Immediately on bringing wild rats into the laboratory, then, there was a tight genetic bottleneck where unintentional selection culled most individuals simply because they reacted adversely to their new environment. Continued breeding of the few remaining animals resulted in a decrease in the incidence of infertility to only 6 percent in eight generations. Correlated with this enhanced reproduction was a decrease in the age of fertility onset in both sexes, an increase in body weight of both sexes, greater docility, and a decrease in the variation seen in all these characteristics (reviewed in Berry 1969).

The secondary action of selection for other traits on puberty has been documented many times now in mice. Selection for either increased body weight or increased appetite, for example, routinely is accompanied by a decrease in the age of puberty in these animals (e.g., Crane et al. 1972; Brien et al. 1984; Falconer 1984). As a demonstration of how indirectly selection can influence age of puberty in mice, Uchida and Mizuma (1983) even report a decrease in age of vaginal opening in females while selecting for increased aggressiveness in males. Apparently, this was done by somehow altering activity of the pituitary/gonadal axis.

Drickamer (1981a, 1981b) has shown in detail how a response to an environmental influence can be lost during domestication. As noted earlier, and as will be described in detail later, pheromonal and tactile cues associated with male house mice stimulate the most rapid reproductive development of young female house mice, while female-originating cues decelerate their attainment of puberty. Drickamer selected domestic mice for early and late appearance of first estrus. After six generations of such selection, these mice were tested for their capacity to respond to social cues. Females of the rapidly developing line could no longer respond to a male with an acceleration of puberty, and female stimuli could no longer decelerate reproductive development in the line selected for delayed puberty. Thus, Drickamer's selection seems to have achieved both a ceiling and a basement effect, thereby preventing further acceleration or deceleration by the appropriate social cues.

Another example of a specific loss of environmental responsiveness during domestication is shown in figure 2.7. In this example, 12 years of laboratory existence completely masked the capacity of prairie voles (*Microtus ochrogaster*) to react to short daylengths. This comparison was made with individuals caught in the wild at the same location as that which provided the founders for the laboratory stock.

Comparisons between domestic stocks and their presumed ancestral stocks have been made many times now in other species for many reasons. Almost always, these studies have supported the conclusions drawn earlier here about the action of domestication. The following references either compare domestic and wild stocks or consider the difficulties encountered when making such comparisons: Richter (1954); Barnett et al. (1979); Clark and Galef (1980); Clark and Price (1981); Price (1984); and Reimov, Adamczyk, and Andrzejewski (1968). An example of such a comparison is shown in figure 2.8.

Given the breadth and depth of our knowledge about the endocrinology of domestic livestock, particularly cattle and sheep (*Ovis aries*), it is unfortunate indeed that we know so little about the precise effects of domestication in these animals. Intuitively, one might sus-

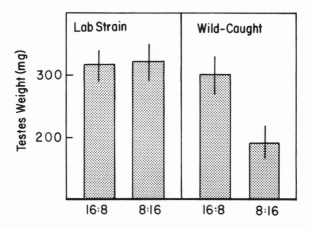

Figure 2.7. Paired testes weight (mean ± SE) in two populations of prairie voles (*Microtus ochrogaster*) when housed during their development on long (16L:8D) versus short (8L:16D) daylengths. One population was caught in the wild, while the other had been maintained in the laboratory for 12 years. Redrawn from Nelson (1985).

pect that, since they are normally housed in open pens or pastures and therefore subjected to considerable climatic variation, domesticated livestock may yield a somewhat better appreciation of the normal environmental responsiveness of their wild ancestors than do laboratory animals.

Even here, however, it should be remembered that these animals have been selected vigorously for early reproduction in an environment that often is stabilized seasonally by supplemental feeding. Reminiscent of Drickamer's observations in mice, then, is the fact that heterosis, the expected increase in vitality (in this case, accelerated puberty) that normally accompanies cross-breeding, usually is seen in cattle only when the animals experience poor nutrition, or in winter, or both (e.g., Smith et al. 1976a, 1976b; Stewart, Long, and Cartwright 1980; Long 1981).

Another complication arising during the domestication of livestock relates to the "unnatural" mating system normally used in their management, namely one male servicing many females without competition from other males (this is usually true in laboratory rodents as well). As mentioned earlier, physical competition between males for mates must be one of the most potent selective forces operating in natural populations. As suggested by Price (1985), negating this potent force, and emphasizing instead the ability to produce semen, undoubtedly has had an effect on the rate of reproductive maturation in today's breeds of livestock.

All in all then, how generalizable is our detailed knowledge of

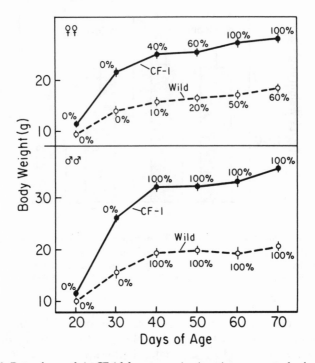

Figure 2.8. Rate of growth in CF-1 laboratory mice (●–●) versus a stock of wild house mice (○--○). Vertical bars total two standard errors. The cumulative proportion achieving fertility in each case is shown at 10-day intervals. Fertility is defined here as the first ovulation for females and as the ability to inseminate a female for males. The CF-1 mice also ate more food each day, and they were less active on a running wheel than their wild counterparts. Extracted from Bronson (1984).

reproductive development in the few domestic animals that have been studied so intensely by physiologists? Their most basic molecular-, tissue-, and organ-level functions are probably quite similar to those of their wild ancestors. They are undoubtedly less variable genetically, individual to individual, than their wild ancestors were, however, and they are probably much less responsive to environmental factors, both physical and social. Depressed responsiveness implies a somewhat altered neural organization, and this may be the most important difference of all.

Are the few domesticated species of rodents and livestock that have been studied so intensively actually representative of the variation that exists in the class Mammalia? Undoubtedly not. There are many fascinating pubertal strategies in this class of animals, and much associated physiological variation, about which we know nothing. On the other hand, one might question whether we could ever learn much about normal physiology by studying an undomesticated mammal in the strange environment we call a laboratory.

Conclusions

The object of this chapter was to establish some general principles about the way the environment regulates reproduction in a mammal. This was done while focusing on only a limited facet of the process of reproduction, namely the age at which a mammal becomes fertile. This is an event that is traditionally of great mechanical interest to the reproductive neuroendocrinologist. The time of fertility onset is of great statistical interest to the population ecologist but of only indirect interest to most behaviorists.

Pubertal development is viewed here as being strictly controlled by genes, at least at some level. The genes of concern can act with different levels of directness, however. Some directly limit the rapidity with which the first stage of reproductive development can occur, and some allow modulation by specific environmental cues for obviously adaptive purposes. Some allow indirect modulation via effects on somatic growth by a host of factors that operate at all stages of prepubertal existence and that are applied randomly to individuals. The result is a complicated, genetically programmed, yet environmentally susceptible and thus somewhat stochastic process whose limits vary from individual to individual.

There is no such thing as a typical mammalian gene pool or a typical strategy for achieving fertility onset. These can vary greatly between species, and they can vary just as greatly between populations of the same species. This is because the environments in which these populations exist can differ greatly one from another. Furthermore, sex-specific strategies are common in mammals simply because the forces controlling selection for the time of fertility onset differ markedly for the two sexes. The result of all this is great variation in mammals as a whole.

Most of what we know about the physiological underpinnings of fertility onset has been learned by studying a few highly domesticated stocks under carefully controlled conditions. Much has been learned using this approach, and at this time we probably have a reasonably detailed view of the most important internal mechanisms that *directly* govern fertility onset in rodents and livestock. What we do not have now is sufficient comparative information to appreciate fully the richness of the internal and external controls that regulate fertility onset in mammals as a whole.

3

Seasonal Strategies: Ultimate Factors

Mammals often show seasonal variation in their reproduction. Sometimes this variation is dramatic, with all a population's reproductive activities, or at least all of one kind of activity such as mating or birth, taking place during a markedly restricted part of the year. Sometimes seasonal variation amounts to only a tendency to concentrate reproductive activities, and sometimes it is absent entirely. As should be expected, often the two sexes differ somewhat in their precise seasonal patterns. In its dramatic form, seasonality is the most obvious effect of the environment on mammalian reproduction, and traditionally this is the phenomenon that has captured the most interest among both ecologists and physiologists interested in reproduction (e.g., Zuckerman 1953).

Whether a mammal reproduces seasonally or continuously depends mostly on its environment. Furthermore, as noted some time ago by Baker (1938), one can visualize the environmental forces of concern here as operating at two levels: the ultimate and the proximate (see also Negus and Berger 1972). Ultimate factors are those that are important in a long-term, evolutionary sense. Proximate factors are those that actually provide the immediate cuing for the onset and cessation of reproduction.

From a purely ultimate perspective, most cases of seasonal reproduction reflect variation in a complex of interacting dietary and climatic factors: food, rainfall, and temperature. All physiological processes, reproductive and otherwise, are limited by the amount of available food. Rainfall and temperature determine plant growth and hence the amount of food available for plant-eating animals, which in turn provide the food for invertebrate- or vertebrate-eating mammals. Temperature can exert more direct effects on reproduction as well. In environments characterized by seasonal variation in climate and diet, natural selection will tend to favor reproduction during whatever season maximizes the potential for success.

Two other factors can act in the ultimate sense to influence seasonality. These are competition between populations for similar types of resources and strategies to avoid predation by either concentrating or spacing births. These are minor influences compared to dietary and climatic variation, however.

Most habitats exploited by mammals experience at least some degree of seasonal variation in climate and diet. This is most obvious in the higher latitudes, where annual variation in temperature can be extreme. It is true in the tropics as well. Temperature varies little in the tropics, but rainfall patterns can be strongly seasonal (Walter 1971; MacArthur 1972). Thus, the expectation is that most mammals will show at least some seasonal tendency in their reproduction. Several factors intrinsic to the mammal itself can ameliorate or potentiate this expectation. These are its average life span, the nature of the mammal's feeding strategy, and the presence or absence of certain survival mechanisms.

Short-lived mammals, for example, must always gamble somewhat with their reproduction. They must reproduce as continuously as possible to counterbalance their short life expectancy. Longer-lived mammals can afford to be more selective. All other things being equal then, short-lived mammals tend to be more opportunistic and less seasonal in their reproductive effort than do long-lived mammals.

Likewise, a mammal's feeding strategy can potently modify the expectation of seasonal breeding in seasonally changing habitats. Some mammals feed only on highly specific food items. These animals tend to be more seasonal in their reproduction than mammals that have evolved a generalist feeding strategy. Extreme generalists can shift easily from one food source to another, depending on the relative availability of each, thereby buffering seasonal change in specific foods. Finally, the evolution of such seasonal survival mechanisms as hibernation and migration can potently exaggerate the need to reproduce seasonally.

If these intrinsic considerations interact with each other and with habitat characteristics in a way that dictates seasonal reproduction, another intrinsic consideration determines the precise time during the year when a mammal will actually initiate this process. This is the length of the female's reproductive cycle. More specifically, it is the interval of time between ovulation and the most environmentally sensitive phase of the female's cycle. This is commonly late lactation, when the female must find and consume enough food to nourish both herself and her rapidly growing mass of offspring. The most critical time for some populations, however, is the immediate post-birth period, when neonatal mortality can be great, and for others it is the period immediately following weaning.

Long reproductive cycles sometimes require that breeding occur during the harshest part of the year in order to synchronize the most environmentally sensitive phase of the female's cycle with the most propitious season (Clarke 1972, 1981). Correlatively, this may mean that all the reproductive activities of the males of this species must take place during the harshest season.

The way in which all these intrinsic and extrinsic considerations interact to forge a mammal's seasonal strategy is viewed diagrammatically in figure 3.1. At the bottom of this figure are the intrinsic factors of concern. At its center are four temporal patterns of variation in dietary and climatic conditions. These four patterns are only representative of the many such variations that exist on this planet (see Southwood 1977). Panel A represents the unpredictable conditions found in many desert and semiarid regions. Annual variation in temperature is more or less predictable in such environments, but rainfall occurs in unpredictable episodes, and hence food availability likewise is unpredictably episodic.

Panel B represents the more predictable changes found in many environments in the higher latitudes of the temperate zones and sometimes in the tropics, where only short-lived windows in a region's annual climatic and dietary cycle permit reproductive success. In many such habitats, there is considerable year-to-year variation in the dietary and climatic conditions experienced during the preferred season for reproduction, however, and also in the degree to which these conditions allow reproduction during the "off season." Panel C is an exaggeration of such variation. This pattern of variation is relatively common in the tropics but rare in the temperate zone.

Finally, panel D illustrates the more constant conditions that can be found in a few parts of the tropics. As indicated in figure 3.1, competition between populations for similar resources and strategies to avoid predation probably plays the greatest role in shaping the annual reproductive strategies of mammals in these more constant environments.

Sometimes variation in climatic and dietary factors acts directly to determine whether a mammal will reproduce continuously or seasonally. In such cases, these factors are acting in both the ultimate and the proximate sense. As noted in the preceding chapter, in other cases natural selection opts to use a purely proximal predictor, such as photoperiod. This allows a period of metabolic preparation before the

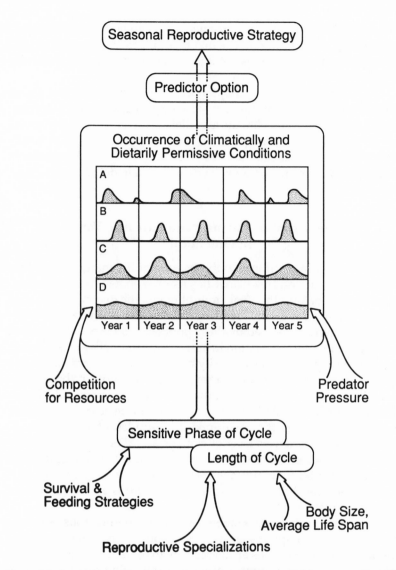

Figure 3.1. Interaction of intrinsic and extrinsic variables to yield a mammal's annual reproductive strategy. At the bottom of this figure are the intrinsic factors of concern. At the center are four temporal patterns of climatic and dietary variation. Temporal variation of this kind plus predator pressure and potential competition for resources are the extrinsic factors of concern. As suggested at the top of this figure, a mammal's annual reproductive strategy may or may not include the use of a seasonal predictor. For a detailed explanation of this figure, see the text.

arrival of the best season to reproduce. This can be an advantage or a disadvantage, depending on the mammal of concern and the characteristics of its habitat. The use of this option is shown toward the top of figure 3.1.

The remainder of this chapter will consider the ultimate forces shaping the annual reproductive strategies of mammals. Most emphasis will be placed on climatic and dietary factors. Lesser emphasis is given to competition and predator pressure because these are probably less important factors and because we know much less about them anyhow. Proximal cuing will be discussed in detail in later chapters.

The Interaction of Intrinsic and Extrinsic Variation in One Locale

As noted earlier in relation to puberty, each of the many populations of mammals living on this planet has its own somewhat unique evolutionary history, and the total amount of genetic diversity among all these populations is great. The dietary and climatic characteristics of the environments inhabited by these populations are equally diverse. The result is immense variation in seasonal reproductive strategies.

An initial hint of this diversity can be seen in figure 3.2, which examines the typical annual patterns of reproduction of three mammals, all of whom live in Kansas: the coyote (*Canis latrans*), the blacktailed jackrabbit (*Lepus californicus*), and the prairie vole (*Microtus ochrogaster*). Situated in the lower-middle latitudes of the temperate zone, Kansas experiences a set of climatic and dietary conditions intermediate between those shown earlier in panels B and C of figure 3.1. That is, winter there normally is a time of cold temperatures, low precipitation, and little plant growth, but there is an expectation of some year-to-year variation.

The vole and the jackrabbit are strictly herbivorous. Coyotes prey on these two species as well as on other small mammals and ground birds. The vole has an average life expectancy at birth of a few weeks, perhaps 2 or 3 months at most. Countering this high rate of mortality is an exceptionally high reproductive potential. Indeed, voles are classic r-strategists (Stenseth et al. 1985; Negus and Berger 1987). They have the capacity to mature quickly, and thereafter to produce litter after litter of offspring rapidly and continuously if allowed to do so by their environment. Voles experience a postpartum estrus. They can suckle one litter while carrying another in the uterus with only a small increase in the duration of pregnancy.

The larger jackrabbit has a somewhat longer life span, 3–6

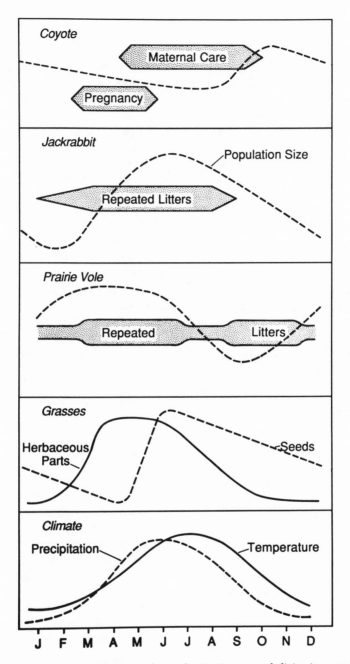

Figure 3.2. Typical annual patterns of reproduction in mammals living in central Kansas, modeled after Gier (1957), Bronson and Tiemeier (1958, 1959), and Rose and Gaines (1978). Vole populations are highly variable, and the pattern shown here may or may not occur in any given year (see Gaines and Rose 1976). Climatic data are 30-year averages recorded at Condordia, Kansas. For a similar comparison involving five species of rodents in a desert, see Kenagy and Bartholomew (1985).

months on the average, and it also experiences a postpartum estrus. Thus, it also has the capacity to produce litters of offspring repeatedly, again if allowed to do so by environmental factors. The jackrabbit takes somewhat longer to produce a weaned litter, however—7 or 8 weeks, as opposed to 5 or 6 weeks for the vole. In contrast, the average life span of the still larger coyote is 2 or 3 years. This longer life span is balanced by a maximum production of a single litter of offspring each year, an effort requiring 7 or 8 months.

Both the coyote and the jackrabbit routinely reproduce only during a limited part of the year in Kansas. The prairie vole does not always show this restraint in this locality. Temperature and food availability vary from winter to winter, and whenever possible the vole continues to reproduce throughout this harsh part of the year. Heavy snow cover actually can facilitate this effort because it moderates ground-level temperatures (see Jannett 1984a; Spencer 1984). For reasons that are still uncertain, prairie voles often achieve only a limited amount of reproduction in midsummer in Kansas.

Environmental conditions can change extremely rapidly in Kansas, and many attempts by these voles to reproduce during midsummer and midwinter must end in failure, but some are successful. Obviously, the gamble is worth the effort; otherwise, it would not be a routine part of this population's reproductive strategy. As noted earlier, the ultimate driving force here is short life expectancy. Verifying that simple biological rules always have exceptions, however, the small and equally short-lived harvest mouse (*Reithrodontomys megalotus*) never breeds during the winter in Kansas (Johnson and Gaines 1988).

Both jackrabbits and coyotes begin mating well before the beginning of the period of maximum food availability—indeed, well before ambient temperatures begin to rise in the spring. Obviously, they do so in response to a proximal predictor of some kind. In both species, the most demanding phase of the female's reproductive cycle is after birth, when she must provide nourishment both for herself and for a large and rapidly growing mass of offspring. As shown in figure 3.2, the jackrabbit's repeated periods of lactation coincide with the maximum availability of the vegetative part of grasses and other plants on which it feeds. The period of maternal care in the coyote, which includes both lactation and a period of time during which the young take solid food, coincides with the maximum availability of jackrabbits but not with that of voles, which can vary greatly from year to year (Gaines and Rose 1976).

Beginning to breed so early in the year is a gamble that can backfire for the jackrabbit. Occasionally, this region experiences intense and prolonged blizzards in March and early April. When this happens, all access to food is blocked, and the jackrabbit population experiences massive prenatal and neonatal mortality (Bronson and Tiemeier 1958; see also Clark and Innis 1982). Thus, like the vole, the jackrabbit also shows a degree of opportunism in its annual reproductive strategy, just not so much as the shorter-lived animal.

The coyote, with its longer life span and lower reproductive potential, has little need to gamble. Its annual reproductive strategy is much more rigidly programmed. Nevertheless, coyote reproduction can suffer in years when its prey is scarce (e.g., Todd and Keith 1983). Also of interest here is the fact that the coyote has developed a social system that promotes pup survival. As recorded by Bekoff and Wells (1982), nonbreeding yearling coyotes often bring food to the younger generation of their mother's pups (see also Kleiman 1980; Andelt 1985). Such cooperation is never seen in the shorter-lived, herbivorous voles and jackrabbits.

In general then, figure 3.2 shows three different reproductive strategies that have evolved in a reasonably common type of temperate environment. The strategy of each species includes a balancing of the female's life expectancy with her reproductive potential, invoking a greater and greater degree of opportunism, as opposed to temporal rigidity, as life span decreases.

As far as the males of these three species are concerned, both the jackrabbit and the coyote show a marked seasonal cycle of testicular development and decline, and in each case males achieve full reproductive development well before the time that breeding actually commences. This is an expected consequence of natural selection operating on males that must compete with each other for chances to mate (see Blackshaw 1977; Lincoln 1981). Most male voles are capable of breeding at all times of the year in Kansas. This of course is a necessity for a real opportunist.

Latitude and Seasonality

Another way to view the diversity of mammalian annual strategies is in relation to latitude. Even though it is a poor predictor of rainfall patterns, latitude is a crude predictor of annual extremes in temperature. Thus, one expects to see some correlation among latitude, plant growth, and the tendency to reproduce seasonally, but also a great deal of variation that is not accounted for by this single factor. This fact is demonstrated in figures 3.3–5, which present the annual patterns of reproduction of three sets of North American herbivores: small, short-lived mice of the genus *Peromyscus*, intermediate-sized

Figure 3.3. Observed breeding seasons (percentage of females pregnant each month) in several populations of the genus *Peromyscus*. The left axis of each rectangle represents January, the right axis represents December, and the stippled area between indicates the annual breeding pattern observed over a 12-month period. The rectangles marked with an X are the patterns reported for the deer mouse *P. maniculatus*. These data were extracted from Baker (1956), Beer and MacLeod (1966), Blair (1958), Brown (1964, 1966), Christian (1980), Cornish and Bradshaw (1978), Davenport (1964), Drickamer (1978), Fuller (1969), Halfpenny (1980), Harland, Blancher, and Miller (1979), Howard (1949), Jameson (1953), Judd, Herrera, and Wagner (1978), Krebs and Wingate (1985), Layne (1966), Long (1973), Merritt and Merritt (1980), Millar, Wille, and Iverson (1979), Millar and Innes (1983), Redfield, Krebs, and Taitt (1977), Rintamaa, Mazur, and Vessey (1976), Robertson (1975), Scheffer (1924), Svendson (1964), and Wolff (1985). Modified from Bronson (1985).

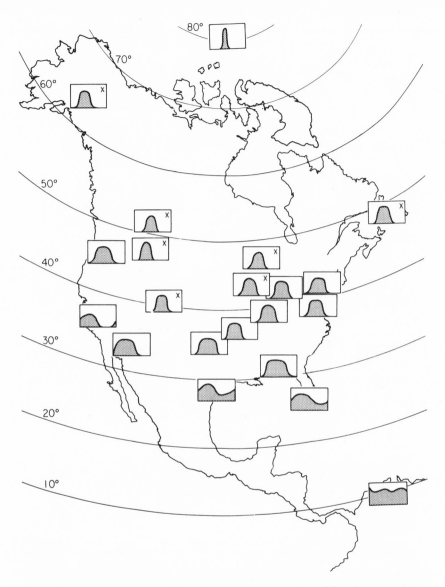

Figure 3.4. Breeding seasons of three lagomorphs (percentage of females pregnant in monthly kill samples). Those patterns observed for the snowshoe hare are marked with an X. These data were extracted from Adams (1959), Bigham (1966), Bookhout (1965), Bothma and Tern (1977), Chapman and Harman (1972), Conaway, White, and Sadler (1963), Dodds (1965), Dolbeer and Clark (1975), Evans et al. (1965), Fitch (1947), Hamilton (1940), Hill (1972), Holler and Conaway (1979), Ingles (1941), Keith and Windberg (1978), Keith et al. (1984), Kuvlesky and Keith (1983), Lord (1961), O'Farrell (1965), Ojeda, Magaly, and Keith (1982), Parker (1977), Powers and Verts (1971), Stevens (1962), Stout (1970), and Trethewey and Verts (1971). Reprinted from Bronson (1985).

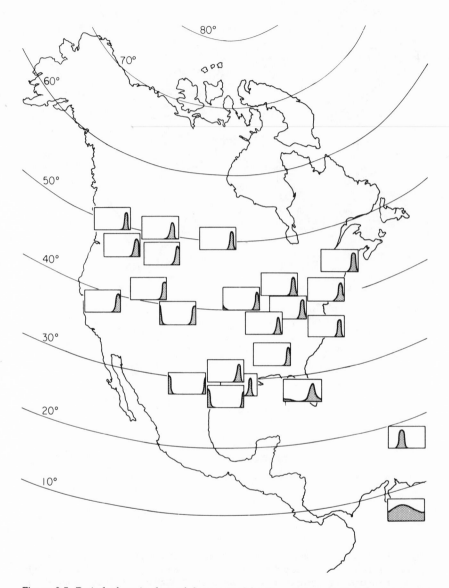

Figure 3.5. Period of rut in deer of the genus *Odocoileus*. Data extracted from Adams (1960), Banasiak (1961), Brokx (1972), Cheatham and Morton (1946), Haugen (1975), Illige (1951), Kucera (1978), Loveless (1959), Mansell (1974), McGinnes and Downing (1977), Mundinger (1981), Nixon (1971), Ransom (1966), Robinson, Thomas, and Marburger (1965), Roseberry and Klimstra (1970), Taylor (1956), Verme (1965), Wallmo (1981), Webb and Nellis (1981), and White (1973). Reprinted from Bronson (1985).

rabbits and hares with modest life expectancies of the order Lagomorpha, and the much larger and longer-lived deer of the genus *Odocoileus*.

The genus *Peromyscus* includes a variety of small-sized rodents known variously as deermice, white-footed mice, beach mice, cactus mice, and so forth. In the laboratory, these animals, like voles, can breed rapidly and continuously if given an appropriate environment. As suggested in figure 3.3, in natural habitats *Peromyscus* may or may not show seasonal inhibition of their reproduction (see also Millar 1984). Indeed, the overall impression created by figure 3.1 is one of immense variation.

While a breeding season limited to 3 summer months has been observed in *Peromyscus* above 60° of latitude, a winter breeding season of 6 months has been recorded in central Texas at 30° of latitude. Two hundred miles south in the Rio Grande River valley, a summer peak in breeding is seen with an occasional winter pregnancy occurring as well. Just west, in the state of Coahuila, Mexico, pregnant females may be found in all months of the year.

Winter breeding of *Peromyscus* also has been recorded in Kansas, coastal South Carolina, Florida, eastern Washington, and southern Mexico. Bimodal patterns of spring and fall breeding are common near 40° of latitude, as is a more simple 5–7 month spring and summer breeding season. Importantly, as noted in figure 3.3, most of these patterns can be seen within even a single species of this genus, the deer mouse (*P. maniculatus*).

The great regional variation obvious in figure 3.3 must be considered in relation to the year-to-year variation in the reproduction of *Peromyscus* living in the same locality. For 3 consecutive years, Sadleir (1974) studied a population of deermice living on the Fraser River delta in British Columbia. The onset of breeding in this population varied by as much as 2 months. This was a period of time almost equivalent to the length of the entire breeding season in one of the three years. All in all then, *Peromyscus* populations show great variation in their annual patterns of reproduction, both from locale to locale and from year to year, even within the same species (see also Millar and Gyug 1981).

Lagomorphs also can breed continuously in the laboratory. The annual patterns shown in figure 3.4 are those recorded for the cottontail rabbit (*Sylvilagus* spp.), the snowshoe hare (*Lepus americanus*), and the arctic hare (*L. arcticus*). Together these animals range from near the equator to over 80° of latitude. Only the extreme northern part of this range is occupied by the relatively large arctic hare; the rest of Canada is occupied by the smaller showshoe hare, as is part of the northern United States, while the still smaller cottontail is limited to the United States and southward.

The large arctic hare lives in a climate so harshly seasonal that it can produce only one litter a year. Obviously, these animals must experience an average life span of at least several months; otherwise, they could not exist in such northern latitudes. Over its broad range, the smaller showshoe hare produces two or three litters during a 5- or 6-month breeding season that extends from early spring into the warm summer months. The timing of these animals' annual pattern of reproduction is remarkably consistent within this broad region.

Almost identical breeding patterns are shown by cottontails living in the northern part of the United States. As one progresses southward, however, the still smaller cottontail's breeding season becomes progressively longer until continuous breeding has been recorded in southern Texas, Florida, and Venezuela. Where the cottontail shows seasonal breeding, some year-to-year variation in the onset of cessation of breeding can be expected, but not of the magnitude seen in the smaller *Peromyscus* (cf. Conaway and Wight 1962).

Deer of the genus *Odocoileus* range from southern Canada to the Amazon River in Brazil. They are relatively long lived, and they breed only once each year in the United States and Canada. Their breeding seasons everywhere above 30° of latitude are predictable, short periods in the fall and early winter (fig. 3.5; also see Lee 1970; Goss 1983). Births and lactation occur the following spring in conjunction with the peak in available vegetation. Breeding occurs sporadically in almost every month of the year in the Everglades, with a marked peak in September, while the peak season on Saint Croix island in the Caribbean is in the spring and early summer. Poorly quantified information suggests that these deer have a somewhat extended midwinter breeding season in northern Mexico (Leopold 1959) and that their peak period of breeding in Panama is in September (D. E. Mendez, June 1984, personal communication).

At the southern extreme of its range, the reproductive strategy of this genus changes dramatically. In Venezuela, these deer experience a postpartum estrus. Thus, females can breed more than once a year, and every month finds individuals in different stages of reproduction (Brokx 1972). Interestingly, the bucks in some populations at these lower latitudes show annual cycles of antler growth and shedding, but these cycles occur asynchronously among the different individuals in a population (Goss 1983).

Three conclusions emerge when one compares the annual patterns of reproduction for the three groups of animals shown in figures 3.3–5. First, all show short, well-delineated breeding seasons in the northern part of their ranges, and all become year-around breeders in the southern part. Second, the latitude at which the shift from restricted to continuous breeding occurs varies with life span; the shift occurs at higher latitudes as life span decreases. Third, while not well documented here, the degree of year-to-year variation as well as locale-to-locale variation decreases as the life span of the animal increases. All these conclusions are generally predictable.

One should expect a long-lived, periodic breeder such as the deer to show a temporally rigid season of reproduction that does not vary much from year to year or from locale to locale, at least in the temperate zone. For reasons that will be discussed later in relation to energetics, the precise timing of the breeding of these animals should be little affected by short-term dietary and climatic challenges. Since evolutionary success is always determined by the number and reproductive success of one's offspring, however, one might also expect even deer-sized mammals to breed as often as possible whenever they dwell in dietarily constant environments. Sometimes these conditions exist in the tropics, but often they do not.

Likewise, one should expect the lagomorphs with their shorter life span to have evolved annual strategies that are more opportunistic and less rigidly programmed. This translates into more locale-to-locale and year-to-year variation in performance (see Lloyd 1970). Also because of their modest life expectancies, one should expect these animals to show more opportunism then deer at higher latitudes. In no case, however, would these attributes be as extreme as they are in the still shorter-lived *Peromyscus,* who must always be as opportunistic as possible (see Smyth 1966; Kemper 1980; Zucker and Chapman 1984; Murua, Gonzalez, and Meserve 1986).

The general relation between life span, body size, latitude, and pattern of reproduction that is suggested in figures 3.3–5 exists in many other groups of mammals, but it also has many important and interesting exceptions that will be discussed in detail later. For now, three modifying principles must be noted.

First, it must be emphasized again that latitude is only a crude indicator of the degree of seasonal variation that exists in a region's climate. Shipp et al. (1963), for example, charted the annual reproduction of a free-living population of domestic rabbit (*Oryctolagus cuniculus*) that had been released on Macquarie Island by visiting whalers. This island is located at 54° S, and its climate is cold and bleak, but largely nonseasonal because of its oceanic environment. The mean difference between the mildest and coldest months is only about 3°C. Rabbits breed continuously on the parts of the island where vegetation growth is adequate, albeit with strong seasonal minima and max-

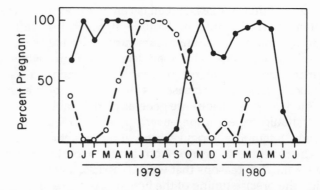

Figure 3.6. Frequency of pregnancy in a population of California voles (●–●) and western harvest mice (o--o) inhabiting a California grassland. Redrawn from Heske, Ostfeld, and Lidicker (1984).

ima. As shown in figure 3.4, one would expect lagomorphs at this latitude to show a short, rigidly limited breeding season if they lived in the interior of a continent. Similarly, altitudinal variation is a potent factor in determining seasonal variation in reproductive strategies, a fact that has been documented in *Peromyscus* (Millar and Innes 1985; see also Smith and McGinnis 1968).

Second, as noted earlier, a mammal's feeding strategy can alter greatly the kinds of general expectations generated by figures 3.3–5. Some muroid rodents, for example, specialize on particular foods, and usually their reproduction can be supported only by those foods. This fact is illustrated by data collected in a California grassland located at the same latitude as Kansas. It contains both California voles (*Microtus californicus*) and western harvest mice (*Reithrodontomys megalotus*). Harvest mice normally eat seeds, wherever possible, while voles eat the vegetative parts of plants, again wherever possible. Thus, as shown in figure 3.6, harvest mice reproduce in this grassland during the summer, when seeds are maximally available, as they do in Kansas, but the herbivorous California voles breed only during the winter, unlike the prairie voles in Kansas. The difference here can be traced to a reasonably predictable winter rainy season in this part of California.

Third, a comparison of figures 3.2, 3.3, 3.4, and 3.5 suggests a potent relation between body size and reproductive potential as well as between life span and reproductive potential. As noted earlier in relation to fertility onset, it must be emphasized again that body size and life span are not always well correlated in mammals, and it is the latter rather than the former that is most instrumental in determining

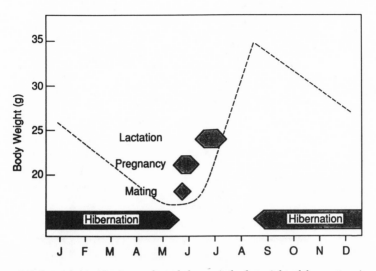

Figure 3.7. Annual reproductive cycle and change in body weight of the western jumping mouse in Utah. Redrawn from Cranford (1983).

reproductive potential. There are many small mammals who are relatively long lived, and these animals have relatively low reproductive potentials. Often the life-history and reproductive strategies of such animals revolve around hibernation.

For example, as shown in figure 3.7, the *Peromyscus*-sized western jumping mouse (*Zapus princeps*) produces only one litter of four or five young each year. In the population studied by Cranford (1983) in the mountains of Utah, these small animals hibernate for 9 months of the year. Males emerge from hibernation first, more or less in full breeding condition. Mating occurs as the females emerge, and then the entire reproductive cycle, plus the fattening necessary for hibernation, must be accomplished in the 3-month period when food is maximally available. Cranford noted that some of these small animals survive for 5 years in the wild. It is obvious that their average life span must be relatively long for their size.

A possibly even more spectacular example of a small mammal with a low reproductive potential was reported by Kenagy and Bartholomew (1981, 1985), who studied the long-tailed pocket mouse (*Perognathus formosus*) in the unpredictable Mojave desert in California. These small hibernators also produce only one litter of young each year, but in drought years they may not achieve even this low potential. Again, obviously, these must be relatively long-lived animals. Otherwise, they could not exist. As will be detailed later, body

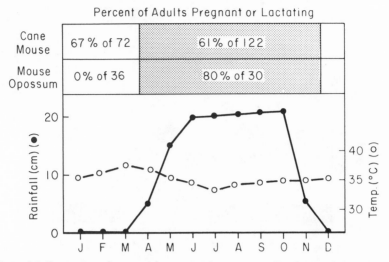

Figure 3.8. Proportion of marsupial mouse and cane mouse females pregnant or lactating in relation to annual changes in rainfall and temperature on the llanos of Venezuela. Data extracted from O'Connell (1981) and previously published by Bronson (1988c).

size usually correlates to some degree with reproductive potential in mammals, but life span is a better correlate.

The Tropics

Most reproductive biologists, whether of an endocrine, a behavioral, or an ecological orientation, live in the temperate zone, and most of the mammals we utilize in our research evolved here also. Four out of every five species of mammals are found in the tropics, however. Thus arises a profound mismatch between effort and geographic distribution. For this reason it is worth making a special effort here to discuss seasonality in the tropics.

An erroneous conclusion that might be drawn from our considerations of *Peromyscus, Odocileus,* and the lagomorphs is that all mammals breed continuously in the warmer climates of the tropics. This is an artifact of the choice of animals for these comparisons, which, in turn, is a reflection of the available literature. As emphasized earlier, the tropics encompass a huge diversity of habitats, and many of these habitats experience great seasonal variation in rainfall. Thus, seasonality of reproduction often is a necessity in the tropics (reviewed in Heideman 1987).

Typical breeding patterns of two mammals in a reasonably common tropical habitat are shown in figure 3.8. The llanos of Venezuela are harshly seasonal grasslands located north of the Orinoco River.

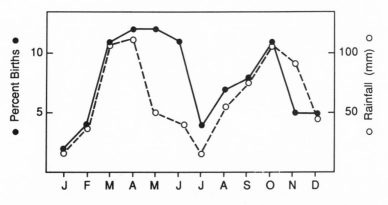

Figure 3.9. Annual variation in births in relation to annual variation in rainfall among African buffalos (*Syncerus caffer*) in equatorial Uganda. Redrawn from Grimsdell (1973).

Their center is about 8° of latitude. There is little meaningful variation in ambient temperature at this latitude, but rainfall is dramatically seasonal. This results in great annual variation in primary productivity.

As one reflection of this variation, the small marsupial mouse (*Marmosa robinsonii*) breeds on the llanos strictly in relation to the rainy season. The slightly smaller cane mouse (*Zygodontomys brevicauda*), on the other hand, breeds continuously, as do most of the other rodents on the llanos (e.g., Vivas and Calero 1985; Vivas 1986). The small marsupial is a highly specialized arboreal frugivore that is relatively long lived for its size (O'Connell 1979). As might be expected from figure 3.8, the cane mouse is a heavily preyed upon generalist (O'Connell 1982). The same kinds of differences noted in figure 3.8 have been seen among even closely related rodents in Kenya, apparently in association with variation in feeding strategies (Neal 1984).

Sometimes rainfall patterns are bimodal in the tropics. This often results in bimodal patterns of reproduction, at least on the part of females. Bimodal patterns similar to that shown in figure 3.9 have been reported for the giraffe (*Giraffa camelopardalis*) and the pygmy antelope (*Neotragus batesi*) in Cameroon by Nje (1983) and Feer (1982), respectively, for the water buffalo (*Bubalu bubalu*) in northern Australia (Tulloch and Grassia 1981), and for the Polynesian rat (*Rattus exulans*) in the Marshall Islands (Temme 1981). Bimodal patterns also can be seen sometimes even in the subtropics (e.g., in the Nyala, *Tragelaphus angasi*, in Natal; Anderson 1984). Usually the males of such bimodally breeding populations show little seasonal variation in either spermatogenesis or sexual capability.

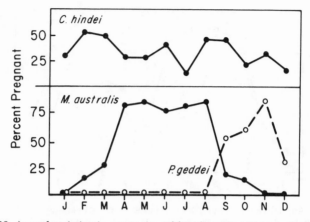

Figure 3.10. Annual variation in proportion of females pregnant in three tropical bats (see text). Data extracted from Baker and Baker (1936) and Baker and Bird (1936) and previously published by Bronson (1988b).

As a final example of annual strategies at the lower latitudes, bats have undergone extensive radiation in the tropics in relation to food sources. One result of this diversity is almost every conceivable annual pattern of reproductive effort imaginable. Three such patterns are shown in figure 3.10. The insectivorous *Chaerephon hindes* shows a continuous pattern of breeding on the equator in eastern Africa. The climate in this particular locale is relatively constant in terms of both rainfall and temperature, a relatively rare occurrence in the tropics.

In contrast, the annual pattern of rainfall is typically monsoonal in the New Hebrides islands at 15° S in the Pacific. In this locale, the insectivorous *Miniopterus australis* reproduces strictly in relation to seasonal variation in insect availability, and the larger and highly specialized *Pteropus geddei* reproduces strictly in relation to the availability of particular fruits. Bimodal patterns often have been reported in tropical bats as well (Racey 1982).

More will be said about reproduction in tropical mammals later in relation to the taxonomic survey that is presented in chapter 9. The point to be made here is simply that the tropics represent an exceptionally diverse collection of habitats that together support most of the mammals that exist on this planet. The annual reproductive strategies of tropical mammals usually reflect three-way interactions between rainfall patterns, feeding strategies, and taxonomic limitations. As a result, almost every conceivable annual pattern of reproduction can be found in this region.

The interested reader might want to pursue the following selection of papers dealing with the reproduction of various kinds of mammals in various parts of the tropics: Harrison (1952), Wade (1958), Taylor and Green (1976), Poulet et al. (1981), Neal (1982), Hubert (1982), Langham (1983), and Dieterlen (1985a, 1985b).

A Purely Energetic Perspective: Small Mammals

Physiological ecologists and evolutionary biologists often have found it rewarding to view the reproductive strategies of wild animals within a framework of purely energetic principles (e.g., Gittleman and Thompson 1988). That is, one can view the question of reproductive success or failure in terms of a simple energetic equation. Assimilated energy must be partitioned among a variety of interlocking yet somewhat competing physiological demands. An increase in any one of these demands must be countered either by an increase in food intake or at the expense of demands having a lower priority.

In this equation, the demands that compete most vigorously with those of reproduction are cellular maintenance, thermoregulation, and the locomotor costs of obtaining food. Once these primary demands have been met, excess energy can be used for growth or for nonforaging behavior, or it can be stored as fat for emergencies, or it can be used to support reproduction. The latter usually has one of the lowest priorities in this competition, at least in nonpregnant females. Good general reviews of this perspective can be found in Calow (1979), Sibley and Calow (1985), and in the many papers collected by Townsend and Calow (1981; see also Hill 1983). Of particular interest here are the many excellent papers in Loudon and Racey (1987).

Viewing reproduction from this admittedly oversimplified perspective offers two advantages. First, it combines the influences of low temperature and the energetic dimension of food to yield a single variable. Second, this variable is quantifiable, both theoretically and experimentally. These are great advantages. The disadvantages are threefold. This approach ignores the direct effects of high temperature on reproduction, and, second and more important, it ignores seasonal variation in the availability of specific nutrients. Reproduction is both an energy- and a nutrient-consuming process, and a deficit in either can curtail reproduction. Finally, laboratory experimenters usually manipulate either food availability or ambient temperature, but not both simultaneously. Thus, the third drawback is that there is not now a well-characterized neuroendocrine framework for conceptualizing the energetic regulation of reproduction.

For now we will take advantage of the utility of the purely energetic perspective, leaving concern for its disadvantages until later. This perspective has proven particularly rewarding when applied to mammals of small size, mostly muroid rodents and insectivores (see Grodzinski and Wunder 1975; Wunder 1978; Ferns 1980; Grodzinski and French 1983; McClure 1987; and an exceptionally well-done theoretical treatment by Porter and McClure 1984). In easily quantifiable, purely energetic terms, reproduction by small mammals is demonstrably not possible in seasons characterized by increased thermoregulatory costs and low food availability.

As has been known for some time now, two energy-related characteristics of small mammals make them exceptionally susceptible to reproductive inhibition. First, their large surface-to-volume ratio results in increased thermoregulatory costs at even mildly low temperatures. To counter this continuing drain of body heat, they rely on a high metabolic rate, which in turn must be fueled by a relatively high food intake (Hart 1971). Second, the energetic costs of a small female's reproductive cycle are extremely high, both in relation to her ability to obtain food and in relation to her fat stores (e.g., Merson and Kirkpatrick 1981, 1983).

The energetic jeopardy that is a constant companion of the small mammal is easily seen in relation to its fat stores (Millar 1988). Even at normal laboratory temperatures, for example, laboratory mice show a dramatic daily cycle in fat storage and utilization when allowed to feed only during the dark phase of their daily light cycle (Bronson 1987b). Their high metabolic rate cannot be sustained during the nonfeeding phase of the daily cycle without converting over *one-third* of their stored fat into energy. This fat is then replaced during the feeding period. In a cooler condition (11°C or 54°F ambient and nest temperatures of 18°C–19°C or 64°F–66°F), these animals cannot store as much fat during their feeding period because of the increased thermoregulatory demand, and they die within hours if they miss a single feeding period (see Howard 1951; Lindstedt and Boyce 1985). Such cool temperatures would not be much of a problem for a larger mammal, but they are a life-and-death challenge for the small mammal (see also Merson et al. 1983).

Rodents in the wild spend much of their day in thermally buffered nests, but to feed they must emerge and forage in whatever climatic conditions prevail. If food is scarce, the locomotor costs of finding it will increase. In itself, this is a relatively minor problem; these small animals are built to run economically. As suggested in the theoretical model shown in the lower half of figure 3.11, however, what is really important here is the amount of time a rodent must spend foraging in relation to the temperature at which foraging is done. If food is scarce and outside temperatures are low, the caloric cost of extended foraging may outweigh caloric gain. The animal loses

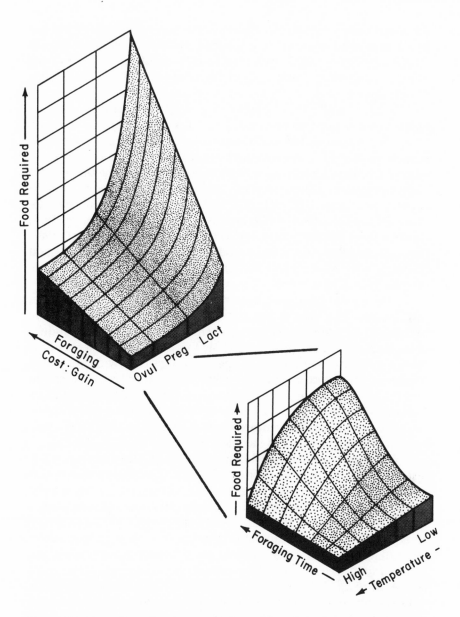

Figure 3.11. Three-dimensional representations of the relation between the energetic costs of reproduction (food intake), ambient temperature, and food availability (foraging time). The lower figure considers the theoretical relation between the amount of food required to maintain a small mammal's ovulatory cycle and the length of time it must forage at different temperatures. The upper figure considers the theoretical relation between the amount of food required to maintain the various stages of reproduction in a small female and the cost/gain ratio of foraging.

too much body heat while foraging in relation to the energy it gains by finding and consuming food. When the caloric cost/gain ratio of foraging reaches a certain minimum level, an ovulatory cycle is a poor investment of energy, and at a still lower level survival itself is compromised.

Once a small female achieves her first ovulation, she risks an enormous energetic drain should she become pregnant and give birth. As demonstrated experimentally in several rodents now, a small female must more than double her food intake during late lactation to nourish herself and her developing mass of offspring, even in the utopian conditions of excess food and warm laboratory temperatures (Kaczmarski 1966; Migula 1969; Myrcha, Ryszkowski, and Walkowa 1969; Millar 1975, 1979; Randolph et al. 1977; Stebbins 1977; Studier 1979; McClure and Randolph 1980; Woodside et al. 1981; Innes and Millar 1981; Morris and Kendeigh 1981; Mattingly and McClure 1982; Merson and Kirkpatrick 1983; Gebczynski and Gebczynska 1984; Bronson and Marsteller 1985).

In the wild, a lactating rodent is confronted with a complex set of problems. She must forage more or less continuously to sustain herself and her litter. While doing so she must continuously produce energy-rich milk. It is important to note that she must budget her time carefully because she must also spend enough time with her young to provide them with adequate warmth (see McNab 1963; Collins and Smith 1976; Randolph 1980; Harland and Millar 1980; Johnson and Cabanac 1982). As suggested in the upper model in figure 3.11 then, even mildly cool outside temperatures, if combined with food shortage, make parental care and lactation energetically impossible.

The theoretical models shown in figure 3.11 have been partially tested in the laboratory. Perrigo and Bronson (1985) designed a caging system to mimic some of the energetic challenges actually facing a house mouse when foraging in the wild. In this caging system, a mouse could stay in a thermally buffered nest, but to feed it had to emerge into whatever temperature was imposed by the investigators and run a set number of revolutions on a running wheel to receive a pellet of food (see Mather 1981). Winter was mimicked by low room temperature and a high running requirement (which equates to low food availability and hence the need for increased foraging activity at a temperature that in itself costs energy).

As shown in figure 3.12, peripubertal female house mice can still gain weight and achieve normal reproductive development when required to run as much as 15 miles a night for their food, provided that the temperature in which they are "foraging" is relatively high (23°C). When faced with this high running requirement at 9°C (48°F), however, these females opt to stay in their nests, not working for food as

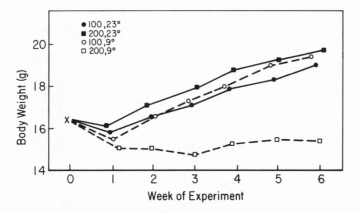

Figure 3.12. Average body weight of young house mouse females required to run either one hundred or two hundred revolutions of a running wheel for a 45mg pellet of food at either 9°C or 23°C. Reproductive development was blocked only in the females who failed to grow when required to work hard for their food at 9°C. Redrawn from Perrigo and Bronson (1985).

much as they could. They give up both growth and reproductive development rather than attempting both while satisfying their additional thermoregulatory demand.

Using this same caging system, the enormous energetic bottleneck of lactation also can be seen. As shown in figure 3.13, nonpregnant house mice will use an exercise wheel for much of the dark period even under conditions of ad lib feeding. This spontaneous activity decreases in late pregnancy, and it almost disappears during lactation. When food availability is made contingent on foraging activity, however, as is normal in the wild, the female must carefully balance the time spent obtaining food against the demands of her growing litter.

The all-important interaction between the need for a greater foraging effort during lactation and the ambient temperature in which the lactating female must forage has not yet been tested empirically in the laboratory, but the consequences of this interaction are fairly obvious from the theoretical model shown earlier in figure 3.11. Even mildly cool temperatures, when combined with the need to forage extensively, make lactation and parental care energetically impossible for the small mammal.

It is important to emphasize that low temperatures per se are not of overwhelming importance for the reproduction of most small rodents. House mice, for example, breed well and produce offspring in the laboratory at −6°C if they are given excess food throughout the day and not made to work for it (Bronson and Pryor 1983; see Mar-

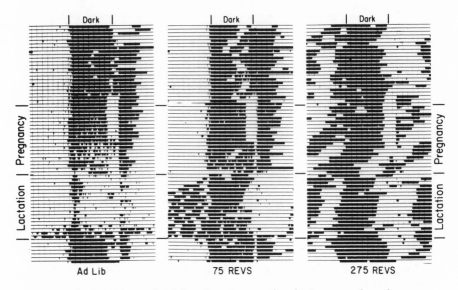

Figure 3.13. Activity records of three house mouse females in cages where they were required to run on a running wheel for food pellets. Each horizontal line represents a 24-hour period, vertical lines indicate hourly intervals, and the dark blocks show when the animal was active on its running wheel. The topmost line is day 1, the line below it is day 2, and so forth. The female on the far left was fed ad lib, and the female on the far right had to run 275 revolutions for each food pellet. The consistently recurring, 2.5-hour periods of inactivity from day 21 of the experiment through day 31 reflect blocking of the running wheel when a male was placed in the cage to allow insemination. Redrawn from Perrigo (1987).

steller and Lynch 1983; Barnett 1973; Barnett and Dickson 1984). They simply remain in their well-constructed nests, coming out only long enough to consume the larger amounts of food necessary to support their increased reproductive and thermoregulatory demands. What ultimately regulates the reproduction of temperate-zone rodents in the wild then is not cold per se or food availability directly; it is the energetic cost/gain ratio of foraging that is determined by both factors (see Millar and Gyug 1981; Pelikan 1981; Wunder 1984; Pennycuik et al. 1986).

Given the sensitivity of the small rodent, and indeed all small mammals, to the combination of low temperature and food scarcity, one can ask why these animals are so successful in exploiting the higher latitudes. The answer is that in these regions small size often is associated with a variety of energy-saving adaptations such as hibernation, daily torpor, food hoarding, seasonal moulting, seasonal metabolic adjustment, and a higher ratio of brown to white fat (e.g., Cherry and Verner 1975; Lynch and Gendler 1980; Wickler 1981; Dark,

Zucker, and Wade 1983; Quay 1984; Wunder 1984; Feist 1984; Blank and Desjardins 1986). Enforced seasonal breeding by using predictors is another such mechanism.

All in all, a purely energetic perspective is exceptionally helpful when visualizing the forces causing seasonal reproduction in mammals of small size. As noted earlier, however, when small size is combined with exceptionally short life span, as it often is, one must always expect an opportunistic dimension to the strategies of these animals as well. This sometimes can be seen even in populations inhabiting harshly seasonal environments at the higher latitudes. One of the best examples of such opportunism was reported by Linduska (1942), who found pregnant deermice in Michigan in January. These particular females were exploiting the energetically good microclimates of shocked corn standing in otherwise harshly open fields where reproduction was impossible. Many other such situations will be noted later in relation to photoperiodic cuing.

Application of an Energetic Perspective to Larger Mammals

A purely energetic perspective can act as a unifying framework within which to organize our knowledge about the annual reproductive strategies of mammals as a whole. To do so, however, requires that we incorporate into this framework all the survival mechanisms that have evolved in this class of animals as well as all their reproductive adaptations. These subjects will be considered later in chapter 9 in relation to a taxonomic survey. For now we will consider only how the general energetic picture changes when we shift our attention from a typical small rodent to a typical large (terrestrial) mammal.

As mammals increase in size, the nature of their energetic constraints changes dramatically. There is less heat loss per gram of body weight from the larger mammal because of its smaller surface to volume ratio. Thus, again per gram of body weight, the larger mammal experiences lower thermoregulatory costs at lower temperatures. Absolute maintenance-level food intake obviously is greater for the larger mammal, but it is less relative to body weight (Kleiber 1975). Locomotion is actually energetically cheaper per gram of body weight for the typical larger animal. Nevertheless, for a variety of reasons, the proportion of the larger mammal's energy expenditure that is devoted each day to foraging is usually much greater on the average than it is for the typical small mammal (Garland 1983). Finally, larger mammals have much greater fat stores with which to counter acute energetic challenges (Pond 1978, 1981).

With regard to reproduction, the mass of young produced by a larger female usually is smaller relative to her own size, and the costs of lactation and postweaning growth of the offspring usually are spread out over longer periods of time (Robbins 1983). Thus, the larger female typically requires less "extra" food during lactation than does the smaller female per gram of body weight. Black-tailed deer (*Odocoileus hemionus*), for example, increase their food intake by only 35 percent during peak lactation when caring for a single offpsring. This figure is increased to 70 percent when the female is nurturing twins (Sadleir 1982). This is well below the more than twofold increase required when rodents suckle a litter and well below the threefold increase required during lactation by some of the still smaller insectivores, even at laboratory temperatures.

Lactational costs have been measured in several average-sized or larger mammals now, including the fox squirrel (*Sciurus niger;* Havera 1979) and the fisher (*Martes pennanti;* Powell and Leonard 1983). Particularly noteworthy among the papers dealing with the energetics of reproduction in larger mammals are those relating to seals (e.g., Fedak and Anderson 1982; McCann 1983; Boness 1984; Stewart 1986; Anderson and Fedak 1987) and ungulates like deer and caribou (Dauphine 1976; Mautz 1978; Moen and Scholtz 1981; Finger, Brisban, and Smith 1981; Thomas 1982; Bobek, Kunelius, and Weiner 1983). An excellent collection of papers dealing with the energetics of herbivores of large size has been produced by Hudson and White (1985).

In general, the available information suggests that the driving force behind the evolution of seasonal reproduction becomes somewhat less dominated by a lactational bottleneck as body size increases. Other concerns, such as the availability of adequate food for the growing offspring immediately after they are weaned, become more important. Success during the larger female's more periodic efforts to reproduce is determined more by long-term food availability and less by low average temperatures, short-term climatic vagaries, and short-term food shortages (e.g., Verme 1965). Indeed, as body size increases, the effects of high temperature may become of greater concern than those of low temperature because burrowing is impossible. Thus, the dramatic interaction seen in small mammals between the low temperature-dominated cost/gain ratio of foraging and lactational costs becomes less important as body size increases.

How good are such generalities? Stated differently, how good is body size as a predictor of annual reproductive strategy? As noted several times earlier, this factor is not as good a predictor as life span, yet body weight is exceptionally important from an energetic standpoint.

There can be no doubt that body size, metabolic rate, and reproductive potential are all generally correlated, and there is no doubt that these correlations are useful in a *superficial* way when visualizing the seasonal reproductive strategies of mammals as a whole. The relation between these three variables has been subjected to elegant mathematical analysis many times now (e.g., Western 1983; Caughley and Krebs 1983; Hennemann 1983; Garland 1983; Reiss 1985; Lindstedt and Boyce 1985). In all cases, the resulting correlations are strongly significant if the spectrum of animals included in the analysis is large and if it contains representatives of both very large and very small mammals.

Particularly germane for the present concern is the fact that such analyses have even been extended to include specific reproductive concerns such as the ratio of testes weight to body weight. Thus, Kenagy and Trombulak (1986) calculate that an average mammal weighing 10g should have testes weighing about 1.8 percent of its body weight. The comparable figure for a 10,000kg mammal is 0.04 percent.

A major source of variation in correlations between body size, metabolic rate, and reproductive potential is phylogenetic in origin (Stearns 1983). The relation between these three variables is poor within the marsupials, for example, and as a group the bats depart radically from the expectations generated by analyzing all other groups of mammals. Some of the total variation can be accounted for by variation in feeding strategies. As noted by McNab (1980, 1984), eutherian mammals feeding on nectar and vertebrate flesh tend to fit the expected relation between body size, metabolic rate, and reproductive potential. Insectivores, frugivores, and folivores tend to have lower than expected metabolic rates and reproductive potentials, and herbaceous grazers tend to have higher rates and potentials. Unfortunately, the factor that is of most importance for shaping a mammal's reproductive potential—life expectancy—is usually missing in such analyses.

In general then, body size is an important variable in determining energetic constraints. It is superficially correlated with reproductive potential, and thus it is a crude predictor of the flexibility that will be seen in a mammal's annual reproductive strategy. Predictability becomes much better when one incorporates concerns for life span and basic diet. As noted earlier, however, good utility from a purely energetic perspective requires incorporation of all the diverse survival and reproductive adaptations that have evolved in the class Mammalia.

Nutrients and Seasonality

A purely energetic perspective ignores the potent role of seasonal variation in the availability of specific nutrients. Nutrients are defined here broadly (and admittedly very loosely) to include all components of a mammal's food except its energy content. There can be no doubt that the availability of key nutrients varies seasonally in many natural habitats, sometimes independently of caloric variation. As with energy, when a nutrient is in short supply, a partitioning process must decide among reproductive and nonreproductive needs.

One of the most important nutrients here is water. Others are the essential amino acids, certain polyunsaturated fatty acids, a variety of minerals, and some vitamins, all of which must be obtained from the mammal's food because none can be synthesized internally. A detailed monograph by Robbins (1983) provides a comprehensive review of this subject.

Many mammals do not drink free water; thus it is reasonable to consider this substance simply as another essential nutrient. Water balance undoubtedly is a more potent seasonal regulator than either energy or other nutrients in deserts and many dry grasslands (e.g., Schmidt-Nielsen 1964; Beatley 1969; Whitford 1976; Christian 1979; Deavers and Hudson 1981; Nelson, Dark, and Zucker 1983). Interestingly, however, reproduction is not always well correlated with rainfall patterns in desert mammals (e.g., in the Namib desert; Withers 1983). Nevertheless, it seems reasonable to expect that the extra water needed for milk production could be an important limiting factor in these environments.

As will be discussed in detail in the next chapter, considerable effort has been devoted now to developing adequate breeding diets for our standard laboratory animals. As expected, diets that are deficient in essential amino acids, vitamins, and so forth deter growth, puberty, and adult reproductive performance. Similarly, it has been documented countless times that nutritional supplements will yield enhanced growth and reproduction for livestock maintained on poor pastures.

Unfortunately, we know little about either the normal diets of wild mammals or their nutritional requirements. We do know that many mammalian habitats vary seasonally in the nutritional quality of the available vegetation (see Stanton-Hicks 1972). For example, a marked seasonal variation in the protein content of forage grasses has been documented many times (e.g., Uresk and Sims 1975; Goldberg, Tabroff, and Tamarin 1980). Thus, one might expect variation in essential amino acids and vitamins to provide an ultimate and sometimes a proximate basis for seasonal breeding in many herbivores.

Likewise, insects vary seasonally in their nutritional makeup, and thus one probably should expect the seasonal breeding of insectivorous mammals to have a nutritional as well as an energetic basis. On the other hand, since vertebrate flesh does not vary much seasonally in its nutritional content, one might predict that the seasonality of reproduction in carnivorous mammals would have an almost purely energetic basis. Tempering all these predictions, however, must be an acknowledgment that relatively few mammals are exclusively grazers, seed eaters, or meat eaters; indeed, a good deal of opportunism seems to reside in the dietary habits of most mammals (Brambell 1972).

Other Ultimate Factors

While climatic and dietary variation underlies most cases of seasonal reproduction in mammals, a reasonable argument can be made that competition and predator pressure should be important ultimate forces in some cases. It has often been argued, for example, that it would be an advantage for some populations of mammals to space out their births as much as possible to avoid concentrating pressure from predators. For other populations with different life-history strategies a concentration of predator pressure actually could be beneficial (Pianka 1976). Likewise, if several populations use the same food resource, it can be argued that they should evolve mechanisms to reproduce at different times of the year, thereby avoiding high energetic demand when the resource is being heavily utilized. Neither of these possibilities has been studied much in relation to the seasonality of reproduction in mammals, but undoubtedly these factors have acted some times in some situations as the ultimate causes of seasonal reproduction.

A possible example of one of these forces in action was provided by Dasmann and Mossman (1962), who studied ten species of ungulates living in the same area at 21° S latitude in Rhodesia (now Zimbabwe). These workers reported restricted breeding seasons in seven of these species and continuous breeding in three. This was in a situation in which there was a dramatic seasonality in rainfall patterns and hence vegetation growth.

It is important to note that many of the ungulates studied by Dasmann and Mossman (1962) ate the same general types of plants. The seasonal breeders bred at different times of the year, however, and some of the continuous breeders showed different seasonal trends. Thus, there was absolutely no uniform pattern of reproduction by these ten species in relation to the marked and predictable change in food availability. The degree to which competition shaped these different responses in unknown, but it certainly could have been an important ultimate cause in this situation.

A recent study of the squirrel monkey (*Saimiri oestedi*) in Costa

Rica may point the way for future explorations of the role of predation in shaping seasonal breeding. In this location, this primate shows a much more synchronized season of births than should be expected by changes in food availability. It also suffers a great amount of predation on recently born young. Thus, Boinski (1987) suggests that the tight birth synchrony exhibited by this population is in direct (ultimate) relation to the predation it faces.

Intuitively, one would guess that neither competition nor predation considerations could override the energetic and nutrient constraints imposed by a strongly seasonal environment. These factors could interact with dietary and climatic factors to fine-tune reproductive strategies in such environments, however. On the other hand, in dietarily and climatically constant environments one would expect that either competition or predation, or both, could often force seasonality on a population's reproductive strategy. Finally, however, since dietarily and climatically constant environments are relatively rare, one would guess that competition and predator pressure are relatively minor ultimate forces when the concern at hand is the seasonal reproductive strategies of mammals as a whole. It must be admitted, however, that there is much we do not know here.

Conclusions

Most of the terrestrial habitats that are exploited by mammals experience some degree of annual variation in rainfall or temperature. Some experience variation in both. In all such cases, the result is annual variation in food availability. Thus, annual variation in reproduction is common in mammals. Sometimes such variation is dramatic, sometimes it is a tendency seen only in females, sometimes it is seen in both sexes, and sometimes it is absent entirely.

Three factors intrinsic to the mammal itself act either to potentiate or to ameliorate the expectation of seasonal reproduction in seasonally changing habitats. These are average life span, feeding strategy, and the presence or absence of survival mechanisms like migration and hibernation. If seasonal reproduction is advantageous, a fourth intrinsic consideration determines when during the year a mammal will actually initiate reproduction. This is the length of time between the onset of oogenesis and the most environmentally sensitive phase of the female's cycle (often late lactation). Males must shape their annual reproductive effort around the pattern that is most advantageous for females.

All in all, it would seem best to conceptualize the annual reproductive strategies of mammals and the ultimate causes of these strategies in as broad a framework as possible. Many distinctly different radiations of mammals emerged from the Paleocene. Each had already established a fundamentally different life-history strategy forged by interacting selection for life span, body size, metabolic rate, food requirements, survival mechanisms, reproductive potential, and specific reproductive characteristics. Since the Paleocene, these radiations have subdivided and diverged genetically over and over again as new environments were exploited. The result must be a myriad of reproductive strategies that can vary within as well as between species.

Viewing all this variation from a purely energetic perspective is a useful organizational ploy, particularly when applied to mammals of small size. This does not mean that small mammals are never regulated seasonally by variation in specific nutrients, either ultimately or proximately. It only means that much of the variation seen in the annual reproductive strategies of these animals as a whole is accountable on a purely energetic basis.

When applied to mammals as a whole, an energetic perspective is still a useful organization tool, particularly if one "corrects" the energetic expectations of variation in body size with concerns for life span, feeding strategies, deficits in specific nutrients, survival mechanisms, and specific reproductive adaptations. Even when this is done, however, one still expects this approach to break down sometimes in interesting ways. Mammals are a diverse lot, and this is an ecologically complex planet. One expects that simple rules about annual reproductive strategies will always have many fascinating exceptions.

4

Food as a Proximate Factor: Neuroendocrine Pathways

Variation in food availability can act as a proximate regulator as well as being an ultimate cause of seasonal reproduction. No wild habitat is characterized by a continuous excess of food. The availability of food can vary greatly from year to year as well as from one season to the next. Furthermore, the food that is available in a typically mammalian habitat is usually distributed in patches, and the highest quality patches are not equally accessible to all individuals. Thus, in most habitats some individuals will either routinely or periodically experience undernourishment. If severe enough, this will curtail their reproduction regardless of other environmental concerns.

The objectives of this chapter are twofold: to consider briefly the finer neuroendocrine workings of the mammalian reproductive axis and to use this information to explore how undernourishment interferes proximately with reproduction. Most of what we know about the actions of undernourishment has been learned from experiments with laboratory rats. Thus, a description of this animal's reproductive axis will form the core of our considerations here. Where possible, and where appropriate, the rhesus monkey and the sheep will be used as comparisons. Emphasis will be placed on mechanisms thought to be more or less universal in eutherians, however. Interesting departures from the way rats, sheep, and rhesus monkeys reproduce will be considered in chapter 9.

Several excellent texts that consider in detail the neuroendocrine bases of mammalian reproduction are now available. The most thorough and up to date of these is the monumental two-volume set edited by Knobil and Neill (1988). Less detailed but more comparative, more biologically oriented, and exceptionally interesting to read is the five-volume set edited by Austin and Short (1982–86). A good clinically oriented text of reproductive endocrinology has been provided by Yen and Jaffe (1986). Unless otherwise noted, the description of the reproductive axis to be presented here is a synthesis of information obtained mostly from the latter two sources.

The Male's Reproductive Effort

In one way or another, the process of reproduction involves every organ system in the male's body. From the standpoint of the classical endocrine physiologist, however, at the core of this process are the hypothalamus, the anterior pituitary gland, the gonads, and a variety of sex accessory tissues. The functions of these various entities are synchronized by the actions of neurotransmitters and blood-borne hormones.

First, very briefly, two gonadotropins, both glycoproteins synthesized in the anterior pituitary, are of central importance for the male's reproductive effort: luteinizing hormone (LH) and follicle-stimulating hormone (FSH). These two hormones act on the testes to promote the production of sperm and steroid hormones. Steroid production also depends in part on a third pituitary glycoprotein, prolactin. The steroids themselves have manifold effects.

The release of the three hormones from the anterior pituitary is under the immediate control of small neuropeptides that act as releasing or inhibiting factors (Weiner, Findell, and Kordon 1988). These factors are synthesized in the hypothalamus and preoptic area and then transported to the anterior pituitary by way of a venous portal system (Padge 1988). Synthesis and release of the releasing or inhibiting peptides, in turn, are regulated by catecholaminergic neuronal networks and peptidergic pathways in the hypothalamus and other parts of the brain and, ultimately, by environmental input, including the amount of available food. Broad views of the interactions of the pituitary and the hypothalamus have been provided by Karsch (1984) and Everett (1988; see also Rennels and Herbert 1980).

In more detail, the physiological underpinnings of the male's reproductive effort, as noted by Bardin (1986), can be conveniently viewed in terms of two somewhat distinct yet interrelated axes: the hypothalamo-pituitary-Leydig cell axis and the hypothalamo-pituitary-seminiferous tubal axis (see also Ewing, Davis, and Zirkin 1980; Hodgson, Robertson, and de Kretser 1983; Williams-Ashman, 1988). In the first of these axes, LH acts on the Leydig cells of the testes to promote the synthesis of steroids (reviewed in de Kretser 1984; de Kretser and Kerr 1988). It is aided in this endeavor by prolactin, which among other things influences the number of LH receptors in these cells. The major steroids produced by the mammalian testes are androgenic in nature, mostly testosterone but with lesser

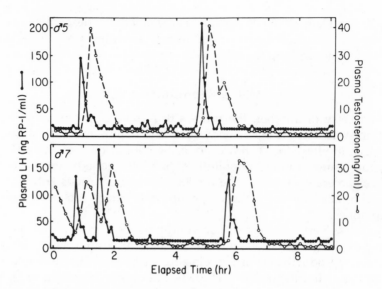

Figure 4.1. Temporal changes in circulating levels of LH and testosterone in two intact male mice bearing indwelling atrial cannulae. Each mouse was living alone in its cage. Small blood samples were collected via the cannula every 5 min. Reprinted from Coquelin and Desjardins (1982).

amounts of such hormones as dihydrotestosterone (Hall 1988). The testes also produce small amounts of estrogens, including such potent forms as estradiol.

The release of LH is under the direct control of a hypothalamic releasing factor, gonadotropin-releasing hormone (GnRH) (Catt and Pierce 1986; Clarke 1987; Fink 1988). The secretion of this peptide, in turn, is regulated by a poorly defined neuronal network acting as an episodic pulse generator (Silverman 1988). Thus, GnRH is released in periodic, short-lived bursts, and, consequently, so is LH and testosterone. This greatly confounds the problem of examining changes in the blood titers of these hormones. Average blood levels analyzed in killed animals or obtained as single "looks" from live animals may be quite misleading because titers of these hormones can vary greatly on a minute-by-minute basis (fig. 4.1).

The state of a male's reproductive potential is a direct reflection of the frequency of the pulse releases of GnRH and hence LH and testosterone (Desjardins 1981). Circadian variation also has been noted repeatedly in the secretory patterns of these hormones in many species (reviewed in Turek, Swann, and Earnest 1984; Turek and van Cauter 1988). One of today's most exciting areas of research in mammalian reproduction involves the complex regulation of GnRH secretion by catecholamines and small neuropeptides in the hypothalamus and other areas of the brain (reviewed in Barraclough and Wise 1982; Kalra and Kalra 1983; Ferin, Van Vugt, and Wardlaw 1984; Kalra and Leadem 1984; Ramirez, Feder, and Sawyer 1984; Van Vugt 1985; Kalra 1986; see also a large collection of papers in Flamigni, Venturoli, and Givens 1985).

The testicular steroids perform a host of diverse functions, and they accomplish these tasks in interesting and complex ways. Early in development, for example, they are responsible for differentiation of the male tract and for fixing a masculine bias in the brain (McEwen 1983). The phrase "masculine bias" usually translates as a lack of estrous-like cyclicity in hypothalamic function and the tendency to show masculine sexual behavior and spontaneous aggression when the mammal reaches adulthood (reviewed in Feder 1981a, 1981b; Sachs and Meisel 1988).

During adulthood, the functions of the testicular steroids include maintenance of the sex accessory organs, including the secretion of seminal fluids by the prostate and seminal vesicles; regulation of the meiotic phase of spermatogenesis; permissive regulation of aggressive and sexual behavior in many mammals; maintenance of external secondary sexual characteristics and some pheromone-producing glands; and, finally, regulation of the secretion of LH, and thereby regulation of their own secretion, in a closed-loop system.

In this closed-loop system, the testicular steroids act both on the anterior pituitary and on the GnRH pulse generator. The latter is known generally as "negative feedback" regulation since high levels of steroids can depress activity of the GnRH pulse generator. As expected then, castration is followed by a dramatic increase in the frequency of LH pulses and thus a much higher average level of LH in the blood. In contrast, blood levels of prolactin fall after castration. Prolactin secretion is regulated routinely by a dopaminergic pathway and probably by a neuropeptide that acts as an inhibiting factor (Neill 1988).

Testosterone is transported in the blood in association with plasma globulins. After dissociating from these proteins, it enters a cell, binds to an intracellular receptor protein, and then modulates genomic expression (Coffey 1988). Often, however, it is converted to a more potent steroid before binding with a receptor. Conversion to the more potent dihydrotestosterone occurs commonly in the tissues of the reproductive tract, and this hormone then is the active agent in these tissues. Likewise, neural tissues often aromatize testosterone to estradiol, and it is the latter steroid that is directly responsible for supporting many of the behavioral dimensions of the male's reproductive process (Crowley and Zemlan 1981).

Regarding the male's hypothalamo-pituitary-seminiferous tubule axis, a cycle of spermatogenesis, as measured from undifferentiated spermatogonia to the appearance of more or less functional sperm, requires anywhere from 5 to 11 weeks, depending on the species (Setchell 1982). Two hormones are directly responsible for this process: FSH and testosterone. FSH acts to establish the epithelium of the seminiferous tubule. Once this has been accomplished, spermatogenesis usually can be maintained in the hypophysectomized male by administering only testosterone. Thus, LH is also necessary for spermatogenesis, albeit indirectly.

The regulation of FSH secretion is still not well understood. This hormone is secreted by the same cells that secrete LH—the pituitary gonadotropes. Its synthesis is regulated by GnRH, but not its release. Thus, FSH is not secreted in a pulsatile manner in most male mammals, and it does not react to steroid feedback in the same manner as LH. Testosterone seems to exert only a relatively minor negative effect on FSH secretion, for example, and estrogens are effective in this regard only if given in supraphysiological doses.

The differential mode of secretion of LH and FSH is somehow related to the pulse frequency of GnRH secretion. It is also related to feedback regulation by a small blood-borne peptide secreted by the Sertoli cells of the testes—inhibin—which acts at the level of the pituitary to depress FSH but not LH secretion (Steinberger and Ward 1988). Inhibin may or may not also act at the level of the hypothalamus. Finally, it is possible that FSH secretion is also regulated by still another hypothalamic releasing factor that has yet to be isolated.

Developmentally, as noted earlier, gonadotropin secretion and hence testicular steroidogenesis peaks early in the life of males, becomes quiescent for a time, and then peaks again to initiate puberty. Thereafter, barring social or seasonal interruption, the male more or less constantly produces sperm and seminal fluids, stores these materials, and awaits the chance to inseminate a female. Often the same hormones responsible for producing sperm and seminal fluids also precondition the male to act aggressively toward other males—his genetic competitors—and otherwise to behave in ways that will promote insemination (and thus his own genes) when a receptive female is encountered.

The Effect of Food Shortage on Male Reproduction

This subject has been reviewed previously (Mann 1974; Leatham 1975; Piacsek 1987). As noted earlier, most of what we know about the effects of food restriction on males has been learned from a horde of studies using the laboratory rat: Widdowson, Mavor, and McCance

(1964); Stewart (1973); Larsson et al. (1974); Srebnik, Fletcher, and Campbell (1978); Glass and Swerdloff (1980); Merry and Holehan (1981); Menendez-Patterson et al. (1982); Nduka, Dada, and Okpako (1983); Glass et al. (1984); Aguilar et al. (1984); and Bazzarre (1984).

These many papers demonstrate that food restriction depresses a male rat's reproductive capacity in complex ways. In the laboratory, the degree of depression resulting from food restriction depends on three factors: the actual amount of food given each day, the length of time food restriction is imposed, and the stage of the life cycle during which the rat experiences it. In general, steroidogenesis is much more sensitive to food restriction than is spermatogenesis. Food restriction imposed early in life, before spermatogenesis begins, will greatly delay the onset of this process. Once spermatogenesis has begun, however, food restriction inhibits it only if severe and prolonged. Steroidogenesis, on the other hand, is extremely sensitive to food restriction throughout the male rat's lifetime.

All the available evidence documents a potent effect of food restriction on LH secretion, while most of it suggests little if any effect on the secretion of FSH, at least in the adult male (Root and Russ 1972; Howland 1975; Sisk and Bronson 1986). Thus arises the relative insensitivity of spermatogenesis and the great sensitivity of steroidogenesis to food restriction. Only small amounts of testosterone (and hence LH) are necessary to maintain spermatogenesis. The situation may be different in the infantile male rat, however (Glass and Swerdloff 1980).

To appreciate the potent effect of food restriction on LH secretion properly, it is necessary to use short-interval, sequential blood-sampling techniques. Thus, as shown in figure 4.2, LH pulsing is completely blocked by restricting a young rat's food intake to a level that allows maintenance of body weight but not growth. A return to ad lib feeding then initiates the pulsatile release of LH. The animals in the experiment from which figure 4.2 was extracted experienced only an average 14 percent decline in FSH titers, however.

Somewhat similar experiments have been done with male rhesus monkeys (Dubey et al. 1986). Chronic food restriction depresses the frequency of LH pulses in castrated males of this species, but again this treatment has little effect on FSH secretion. The frequency of LH pulsing in castrated rhesus males can be increased by infusing GnRH in a pulsatile manner, indicating no impairment of the pituitary itself. Likewise, the inhibitory effect of food restriction on LH secretion in the male rat can be traced it seems largely to a lack of episodic release of GnRH from hypothalamic neurons. Both the pituitary content of LH and the responsiveness of the pituitary to GnRH

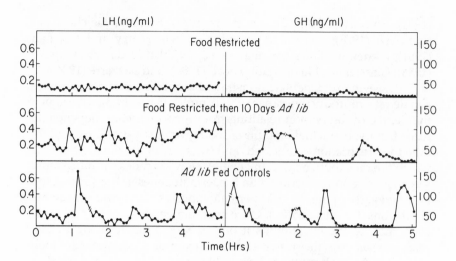

Figure 4.2. Representative temporal patterns of circulating levels of LH and growth hormone (GH) in three 60-day-old male rats that were maintained at 60 percent of their expected 60-day body weight by food restriction (top panel), treated similarly and then given excess food for 10 days (middle panel), or allowed to grow normally (bottom panel). Blood samples were collected every 6 min via atrial cannulae. The general lack of clarity in the LH pulses seen in the normally fed male rats, in comparison to that seen in figure 4.1 for mice, is typical of this species. Extracted from Sisk and Bronson (1986).

remain largely unaltered in starved male rats (e.g., Campbell et al. 1977).

In part, but probably only in part, the rat's failure to secrete GnRH is due to an enhancement of negative feedback sensitivity (e.g., Howland and Skinner 1973; Pirke and Spyra 1981; Piacsek 1984). That is, the normal inhibitory effect of testosterone on GnRH secretion is greatly enhanced in food-restricted animals. Thus, even small amounts of testosterone in circulation are enough to depress LH secretion in a starved rat. A more direct, steroid-independent suppression of LH secretion has been documented in female rats (Bronson 1988a) and male rhesus monkeys (Dubey et al. 1986). This more direct mechanism probably occurs routinely in other mammals as well, including the male rat. A particularly exciting area of endeavor today involves the exploration of the neurotransmitter pathways used by starvation to alter GnRH secretion (e.g., Schweiger, Warnhoff, and Pirke 1985a, 1985b; Philipp and Pirke, 1987).

The depressive effects of food restriction on an adult male's reproduction may or may not result exclusively from a lack of LH pulsing and hence a depression in steroid production by the testes. The sex accessory glands of a starved male rat are not as responsive to exogenous testosterone, nor is his sexual behavior (e.g. Sachs 1965). Such deficits could simply reflect a prolonged absence of stimulation by testosterone. Alternatively, they could find their bases in a more general metabolic impairment or in a depression of prolactin secretion.

Food restriction profoundly depresses the secretion of growth hormone (GH), thyroid-stimulating hormone (TSH), and prolactin, as well as LH, in male rats (fig. 4.2; Campbell et al. 1977). Inhibition of the secretion of the first two hormones could lead to a general metabolic depression, which in turn could result in an insensitivity of the testes and accessory tissues to LH and testosterone, respectively. A lack of circulating prolactin could influence the number or activity of LH receptors in the testes. Figure 4.3 presents an overview of the effect of food restriction on a male's reproductive axis that includes all such presumptive pathways as well as the steroid-dependent depression of the pulsatile release of GnRH, LH, and testosterone noted earlier.

The effects of food restriction on male reproduction have been explored in a few other species, but with much less concern for endocrine pathways: mice (Jean-Faucher et al. 1982; Hamilton and Bronson 1985); guinea pigs (Slob, Vreeburg, and van der Werff ten Bosch 1979); pigs (Dickerson, Gresham, and McCance 1964); wild collared peccaries (*Tayassu tajacu*; Lochmiller et al. 1985); cattle (e.g., Barnes et al. 1980; Almquist 1982; Beeby and Swan 1983); sheep (e.g., Pretorius and Marincowitz 1968; Alkass, Bryant, and Walton 1982); and humans (e.g., Kulin et al. 1984; Chakravarty, Sreedhar, and Gosh 1984).

In general, the conclusions reached in the rat studies seem to hold for other mammals as well. FSH secretion may be more sensitive to food restriction in humans, and apparently spermatogenesis as well as steroidogenesis is adaptively susceptible to chronic food restriction in some adult deermice (Blank and Desjardins 1984).

The Estrous Cycle

A sequential progression of interrelated physiological and behavioral cycles underlies the female's successful production of young. In many but not all species, the first and most basic of these is the estrous cycle, which is itself a combination of cycles. The central feature of the mammalian estrous cycle is the periodic maturation of the eggs that will be released at ovulation and luteinization of the follicles after ovulation to form corpora lutea. Coordinated with this ovarian cycle are cyclic changes in the uterus to prepare it for implantation should fertilization occur. Also coordinated here in most mammals are cyclic changes in the female's receptivity that cause her to be either uninterested or aggressive toward a male except around the time of ovulation. The agents that synchronize these three dimensions of the estrous cycle are of course the pituitary gonadotropins and the ovarian steroids.

The general organizational scheme of hormonal actions and reactions that is shown below for the male (fig. 4.3) can also represent the cycling, nonpregnant, nonlactating female, given the following alterations: changing the testis to an ovary and visualizing the latter

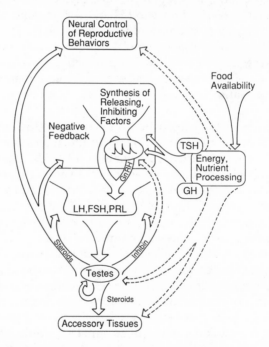

Figure 4.3. A schematic view of the hormonal pathways involved in maintaining reproduction in a male mammal and the influence of food restriction on these pathways. The large box in the middle of this figure represents the neural components involved in the negative feedback regulation of releasing factors by the ovarian steroids. Thus, this figure suggests that food restriction depresses the activity of the GnRH pulse generator both directly and indirectly via enhanced negative feedback sensitivity. The result is an inhibition of the normal episodic release of LH and the testicular steroids. Presumptive pathways are shown here as dashed arrows. An inhibition of GH and TSH secretion could yield a general metabolic depression that in turn could lead to hormonal insensitivity of the testes, the sex accessories, and the neural elements controlling behavior. Not illustrated here (to avoid more visual confusion) is a potential inhibition of prolactin secretion and consequently a depression in LH receptor activity in the testes.

as being more or less dominated during one phase of the estrous cycle by the developing follicles and at a later stage by corpora lutea (Keyes et al. 1983); changing the steroids produced by the gonad to mostly estrogens and progesterone, both of which act via negative feedback to regulate gonadotropin secretion (Lipsett 1986; Karsch 1987); adding a positive feedback dimension by means of which high levels of estradiol promote a dramatic ovulating release of LH from the pituitary after proper steroidal preconditioning (Karsch 1984); giving prolactin a more prominent role in regulating gonadal steroid secretion in some mammals and focusing the actions of this hormone on mammary tissue as well as on the gonad; and adding neural pathways that allow circadian regulation of many facets of the estrous cycle in some mammals, such as the rat (reviewed in Turek, Swann, and Earnest 1984).

The cycle of follicle maturation and luteinization that forms the basis for the estrous cycle is complex, and its regulation by gonadotropins is complex (see Channing et al. 1980; Baker 1982; Ross and Schreiber 1986; Yen 1986c). All female mammals are born with a surfeit of eggs. These are located in primordial follicles, each of which consists of an ovum surrounded by a single layer of granulosa cells. Most of these follicles will develop to some degree, become atretic, and disappear. A relative few will develop fully and be ovulated. A fully developed, immediately preovulatory follicle has many layers of granulosa cells that surround a cavity containing steroid-rich follicular fluid. Outside the thick granulosa layer are thecal cells that are the ovarian counterparts of the Leydig cells of the testes.

As reviewed in Baird (1984), the initial development of a follicle is independent of gonadotropin action, but full development requires a complex synergism between FSH, LH, estradiol, and androgen. LH acts on thecal cells to induce the synthesis of androgens, mostly testosterone, which then diffuse into the follicular fluid. FSH acts on the granulosa cells to induce the formation of an aromatizing enzyme that converts testosterone to estradiol (Gore-Langton and Armstrong 1988). Estradiol then is the mitotic agent that actually causes the granulosa cells to proliferate as well as exerting more systemic effects (Clark and Markaverich 1988).

The gonadotropins also influence receptor regulation in this complex set of interactions. Additionally, there are several inhibiting and activating factors involved in follicular maturation, all produced and acting locally within the ovary (e.g., an oocyte maturation inhibitor that holds meiosis in check until just prior to ovulation; see Channing et al. 1980; Greenwald and Terranova 1988; Tsafriri 1988).

Ovulation—the rupture of a fully developed follicle—is induced by a dramatic surge in circulating LH (Lipner 1988), after which the granulosa cell–thecal cell complex becomes luteinized to a greater or lesser degree (reviewed in Niswender and Nett 1988). The resulting corpus luteum is characterized by progesterone rather than estradiol secretion, at least in most species (the primate corpus secretes considerable estradiol). Both the process of luteinization and the synthesis of progesterone are LH dependent, but other hormonal stimulation may be necessary for full realization of the potential of the corpus luteum. In particular, prolactin plays an important role here in some species.

Much of what we know about the neuroendocrine organization of the female's estrous cycle stems from studies that have focused exclusively on the events immediately preceding the pubertal ovulation. One of the most impressive illustrations of the central role of the GnRH pulse generator for the female's estrous cycle, for example, was provided by Knobil and his colleagues (Wildt, Marshall, and Knobil 1980) when they induced normal puberty in young female rhesus monkeys by administering hourly pulses of GnRH via atrial cannulae (see Plant 1988).

Much of the past effort of physiologists interested in puberty has involved a search for the last component of the reproductive axis to achieve its normal adult level of function. The possibilities here are almost infinite since the axis has many component parts, each of which encompasses a complexity of control mechanisms in itself. Furthermore, the development of some of these control mechanisms depends on the development of others. Many good reviews have focused specifically on these control mechanisms (e.g., Foxcroft 1978; Ramaley 1979; Foster 1980; Levasseur and Thibault 1980; Ojeda et al. 1981; Ojeda, Aguado, and Smith 1983; Reiter and Grumbach 1982; Bronson and Rissman 1986).

A core concept that emerged early in this search was that of the "gonadostat" (Ramirez 1973). GnRH secretion is under tight inhibitory control by steroid negative feedback in the young mammal, but as time progresses it becomes somewhat less sensitive to steroid inhibition. This "resetting" process produces a more rapid rate of firing of the GnRH pulse generator, more LH in circulation, and, consequently, still more gonadal steroid in circulation. The resetting process continues until the adult level of equilibrium is reached.

The gonadostat concept has proved particularly valuable in explaining the onset of fertility in the ewe. Figure 4.4 summarizes the conceptual results of a long series of studies on ewe lambs by Foster and his colleagues (Foster 1988; see also Goodman 1988). As conceptualized in this figure, estradiol negative feedback predominates prior to the pubertal ovulation, while progesterone feedback predominates during the luteal phase of the adult cycle. The gonadostat concept also has proved useful in conceptualizing the onset of fertility in both sexes of humans and in the female rhesus moneky.

As might be expected, recent work suggests that the final step in the development of the reproductive axis probably varies from mammal to mammal. The shift in negative feedback sensitivity to adult levels actually occurs after, rather than before, the pubertal ovulation in the rat, for example (Ojeda et al. 1981). Instead, Ojeda and his colleagues have implicated the development of gonadal LH receptors as the final step in the maturation of the reproductive axis in this animal. This realization, in turn, has led to an increased concern for the role of other pituitary hormones, particularly prolactin and GH,

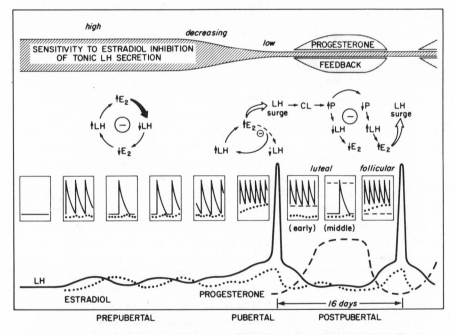

Figure 4.4. "Schematic hypothesis for endocrine events during the transition into adulthood in the female lamb. The hypothesis is based upon a decrease in sensitivity to estradiol inhibition of tonic LH secretion. Width of the crosshatched area at top depicts degree of sensitivity to estradiol negative feedback; after the first ovulation, progesterone assumes the role of feedback regulator of LH secretion. Insets illustrate detailed patterns of hormone secretion during a 6-hour period during the various stages of the pubertal transition, LH, solid line, E_2, estradiol, dotted line; P, progesterone, broken line; ---, negative feedback; CL, corpus luteum." Both the figure and this legend are reprinted from Foster et al. (1986).

as regulators of these receptors (see Ojeda et al. 1983) as well as direct control of the receptors by the sympathetic nervous system (Ojeda and Urbanski 1988).

Other possibilities for the final step that allows fertility onset, for which some support is available in one or more mammals, include maturation of the positive feedback control over LH secretion, a regulatory role for the adrenal steroids (Cutler and Loriaux 1980), and arborization of some key neuronal networks (reviewed in Kalra and Kalra 1983). The concern for the adrenal arises because of the existence of a profound adrenarch in humans (but not in many other mammals; Cutler and Loriaux 1980) and from the experimental observation that adrenalectomy advances the timing of puberty in the female rat (see Ramaley 1978). A key role for circadian maturation in controlling the pulse generator also has been postulated in both rats and humans (e.g., MacKinnon, Puig-Duran, and Laynes 1978; Ramaley 1980), but the evidence for this is weak.

Actually, as will be discussed shortly, the final step allowing fertility onset in most female mammals probably takes place outside the reproductive axis proper. It probably involves a permissive metabolic signal of some kind coupling puberty to some dimension of growth and nonreproductive development.

Once adulthood has been achieved, the precise characteristics of the complex set of cycles that constitute the estrous cycle can vary greatly among species (Feder 1981a; Short 1984). These differences relate to the life of the corpus luteum and, correlatively, the length of the cycle; whether ovulation occurs spontaneously or reflexively in response to copulation; the degree to which sexual behavior requires preconditioning by steroids and whether the steroids of concern are ovarian or adrenal in origin; and the degree to which the cycle is dominated by a circadian organization. There are also species differences in the major steroids produced by the ovary.

Another important source of variation between species is the number of cycles experienced during the breeding season (Sadleir 1969). Some mammals are polyestrous, experiencing cycle after cycle during a breeding season unless interrupted by pregnancy. Others are monestrous; that is, their genetic programming allows only one period of ovulation each breeding season. Finally, some but not all mammals experience a postpartum period of estrus. This allows them to develop one set of offspring in the uterus while suckling another.

Figure 4.5 compares some of the hormonal and behavioral changes observed during the estrous cycles of the laboratory rat and the rhesus monkey when it is maintained in the laboratory. As an adult, the rat experiences a short 4- or 5-day cycle, during which a dozen or more eggs are ovulated. These characteristics reflect the short life span and thus the need for a high reproductive potential by the wild ancestors of our domestic stocks. Traditionally, as shown in figure 4.5, each day of the rat's estrous cycle is named.

The rat's estrous cycle has been reviewed in depth in Freeman (1988). In general, FSH is secreted at low levels throughout the es-

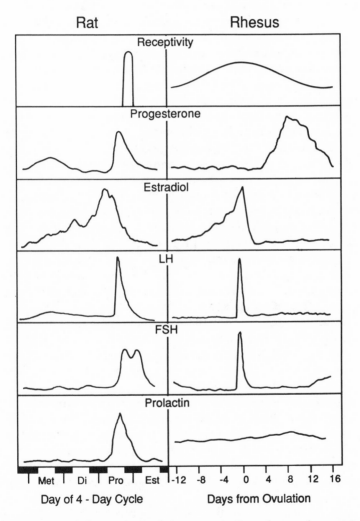

Figure 4.5. Temporal changes in circulating concentrations of some glycoprotein and steroid hormones, and in sexual receptivity, throughout the infertile ovulatory cycle of the rat and the rhesus monkey. A classic 4-day cycle broken up into metestrus, diestrus, proestrus, and estrus is shown for the rat. This figure was compiled and redrawn from Smith, Freeman, and Neill (1975), Beach (1976), Sarkar et al. (1976), Slob et al. (1978), Spies and Chappel (1984), and Yen (1986a).

trous cycle except for a dramatic surge in the release of this hormone around the time of ovulation. This surge requires a relaxation of the normally inhibitory action of both inhibin and the gonadal steroids. The FSH surge accelerates the development of the crop of follicles that will be ovulated during the succeeding cycle. LH is not shown in figure 4.5 as being released episodically. This is a reflection of the scale of the graph. As demonstrated nicely by Gallo (1981a, 1981b), the female rat normally experiences discrete episodes of release of LH about every hour. These pulses are particularly obvious late in the afternoon of metestrus and diestrus. The ovulatory surge of LH release reflects a dramatic increase in the frequency of LH pulses. Pulsatile release becomes so rapid that the individual pulses cumulate as a single massive outpouring of LH from the pituitary.

Because of steroid negative feedback suppression, both the frequency and the magnitude of LH pulses are held in check for a few days after ovulation. These baseline blood levels of LH are sufficient, however, to promote estradiol secretion by the follicular granulosa cells. As these cells proliferate, the total substrate for estradiol synthesis increases, and thus blood levels of this steroid gradually rise. This accelerating process peaks late in the light phase of the day of proestrus when the high levels of estradiol cease inhibiting LH via negative feedback activity and actively promote the ovulatory surge of this hormone. The estradiol titer determines the day of this surge, but the time of day is regulated by a circadian clock. These two forces interact to produce an ovulatory release of LH late in the afternoon of proestrus. Ovulation follows in a few hours.

Searching activity is enhanced by estradiol, and sexual receptivity is programmed steroidally to occur at about the time of ovulation (fig. 4.5). Estradiol is the primary steroid responsible for promoting sexual receptivity in the rat, but progesterone may enhance this effect, and it may also be important in terminating receptivity (Beach 1976; Feder and Marrone 1977; Pfaff 1980, 1982; Fahrbach and Pfaff 1982; Feder 1985; Pfaff and Schwarz-Giblin 1988). The source of the progesterone peak that occurs late in proestrus is partly adrenal in origin. Circulating levels of prolactin also peak at this time, and this hormone plays a major role in producing the rat's short-lived corpus luteum, which secretes modest amounts of progesterone for a day or two.

The estrous cycle of the rhesus monkey differs in several respects from that of the rat. First, correlated with the longer life span of this species, only one egg is ovulated each cycle. The cycle is also much longer and features a much longer-lived corpus luteum. Second, the cycle is characterized by obvious and prolonged follicular and luteal phases, with estradiol being the dominant steroid secreted during the former and progesterone secretion dominating the latter (fig. 4.5). Third, blood titers of prolactin do not change greatly during the rhesus' cycle, leaving open the question of the degree to which this hormone participates in corpora lutea formation and function. Fourth, unlike the rat, the female rhesus copulates throughout her estrous cycle, albeit with a greater frequency around the time of ovulation. Gonadal steroids apparently play little role in supporting this behavior, but adrenal steroids might (cf. Baum et al. 1978; Goldfoot, Wiegand, and Scheffler 1978). Finally, the rhesus's cycle lacks the circadian domination that characterizes the female rat's cycle (Pohl and Hotchkiss 1983).

Not all the variations that can occur in the estrous cycles of mammals appear in this detailed comparison of the rat and the rhesus. Classifications of mammalian estrous cycles have been provided by Conaway (1971), Rowlands and Weir (1984), and Short (1984). Many of these variations will be discussed later. One type of variation should be given special emphasis here, however, namely spontaneous versus reflexive ovulation. Both the rat and the rhesus are spontaneous ovulators. That is, they ovulate every cycle whether or not copulation occurs.

In contrast, in some other mammals, such as the cat (*Felis catus*), the lagomorphs, and the voles, ovulation is induced by copulation. In the absence of copulation, the ovaries of these animals experience recurring waves of follicular development and atresia; as a result, one crop of eggs is always mature and ready for ovulation, at least during the breeding season. This means that blood estradiol levels are always relatively high during the breeding season, and thus so is receptivity. Tactile stimulation of the cervix during copulation then elicits a neurogenic signal that reflexively elicits the ovulatory release of LH in these animals.

Food Shortage and the Estrous Cycle

There is a solid literature on the effects of food restriction on the ovulatory cycle of rats, starting with the papers by Kennedy and Mitra (1963a, 1963b) and Widdowson, Mavor, and McCance (1964), which focused on the pubertal ovulation. It has been obvious since these landmark papers that fertility onset in the female mammal is somehow regulated permissively by some facet of growth and nonreproductive development. Since food restriction depresses growth, it has often been used as a tool to study the relation between growth and reproductive development (reviewed in Glass and Swerdloff 1980; Bronson and Rissman 1986; Piacsek 1987).

Despite this effort, we still do not know how fertility onset in the female is coupled to growth. As of today, there is controversial evidence suggesting that each of the following provides the best correlate of fertility onset in the female mammal: body weight, rate of growth, fat content, fat-to-lean ratio, and food intake (Frisch, Hegsted, and Yoshinaga 1977; Frisch 1980, 1984; Glass et al. 1979; Perrigo and Bronson 1983).

While one of these parameters indeed may provide the best correlate for fertility onset in the rat, or the mouse, or the human female, the same parameter probably would not provide the best correlate for all three, and certainly not for all populations of all four thousand-odd species of this class of animals. The energetic challenges faced by these mammals during evolution, and their genetic solutions, must have been markedly different simply because of the profound differences in body size.

At a more proximate, mechanistic level, there is probably specific regulation of gonadotropin secretion by some as yet unknown, more universally constant facet of the body's energy- or nutrient-processing systems (Steiner et al. 1983). According to this hypothesis, the female's prepubertal increase in gonadotropin secretion could occur only when both internal and external energetic conditions predict success for lactation (Bronson and Rissman 1986).

Quite a bit has been learned about the effects of food restriction (or lack of growth) on endocrine function in the young female rat. As in the male, chronic food restriction profoundly depresses GnRH secretion and, hence, LH and gonadal steroid secretion in the female, but it has less effect on FSH secretion (Schenck et al. 1980; Meredith, Kirkpatrick-Keller, and Butcher 1986). Also as in the male, accessory organ responsiveness to exogenous steroids is depressed by chronic food restriction, possibly indirectly via either prolactin insufficiency or metabolic depression (see Howland 1971; Ronnekleiv, Ojeda, and McCann 1978; Glass and Swerdloff 1980; Dyer and McClure 1981; Hamilton and Bronson 1986).

As might be expected from the minimal effect of food restriction on FSH secretion, folliculogenesis per se is little impaired by this insult. Indeed, food restriction seems to delay follicle atresia somehow, at least in the adult (Lintern-Moore and Everitt 1978). On the other hand, ovulation occurs less frequently in response to exogenous gonadotropin in starved mice (Hamilton and Bronson 1986; see also Wilson et al. 1983).

The ease with which LH secretion can be manipulated in the female rat by varying food availability is best documented in relation to puberty. In figure 4.6, for example, young females were maintained for several weeks at 50 percent of their expected adult weight by re-

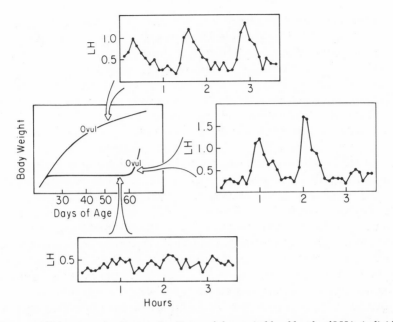

Figure 4.6. Representative temporal patterns of change in blood levels of LH in individual female rats depending on their body growth, which, in turn, was manipulated in some individuals by varying food availability. Growth was stopped in some females prior to puberty by limiting food availability. This depresses the pulsatile release of LH. At 60 days of age, these rats were returned to ad lib feeding, the result being rapid body growth, LH pulsing, and ovulation. The LH pattern shown at the top is typical of female rats when examined during the afternoon of diestrus. Redrawn from Bronson and Rissman (1986).

stricting their food intake. This suppressed the episodic release of LH. After several weeks of such treatment, these rats were returned to ad lib feeding. Repetitive LH pulsing was initiated in some rats within 12 hours, most were pulsing strongly within 24 hours, and most ovulated during the third or fourth dark period. The core effect of food restriction on GnRH secretion has been verified for this situation. Administering this peptide in a pulsatile manner to food-restricted females yields a normal sequence of endocrine and ovarian changes that culminates in normal pubertal development and ovulation, all despite a total lack of body growth (Bronson 1986).

Food restriction depresses GnRH secretion in the young female rat both directly and by enhancing negative feedback sensitivity to estradiol (Howland and Ibrahim 1973; Piacsek 1985; Bronson 1988a). Upstream from GnRH, there is no doubt that food restriction during development has broad effects on the nervous system, including even a general suppression of myelin formation (e.g., Wiggins and Fuller 1978; Wiggins 1982). There is some evidence that the activity of an inhibitory opioid pathway controlling GnRH secretion is enhanced by food restriction in the adult female rat (e.g., Corbet, Dyer, and Mansfield 1982; Dyer, Mansfield, and Dean 1985). Much remains to be learned, however, about the neural pathways mediating the effect of food restriction on GnRH secretion.

As far as the adult female rat is concerned, we know little about the relative sensitivity of the various stages of the estrous cycle to acute food restriction. This question has been explored in laboratory mice (Bronson and Marsteller 1985), however. This was done using 1 or 2 days of total food deprivation preceded and followed by ad lib feeding. Not surprisingly, if this acute insult is initiated on the day of estrus, just after ovulation has occurred, the end result is only a modest prolongation of the following ovulatory cycle. Mice have the capacity to recover body weight and energy reserves rapidly by consuming large amounts of food in a short period of time. If 2 days of food deprivation are imposed on a female mouse during diestrus, however, when the next cycle is at a critical stage of development, the result is as much as a full week's delay in the next ovulation.

The estrous cycle of the mouse is not greatly different than that of the rat. Thus, the results described above are probably generally applicable to it. On the other hand, the rat is a larger mammal with larger energy stores. Thus, the effects of acute food deprivation probably would not be quite as dramatic in the rat. Morin (1986b) reported that total food deprivation blocked the estrous cycle of the Syrian hamster. Interestingly, this block was overcome by giving the hamster unlimited access to drinking water containing glucose, without access to any protein or fat.

The potent effect of chronic food restriction on the estrous cycle has been demonstrated many times now in livestock, often in relation to puberty and sometimes in relation to the onset of seasonal breeding. The following recent papers will serve as an entrée into this vast literature: Oyedipe et al. (1982); Baishya et al. (1982); Fitzgerald, Michel, and Butler (1982); Dufour, Adelakoun, and Matton (1981); Haresign (1981a, 1981b); Ducker, Yarrow, and Morant (1982); Hixon et al. (1982); Kaur and Arora (1982); Etienne, Camous, and Cuvillier (1983); Rhind et al. (1984); Crump, Rodway, and Lomax (1985); Johnsson and Obst (1984); Kazmer, Barnes, and Canfield (1985); Erasmus and Barnard (1985); Day et al. (1986).

The general picture emerging from the studies with livestock is much like that seen in rats and mice, as amended for larger body size. That is, these larger animals with their much larger energy reserves are much less susceptible to short-term food deprivation, but chronic underfeeding apparently suppresses ovulation in much the same way as it does in rodents (see Martin 1984; Foster and Olster 1985).

Pregnancy and Lactation

From the endocrine standpoint, one can consider pregnancy in the eutherian mammal as a progressive change from one major mode of regulation to another (Metcalfe, Stock, and Barron 1988). In the first of these modes, the pituitary and the corpus luteum collaborate to prepare the uterus for implantation. In the second mode, the uterus and the embryo collaborate to form a placenta that in many species assumes both the trophic function of the pituitary and the steroidogenic function of the ovary (Solomon 1988; Talamantes and Ogren 1988). Thus, in many species either the pituitary or the ovary, or both, can be removed at some time during pregnancy without terminating it. There are profound species differences in all this, however (Heap and Flint 1984).

Meiosis is well under way at the time of ovulation in the rat, and fertilization occurs in the ampulla of the oviduct (reviewed in Bedford 1982). About 3 days are required for passage through the oviduct, at which time the embryo has reached the blastocyst stage (Harper 1982). Preparation of the rat uterus for implantation requires estrogen priming followed by prolonged exposure to progesterone, a process already initiated during the normal estrous cycle.

The tactile facet of copulation neurogenically enhances the release of prolactin and more LH. This, in turn, changes the short-lived corpus luteum of the rat's infertile estrous cycle into a more enduring and more functional organ secreting large amounts of progesterone. The relatively high levels of circulating progesterone in turn act on the uterine endometrium to enhance the formation of decidual cells. These are energy- and nutrient-rich cells that will first nourish the implanting blastocysts and then interact with them to form a placenta. Copulation with a vasectomized male results in pseudopregnancy in the rat, a state in which decidualization, the initial stage of placental formation, is easily induced by irritating the endometrium mechanically. Renfree (1982) has provided a broadly comparative look at implantation in mammals, as has Weitlauf (1988).

By mid-pregnancy, the high levels of circulating steroids have largely shut down gonadotropin secretion by the anterior pituitary in the rat, and the responsibility for secreting these hormones has passed almost entirely to the placenta. The placenta has no known negative feedback dimension.

Maintenance of the developing embryo to term requires steroidal, glycoprotein, and peptide hormones, all produced by the rat's placenta in carefully balanced amounts. Progesterone depresses contractility of the uterine myometrium, for example, while estrogen stimulates it. Thus, for this and many other reasons the former rather than the latter steriod must dominate pregnancy. Progesterone is aided in suppressing uterine contractions by relaxin, a small peptide hormone secreted by the ovary. Secretion of these hormones, in turn, requires the presence of LH- and prolactin-like substances.

The signal that triggers birth in the rat and its origin are poorly understood (Challis 1980; reviewed in Liggins 1982; Hodgen and Itskovitz 1988). Signals from the fetus seem to play the central role in eliciting birth in the sheep (Liggins, Fairclough, and Grieves 1973). The endocrine changes seen just prior to birth in the rat include a depression of progesterone secretion and much higher blood levels of estrogens and adrenocortical hormones. Oxytocin is secreted from the posterior pituitary at the time of birth, the result being intense uterine contractions.

The early stages of pregnancy in the rhesus monkey differ endocrinologically from those of the rat. As noted earlier, the corpus luteum of the nonpregnant rhesus secretes large amounts of progesterone throughout the latter half of the infertile cycle. Thus, uterine preparation for implantation is well started even in an infertile cycle. This is best seen in relation to the extensive menstrual sloughing that occurs in another primate, the human. Copulation has no luteotrophic action in the rhesus. Instead, the developing embryo must signal the mother that she is pregnant. How this is done is not well understood (Hodgen and Itskovitz 1988).

As in the rat, early in the rhesus monkey's pregnancy the production of gonadotropins by the anterior pituitary begins to decline owing to negative feedback inhibition. The decidual cells rapidly begin releasing a glycoprotein with LH-like activity, and shortly thereafter another glycoprotein with prolactin-like activity appears in circulation. These substances—human chorionic gonadotropin (hCG) and human chorionic somatomammotropin (hCS), respectively— have been well characterized in the human. The latter has both prolactin- and GH-like activity.

The rhesus placenta is a rich source of GnRH and steroids. As emphasized by Jaffe (1986), however, hormone production by the developing fetus can interact importantly with that of the placenta. Indeed, in the rhesus the maternal adrenals and ovaries, the placenta, and the fetal pituitary, adrenals, and ovaries seem best viewed as a single unit when considering steroidogenesis during pregnancy.

Preparation for lactation begins early in pregnancy in most eutherian females. The mammary glands grow proportionally to body size before puberty, and except in humans they experience only a minor acceleration in development at puberty. The major development of these glands normally occurs only after the first fertilization, when a complex of broadly acting hormonal changes readies the female for lactation and its consequent drain of energy and nutrients. An excellent review of these changes, from a comparative point of view, has been provided by Peaker, Vernon, and Knight (1984; see also Cowie 1984; and Tucker 1988). In the pregnant rat, the hormones necessary for mammary duct formation are estradiol, the corticosteroids, and the placental counterpart of GH. Progesterone and placental prolactin are also necessary for proliferation of the alveolar secretory cells that produce milk. Thyroxin and insulin play permissive roles here.

Concurrent with mammary development during pregnancy is a prolonged period of lipid deposition in adipose tissue in other parts of the body. These deposits form an energy reserve that can be used during lactation to supplement the lactating female's diet. Both progesterone and insulin play a role in inducing lipid deposition, at least in cattle and rats, both by increasing appetite and hence food intake and by shunting lipid metabolism away from lipolysis (see Wade 1975; Cripps and Williams 1975). The drive to increase lipid deposition in adipose tissue, as opposed to lipolysis, is then reversed during lactation under the influence of prolactin and sometimes growth hormone.

The major energy-transferring agent in milk is lipid. The other components of milk are protein, sugars (mostly lactose), minerals, and water. Mammalian milk varies somewhat from species to species. A detailed comparison of the characteristics of the milk of different species has been provided by Oftedal (1984). For the first few hours or days of lactation, a different type of milk—colostrum—is produced. This substance is typically lower in fat and sugar and higher in protein than real milk. It is also typically rich in antibodies.

Delivering calories and nutrients in the form of milk is only one facet of the maternal care that must be given to neonates. In many species, the female also is responsible for aiding them to thermoregulate. She helps them eliminate wastes, and, later, she retrieves them when they wander off. This has been a rich area for research by endocrine-oriented behaviorists, working mostly with rats (e.g., Woodside et al. 1981; Leon and Woodside 1983; Leon, Adels, and Coopersmith 1985). Numan (1988) has provided an exceptionally detailed and broad overview of maternal care.

Typically, the hormones necessary for lactation also drive the female's maternal behavior (reviewed for the rat in Rosenblatt, Siegel, and Mayer 1979). Milk delivery itself also is affected by a behavioral-hormonal interaction (Wakerley, Clarke, and Summerlee 1988). Suckling reflexively stimulates prolactin secretion, which, in turn, increases milk production in the alveolar cells. Suckling also reflexively stimulates the release of oxytocin, which causes contraction of the myoepithelial cells that surround the alveolar cells. The result is "milk letdown," or the squeezing of milk into the ducts.

Food Shortage, Pregnancy, and Lactation

Detailed exploration of the effects of long-term food restriction on pregnancy and lactation has proved difficult. These later stages of the female's reproductive cycle obviously do not occur, and hence cannot be studied, if food restriction is severe enough to block ovulation. To study the effect of food restriction on pregnancy and lactation, the amount of food available must be insufficient for these later stages but sufficient for ovulation. Alternatively, one can employ short-term food deprivation after pregnancy or lactation has already been initiated. Both kinds of studies have been done with rats and mice (e.g., Berg 1965; Hsueh et al. 1974; Fleischer and Turkewitz 1977; Zamiri 1978; Lederman and Rosso 1980; Grosvenor and Mena 1983; Kanarek, Schoenfeld, and Morgane 1986).

As an example of this literature, figure 4.7 illustrates the relative effects of 24 or 48 hours of total food deprivation on pregnancy and lactation in CF-1 domestic house mice. As assessed by food intake, the CF-1 female's demands for energy and nutrients increase only slightly in late pregnancy and early lactation. Late in lactation, the female's demands are greatly exaggerated, and, indeed, her fat reserves are slowly depleted as she nurses a mass of young much greater than her own body weight.

As might be expected on energetic and perhaps on endocrine grounds as well, food deprivation initiated on day 2 of pregnancy has little effect on the number of young born later (fig. 4.7; but see Mc-Clure 1962, 1966; Bruce 1963). Likewise, later in pregnancy even 48 hours of total food deprivation causes only a modest loss of young in utero. In sharp contrast, 48 hours of food deprivation initiated on day 2 of lactation causes CF-1 females to consume over three-quarters of their young to make up for their food deficit. Later in lactation, after having invested a great deal of effort in their young, CF-1 mothers often will die before consuming any of their young (Bronson and Marsteller 1985). This is in spite of their depleted fat reserves and their greatly increased need for food.

It is obvious from figure 4.7 that the CF-1 female's reactions to food deprivation are much more complicated than might be predicted on a simple energetic basis. Apparently, as part of this species' opportunistic reproductive strategy, in early lactation females will consume some of their young when confronted with an absence of food, keeping some alive if possible. Later in lactation, they will sacrifice themselves to promote the survival of their offspring. Deermouse females employ a totally different strategy. Whenever their energetic constraints become too great during lactation, early or late, they simply consume their entire litter and then reinitiate an estrous cycle (Perrigo 1987).

As a general principle, one would expect mammals larger than

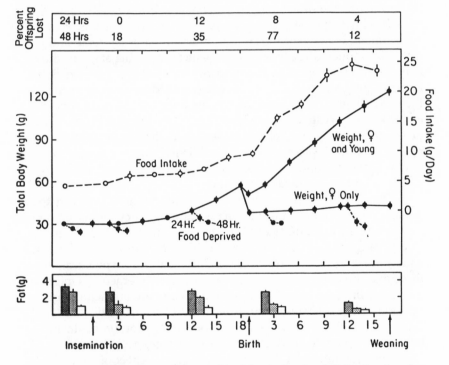

Figure 4.7. The effects of 24 or 48 hours of food deprivation in adult female mice when nonpregnant, 2 or 12 days pregnant, or on days 2 or 12 of lactation. The upper panel shows the effect of these treatments on the production of offspring. Loss during pregnancy was determined at birth. Loss during lactation was determined immediately after ad lib feeding was resumed. The middle panel shows the normal body weight and food intake of CF-1 females during pregnancy and lactation and the effect of 24 or 48 hours of food deprivation on their body weight. The lower panel shows the effects of 24 or 48 hours of food deprivation on fat reserves. The heavily stippled bars represent ad lib–fed controls, the lightly stippled bars represent females subjected to 24 hours of food deprivation, and the open bars indicate females food deprived for 48 hours. Redrawn from Bronson and Marsteller (1985).

mice to be much less susceptible to 1 or 2 days of food deprivation, even during lactation, because of their much larger energy reserves. Whether large or small in size, however, it seems reasonable to expect great variation among species in the way pregnant or lactating mammals react to the challenge of food shortage. As will be noted in chapter 7, for example, both the bats and the marsupials possess interesting mechanisms for regulating pregnancy in relation to food availability. All in all, however, it is unfortunate that we have so little comparative data here. There must be many fascinating strategies dealing with food shortage during pregnancy and lactation in mammals about which we know absolutely nothing.

Somewhat surprisingly, we also know very little about the endocrine pathways involved when food restriction yields deficits in either pregnancy or lactation. The problem in pregnancy is of course very difficult because of the large number of maternal, fetal, and placental hormones directly involved in sustaining this stage of the female's reproductive cycle. It is known, for example, that circulating levels of progesterone are probably depressed by food restriction in the early pregnant ewe, but the trophic hormone basis for this effect is not known (Williams and Cumming 1982). Intuitively, one would expect the same general effects as described already for the nonpregnant animal until placentation is established, but we remain almost totally ignorant about what happens endocrinologically when food restriction is applied in late pregnancy.

There is an extensive literature on the relation between food availability, hormones, and the success of pregnancy and lactation in livestock (e.g., Koritnik et al. 1981; Johnsson and Obst 1984; Gauthier, Terqui, and Mauleon 1983; Scales, Burton, and Moss 1986). Unfortunately, much of this effort has had limited and purely practical objectives, and thus no general set of principles has emerged. As might be expected, the loss of milk production accompanying acute food restriction can be overcome with prolactin, at least in rabbits and cattle (Mena et al. 1981), but the effect of food restriction on oxytocin has not been investigated extensively (see Grosvenor and Mena 1983).

Considerable work has been done on the effect of food restriction on ovulation and estrus in the suckling cow, and the results are confusing. Circulating levels of LH, FSH, and prolactin are all reduced by food restriction in these animals, and thus ovulation and estrus are often blocked (Echternkamp, Ferrell, and Rone 1982; Gauthier, Terqui, and Mauleon 1983; Easdon et al. 1985). Unexpectedly, however, this is not due even in part to a depression of GnRH secretion or low pituitary responsiveness to this peptide, nor is mating behavior enhanced in food-restricted animals by exogenous steroids

(Walters, Burrell, and Wiltbank 1984; Whisnant et al. 1985; Sides et al. 1986). All in all, the pathways by which food restriction interferes with pregnancy, lactation, and postpartum estrus constitute a richly unexplored area of endeavor.

Energy versus Nutrients

It is a truism that reproductive development, reproduction in the adult, and the behaviors associated with these processes all demand energy. This energy must be obtained from the mammal's diet, usually in the form of carbohydrates and fats. Successful growth and development of young mammals also require a diet containing minimum amounts of total protein, essential amino acids, vitamins, and minerals (e.g., Rao, Chalam Metta, and Johnson 1959; Underwood 1977). At first, these substances must be supplied by the mother, but after weaning they must be obtained by foraging. Beyond these generalities, we know little about the relative importance of calories versus specific dietary nutrients for regulating gonadotropin secretion.

Our most detailed experimental information about the role of specific dietary components in regulating reproduction, particularly gonadotropin secretion, again comes from studies with rats. Much of this effort has been directed specifically toward understanding the metabolic coupling of body weight and puberty. Thus, body growth and hence puberty can be manipulated easily by grossly varying the amount of fat and protein in a young rat's diet or by using a diet that is deficient in an essential amino acid (e.g., Innami et al. 1973; Massaro, Levitsky, and Barnes 1974; Frisch, Hegsted, and Yoshinaga 1975; 1977; Glass, Harrison, and Swerdloff 1976; Glass, Dahms, and Swerdloff 1979; Glass et al. 1979; Glass et al. 1984; Glass and Swerdloff 1977, 1980; Wilen and Naftolin 1977, 1978; Kirtley and Maher 1979; Ramaley 1981a; Aguilar et al. 1984; Pau and Milner 1984; Kanarek, Schoenfeld, and Morgane 1986).

Similar studies involving similar motives have been done with mice (Vandenbergh, Drickamer, and Colby 1972; Day et al. 1986; see also Bomford 1985), dogs (Rosmos et al. 1981), and cattle and sheep (e.g., Hansen et al. 1983; see also Crichton, Aitken, and Boyne 1959; Lamming 1966; McCartor, Randel, and Carroll 1979; Martin 1984). General reviews of interest here may be found in Frisch (1980) and Bronson and Rissman (1986).

In the studies noted above, sometimes gonadotropin secretion has been found to be altered, and sometimes not. Certainly, no clear picture has emerged yet in either prepubertal or adult animals relating a specific action of a specific dietary constituent to the secretion of either LH or FSH (but see Steiner et al. 1983; Cameron et al. 1985). Likewise, at this time we have no clear picture about the role of energy per se.

One reason why so little information is available here is that these are extremely difficult questions to ask, both technically and conceptually. Inhibiting gonadotropin secretion with a diet that is grossly deficient in either total calories or total protein may or may not imply a specific relation between gonadotropin secretion and available calories, total protein, or specific amino acids, for example. It is almost impossible to separate the long-term effects of caloric versus protein deficiency because a deficiency in calories must be accommodated ultimately by protein catabolism. Unfortunately, at least from an experimental standpoint, deficiencies in energy and specific nutrients are all intertwined metabolically in an animal adjusting to food deprivation.

Also unfortunately, as of now we do not have a good conceptual basis for visualizing the metabolic partitioning of a specific nutrient between reproductive and nonreproductive needs. This is why the preceding chapter emphasized energetics in relation to seasonality. This approach may be misleading sometimes, but at least it is a practical one. Both ecologists and physiologists have provided us with strong theoretical concepts for visualizing reproduction within an energetic framework (see Le Magnen 1983). Nothing like this exists for the relation between specific nutrients and reproduction. The metabolic partitioning of nutrients, the actions of specific nutrients on gonadotropin secretion, and the neuroendocrine pathways involved in such relations would seem like another rich but particularly frustrating area for future endeavor (see Platt and Stewart 1971; Wurtmann, Cohen, and Fernstrom 1977; Wiggins, Fuller, and Enna 1984).

Food Availability as a Proximate Regulator in Wild Populations

Food availability undoubtedly acts as both the ultimate and the proximate cause for seasonal reproduction in many wild populations of mammals. Additionally, as suggested in the introduction to this chapter, it probably is a factor of consequence for some individuals in many populations even during the best of years and even during the best season for reproducing during some years.

The routine way food availability probably regulates reproduction in the wild can be illustrated by comparing the reproductive performance of penned versus wild populations of the same species. The former typically are provided with food supplements. As a result, they routinely reproduce better than their counterparts in wild habitats. Mueller and Sadleir (1979), for example, reported that 50 percent of their captive female black-tailed deer conceived during their first year of life when held in large outdoor pens, whereas none do so normally in wild habitats. Several other examples of this phenomenon are presented in Sadleir (1969).

Even domesticated livestock often require food supplements during the winter in order to maximize their reproductive performance. Particularly germane here is the well-studied phenomenon of flushing in sheep. The number of eggs ovulated, and ultimately the number of lambs born, can be increased in ewes kept on poor pasture by giving them supplemental food for a few weeks prior to mating. Sometimes this is related to a gain in body weight, and sometimes it is not (cf. Coop 1966; Gherardi and Lindsay 1982; see also Allen and Lamming 1961; Den Hartog and Van Kempen 1980; Ensthaler and Holtz 1986). In either case, this phenomenon illustrates nicely the close relation between food availability and ovulation in mammals living in a dietarily poor habitat.

Most of what we know about food as a proximate regulator in the wild stems from studies with rodents. There is a vast literature correlating the reproductive performance of wild rodents with various indices of food availability (e.g., Taylor and Green 1976; Gashwiler 1979; Kemper 1980; Swanepoel 1980; Cockburn 1981; Yabe and Wada 1983; Ford and Pitelka 1984). Indeed, there have been many experiments in which food supplements are given to seasonally reproducing wild populations during the temperate-zone winter to see if this would improve their reproductive performance. In most cases, the result has been a marginal but definite improvement. Often this has taken the form of earlier than expected breeding in the spring or an extension of the breeding season during the fall.

Figure 4.8, for example, illustrates the effect of food supplements on a wild population of house mice living in and around grain fields in Australia. In this particular region, these animals usually breed during the spring and summer, but always in relation to the availability of wild grass seeds or domestic crops. When food supplements are added during the late winter, the animals respond quickly. Interestingly, Bomford (1987a) found no difference between the effects produced by supplements of wheat seeds and commercial rodent chow, suggesting an energetic basis for the winter depression of reproduction. In other studies, however, Bomford (1987b) obtained indirect evidence that total protein availability could be an important limiting factor in these populations. Again, however, this is a difficult distinction to make in any long-term study.

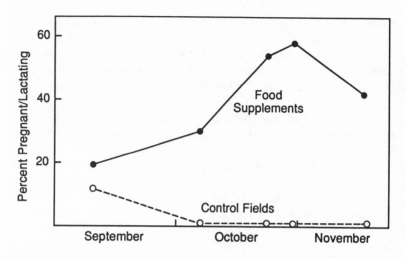

Figure 4.8. The effect of adding food supplements in the form of wheat or lab chow to natural habitats containing wild mice in Australia. This was done in the late winter, when reproduction in control fields was minimal. Redrawn from Bomford (1987b).

Many studies such as that shown in figure 4.8 have been done with a variety of cricetid rodents, usually with the same kinds of results (e.g., Newsome 1970; Watts 1970; Smith 1971; Fordham 1971; Flowerdew 1973; Andrzejewski 1975; Taitt and Krebs 1981). Adding food supplements to a wild habitat is not always successful in stimulating the reproduction of rodents, however, and correlational studies often indicate that food is not the only factor shaping the breeding season in some situations (e.g., Andersson and Jonasson 1986). As will be discussed in detail later, in chapter 6, a major concern here is the degree to which the population is genetically heterogeneous for photoperiodic responsiveness.

Finally, supplements of free water have been provided to some rodent populations in deserts or dry grasslands, where this might be the most potent limiting factor in operation. As shown by Christian (1979) and Newsome, Stendell, and Myers (1976), such supplements sometimes can improve reproductive success, at least marginally.

Conclusions

Of the many environmental factors that can influence a mammal's reproduction, food availability must be accorded the most important role. This is particularly obvious in relation to seasonal variation in reproduction. Variation in either the quantity or the quality of a mammal's food can serve as either an ultimate or a proximate cause for annual variation in the patterns of reproduction seen in mammals, or it can act in both ways at the same time. Indeed, food availability probably acts routinely as a proximate regulator of reproductive performance in many individuals in many populations, even during the normally preferred season to reproduce.

Experimentally, most of what we know about the proximate effects of food restriction has been learned from studies with laboratory rats or livestock. Food restriction suppresses the pulsatile release of GnRH directly, and it also acts indirectly by enhancing negative feedback sensitivity to the gonadal steroids. LH secretion is much more affected by food restriction than is FSH secretion. As a result, steroidogenesis usually is much more affected by food restriction than is gametogenesis, at least in the adult.

Spermatogenesis can be seriously affected by food restriction if it is experienced early in the life of a male, before this process is well started. Oogenesis, on the other hand, is little affected by food restriction, regardless of when it occurs. Food restriction probably also depresses reproductive performance indirectly by inhibiting the secretion of GH, TSH, and prolactin.

Levels of food restriction that allow ovulation seem to have little effect on pregnancy despite the increased need for energy and nutrients. This conclusion is based primarily on studies with rodents, however, and there are suggestions that late pregnancy might not be so well buffered from food restriction in some other types of animals.

As should be expected, food restriction has its most potent effects on the lactating female when the demands for calories and nutrients are highest. In part this is due to a decrease in prolactin secretion, but the situation is probably much more complicated than this. There is much we do not know about the effects of food restriction on pregnancy and lactation, and it is probably much too early to attempt generalizations about mammals as a whole.

Likewise, at this time we have an inadequate understanding of the relative importance of energy versus specific nutrients in regulating reproduction. Missing is a good theoretical basis for conceptualizing the way an inadequate supply of specific nutrients is partitioned metabolically between reproductive and nonreproductive needs. We have such a theoretical framework for visualizing the relation between available energy and reproduction, and both physiologists and ecologists continue to rely on the latter framework, even if it is misleading at times.

5

Ambient Temperature as a Proximate Factor

It is difficult to conceptualize in a truly meaningful way the neuroendocrine pathways involved in the proximate regulation of reproduction by ambient temperature. Indeed, to my knowledge this has not been attempted before for mammals, at least more than cursorily. In one sense this is surprising, but in another it is not. The effect of temperature on reproduction is an immensely complex and multifaceted problem whose many dimensions have never been explored systematically in the laboratory. Thus, there is no adequate data base on which to develop a conceptual overview. The scheme that will be proposed here is speculative, and it is meant to serve only as a target for future research. There are simply too many unknowns at present to do otherwise.

By way of background, some general principles about the way mammals react metabolically and behaviorally to temperature challenge must be noted before tackling the question of how reproduction is modulated proximately by ambient temperature. Several reviews on the subject of thermoregulation are available, including Hill (1976), Bartholomew (1977), and the excellent book by Mount (1979). The interested reader also might want to consult the short reviews by Chatonnet (1983) and Hammel (1983), which focus on some interesting evolutionary considerations, and those by Thompson (1977) and Robertshaw (1977), which are more endocrine oriented.

The first principle of importance here is simply that a mammal's reaction to temperature challenge depends on both its genes and its prior experience. Species and even populations of the same species differ inherently in determining which temperatures require metabolic and behavioral adjustment and which do not. Furthermore, previous exposure of an individual to a particular high or low temperature predisposes that animal metabolically to function better at that temperature. In the laboratory, this is known as acclimation. The ecologically more complex but somewhat analogous seasonal situation in the wild is known as acclimatization (Roberts and Chaffee 1976; Wickler 1981; Böckler and Heldmaier 1983; Cannon and Nedergaard 1983; Feist and Feist 1986).

Second, when visualizing a mammal's metabolic responses to temperature variation, one must mechanically separate its reactions to high and low temperatures. The zone of thermoneutrality—the range of ambient temperature within which the caloric costs of maintenance are minimal—is well below normal body temperature for all mammals. Thus, exposure to lower temperatures simply exaggerates the metabolic adjustments that are already occurring routinely anyhow (Thompson 1977). As noted in chapter 3, depending on both the severity of the low-temperature challenge and the body size of the mammal of concern, the adverse effects of cold can often be countered simply by increasing food intake.

In contrast, even a small increase in ambient temperature above thermoneutrality must be met with a totally new set of metabolic and behavioral adjustments. Usually, these are related to evaporative cooling, which increases the mammal's demand for water. These adjustments are also energetically expensive, but this expense cannot be countered by increasing food intake. This would add to the mammal's heat load. Searching for food would compound this problem even further (Taylor 1977; Nadel 1983). Thus, both food intake and locomotor activity normally decrease at high temperatures.

For all these reasons, a few degrees of temperature elevation above thermoneutrality can have far more potent effects than a much larger decrease below thermoneutrality. Indeed, in most mammals only a very narrow range of temperature separates the upper limit of thermoneutrality from the temperature at which survival is compromised, even with excess water available. In the presence of excess food, the comparable range below thermoneutrality is broad, and it becomes progressively broader as body size and food availability increase.

Finally, it is important to emphasize the potency of the thermoregulatory demand of the mammal and thus its potential for antagonizing reproduction. According to Bartholomew (1977), between 80 and 90 percent of the oxidative energy produced from consumed food is used to maintain thermal homeostasis in the mammal of average size under average conditions. This leaves little energy available for other functions. Thus, one always expects a close coupling between reproduction and ambient energetic conditions, regardless of which mammal is under consideration and where it lives.

Temperature, Reproduction, and Genetic Adaptation

The genes of most immediate concern for modulating reproduction in relation to ambient temperature must act in one of two general ways. First, natural selection will hone the mechanisms coupling ambient temperature and reproduction in a population to fit the particular demands imposed on that population. As will be shown later, geographic populations of the same species can vary greatly in this regard. Second, enough flexibility must be left in this system to allow individuals to acclimatize to changing temperature, particularly in seasonally changing environments. The result should be a population-specific range of temperatures within which reproduction is both permissible and profitable. The capacity for acclimatization would add flexibility at both ends of this range, but much less so at its upper end.

Experiments with wild house mice and their laboratory counterparts can be used to demonstrate these generalities. As shown in a large series of studies done by Barnett and his colleagues (e.g., reviewed in Barnett 1965; 1973; see also Barnett et al. 1975; Barnett and Dickson 1984), wild-caught house mice reproduce normally at 21°C in the laboratory but poorly at −3°C, even when given excess food. As expected, mice born under cold conditions reproduce better in the cold as adults than do mice acutely exposed to cold for the first time during adulthood. What is also important here is that these workers have shown that as little as eight generations of selection can yield a combination of genetic changes and maternal effects that allows normal reproduction in wild-derived mice at −3°C (fig. 5.1).

In contrast, similar experiments done with house mice maintained at high temperatures failed to produce a stock that reproduced normally (Pennycuik 1969). Indeed, only a relatively minor improvement was seen in the reproduction of Pennycuik's animals after many generations of selection at 34°C. The upper limits of temperature are difficult to surmount, even in a small mammal that can more easily eliminate heat through its skin.

We have little knowledge of the variation that exists in the reproductively optimal and reproductively permissible range of temperatures in the class Mammalia. Only a very few animals have been tested under controlled conditions. A hint at how interesting genetic adaptation for temperature sensitivity can be at the population level, however, is presented in figure 5.2. As shown in this figure, deermice from Alberta actually reproduce best in the laboratory at ambient temperatures much higher than those preferred by deermice living in Texas. At first glance, this seems like a paradox: the animals from the

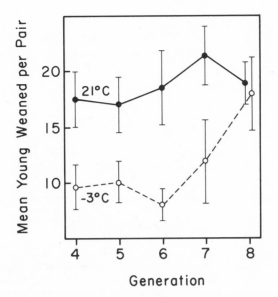

Figure 5.1. Selection for productivity among wild house mice maintained at −3°C for eight generations. Redrawn with permission from data collected by S. A. Barnett, K. Matt Munro, J. L. Smart, and R. C. Stoddart and published in Barnett (1973).

colder climate breed best at a higher temperature than is preferred by the animals from the warmer climate.

This really is not a paradox at all. The Texas population of deermice under consideration in figure 5.2 reproduces during the winter, while deermice breed in the late spring and summer in Alberta. Mean nocturnal temperatures (when the animals are foraging) are actually lower during a Texas winter than they are during an Alberta summer. Thus arose the difference seen in figure 5.2.

While we know little about population-to-population variation in the range of temperatures that permit unfettered reproduction in mammals, much of this variation must be accounted for simply by sex and body size. The reproductive capability of male mammals seems little affected by low temperatures per se, for example, regardless of species or size (e.g., Nazian and Piacsek 1977).

In contrast, females of small size, like house mice, show a variety of specific responses to low temperature that can cumulate to depress their productivity, even when given excess food. In the laboratory, these include a delay in puberty, a decreased frequency of ovulation after puberty, fewer young born per litter, and a longer interval between litters (Biggers et al. 1958; Barnett 1965). Similar observations have been made in rats (Piacsek and Nazian 1981; see also Chang and

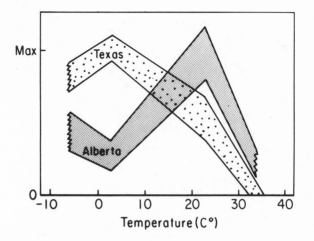

Figure 5.2. Litter productivity in two populations of deermice whose progenitors were wild trapped in Alberta or Texas. The stippled area encompasses the mean ±1 standard error as determined at each of four temperatures for each population. The data are expressed as percentages of maximum possible productivity for each population. Extracted from Bronson and Pryor (1983).

Fernandez-Cano 1959). Again as expected, these effects are greatly exaggerated if the animal is not allowed to increase its food intake to compensate for its increased thermoregulatory demand (e.g., Perrigo and Bronson 1985).

On the other hand, ecologically reasonable low temperatures seem to have little effect on the reproduction of large mammals such as cattle, at least if excess food is available (e.g., Young 1983). Unfortunately, we know little about the effects of low temperature on large mammals not genetically cold adapted, for example, large tropical mammals.

Exposure to temperatures above thermoneutrality seems to depress the reproductive processes of females in all species studied so far, regardless of body size: mice (Pennycuik 1967, 1969, 1971; Paris and Ramaley 1973; Paris, Kelly, and Ramaley 1973; Garrard, Harrison, and Weiner 1974; Yamauchi et al. 1983); rats (Chang and Fernandez-Cado 1959; Hensleigh and Johnson 1971; Benson and Morris 1971; but see Piacsek and Nazian 1981); sheep (Neville and Neathery 1974); and cattle (e.g., Collier et al. 1982; Francos and Mayer 1983; Badinga et al. 1985; see Morrison 1983).

The effects of high temperature manifest themselves throughout the female's reproductive cycle, depressing ovulation and increasing both pre- and postnatal mortality. Probably the best-studied effect here relates to the high mortality of early embryos that is often seen in livestock exposed to high temperature (e.g., Hafez 1964; Thwaites 1967; Ulberg and Sheean 1973; see also Banai and Sod-Moriah 1976, who explored this phenomenon in rats). As will be detailed later, males face a problem in a hot environment not encountered by females, namely a direct action on the gonad. Local heating of the testes inhibits spermatogenesis; thus, a scrotum evolved to maintain the temperature of these organs below that of the rest of the body.

Set against this experimental and theoretical background, one can ask what kinds of temperature challenges actually face the mammals living on this planet? Answering this question is a necessary prerequisite for conceptualizing mechanically how their reproduction should be modulated by these challenges. The most severe environments in which mammals exist are the polar regions, high mountains, and low-latitude deserts, the latter because water for evaporative cooling is a limiting factor in these environments by definition. Mountain environments are characterized not only by harsh, cold winters but also by sudden changes in temperature in all seasons. The typical temperate-zone habitat experiences marked seasonal change in temperature as well as more abrupt fluctuations as storm fronts progress across them. The tropics, on the other hand, are where most mammals reside, and the temperatures there are both warm and relatively constant.

As suggested earlier in figure 5.2, one would guess that all mammals are well adapted to reproduce wherever temperatures are relatively constant or where they experience gradual seasonal change to which they can acclimatize. An exception might be in the hot deserts, where some mammals seem to be existing near their physiological limits. Another exception relates to domestic livestock that originally evolved in the temperate zone but that have since been moved to the tropics by man. This is an important consideration because most of what we know about the endocrine responses to temperature challenge has been learned by exposing livestock to high temperatures. On the other hand, sudden changes in temperature could present problems in many habitats in which mammals exist, even where these mammals can become well acclimatized to slowly varying weather conditions. Thus arises a concern for the effects of stress on reproduction.

The Concept of Stress

Endocrinologists traditionally view the regulation of a mammal's reproduction by ambient temperature almost exclusively within the framework of the classic Selyean concept of stress (Selye 1980). That is, animals exposed to temperatures above or below those of thermoneutrality are considered to be either heat stressed or cold stressed, and this is further considered within a temporal framework of acute versus chronic exposure. This is a purely laboratory-oriented perspective, and by itself it is inadequate for the problem at hand. There are three reasons why this is so.

First, the term *stress* is used in so many different ways now, even by endocrine physiologists, that its application in any situation is confusing. Second, drawing close parallels between high- and low-temperature challenge and all other potentially noxious stimuli, particularly the large assortment of stressors that have been devised by laboratory scientists, undoubtedly leads to unbiological oversimplification. Finally, as argued above in relation to the temperature challenges actually facing the wild mammals on this planet, the stress concept can encompass only a limited dimension of the way temperature must act to regulate reproduction in wild habitats.

In the first regard, stress was originally defined endocrinologically in relation to a common set of stereotyped, nonspecific responses to diverse noxious agents, at the core of which was increased adrenal activity (Seyle 1936). Today, stress seems to be defined in two markedly different ways. First it is defined classically as hyperactivity of the corticotropin-releasing hormone (CRF)–adrenocorticotropin (ACTH)–adrenal steroid axis caused by some change in an animal's internal or external environment (Ganong 1977).

Alternatively, stress is often defined arbitrarily by an experimenter in relation to his or her subjective evaluation of the environmental change itself. That is, any perturbation in an animal's environment that is deemed noxious by an experimenter will evoke a condition of stress in that animal, at least in the mind of the experimenter, regardless of what happens to the secretion of ACTH and the adrenal steroids (e.g., Makhmudov and Khaibullina 1977; Ramaley 1981b; Armstrong 1986). The result of this semantic difference is an exceptionally confusing literature in which one is never quite sure how a particular author is using the term.

There is no doubt that diverse kinds of stimulation can enhance the secretion of ACTH and the adrenal steroids. These range from sexual arousal in a male mouse, to the immobilization or cold exposure of a rat, to pre-exam anxiety in a medical student (e.g., Blake 1975; Vernikos et al. 1982; Bronson and Desjardins 1982).

Stimuli that have been deemed stressful by endocrinologists, whether or not adrenal activity is elevated, include the following conditions and stimuli: caloric deficiency, nutrient deficiency, infectious disease, electroejaculation, hypoxia, the sound of a bell ringing, transport between animal rooms, capture in large cages, fighting, social subordination without physical contact, exposure to low air pressure, removal of offspring from their mother, sudden exposure to the sun, gentle handling early in life, inserting gauze under the skin, footshock, exposure to nembutal or ether, intense exercise, noise, surgery such as laparoscopy or ovariectomy, broken bones, and exposure to high or low temperature. A common presumption pervading the field of stress endocrinology is that all these stimuli yield a stereotypical set of common, nonspecific, endocrine responses that have adaptive consequences for reproduction. To biologists this makes little sense, particularly in relation to our concern here, which is the regulation of reproduction by temperature in the class Mammalia.

Evolutionarily, mammals have not had to deal with most of the stimuli employed by endocrinologists in the laboratory. On the other hand, they have had a great need to evolve adaptive ways of regulating their reproduction in relation to variation in food availability and ambient temperature. This, along with survival, is the core challenge for evolutionary success, and its genetic solution should have been relatively specific. Thus, looking for commonality in a mammal's reproductive response to low temperature, nembutal, and loud noise, for example, seems biologically irrational. Likewise, conceptually linking a mammal's response to sexual arousal, surgery, and food shortage simply because all these conditions cause an increase in circulating adrenal steroids also seems of questionable evolutionary significance (see Armario and Castellanos 1984).

Nevertheless, having criticized on biological grounds the confusing stress concept as it stands today, there is absolutely no doubt that a wide variety of laboratory stressors do routinely depress various dimensions of the reproductive process by depressing the secretion of the gonadotropins and the gonadal steroids. There also is no doubt that this often occurs in conjunction with increased activity of the CRF-ACTH-adrenocortical axis. Representative papers in this voluminous literature include Krulich et al. (1974), Euker, Meites, and Riegle (1975), Nakashima et al. (1975), Nequin, Alvarez, and Campbell (1975), MacKinnon, Mattock, and ter Haar (1976), Gray et al. (1978), Ramaley and Schwartz (1980), Forrest, Rhodes, and Randel (1980), Charpenet et al. (1981), Martin, Oldham, and Lindsay (1981), Welsh and Johnson (1981), Stoebel and Moberg (1982), Barb et al. (1982), Rasmussen and Malven (1983), Hennesey and Williamson (1984), Carter et al. (1984), Fuller et al. (1984), Goncharov et al. (1984), Rivier and Vale (1984), and Rivier, Rivier, and Vale (1986).

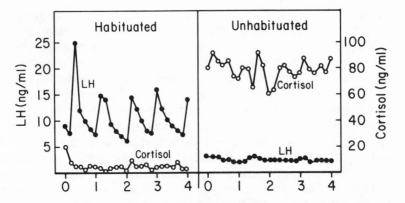

Figure 5.3. Temporal changes in plasma LH and cortisol in two ovariectomized cows shortly after being immobilized, haltered, and surgically fitted with jugular cannulae for blood collection. One individual was experiencing this set of procedures for the first time (Unhabituated), while the other had experienced it several times previously (Habituated). Redrawn from Echternkamp (1984).

A good example of a reciprocal relation between adrenocortical activity and luteinizing hormone (LH) secretion in relation to an aversive emotional state can be seen in figure 5.3. When cattle are placed for the first time in a stanchion, haltered, and prepared surgically for sequential blood collection via jugular cannulae, the result is a greatly elevated blood titer of cortisol and no pulsatile release of LH. In sharp contrast, after these cattle are habituated to this procedure by repeated exposure, they show low titers of cortisol in their plasma and normal episodic patterns of LH secretion.

There is no doubt that such reciprocity between LH secretion and adrenocortical activity occurs in relation to many unbiological stressors. There is also no doubt that it can sometimes be seen in relation to some kinds of temperature challenge (e.g., Schillo, Alliston, and Malven 1978; Hill and Alliston 1981; Plas-Roser and Aron 1981; Magal et al. 1981; Larsson et al. 1983). Thus, the job at hand is to take the unwieldy and somewhat unbiological concept of nonspecific stress and incorporate it into a specific concern for the regulation of reproduction by ambient temperature in mammals living in the wild as well as in the laboratory.

Endocrine Pathways: A Speculative Scheme

Figure 5.4 combines the concerns and expectations discussed earlier with what has been learned by viewing temperature challenge as a stressor in the laboratory. Added to this are some speculative guesses.

In this figure, high and low temperatures are defined in relation to a somewhat flexible range of temperatures within which reproduction can proceed unimpaired. Considerable population-to-population variation and considerable variation between the sexes are acknowledged here, as is the potential for considerable acclimatization. In the laboratory, the latter equates to the duration of the temperature chal-

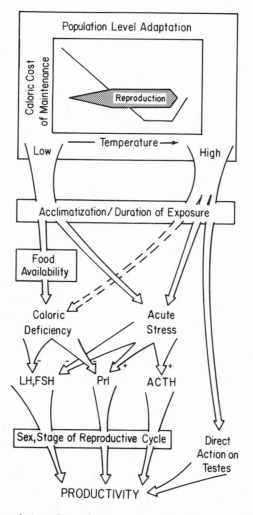

Figure 5.4. A speculative scheme for the way reproduction is modulated by ambient temperature when this factor is acting proximately but not as a predictor. The dashed arrow indicates a pathway that in theory should exist but for which no support is available. For a detailed description of this scheme, see the text.

lenge experienced by an animal prior to the time an endocrine measurement is made.

Figure 5.4 proposes four general ranges of temperatures that are important for the inhibition of reproduction. Two are interlocked above and two below thermoneutrality. Immediately above and below thermoneutrality should be a range of temperatures wherein reproduction will be suppressed to some degree if the shift from thermoneutrality to one of these temperatures is sudden. Gradual change or prolonged exposure to these temperatures will allow reproductive acclimatization, however. Beyond these two ranges of temperatures should be two more extreme ranges within which survival is possible but reproduction will remain suppressed regardless of the length of exposure.

The reader should be aware that there is a semantic problem inherent in this scheme, namely the supposition that there are some temperature ranges where acclimatization will allow survival but not reproduction. The remainder of this chapter will define *acclimation* and *acclimatization* purely in terms of survival mechanisms, without any accompanying assumption about reproduction.

In that vein then, temperature challenge is visualized in figure 5.4 as affecting reproduction via any one of several pathways. Excluded here is the possiblity that temperature variation could act as a predictor for some mammals. This will be discussed in the next chapter. In any case, the most fundamental pathway operating at low temperature in an acclimatized animal should be purely energetic. Downstream from the hypothalamus, this pathway should be more or less identical to that used by food insufficiency, at least in theory. That is, as noted in the preceding chapter, LH and prolactin secretion should be depressed whenever the animal experiences energetic insufficiency, whether because of an increased thermoregulatory demand or food insufficiency. Again, at least in theory, the secretion of follicle-stimulating hormone (FSH) should be much less affected by these insults, at least in adults.

The secretion of growth hormone (GH) should also be depressed in an acclimatized animal by low-temperature challenge with important secondary effects on reproduction. For this and other reasons, the target organs of the gonadal steroids should become less responsive to steroids at low temperature. Indeed, the end result of all this should be quite similar to that discussed earlier in relation to food restriction, with the probable exception of the control of thyroid-stimulating hormone (TSH) secretion. Whether the concern is proximate or ultimate, this energetic pathway should be the most fundamental one operating to regulate reproduction in relation to seasonal decreases in temperature.

The second pathway of concern at low temperature is the classic stress response, which is viewed here as being activated under only two conditions: when a mammal attempts to reproduce at temperatures that are below those to which it can acclimatize or when an unacclimatized animal experiences a sudden and dramatic decrease in ambient temperature. The latter certainly could occur in natural habitats in relation to sudden storms, but the former undoubtedly is a rarity outside the laboratory.

To the degree that the known endocrine responses to unbiological laboratory stressors can be extended to include the unacclimatized animal's response to cold, an increase in ACTH/adrenal activity could interfere with reproduction in several ways. As reviewed in Rivier and Vale (1984), these include a depression of gonadotropin-releasing hormone (GnRH) secretion associated directly with enhanced secretion of CRF, direct effects of ACTH on LH secretion and on gonadal steroidogenesis, and the negative feedback inhibition of gonadotropin secretion by adrenal androgens and progesterone. The latter could occur via an action on the neurons secreting GnRH or on the pituitary gonadotropes themselves. A smattering of papers that may prove of interest to the reader in relation to this problem include Christian (1964), Cohen and Mann (1979), Stoebel and Moberg (1982), Padmanabhan, Keech, and Convey (1983), Matteri, Watson, and Moberg (1984), Fonda, Rampacek, and Kraeling (1984), and Rivier, Rivier, and Vale (1986).

Any or all of the effects noted above could decrease reproductive success by acting at many stages of the female's reproductive cycle, including the behavioral dimensions of this cycle. Likewise, these actions could interfere with gametogenesis, steroidogenesis, and the reproductive behavior of males. It is important to note that an integral part of the endocrine response to many laboratory stressors is an increase in the secretion of prolactin (e.g., Aidara, Tahiri-Zagret, and Robyn 1981), and this could have manifold effects on reproduction, depending on the sex and stage of reproduction of the mammal experiencing it. More will be said about this shortly.

There is little endocrine data to support any conceptualization of the effect of low temperature on reproduction in either sex of any mammal. This is particularly true for the two-mode scheme being proposed here. Probably the most extensive set of data are those obtained in male rats by Piacsek and Nazian (1981). The rats studied by these authors were born at low temperature and then examined at various times during maturation; thus they were well acclimated. Only minor alterations were seen in LH, FSH, and prolactin concentrations in the blood of these rats, but their seminal vesicles were less responsive to testosterone.

Table 5.1 Effect of Maintaining Male Rats at 35°C for 30 Days, Starting at 4 Weeks of Age

	21°	35°
Rectal temperature	37.5 ± 0.1	39.6 ± 0.2
Body weight (g)	288 ± 6	214 ± 4
Testes weight	2.8 ± 0.1	2.5 ± 0.1
Serum LH (ng/ml)	3.4 ± 0.3	2.1 ± 0.2
Serum testosterone (ng/ml)	3.2 ± 0.4	1.9 ± 0.2
Serum corticosterone (μg/ml)	2.2 ± 0.3	8.4 ± 2.3

Source: Data from Magal et al. 1981.
Note: All the values shown are significantly different for the two temperature treatments.

As discussed earlier in chapter 2, however, from the standpoint of evolutionary strategies, one would expect less effect of low temperature per se on males than on females of any species, even in unacclimatized animals. Thus, not surprisingly, Tache et al. (1978) also found no significant change in the secretion of LH, FSH, or prolactin after a few days to several weeks of exposure to cold in their male rats. Unfortunately, little concern has been shown for assessing the pulsatile patterns of ACTH, LH, and prolactin release in either acclimatized or unacclimatized females of any species when exposed to low temperatures.

In theory, the same two pathways proposed as operating at low temperature should also operate in the animal experiencing high-temperature challenge. That is, since high-temperature challenge also requires energetically expensive metabolic adjustments, even the acclimatized animal experiencing a modest degree of hyperthermy should show endocrine responses similar to those of food insufficiency. From this perspective then, one would expect to see a classic stress response only at extremely high temperature or in an unacclimatized animal confronted with a sudden increase in temperature. The available data, however, do not support these theoretical predictions.

As shown in table 5.1, for example, male rats maintained for 30 days at 35°C grow more slowly and show smaller testes at the end of this period, even though this is adequate time for acclimatization, if indeed it could occur. Correlated with the slower testicular development of these rats were lower blood levels of LH and testosterone and higher blood levels of corticosterone, presumably because of enhanced ACTH secretion. This certainly looks like a classic stress response in an animal maintained for a long time at high temperature.

On the other hand, similar studies with rats conducted by Piacsek and Nazian (1981) at 34°C yielded none of the effects noted above. Interestingly, Bedrak, Chap, and Fried (1979) kept male rats at 33°C–35°C for up to 7 months starting at 3 months of age and found a continuous depression in circulating levels of testosterone without accompanying change in blood levels of either LH or FSH. Adrenal activity was not measured.

The same kinds of experiments have been conducted many times now with adult sheep, cattle, pigs, and goats of both sexes, usually, however, over much shorter periods of time (e.g., Larsson et al. 1983; Hoagland and Wettemann 1984). Sometimes these studies report depressed gonadotropin and gonadal steroid secretion in conjunction with enhanced adrenal activity, and sometimes only one or the other effect is seen. Sometimes no effect at all is seen. Also, as in rats, sometimes depressed gonadal steroid secretion is seen in the absence of either a change in blood levels of LH or enhanced adrenal activity (e.g., Madan and Johnson 1973; Schillo, Alliston, and Malver 1978; Hooley, Findlay, and Stephenson 1979; Schams, Stephan, and Hooley 1980; Minton et al. 1981; Gwazdauskas et al. 1981; Hill and Alliston 1981).

Part of the reason for such variation in results undoubtedly resides in the varying degree of acclimatization allowed by the various researchers before testing. Some of it undoubtedly reflects variation in humidity, and some of it may relate to true species differences. Additionally, part of the confusion may relate to the potential for the nature of the LH molecule itself to change in animals exposed to heat (e.g., Wilson, Buckingham, and Morris 1985). Some of this variation undoubtedly relates to the well-known problem of interpreting average hormone levels in the blood of an animal that is secreting these hormones episodically.

Another major source of variation here probably resides in the degree to which high temperature damages the testes directly. This is the one well-established pathway through which high temperature acts on the reproductive capabilities of the male mammal (Van Demark and Free 1970; Blackshaw 1977). Local heating depresses spermatogenesis, possibly with accompanying alteration in steroidogenesis (see Braden and Mattner 1970; Sod-Moriah, Goldberg, and Bedrak 1974; Magal et al. 1981).

Presumably, heat-induced testicular damage is a problem encountered outside the laboratory only in large mammals. Small mammals show it in the laboratory (e.g., the hamster; Kaplanski et al. 1983), but in the wild such animals normally remain in thermally buffered burrows during the hot part of the day. Larger males can seek out shade, but other than employing this behavior they cannot buffer

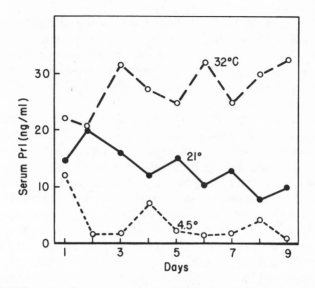

Figure 5.5. Differential effect on serum levels of prolactin in heifers when ambient temperature is elevated to 32°C or lowered to 4.5°C. Redrawn from Wettemann and Tucker (1974) and Tucker and Wettemann (1976), excluding data obtained during the first few hours, when the animals were being subjected to rapidly changing temperature. For similar results, see Smith, Hacker, and Brown (1977).

their testes from high air temperature. Thus, testicular damage is often seen in livestock subjected to tropical summers, and this phenomenon may occur in some large wild mammals as well (e.g., the red kangaroo; Newsome 1973). In the latter case, however, this effect has never been seen in the wild in isolation from other factors such as food or water insufficiency.

Another pathway of potentially great importance here relates to the secretion of prolactin. As illustrated in figure 5.5, prolactin secretion usually reacts in a dramatically different manner to high- and low-temperature challenge. This of course is not predicted at all by the simple concept of stress (e.g., Tache et al. 1978). As it does in response to food insufficiency, prolactin secretion decreases dramatically in response to prolonged exposure to cold. This is expected on energetic grounds.

In contrast, prolactin secretion increases dramatically in animals experiencing high temperatures, at least in livestock (Wettemann and Tucker 1974; Smith, Hacker, and Brown 1977; Schillo, Alliston, and Malver 1978; Schams, Stephan, and Hooley 1980; Hill and Alliston 1981; Sergent et al. 1985). Given the importance of this hormone for so many dimensions of the reproductive process, including steroidogenesis (e.g., Yen 1986b) and modulation of the negative feedback regulation of LH secretion by steroids (e.g., McNeilly, Sharpe, and Fraser 1983), prolactin could be a major key in determining how reproduction is regulated by high temperature.

Conclusions

Conceptualizing the physiological pathways involved in the regulation of mammalian reproduction by ambient temperature is difficult because of the complexity of these pathways and because of an inadequate data base. Never has this relation been studied *systematically* under controlled conditions in either sex of any species. These problems are compounded by the fact that temperature challenge has been traditionally viewed by the laboratory researcher within the limited and somewhat unbiological framework of stereotypic, nonspecific stress.

The broad scheme proposed here is meant only to be a target for further research. In this scheme, natural selection is viewed as providing the diverse populations of mammals with diverse ranges of temperatures within which reproduction is both permissible and profitable. The potential for acclimatization would add a little flexibility to the higher end of this range, but not much. The lower end of the range would depend heavily on the degree of acclimatization experienced, the amount of food available, body size, and sex.

Low temperature probably exerts its effects on reproduction via two pathways. The first would be the same energetic pathway used by food insufficiency, whereby the secretion of LH and prolactin are depressed by caloric insufficiency, while FSH secretion is less affected. The reproductive effort of females would be more sensitive to energetic challenge than would that of males. At least in theory, this must be considered the core pathway from both the ultimate and the proximate standpoints.

The second pathway proposed for low temperature is that encompassed within the classic concept of nonspecific stress, whereby gonadotropin (mostly LH) secretion is depressed and prolactin secretion is enhanced in association with the nonspecific enhancement of activity of the CRF-ACTH-adrenocortical axis. This pathway would be brought into play when an unacclimatized animal is suddenly confronted with a sharp drop in temperature or at low temperatures so extreme that an animal cannot acclimatize to them. The first possibility probably occurs routinely in many temperate-zone habitats, but the second is probably only a laboratory phenomenon.

The pathways involved in the regulation of reproduction by

high temperature are particularly confusing. Only two effects seem well established. The first of these is the local and direct action of heat on the testes, whereby spermatogenesis is inhibited. This is easily seen in the laboratory and sometimes observed in nonburrowing (usually large) mammals in hot environments in the wild. The second is a dramatically increased secretion of prolactin in response to high temperature. This has been best demonstrated in livestock, but incidental observation suggests that this may be a general response among many mammals. Elevated levels of prolactin in the blood could have manifold effects on a mammal's reproductive cycle.

The degree to which a purely energetic pathway similar to that used by low temperature and food insufficiency actually exists in relation to high temperature is debatable. In theory it should exist, but there are no data available to support this presumption. It may exist and simply be routinely overridden by other factors, in which case its functional significance is negligible anyhow.

Likewise, the degree to which the classic concept of nonspecific stress is useful in understanding the effects of high temperature on reproduction is debatable. Some data collected in rats and livestock seem to show enhanced adrenal activity in association with depressed LH secretion and elevated prolactin secretion, but often this is not the case.

It is probably important to remember here that in all mammals there is only a narrow range of temperatures separating the upper limit of thermoneutrality from the temperature at which survival is threatened. The potential limitations imposed by this fact must have been a potent focus for natural selection. Thus, one would guess that, rather than natural selection having relied on the nonspecificity of the classic stress response, specific adaptations have evolved to regulate reproductive attempts in relation to high temperature. In any case, as of now we probably do not yet have a rational conceptual grasp of any of these mechanisms.

Little more can be said here because of a lack of systematic studies in which detailed changes in hormonal parameters are explored in acclimatized and unacclimatized mammals of both sexes and different species when challenged with graded changes in both high and low temperature. Only when such studies have been done will we be able adequately to conceptualize the way reproduction is regulated by ambient temperature.

6

The Predictor Option

Regardless of whether seasonal variation is required ultimately because of energetic or nutrient variation, or both, it has long been recognized that a mammal may opt to use a proximal predictor of this variation rather than reacting directly to it. That is, natural selection can couple a mammal's reproduction to an external cue that in itself is not a required substrate for reproduction but whose variation can be used to predict oncoming periods of time when climatic and dietary conditions will promote reproductive success.

Use of such a predictor allows metabolic preparation in advance of the time reproduction actually will be profitable. On the other hand, its use antagonizes opportunism. Thus, the use of a predictor can be an advantage, a disadvantage, or selectively neutral, all depending on the mammal and the habitat of concern.

The most widely used seasonal predictor in the temperate zone, and certainly the best-understood predictor overall, is the changing length of the daily photoperiod (Reiter and Follett 1980; Follett and Follett 1981; Nicholls et al. 1988). As noted by Turek and Campbell (1979) and Keefe and Turek (1986), this is the most noise-free seasonal predictor available to a mammal. The use of photoperiod as a predictive cue is the classic basis for distinguishing between the ultimate and the proximate causes of seasonal breeding (Baker 1938). Its use also distinguishes between the "obligatory" and the "facultative" strategies proposed by Negus and Berger (1972). Most of this chapter will focus on photoperiodic prediction, but other possibilities will be discussed toward the end.

The use of photoperiod as a predictive cue was first demonstrated in a mammal by Baker and Ransom (1932). These investigators observed normal reproduction in field voles (*Microtus agrestis*) maintained in the laboratory on 15 hours of light each day. Exposure to 9 hours of light a day blocked their reproduction.

In the several decades since Baker and Ransom made their observations, the phenomenon of photoperiodic prediction has attracted intense interest among laboratory physiologists. Unfortunately, it has attracted much less interest among comparative biologists. The result is a present-day body of knowledge that is truly elegant and extensive on the one hand and remarkably shallow on the other. That is, we know a great deal about the way photoperiod and reproduction are linked neuroendocrinologically in a few domestic animals, but, in sharp contrast, we have little information about how commonly and in what ways photoperiod is used to time reproduction in mammals as a whole.

Leaving aside for a moment these larger and more difficult questions, we can begin our consideration of photoperiodic regulation by surveying what has been learned by experimenting with mammals in controlled environments. The two species that have been most intensely studied by physiologists are the Syrian hamster (*Mesocricetus auratus*) and the sheep.

The Syrian Hamster

This is the species traditionally favored by most laboratory physiologists interested in the photoperiodic regulation of reproduction. All of today's laboratory stocks of this animal are descended from one mother and her litter captured in 1930. Thus, our present stocks of Syrian hamsters must be considered highly domesticated and inbred. Little is known about this species' annual reproductive cycle in its native habitat, but a truly voluminous literature generated in the laboratory suggests that it is regulated by photoperiod via the interaction of two mechanisms: (a) the recognition of a critical daylength below which reproduction ceases and (b) endogenously generated, photoperiodically entrained periods of photosensitivity and insensitivity that alternate with each other on an annual basis (reviewed in Reiter 1980; Stetson and Tate-Ostroff 1981; Elliott and Goldman 1981; Steger, Matt, and Bartke 1985). As will be discussed in detail later, and as noted already by Brainard, Vaughan, and Reiter (1984), photoperiod is not the only environmental factor that regulates the annual reproductive cycle of this hamster. It undoubtedly is a factor of major importance, however.

In more detail, daylengths below 12.5 hours of light inhibit reproduction in our domestic stocks of Syrian hamsters in the laboratory, while photoperiods greater than 12.5 hours of light stimulate reproduction (fig. 6.1). Thus, on a Paris rooftop where hamsters experience the natural light cycles of 49° N, breeding ceases at about the time of the autumnal equinox when daylengths drop below 12.5 hours of light. Hamsters maintained on short daylengths in the laboratory become refractory to this inhibitory cue in 4 or 5 months, however, at which time they spontaneously recover reproductive capability. Thus, under the natural photoperiods of 49° N, these hamsters begin breeding in the late winter when daylength is still well below the critical level of 12.5 hours of light. Exposure to the long daylengths of spring and early summer (or for 10 or 12 weeks in the laboratory) then resensitizes the animals to the inhibitory effect of short days, and the cycle can continue.

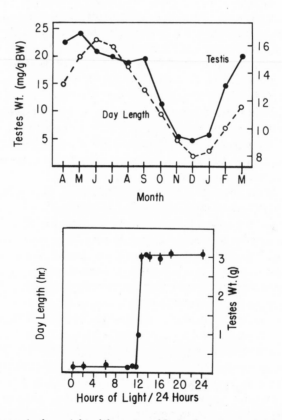

Figure 6.1. Change in the weight of the testes of Syrian hamsters maintained outdoors at 49° of latitude (upper panel) or under conditions of controlled manipulation of photoperiod in the laboratory (lower panel). Redrawn from Vendreley et al. (1971) and Elliott (1976), respectively.

The result of these complex interactions between daylength and internal mechanisms must be an annual reproductive cycle in the hamster's native Syria that accommodates two needs: the need to hibernate during the late fall and early winter (e.g., Frehn and Liu 1970; Jansky et al. 1984) and the need to emerge from hibernation and start breeding in late winter in anticipation of the approaching spring conditions that will support lactation. It is unfortunate that we know so little about the annual cycle of reproduction and hibernation of these animals in their native habitats. It would be of great interest, for example, to see how the conflict between the energetic drain of lactation and the need to store fat prior to hibernation actually is resolved at the end of the breeding season in Syria.

Knowledge about this animal's biology in its home environment might also suggest an answer for an apparent enigma: the reproductive development of young Syrian hamsters occurs independently of photoperiod for the first 7 weeks of life, that is, until they achieve an approximation of sexual maturity (Darrow et al. 1980). This independence of sexual maturity and photoperiod is not dependent on intact gonads (Sisk and Turek 1983). The adaptive advantage here is not readily apparent, but it must have something to do with short life span (and hence the need to reproduce whenever possible) and the need to hibernate among late-born litters. Interestingly, a nonhibernating hamster of a different genus living north of Syria, the Djungarian hamster (*Phodopus sungorus*), is responsive to photoperiod throughout its development (fig. 6.2).

Obviously, the Syrian hamster measures time in at least two ways in relation to its annual reproductive cycle. The way it measures daylength is well understood now. As reviewed in Elliott (1981) and Elliott and Goldman (1981), a large number of elegant experiments, many of which used either a "resonance" design or skeleton photoperiods, have shown that the hamster measures daylength by determining whether light impinges on an endogenous circadian rhythm of sensitivity to light. This rhythm is entrained by the light cycle. Reproductive stimulation occurs when daylength is long enough to overlap with the sensitive phase of the endogenous rhythm. When daylength is not long enough to do this, the result is reproductive inhibition.

As little as two 1-sec pulses of light each day are adequate to promote gonadal growth in a hamster maintained in an otherwise continuously dark environment in the laboratory, provided that one such pulse is given during the hamster's subjective night, that is, during the active phase of its activity-rest cycle (Earnest and Turek 1983a). Exploring the circadian basis for photoperiod recognition is a

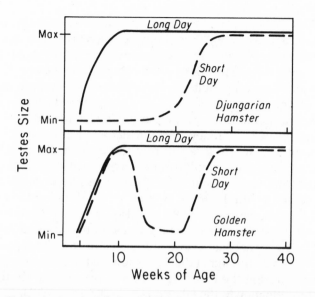

Figure 6.2. Change in testes weight in weanling Syrian and Djungarian hamsters maintained in long (16:8, L:D) versus short (8:16) daylengths. Redrawn from Hoffman (1978) and Darrow et al. (1980).

fascinating area of research. A related and equally fascinating line of work concerns the circadian regulation of ovulation in the female hamster (e.g., Moline et al. 1981; Swan and Turek 1985). Unfortunately, how the hamster measures the dimension of time encompassed by its annually alternating periods of photosensitivity and insensitivity is not understood. This story therefore remains unfinished.

The neuroendocrine coupling between the hamster's measurement of time and its reproduction has been reviewed many times recently (e.g., Reiter 1980; Bittman 1984; see also Reiter 1986). Much of today's immense research effort in this area was stimulated by the observation made by Czyba, Girod, and Durand (1964) and by Hoffman and Reiter (1965) that removal of a hamster's pineal gland blocks the reproductively suppressive effects of short daylengths. The conclusions that have emerged from the many experiments that have explored the ramifications of these observations are as follows.

As reviewed most recently in Tamarkin, Baird, and Almeida (1985), light impinging on the retina of the eye stimulates nerve impulses that travel along the retinohypothalamic tract to the suprachiasmatic nucleus (SCN) in the hypothalamus (Rusak and Morin 1976; Stetson and Watson-Whitmyer 1976; see also Mess and Ruzsas

1986). This nucleus functions as an autonomous circadian oscillator (Rusak and Zucker 1979). These impulses then pass, by a surprisingly circuitous route, through the paraventricular nucleus (e.g., Lehman, Bittman, and Newman 1984) via the sympathetic nervous system to the superior cervical ganglia in the spinal cord and on to the pineal gland. There, the nature of the signal is transduced from a nerve impulse to a biochemical—the indoleamine, melatonin (Hoffman 1981).

As reviewed in Binkley (1988), melatonin is secreted at high levels at night and at low levels during the daylight hours. This is an endogenous circadian rhythm that is entrained by the light cycle. Thus, the duration of nocturnal melatonin secretion varies from season to season in the hamster; it is of longer duration in short daylengths (e.g., Roberts et al. 1985; see also Carter and Goldman 1983). The duration and possibly the magnitude of nocturnal melatonin secretion is the signal that either stimulates or inhibits reproduction. Melatonin is also the signal that somehow restores sensitivity to short daylengths during the breeding season in preparation for the cessation of reproduction in the fall (Bittman and Zucker 1981).

How melatonin inhibits the hamster's reproduction is not well understood (see Reiter 1982). This hormone affects both the pituitary and peripheral tissues, but its main effect probably is to modulate the secretion of hypothalamic-releasing and -inhibiting peptides and hence gonadotropin secretion. Circulating levels of luteinizing hormone (LH), follicle-stimulating hormone (FSH), and prolactin have often been measured in male Syrian hamsters undergoing short-day-induced testicular atrophy as well as spontaneous or long-day-induced recovery (e.g., Berndtson and Desjardins 1974; Tamarkin, Hutchinson, and Goldman 1976; Bex et al. 1978; Steger, Matt, and Bartke 1986; see Stetson and Tate-Ostroff 1981). Usually, but not always, short-day exposure slowly lowers the circulating titers of these hormones. Results with the Djungarian hamster are less equivocal. Yellon and Goldman (1984), for example, showed striking changes in males of this species in relation to photoperiod.

There really should be no doubt that the secretion of LH, FSH, and prolactin should be profoundly suppressed in the seasonally quiescent Syrian hamster. The testes of males housed in short photoperiods are small, and they show no evidence of spermatogenesis. Likewise, the accessory organs of these animals are small, and they are obviously not being stimulated by testicular androgens. Females show no evidence of ovulation, and they exhibit small uteri when maintained on short daylengths. The historic inability to verify the expected short-day suppression of the secretion of pituitary hormones in this animal may relate to the way blood samples have been

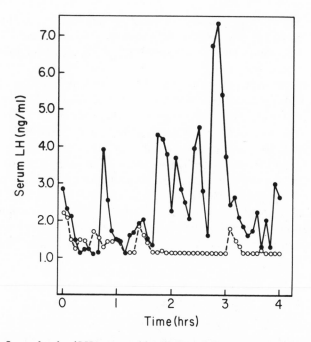

Figure 6.3. Serum levels of LH in two golden hamsters. One (●—●) was housed on long days (14 hours of light, 10 hours of dark), and the other (o—o) was housed on short days (6 hours of light and 18 hours of dark). Unpublished data kindly provided by J. Swann and F. Turek.

collected (e.g., under chronic anesthesia; see Chen 1983), or to the time of day collections are made, or to the episodic nature of the secretion of these hormones, at least LH.

Indeed, when short-term, sequential blood-sampling procedures are employed, the effect of short days on LH secretion is easily seen in unanesthetized, freely moving hamsters (fig. 6.3). Furthermore, simple injections of gonadotropin-releasing hormone (GnRH) can partially overcome the gonadal suppression induced by exposure to short photoperiod (Chen 1983; see also Steger, Matt, and Bartke 1986). One would guess that pulsatile infusions of this neurohormone might totally override the effect of short daylengths, but this has not been attempted.

Short daylengths apparently suppress the secretion of LH in the Syrian hamster both directly, in a steroid-independent manner, and indirectly, by enhancing negative feedback sensitivity to the gonadal steroids (e.g., Turek 1977; Ellis and Turek 1979; Urbanski et al. 1983; Turek, Losee-Olsen, and Ellis 1983; Steger, Matt, and Bartke 1986).

Much of the current research in hamster reproductive biology is related to clarifying this possibility as well as to understanding the role played by prolactin and to determining the neurotransmitter systems and brain pathways most directly related to the regulation of gonadotropin secretion by daylength and hence melatonin (e.g., Panke et al. 1978; Earnest and Turek 1983b; Steger et al. 1984; Bartke et al. 1984; Lehman, Bittman, and Newman 1984; Roberts et al. 1985; Nunez, Brown, and Youngstrom 1985; Hastings et al. 1985; Shin-ichi and Turek 1986). An interesting approach that has been employed is to modify sensitivity to daylength by manipulating the amino acid content (i.e., the precursors of some neurotransmitters) of a hamster's diet (e.g., Wilson and Meier 1983).

Much remains to be learned about the neural and neuroendocrine mediation of photoperiod in the regulation of the Syrian hamster's reproduction, but amazing progress has made been in only two decades.

The Sheep

Sheep have been domesticated for eight to ten thousand years. Our modern breeds are probably descended from several different populations of more than one species, most of which are now extinct (Zeuner 1963). These breeds, in turn, have been shifted around the world, being selected over and over again under different conditions. Correlated with the magnitude of seasonal changes in photoperiod, there is a general tendency for continuous, year-round breeding near the equator and for fall breeding at higher latitudes (fig. 6.4).

More will be said later about the many possible meanings of correlations such as that suggested in figure 6.4. For now, it is important to note only that the major factor driving the seasonality of temperate-zone sheep is indeed photoperiod (Karsch 1987). Nevertheless, there can be considerable variation in breeding seasons from locale to locale at the same latitude in sheep and some variation between breeds even in the same locale (e.g., Wheeler 1973; Jeffcoate, Rawlings, and Howell 1984). Hafez (1952) has compiled an extensive data base on the breeding seasons of sheep in various parts of the world.

The hormonal changes accompanying the seasonal breeding of sheep in the temperate zone have been examined several times. Martin (1984) has provided an exceptionally broad perspective of the way LH secretion is regulated by the environment in sheep. He emphasizes both the control by photoperiod and the interacting influence of other environmental factors, both dietary and social.

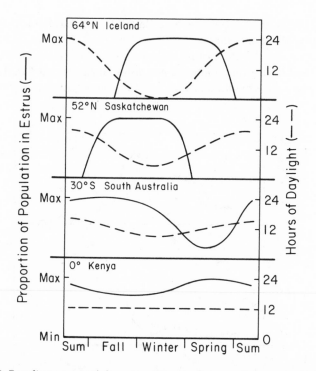

Figure 6.4. Breeding season of sheep in relation to the annual change in daylength in four locations. The location and its latitude are shown in each panel. Data extracted from Anderson (1964), Dyrmundsson (1978), Phillips et al. (1984), and Jeffcoate, Rawlings, and Howell (1984).

One of the most extensive sets of data relating hormone titers to seasonality in sheep has been collected on Soay rams by Lincoln and his colleagues (e.g., Lincoln and Short 1980). The Soay breed of the St. Kilda Islands, located off the northwest coast of Scotland, probably has been subjected to less genetic selection by man in recent times than any other breed. The Soay show a strongly seasonal pattern of reproduction wherein breeding occurs over a 2½-month period in the late fall and lambing takes place in the spring, when grasses are becoming maximally available and maximally digestible.

As shown in figure 6.5, sequential blood samples of penned rams reveal the presence of some LH pulsing throughout the year, but the amplitude and the frequency of these pulses increases dramatically in the late summer. Mean blood levels of FSH, which is not secreted in a pulsatile manner, increase at this time also. The result of these hormonal changes is testicular growth, spermatogenesis, and elevated testosterone titers, all in preparation for the period of rut that will begin in October (see also Ravault 1976; Sanford and Yarney 1983; Darbeida et al. 1986).

The increased titers of testosterone either elicit or support indirectly a variety of morphological and behavioral changes that accompany the rutting season: a sexual flush in the inguinal region, phero-

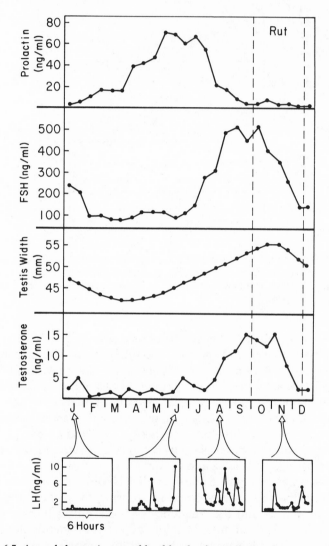

Figure 6.5. Annual change in mean blood levels of reproductive hormones and testes size in confined Soay rams. Short-term temporal patterns of change in LH titers in four individuals are shown at the bottom; each record is typical for the time of year indicated. Redrawn from Lincoln and Short (1980).

monal secretion and the Flehman response to pheromones emanating from females, development of the greater neck musculature that subserves aggressive activity, and, of course, copulatory behavior itself. LH, FSH, and testosterone secretion decreases during the late fall, bringing the rut to an end by mid-December (see also Loubser, Van Niekerk, and Botha 1983). As a contrast to the Soay ram, McNeilly, Sharpe, and Fraser (1983) provide a less-detailed annual profile of hormonal changes in the African elephant (*Loxadenta africana*), a nonseasonal breeder that shows no seasonal change in blood levels of the gonadotropins.

In a long series of studies, Lincoln and his coworkers have documented the central role of photoperiod in producing seasonality in the Soay ram. They have also indirectly documented the fact that seasonal changes in the pattern of secretion of GnRH can account for all the observed seasonal changes in both the frequency of episodes of LH secretion and the rate at which FSH is secreted nonepisodically in Soay rams. Downstream there are other changes, however. The pituitary gonadotropes change seasonally to some degree in their responsiveness to GnRH, and the capacity of the testes to secrete testosterone in response to LH changes dramatically with season. As shown in other breeds of sheep, Leydig cells decrease in number and size during the nonbreeding season, and the number but not the affinity of testicular LH and FSH receptors also changes seasonally (e.g., Barenton and Pelletier 1980, 1983; Garnier et al. 1981).

The seasonal changes in blood prolactin levels shown in figure 6.5 are particularly interesting since they occur out of phase with the seasonal LH and FSH rhythms. One could argue that the Soay's out-of-phase prolactin rhythm evolved to prepare the ram to respond maximally to the increased LH secretion that will follow at a later season. This may be true, in part. On the other hand, the seasonal peak in prolactin in the Soay ram is truly massive. Indeed, the amount of prolactin in circulation here seems far in excess of that necessary to prepare the brain and testes to respond to later enhanced LH secretion. Furthermore, the prolactin peak precedes testosterone secretion by several months. The timing of the prolactin peak in the male Soay actually correlates much better with the period of lactation in the female (see Yenikoye and Ravault 1981). Thus, the profound rise and fall of prolactin secretion in the male might simply reflect selection for seasonal lactational support in the female, with its occurrence in the male being of only secondary importance.

It is dangerous to generalize from breed to breed (e.g., Webb et al. 1985), from one sex to the other, and from locale to locale in sheep (or any other mammal). Indeed, unlike the Soay, rams of some other breeds in some other locales show little sign of seasonality in their

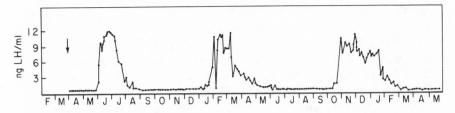

Figure 6.6. Free-running rhythm in blood levels of LH in an ovariectomized ewe maintained on short daylengths (8 hours of light) for 2.5 years starting at the arrow. Unpublished data kindly provided by F. Karsch.

reproductive effort. Ewes of some of the other temperate breeds have been examined almost as extensively as the Soay ram, with interesting results.

Follicular development in these breeds is apparently begun early rather than late in anestrus. Indeed, the anestrous ovary has similar numbers of preovulatory follicles and greater numbers of antral follicles than does the ovary during the breeding season (Cahill et al. 1985; McNatty et al. 1984). Correlatively, while LH pulses are of greater magnitude during the breeding season in these ewes, average FSH and prolactin levels are actually much lower during the breeding season than they are in seasonal anestrus (Levasseur and Thibault 1980; McNatty et al. 1984; Montgomery, Martin, and Pelletier 1985; see also Shailaja and Kumari 1984).

Many other studies document the importance of photoperiod in regulating the breeding season of temperate-zone sheep, including some using skeleton photoperiods (e.g., Lincoln 1978; Schanbacher, Nienaber, and Hahn 1985; Schanbacher 1988). Unlike the hamster, the temperate-zone sheep begins breeding in decreasing photoperiods to accommodate its longer period of gestation. Recent papers in this area include Walton et al. (1977), Jackson and Davis (1979), Ortavant et al. (1982), Hackett and Wolynetz (1982), Almeida and Lincoln (1984), Lindsay et al. (1984), D'Occhio, Schanbacher, and Kinder (1984), Cahill et al. (1984), Pelletier et al. (1986), and Slyter, Roigen, and Schanbacher (1986).

The consensus of these workers is that the annual reproductive cycle of the temperate-zone sheep is driven by a circannual clock that is entrained by light (Karsch et al. 1984). Figure 6.6, for example, shows a free-running cycle in LH secretion in ewes maintained continuously on short photoperiods for 2½ years. The periodicity of this cycle in the free-running form is about 9 months, but with considerable individual variation (see also Smith 1967; Howles, Webster, and Haynes 1980; Howles, Craigon, and Haynes 1982).

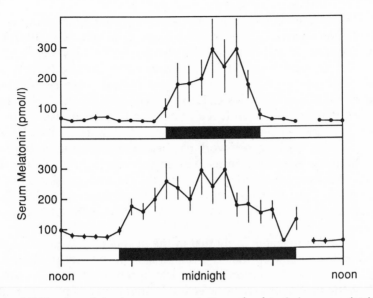

Figure 6.7. Hourly variation in serum concentrations of melatonin in ewes maintained on long versus short daylengths. The light cycle is indicated at the bottom of each panel. Redrawn from Kennaway et al. (1983).

How photoperiod actually entrains the sheep's circannual clock is still uncertain. Indeed, the whole issue of how refractoriness relates to circannual rhythms is poorly conceptualized. This may be a quite complicated process, however. Robinson and Karsch (1984) and Robinson, Wayne, and Karsch (1985) have gathered evidence suggesting that the onset of breeding in the sheep is actually due to the development of refractoriness to the previously inhibitory effects of long days and that cessation of breeding is due to the development of refractoriness to the previously stimulatory effects of short days. This interesting and complicated hypothesis certainly deserves further testing.

On more solid ground is the fact that, as in the hamster, the pathways by which photoperiod regulates reproduction in the sheep include an alteration of the negative feedback sensitivity of LH (and presumably GnRH) secretion to gonadal steroids. This alteration, in turn, is associated with seasonal shifting patterns in melatonin secretion. Figure 6.7, for example, documents the fact that the duration of melatonin secretion reflects the length of the daily dark period in the ewe. Indeed, the use of melatonin implants to regulate the onset of breeding in sheep has moved from the experimental arena to practical application in the livestock industry (e.g., Chemineau et al. 1988; Williams and Ward 1988).

The way melatonin regulates seasonal breeding in sheep is an exceptionally active area of research (e.g., Goodman et al. 1982; Legan and Winans 1981; Nett and Niswender 1982; Tulley and Burfening 1983; Kennaway et al. 1983; Kennaway and Gilmore 1984; Yellon et al. 1985; Lincoln, Ebling, and Almeida 1985; Bittman 1985; Foster, Olster, and Yellon 1985; Foster 1986; Karsch 1986; Foster 1988; Robinson and Karsch 1988; Arendt et al. 1988; and Kennaway 1988). One of the best-conceived reviews is that provided by Karsch et al. (1984). Also, as with the hamster, work has begun on determining the fine details of the neurotransmitter pathways involved in mediating the effects of photoperiod and melatonin in the sheep (e.g., Lincoln 1979; Pau, Kuehl, and Jackson 1982; Goodman and Meyer 1984; Schillo, Kuehl, and Jackson 1985; Meyer and Goodman 1985, 1986; Lincoln 1988).

All in all, it seems likely that in the next decade we will see the emergence of an exceptionally detailed look at the way photoperiod regulates the annual reproductive cycle of temperate-zone sheep as well as the results of genetic selection for resistance to photoperiodic regulation (e.g., Fahmy, MacIntyre, and Chancey 1980). We can also hope to see the development of an understanding of how all this is related to the presumed circannual clock. Unfortunately, no one seems to be concerned with the question of photoperiodism in non-seasonally breeding sheep in the tropics. Do they have this capacity but not use it? Interestingly, there are some reports even from the temperate zone of a lack of response to photoperiod in sheep (e.g., Radford 1961; Ducker, Bowman, and Temple 1973; Fitzgerald, Michel, and Butler 1982). This might be the result of local selection, or it might relate to founder effects, or both. As with the hamster, there is still more to learn about photoperiodic regulation in sheep.

Other Species Studied under Controlled Conditions

Reproductive photoresponsiveness of one kind or another has been documented in well over fifty species of wild and domestic mammals. This fact will be explored more fully later in this chapter in relation to the influence of latitude. As far as physiological pathways are concerned, two important conclusions have emerged from detailed studies in mammals other than the hamster or the sheep. First, the fact that the sheep and the hamster can measure time in different dimensions probably has broad applicability in mammals. Second, the coupling of these time-measuring capacities to reproduction by way of the SCN and the pineal likewise probably has broad applicability.

In the first place, a circadian cycle of photosensitivity has been documented in mammals as diverse as the mink (*Mustela vison*; Boisin-Agasse and Boisin 1985; Boisin-Agasse, Ortavant, and Boissin 1986) and the white-footed mouse (*Peromyscus leucopus*; Sullivan and Lynch 1986). Alternating phases of sensitivity and insensitivity to photoperiod over a period of months have also been well documented in other species, most notably in the Djungarian hamster (Hoffmann 1985; see also Simpson, Follett, and Ellis 1982; Duncan et al. 1985). Direct evidence of a circannual clock has been obtained in golden-mantled ground squirrels (*Spermophilus lateralis*; Kenagy, 1980; Zucker and Licht 1983). Indirect evidence for such a clock has been seen in a marsupial (*Antechinus stuartii*; Dickman 1985) and the pallid bat (*Antrozous pallidus*; Beasley, Pelz, and Zucker 1984).

Daily or seasonal variation in melatonin secretion and/or reproductive responsiveness to exogenous melatonin has been documented in cattle (e.g., Petitclerc et al. 1983), the marmot (*Marmota flavientris*; Florant and Tamarkin 1984), the domestic cat (Leyva, Addiego, and Stabenfeldt 1984), the mink (Martinet, Allain, and Meunier 1983), two species of *Peromyscus* (Johnston and Zucker 1980; Whitsett, Lawton, and Miller 1984; Hall et al. 1985), the Djungarian hamster (Yellon et al. 1982; see also Pevet 1988), the white-tailed deer (Bubenik 1983), and two marsupials of the genus *Macropus* (Loudon, Curlewis, and English 1985; McConnell and Hinds 1985).

All in all, it seems reasonable to assume that several types of timing mechanisms exist in mammals and that the pineal routinely plays a central role in coupling these mechanisms to gonadotropin secretion (reviewed in Tamarkin, Baird, and Almeida 1985). The reader interested in the comparative aspects of pineal action should consult the reviews in Ralph (1975), Mess, Ruzsas, and Trentini (1984), Lincoln (1984), and Menaker (1985). The recent book by Binkley (1988) provides an invaluable summary of pineal research.

One outcome of laboratory experimentation with wild rodents deserves special mention here. As noted in an earlier chapter, much of reproductive biology remains firmly wedded to the integrity of the taxon we call a species. This is in spite of the modern view of population biology that this is not a very meaningful concept because it obscures a great deal of population-to-population variation. Recent findings in rodents both verify the latter position and speak to an important source of variation in photoresponsiveness.

Testing wild rodents under controlled conditions has led to the conclusion that populations of the same species and even subsets of individuals in the same population can differ dramatically in photoperiodic control. This has been established best in the rodent genus *Peromyscus*. Desjardins and Lopez (1980), for example, reported a lat-

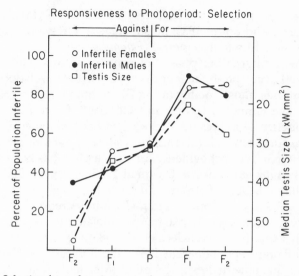

Figure 6.8. Selection for and against reproductive photoresponsiveness for two generations in a population of deermice. Infertility was judged on the basis of organ size, not by mating tests. Reprinted from Desjardins, Bronson, and Blank (1986). Reprinted by permission from *Nature*, vol. 322, pp. 172–73. Copyright © 1986 Macmillan Magazines Ltd.

itudinal gradient in which a few deermouse males collected in Alberta (56° N latitude) were unresponsive to photoperiodic cuing, more were unresponsive in South Dakota (44° N), while all were unresponsive in Texas (30° N). The same phenomenon has been observed by Dark, Zucker, and Wade (1983) in other populations of this species (see also Whitsett, Lawton, and Miller 1984) and by Lynch, Heath, and Johnston (1981) in white-footed mice in the eastern United States (see also Johnston and Zucker 1980; Lynch et al. 1982). Altitudinal variation in critical daylength has also been documented in different populations of this genus (Weiner, Schlechter, and Zucker 1984).

The genetic basis for the within-population heterogeneity of photoperiodic responsiveness seen in deermice has been documented by selection experiments. Using a population in which somewhat over half the individuals normally were reproductively photoresponsive, Desjardins, Bronson, and Blank (1986) reduced this proportion to less than one-quarter in just two generations of selection. Correlatively, in a second stock of animals, they increased the proportion that were not responsive to photoperiod to over three-quarters (fig. 6.8).

Except in the very northern part of their range, deermice commonly produce at least two generations during a single breeding season. Thus, the proportion of deermice that are reproductively photoresponsive must be a highly labile statistic in the wild, shifting easily from year to year in the same population and, just as easily, from one locale to another. Such population heterogeneity has been documented in several other rodents (Desjardins 1981). Indeed, even the highly domesticated Syrian hamster apparently shows some degree of such heterogeneity, perhaps as high as 10 percent in some stocks (Eskes and Zucker 1978).

Another interesting source of variation in photoperiodic responsiveness has also emerged recently from laboratory studies involving rodents, namely an individual's photoperiodic experience. Hoffmann (1984) showed that the critical daylength to which a Djungarian hamster reacts is dependent in part on the daylength it experienced previously (see also McAllan and Dickman 1986). Furthermore, Horton (1984, 1985) has shown that the daylength to which the montane vole (*Microtus montanus*) reacts as an adult depends not only on the daylength to which it was exposed prior to weaning but also to some degree on the daylength its mother experienced when pregnant (see also Whitsett, Lawton, and Miller 1984; Reppert, Duncan, and Goldman 1985). These observations suggest that the critical daylength to which an individual responds may not be immutably inherited but rather dependent to some degree on its experience, starting even before birth.

These findings speak against the simplistic approach of describing a particular species as being either photoperiodic or not photoperiodic. They also argue against generalizing from a few representatives studied in the laboratory to entire populations or species living in the wild.

Natural Selection and Photoperiodic Cuing

As noted in the beginning of this chapter, we really know very little about how often and in what way photoperiod is used to regulate reproduction in the multitude of mammalian populations that exist on this planet. How then does one extrapolate from detailed laboratory findings based on representatives of a few species, many of which are domesticated, to meaningful generalities about the use of photoperiodic cuing in mammals as a whole? Obviously, one can only speculate. This will be a two-step process. First, we can conceptualize the way natural selection probably acts to shape the use of photoperiodic cuing in the diverse populations of mammals. Then, we can consider how this shaping process might relate to latitude of residence, life span, and other factors of importance.

The way natural selection probably influences photoperiodic

cuing is conceptualized in figure 6.9. In general, this figure suggests that a variety of intrinsic and extrinsic factors determine how natural selection will act on the neuroendocrine substrate for photoperiodic cuing. Given the diversity of mammalian populations and the variation in the habitats in which these populations dwell, the result should be a truly large array of strategies for using photoperiodic information.

In more detail, figure 6.9 assumes that mammals measure time relative to the phenomenon of seasonal breeding by using at least three general kinds of timing mechanisms: an entrainable circadian clock, an entrainable circannual clock, and an interval timer whose characteristics vary qualitatively as well as quantitatively from the other two timing mechanisms. The latter concept was employed by Silver and Bittman (1984) to account for functions of less than 24 hours that are potentially rhythmic but that do not necessarily oscillate. This concept is borrowed and altered here simply to acknowledge the mammal's ability to vary its sensitivity to photoperiod over periods of weeks or months. As noted earlier, little is known about this mechanism, and therefore its inclusion here represents only a necessary theoretical construct.

Obviously, the three-dimensional construct used to denote the need to measure time in figure 6.9 is a great oversimplification. Just the circadian dimension alone probably involves complex interactions between multiple oscillators (e.g., Pittendrigh 1981; Follet et al. 1981). Certainly, it is not known how the three kinds of timing mechanisms shown in figure 6.9 actually relate to each other. Thoughtful reviews on this subject, however, include Pengelley and Asmundson (1974), Mrosovsky (1978), Zucker, Johnston, and Frost (1980), Gwinner (1981), Follet et al. (1981), Zucker (1983), Silver and Bittman (1984), and Morin (1986a). A particularly important recent contribution is the book by Gwinner (1986), which focuses broadly and thoughtfully on the evolutionary significance of circannual rhythms and their relation to circadian timing mechanisms (see also Gwinner and Dittami 1986).

As well as visualizing at least three types of timing mechanisms, figure 6.9 also assumes that all mammals possess at least some elements of the basic retina-SCN-pineal-hypothalamic peptide pathway by way of which gonadotropin secretion can be modulated by photoperiod.

The presumption here is that the functional development of the physiological complexity shown at the core of figure 6.9 reflects the actions of many genes. Furthermore, an assumption inherent in this scheme is that all mammals possess in a functional state many and perhaps most elements of this entire complex of mechanisms. De-

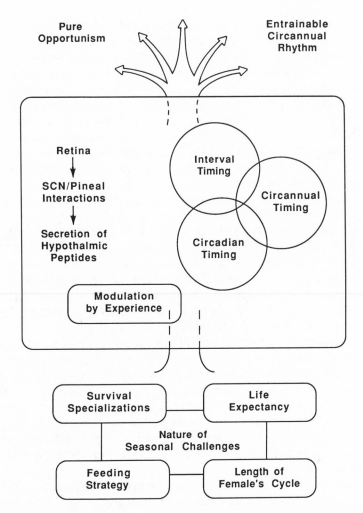

Figure 6.9. Theoretical scheme for visualizing the action of natural selection on photo-responsiveness in mammals to yield an array of reproductive strategies. The bottom third of this figure shows the intrinsic and extrinsic factors that determine whether, and how, a mammal will use photoperiodic information to time its annual reproductive effort. These factors are discussed in detail in this chapter as well as in chapter 3. The physiological substrate on which natural selection will act is shown in the large box that occupies the center of this figure. It is assumed that all mammals have at least most of the elements shown here: a minimum of three kinds of timing mechanisms and a neural/neuroendocrine link between the retina and the secretion of the hypotha-lamic releasing or inhibiting factors. Natural selection could act on this complexity to yield an array of reproductive strategies ranging from pure opportunism to the rigid use of an entrainable circannual clock. Reprinted from Bronson (1988c).

pending on the characteristics of a mammal's habitat and its need to breed seasonally then, natural selection could act on many facets of this neural substrate to yield different strategies. For example, natural selection could either allow or block reproductive responsiveness to photoperiod simply by acting on any one of the many elements of the neuroendocrine pathway linking the mammal's measurement of time to gonadotropin secretion. Alternatively, it could accomplish the same result by acting on the linkage between these two entities itself. If photoperiodic cuing is favored by natural selection, the way that this is actually accomplished could be shaped by manipulating the timing mechanisms themselves.

Most of the extrinsic and intrinsic considerations that will determine the way natural selection will act on the neuroendocrine basis of reproductive photoresponsiveness have been discussed previously in relation to seasonal breeding. A few additional comments are necessary here, however. First, much has been made in the past of the importance of the predictability of the seasonal challenges offered by a mammal's habitat in shaping its use of photoperiodic cuing. It must be emphasized that the predictability of a changing environment is in part a function of the life span of the individual perceiving it.

The simple fact that good and bad seasons alternate with each other on an annual basis may be an adequate level of predictability for a long-lived mammal that will have many years in which to produce offspring. This is a poor level of predictability, however, for small mammals that have average life spans of only a few weeks to a few months at best. For this reason one should expect commonly to see some degree of opportunism in the reproductive strategies of all short-lived animals. Rigid use of photoperiodic prediction would not allow such flexibility.

Second, the length of the female's reproductive cycle becomes of paramount importance in determining the advantage of photoperiodic cuing for a particular mammal. The need for advance cuing obviously becomes of greater and greater importance as the length of the female's cycle becomes longer, at least until it reaches 1 year in length. Temperate-zone females with cycles of intermediate length (i.e., about 6 months) often must ovulate and mate during the energetically and nutritionally harsh part of the year in order to synchronize the more environmentally sensitive phase of their cycle with the most propitious season. This requires the use of a predictive cue of some kind.

Third, survival mechanisms such as hibernation and migration exaggerate the need for photoperiodic predition. Indeed, opting for the use of a circannual clock, as opposed to some other type of timing, makes great theoretical sense for such animals. This has been noted before in relation to some of the larger ground squirrels (Pengelley and Asmundson 1974; see also Davis 1976). The average life span of these animals encompasses more than one breeding season (Murie and Michener 1984), and they live in seasonally harsh climates, but ones where food resources allow considerable fat storage during the summer. Therefore, hibernation is both advantageous and possible. Finally, they begin breeding on arousal, and they must prepare for this activity while still in deep hibernation.

Thus, successful hibernation and reproduction in ground squirrels requires the proper sequencing throughout the year of many physiological activities, most of which require considerable metabolic preparation. The use of a circannual clock would ensure the proper sequencing of all these related needs. As noted earlier, direct evidence of a circannual clock has been obtained in the golden-mantled ground squirrel (Kenagy 1980). An intriguing question then is why some ground squirrels have opted for the use of a circannual clock but the Syrian hamster has not. The answer may lie in the life expectancy of the predecessors of these two stocks. Short life span may preclude the use of a circannual clock.

In that vein, while not noted in figure 6.9, the importance of a mammal's recent evolutionary history for determining how it uses photoperiodic information must be emphasized. When considering whether a particular mammal uses photoperiodic information to time its reproduction and how it uses it, one should probably ask immediately whether its environment has changed markedly in the past few thousand years or if it has invaded a new area. A particularly interesting situation involving circannual rhythms has been seen in the antelope ground squirrel (*Ammospermophilus leucurus*), for example. This animal lives in the dry southwestern United States, where rainfall is highly unpredictable. At least in theory this animal should be an opportunist; it is the only ground squirrel that neither hibernates nor estivates. Nevertheless, it shows a short, reasonably well-timed breeding season in the spring, similar to those of other ground squirrels, and it shows a circannual rhythm of testes change when maintained under constant conditions in the laboratory (Kenagy 1981).

As another example, the California vole (*Microtus californicus*) acts as a long-day breeder when tested in the laboratory, but it breeds during the winter in the San Francisco Bay area. Obviously, the photoperiodic strategies of the antelope ground squirrel and the California vole were shaped in another time when conditions were different or in another place entirely. Why selection has not altered the way photoperiodic information is used today by these animals is an exceptionally interesting question.

Finally, in relation to figure 6.9, when visualizing the array of strategies for using photoperiodic cuing that must have been produced by natural selection in mammals, obviously at one extreme will be "pure" opportunism. By definition, no seasonal predictors, photoperiod or otherwise, are used in this strategy. In its extreme form, opportunism would dictate that males remain sexually ready at all times of the year and that females breed either seasonally or continually, depending on moment-to-moment energetic and nutritional considerations.

This is the strategy that has been adopted by the wild house mouse and the Norway rat, both of which live either commensally with man or in totally wild habitats (Davis 1953; Bronson 1979b). The house mouse reproduces well even in constant darkness (Stoddart 1970; Bronson 1979a). While there is a voluminous literature on the detrimental effects of constant light on the laboratory rat, this is probably best considered as an artifact of pathological circadian development (see Turek and Campbell 1979). The fact is that pairs of domestic rats produce well in all photoperiods except constant light, and, like the house mouse, the wild Norway rat reproduces either seasonally or continuously, depending on the habitat of concern (Davis 1953).

As predicted by the scheme proposed in figure 6.9 then, the domestic rat shows many characteristics of a reproductively photoresponsive animal (e.g., Nelson, Bamat, and Zucker 1982; Illnerova and Vanecek 1988), but its secretion of GnRH is not particularly sensitive to melatonin (e.g., Wallen and Turek 1981; Lang et al. 1983). In contrast, the ability to synthesize melatonin in the pineal has been lost in one stock of laboratory mouse, apparently because of an inadvertent action of selection during domestication (Menaker 1985). In all likelihood, natural selection has found many weak links in the retina-SCN-pineal-GnRH pathway, each of which could be exploited in one way or another in one population or another to block reproductive photoresponsiveness.

At the other extreme of the array of strategies suggested in figure 6.9 is the rigid use of an entrainable circannual rhythm, possibly something like that found in the sheep. It is unfortunate that we have only one partially explored model of this type of photoperiodic regulation. It must be a common mechanism in long-lived mammals. It is not improbable, for example, to suppose that some mammals have a circannual clock that is entrained by only one brief period of stimulation each year. Of necessity this would require recognition of the direction of change of photoperiod with time, however.

In between the two extreme strategies represented by the rat and the sheep in figure 6.9 are many possibilities, including that of the Syrian hamster. Probably seldom is the period for ecologically profitable reproduction precisely bracketed by the same critical day-length. Thus, one would guess that there are many mammals that use the perception of a critical daylength to trigger either the onset or the offset of breeding, but not both. On the other hand, there probably are many mammals that, unlike the hamster, trigger the onset rather than the offset of breeding photoperiodically and thus many cases in which one or the other is controlled exclusively by nonphotoperiodic factors. Likewise, given the diversity of challenges facing mammals, one would expect that refractory mechanisms might be used in many ways here, as would the modifying action of experience. There is a world of unknowns here.

Latitude and Photoperiodic Cuing

Latitude of residence determines the annual variation in daylength that a mammal will experience. There is no variation in daylength on the equator; thus, photoperiodic cuing could not be used there to enforce seasonal breeding. There is about 1 hour of annual variation at 8° of latitude. The middle latitudes of the temperate zone experience 8–12 hours of annual variation, and the subpolar and polar regions experience 24 hours of annual variation in daylength.

While it is obvious that the potential for using photoperiodic cuing increases as one leaves the equatorial regions, it is important to emphasize that latitudinal gradients in seasonal patterns of reproduction do not automatically imply gradients in photoperiodic control. This assumption often has been made in relation to sheep (e.g., Hafez 1952; see fig. 6.4) and other mammals (e.g., deer; Lee 1970).

The ultimate factors that promote seasonal breeding, as well as the photoperiodic cue itself, all change in unison with season, and the entire complex shifts in unison with latitude. It is also worth remembering that photoperiod can exert an indirect as well as a direct control over the breeding of a mammal. It can control the reproduction of the plants and insects on which a mammal feeds, thus indirectly regulating the mammal's breeding (e.g., see Epstein et al. 1986). Direct photoperiodic control—the kind we are interested in here—can be established only by manipulation of the light cycle in an artificially controlled environment, not by latitudinal correlation.

Against this background then, representatives of the wild species that have been documented now as being reproductively photoresponsive in one way or another are shown in figure 6.10. The most obvious conclusion that can be drawn from this figure is that most of what we know about this trait stems from studies done on animals living at the higher latitudes. Unfortunately, there are few reports in

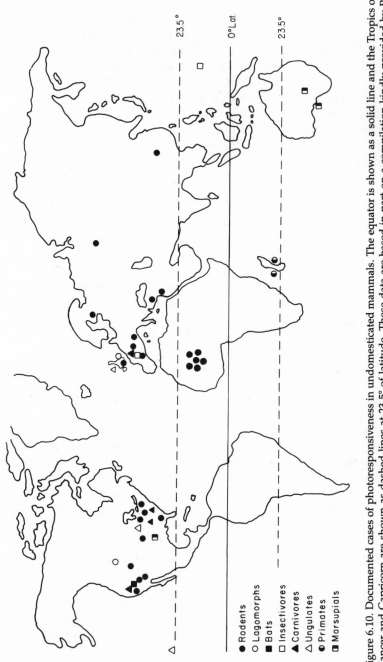

Figure 6.10. Documented cases of photoresponsiveness in undomesticated mammals. The equator is shown as a solid line and the Tropics of Cancer and Capricorn are shown as dashed lines at 23.5° of latitude. These data are based in part on a compilation kindly provided by R. Nelson and specifically on Baker and Ransom (1932), Bartke and Parkening (1981), Beasley and Zucker (1984), Bedford and Marshall (1942), Bissonnette and Csech (1937, 1939), Boyd (1985), Budde (1983), Canivenc and Bonnin (1979), Dark, Zucker, and Wade (1983), Davis and Meyer (1972), Farris (1950), Frost and Zucker (1983), Godfrey (1969), Hall and Goldman (1980), Hoffman, Hester, and Towns (1965), Hoffman (1973), Johnston and Zucker (1979), Joy, Melnyk, and Mrosovsky (1980), Kenagy and Bartholomew (1981), Lecyk (1962), Mead (1971), Moos, Treagust, and Folk (1979), Muul (1969), Nelson, Dark, and Zucker (1983), Ostwald et al. (1972), Petter-Rousseaux (1972), Pinter and Negus (1965), Rissman et al. (1987), Roux, Richoux, and Cordonnier (1977), Saboureau (1981), Sadleir and Tyndale-Biscoe (1977), Selwood (1985), Sicard et al. (1988), Smith, Bennett, and Chesson (1978), Soares and Hoffmann (1982), Tähkä et al. (1983), Van Horn (1975, 1980), Walter et al. (1968), Whitaker (1940), and Whitsett, Lawton, and Miller (1984).

the literature of a failure to find a response to photoperiod, even though this must have been a common observation. An exception here is the report by Racey (1978) of a lack of reproductive photoresponsiveness in one of the pipistrelle bats (*Pipistrellis pipistrellis*).

Only ten species of tropical mammals have been tested in the laboratory under controlled conditions: two lemurs from Madagascar (*Lemur catta* and *Microcebus murinus;* Petter-Rousseaux 1970; Martin 1972; Van Horn and Resko 1977), seven rodents from the African Sahel (Sicard et al. 1988), and the musk shrew (*Suncus murinus*) from Guam (Rissman et al. 1987). Interestingly, nine of the ten species showed indications of being reproductively photoresponsive.

The musk shrew, a small insectivore, is particularly interesting in this regard. This animal acts like an ecological opportunist, sometimes living commensally with man and sometimes not, but always breeding continuously, year-round, wherever it exists, even in temperate Japan. Nevertheless, when tested in the laboratory, gonadal steroidogenesis but not gametogenesis is decidedly photoresponsive in both sexes of the population of these animals on Guam. The best explanation for this phenomenon is that reproductive photoresponsiveness in the Guam population at 14° N must be a relic from another time and place. Reproductive photoresponsiveness obviously can be carried along as a selectively neutral trait in the gene pool of a tropical mammal.

Also of particular interest here are the seven species of rodents from the African Sahel that were examined by Sicard et al. (1988). Six showed indications of being reproductively photoresponsive. There is less than 2 hours of annual variation in daylength where these animals were collected at 14° N latitude. Sicard et al. argue that these rodents could indeed be using this amount of photoperiodic variation to time their annual reproductive effort. This seems unlikely, however, given the unpredictable, almost desert-like conditions in the Sahel. At least it seems highly unlikely that these rodents are using this one kind of cue exclusively.

A speculative scheme for the use of photoperiodic cuing in relation to latitude and life span is shown in figure 6.11. This scheme is not meant to be an end in itself. It is only a challenge to researchers to collect the kinds of information that would either verify or disprove it.

An assumption inherent in figure 6.11 is that mammals could use less than 2 hours of annual variation in daylength to modulate their reproduction in the wild. The inbred Syrian hamster can do much better than this in the controlled confines of the laboratory, of course (fig. 6.1). The problem facing a wild population is different, however. How could a population of genetically diverse individuals,

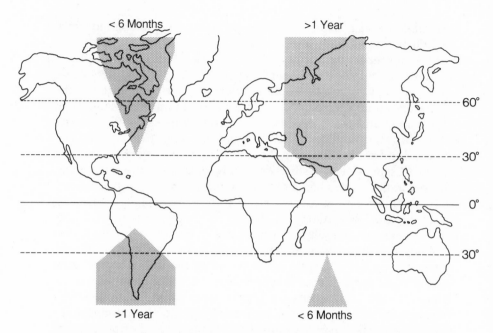

Figure 6.11. A theoretical (and highly speculative) scheme relating the use or disuse of photoperiodic cuing to latitude and life span. For long-lived mammals, the stippled areas suggest the proportion of populations that use proximal photoperiodic cuing. For short-lived mammals, the shaded areas suggest the proportion of individuals that use this kind of predictive cuing (see text).

each influenced by a somewhat different set of environmental variables, achieve a reasonable degree of sexual synchrony when daylength is changing only a few seconds a day? The answer of course is that they could not, unless they utilized supplementary social mechanisms to enhance synchrony. This is an interesting possibility that will be considered in more detail in chapter 8. For now we will adopt a conservative approach, suggesting that photoperiodic cuing could not be a major factor enforcing seasonal breeding much below 15° of latitude. Obviously, the scheme shown in figure 6.11 will have to be modified if the arguments presented by Sicard and his coworkers prove correct.

Because of short-lived mammals' need for flexible opportunism whenever possible, figure 6.11 suggests that photoperiodic cuing is probably of universal importance to them only at the very highest latitudes, and possibly not even there. Few truly short-lived mammals live above the Arctic circle. Those that do live there face exceptionally harsh winters, and one would expect that selection for photoperiodic regulation of both reproduction and survival processes would be common at these latitudes. Nevertheless, short life expectancy is a potent force, and thus one would also expect a degree of opportunism in this animal whenever possible, regardless of latitude.

The ubiquitous microtine rodents that exist throughout the world in the northern temperate and subpolar regions provide a case in point (see Clarke 1977; Mihok, Turner, and Iverson 1985; Stenseth et al. 1985; Negus, Berger, and Brown 1986). Some populations of some species of microtines seem to be mostly photoperiodic (e.g., the field vole, *M. agrestis;* Baker and Ransom 1932), some are decidedly not photoperiodic despite living in the far north (e.g., the collared lemmings, *Dichrostonyx groenlandicus,* collected at 58° N by Hasler, Buhl, and Banks 1976), and two species seem best described as "marginally photoperiodic": the population of montane voles (*M. montanus*) studied by Pinter and Negus (1965) and the population of meadow voles (*M. pennsylvanicus*) examined by Dark, Zucker, and Wade (1983). One species, the field vole (*Microtus arvalis*), is known to be highly variable with regard to photoperiodism from population to population in Europe (cf. Marshall and Wilkinson 1957; Lecyk 1962; Dobrowolska and Gromadzka-Ostrowska 1983; Rychnovsky 1985). Such variability is probably characteristic of most other microtines as well, though it has yet to be proved (see Clarke 1977; Spears and Clarke 1988).

On purely theoretical grounds, one should expect to find a high degree of within-population genetic heterogeneity in many small mammals living at the higher latitudes. This seems like an expected consequence of natural selection operating on short-lived animals in unpredictable environments (which include most environments if one is short lived). There is independent evidence of this, again in the microtines. Winter breeding by some individuals in some microtine populations occurs sporadically even above the Arctic circle in Finland (Kaikusalo and Tast 1984). It occurs more commonly in Denmark, Sweden, and Britain (respectively, e.g., Jensen 1982; Hansson 1984; and Smyth 1966). It is important to note that within-population heterogeneity has been confirmed in some microtines when tested in the laboratory, and there is some evidence that this variation is amenable to artificial selection (Spears and Clarke 1988).

Thus, figure 6.11 suggests that there probably is a broad range above 30° of latitude in which selection acts progressively against photoperiodic cuing in short-lived mammals as latitude decreases. This would depend on the precise set of environmental challenges facing each population as well as on its feeding strategy and its reliance on survival mechanisms such as hibernation. Again, short life span is a potent driving force. Thus, within-population genetic heterogeneity may always be a routine consequence of natural selection operating in short-lived animals at these latitudes.

As will be discussed later, short-lived mammals living above 30° probably also routinely use multiple cuing to supplement photoperiodic regulation, when present, thereby allowing still more flexibility (Bronson and Perrigo 1987). They may also routinely modify their critical daylength by experience, again promoting flexibility.

Below 30° of latitude, most short-lived mammals probably breed purely opportunistically in relation to food availability and hence often in relation to rainfall patterns. The capacity to respond reproductively to short daylength is undoubtedly often carried along as a selectively neutral trait in many of these animals below 15° of latitude, however, depending on their evolutionary history.

It is unfortunate that we know so little about the normal breeding patterns of tropical mammals facing a short life expectancy. A notable exception has been provided by Lam (1983), who studied the rice field rat (*Rattus argentiventes*) with great thoroughness both in the laboratory and in the field in Malaysia. Male rice rats in this region remain fertile year-round. Females breed when rice is in the reproductive and ripening stages. In areas where one rice crop is grown each year, the seasonal pattern of reproduction of this species in unimodal; in areas where two crops are grown, the pattern is bimodal. This variation certainly suggests a purely opportunistic strategy, and such a strategy is probably common at these latitudes in short-lived mammals. Delaney and Neal (1969) provide other such examples in equatorial Kenya.

As far as longer-lived mammals are concerned, certainly pure opportunism can be seen occasionally in these animals even in the temperate zone. Several examples of such opportunism will be presented in chapter 9 in the sections on marsupials and carnivores. In general, however, most temperate-zone mammals with relatively long life spans breed only seasonally, and they probably do so routinely in response to photoperiod. The latitudinal comparison of deer populations examined in chapter 3 is a case in point (see French et al. 1960; Fletcher 1974; Bubenik 1983; Skinner, van Aarde, and van Jaarsveld 1986). Long-lived females tend to have long reproductive cycles, and this accentuates their need for advance cuing. For the same reason one would expect to find little population heterogeneity in these animals at these latitudes, and one would expect to see little modulation of critical daylength by experience. Thus, figure 6.11 suggests that photoperiodic cuing is more or less always selectively advantageous for long-lived mammals that live above 30° of latitude.

Below 30° one probably finds a relatively narrow band of latitudes where photoperiodic cuing is selected for or against in long-lived mammals, depending on local conditions. Below this band one probably finds this trait carried in a selectively neutral state in some populations (or in some individuals) and not in others. Again, unknown here is the potential importance of supplemental social cuing to allow the use of photoperiodic regulation to penetrate deeper into the tropics and, as will be discussed shortly, the possibility that plant predictors could be used in the same way.

All in all, the scheme offered in figure 6.11 seems reasonable, but our lack of knowledge about tropical mammals makes it tenuous at best. The burning issues here would seem to be whether photoperiod can be used to track the more or less predictable rainfall patterns that are common in the higher latitudes of the tropics and the way other cues could interact with photoperiodic cuing to enforce seasonal breeding at still lower latitudes.

Other Predictors

At least in theory a variety of environmental factors other than photoperiod could be used as predictive cues. There is some evidence that the entraining agent for the circannual clock controlling reproduction in some ground squirrels is actually ambient temperature (Pengelley and Fisher 1963). This is somewhat surprising. Air temperature is a particularly noisy signal that would seem to possess too much day-to-day variation to be of much use as a predictor. Ground temperature at the depth of a ground squirrel's hibernaculum might be an entirely different situation, however. In any case, separating the potentially direct effects of temperature from its use as a zeitgeber is something that needs to be explored much more fully, as does the potential for separate or interacting photoperiodic regulation.

On firmer ground is the fact that some animals can use short-term predictors obtained from plants. Our best evidence for the existence of plant predictors comes from work on the montane vole. This species lives in the Rocky Mountains, where the season of maximum food availability varies anywhere from 3 to 6 months each year. Daylength by itself is not a good predictor of the precise onset and cessation of plant growth at these high altitudes (Negus, Berger, and Forslund 1977). As shown convincingly by Negus, Berger, and their coworkers (e.g., Sanders et al. 1981), a secondary plant compound found in newly emerging grass, 6-methoxybenzoxalinone (6-MBOA), is used by these voles to predict accurately the oncoming period of maximum availability of green grass. Indeed, reproduction can be stimulated in these voles in midwinter under a heavy snow cover by feeding them fresh green shoots (Negus and Berger 1977; see also Berger, Negus, and Rowsemitt 1987).

The capacity to predict accurately an oncoming period of food availability is exceptionally important to montane voles since their potential breeding season is short and unpredictable, their mortality rate is exceptionally high, and they must produce large numbers of rapidly maturing offspring on a calorically poor but seasonally abundant diet. The grass that is their stable foodstuff is worth only about 40kcal/100g, compared to more than 100kcal/100g for insects and more than 300kcal/100g for seeds (Brambell 1972).

Thus, massive lactational costs must be supported by this vole under particularly trying conditions. The result is a strategy in which males, but not females, apparently are regulated by photoperiod (e.g., Vaughan, Vaughan, and Reiter 1973; P. J. Berger, 1982, personal communication). Males come into breeding condition early and await the emergence of fresh grass, which contains the melatonin-like phenol that, in turn, stimulates females to initiate breeding (see also Pinter and Negus 1965). As will be discussed later, social synchrony plays an important supplementary role in these animals as well.

In general, one might suspect that the use of plant predictors would be advantageous for many strict herbivores of short life span that live in highly unpredictable climates. Many deserts and some grasslands offer these conditions (Prakash and Gosh 1975), and, indeed, there is indirect evidence that this type of prediction might be important in such areas (e.g., van de Graaf and Balda 1973; Beatley 1976; Kenagy and Bartholomew 1981). On the other hand, many mammals living in more stable habitats also respond to 6-MBOA when tested in the laboratory. These include other microtines (e.g., Alibhai 1985) and *Peromyscus* (Cranford and Wolff 1986). Whether these other mammals actually use this kind of predictive cue in the wild is not known, however.

Plant prediction might also be of great use in the tropics. In this vein, Whitten (1983, 1984) provides strong correlational evidence that the seasonality of reproduction in the vervet monkey (*Cercopithecus aethiops*) is more closely attuned to the availability of acacia flowers than it is to any other environmental factor. These flowers are rich in flavenoids that have estrogenic properties. Even if this turns out to be a true cause-and-effect relation, however, there still remains the important question of whether the vervet is using the flavenoids as a predictive cue or simply responding directly to them.

Conclusions

It is often advantageous for a mammal to couple its reproduction to a cue that predicts oncoming periods of time when prevailing climatic and dietary conditions will enhance the chances of reproductive success. While plant compounds can be used in this way on a short-term basis, by far the best and most noise-free seasonal predictor is photoperiod.

Use of photoperiod as a predictive cue is most advantageous for long-lived mammals having long reproductive cycles (as measured in the female from ovulation to weaning of offspring) that live in the higher latitudes. Pure opportunism, defined here as the lack of predictor use, becomes more advantageous as life span decreases, as reproductive cycles shorten, and as latitude of residence decreases. Unfortunately, this is all theoretical speculation because we really know almost nothing about the use of photoperiodic cuing in the tropics, where most mammals reside.

Our best information about how photoperiod regulates reproduction, when it does so, comes from a long and elegant series of studies on sheep and Syrian hamsters. On the basis of these studies and data from a few other species, it is apparent that mammals have the ability to measure time in several different dimensions. To account for the photoperiodic modulation of seasonal breeding in mammals as a whole, one must visualize at least three types of timing mechanisms: an entrainable circadian clock, an entrainable circannual clock, and some kind of an interval timer that regulates annually alternating phases of photosensitivity and insensitivity.

These timing mechanisms interact somehow with a pathway that starts as a neural signal from the retina, passes to the SCN of the hypothalamus (an autonomous oscillator), and then travels by a circuitous route to the pineal, where the result is modulation of the secretion of melatonin. The daily pattern of melatonin secretion changes with the length of the dark phase of daily photoperiod, and this pattern then is a key signal that regulates gonadotropin secretion and hence seasonality in some mammals.

It is assumed that natural selection has operated on this complex of timing mechanisms and neural and hormonal pathways to yield a truly large array of strategies involving the use of photoperiodic information to regulate reproduction. Only a few of these strategies have been described so far.

The action of natural selection on reproductive photoresponsiveness should be viewed in a dynamic context. Apparently, this is a highly labile trait in short-lived mammals, in which it can vary immensely from one population to another even in the same species and from one subset of animals to another even in the same population. In long-lived mammals, this trait probably is labile only in the long-term evolutionary sense.

7

Regulation by Social Cues

Mammalian populations vary greatly in the way their individual members are dispersed in space relative to each other. At one extreme are many small insectivores and rodents who live exceptionally isolated existences. These animals seldom confront other members of their own species face to face. At the other extreme are the cohesive family groupings of some carnivores and the complex multifamily groupings often seen in primates, wherein individuals are always closely surrounded by conspecifics.

Individuals that live in cohesive groups continuously monitor the location, the individual identity, and the immediate intentions of the other members of their group. They do so using whatever sensory modalities are appropriate for the situation. More widely dispersed mammals also monitor as closely as possible the location, characteristics, and activities of their nearest neighbors, again using whatever sensory modalities are most appropriate. While the frequency of information exchange is much lower in the latter situation, these animals are still more or less continually cognizant of the distant presence of conspecifics.

Our concern in this chapter is with the way a mammal's reproductive success is influenced by the presence of other members of its own species. In particular, our concern here will be with the way the social environment can alter the endocrine substrate for reproduction in a mammal. For at least two reasons this is an exceptionally complicated process.

First, many of the behavioral interactions that cause hormonal change in mammals require prior conditioning by the same hormones that are influenced by the interaction. There is an intertwining, two-way relation between the hormones associated with reproduction and the behaviors associated with this process. This blurs cause and effect. Second, in any interaction between two mammals, the participants routinely utilize many modes of communication simultaneously. Only a few of the resulting barrage of social signals can actually influence endocrine secretion, however, and it is often difficult to separate these few from the many that do not.

To illustrate the potential complexity of all this, one can examine the relation between hormones and specific behaviors when a male rodent monitors, detects, searches for, finds, and then copulates with a receptive female. Male and female rodents often occupy different burrow systems in the wild. Thus, they must monitor each other's reproductive states while separated both spatially and temporally, and usually in the dark. To accomplish this end, both sexes routinely mark the ground while foraging with either urine or the products of scent glands, thereby leaving behind chemical cues that denote their identity, sex, and sexual status (Jannett 1984b). These cues are perceived by neighboring animals when they later chance on them during their own daily foraging trips.

Focusing just on the male now, the urinary cues that denote his sex and sexual state are testosterone dependent, and thus, ultimately, they require luteinizing hormone (LH) and gonadotropin-releasing hormone (GnRH) secretion. Likewise, the male's motivation to search for a neighboring female who is sexually receptive is also dependent on testosterone and hence GnRH and LH secretion. When the two individuals find each other, the male uses all available senses to identify the female and to interpret her intentions. This multisensory input enhances his arousal, which in turn leads to repeated attempts to mount, intromit, and eventually ejaculate. These behaviors also are dependent on GnRH, LH, and testosterone.

The behavioral sequence described above causes hormonal changes in the male as well as being influenced by his hormones. Figure 7.1 examines the temporal patterns of change in the circulating levels of four hormones in male mice before and after they are confronted with a receptive female in a controlled situation in the laboratory. The males in this experiment were either sated sexually (to the point where they would not even look at the receptive female) or unsated and highly motivated to copulate. This fundamental difference in emotional state is dramatically reflected in circulating levels of epinephrine. The total lack of arousal in the sated males is obvious. The release of epinephrine seen in the aroused males is a more or less stereotyped response that can be elicited by a wide variety of stimuli such as fighting or electroshock or even by exposure to a strange object such as a tennis ball (Craigen and Bronson 1982).

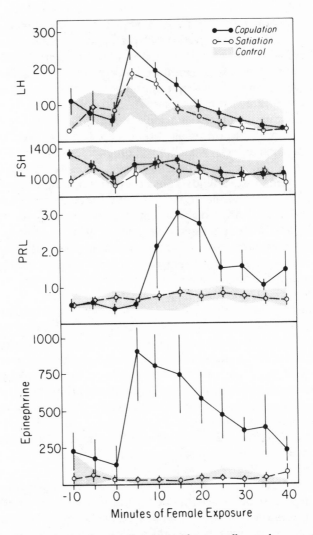

Figure 7.1. Reactions of male mice that were either sexually sated or unsated to a receptive female. Blood was collected via atrial cannulae, starting 10 min before the female was encountered and continuing for 40 min thereafter. All sexually rested males mated with their test females, with ejaculation occurring in as short a time as 10 min in some males and as long as 30 min in others. The stippled area indicates mean ($\pm$1 SE) hormone titers in males not exposed to a female. From F. H. Bronson and C. Desjardins, Endocrine responses to sexual arousal in male mice, *Endocrinology* 111:1286–91, © 1982 by the Endocrine Society.

In contrast, both sated and unsated males show an immediate release of LH in response to the female. While not shown, this pulse of LH must be induced by a pulse release of GnRH, and it is followed shortly by increased testicular secretion of testosterone (Coquelin and Desjardins 1982). This is a passive, almost purely reflexive set of responses elicited by a specific chemical cue in the female's urine and probably elsewhere on her body as well. Follicle-stimulating hormone (FSH) levels do not vary at all in response to this situation, and prolactin levels do not change until being explosively elevated at the time of ejaculation.

In figure 7.1 then, one can see three different kinds of endocrine responses: a nonspecific response of the adrenal to a heightened emotional state called *arousal*, which in turn reflects input via many sensory channels; a highly specific release of GnRH, LH, and thus testosterone in response to a discrete pheromonal cue; and a highly specific release of prolactin associated somehow with the tactile dimensions of ejaculation. These are physiologically independent responses that nevertheless are coupled by the situation.

It is important to note that figure 7.1 focuses only on those social cues that yield hormonal responses in the male. One must realize that in this situation there are a horde of other female-originating signals that influence the male's behavior without causing a hormonal response. One must also realize that the female in this situation is also being barraged with signals from the male and that some of the male's signals are organizing her behavior, some are inducing hormonal changes in her, and some are doing both. A social interaction is a highly complex phenomenon, and isolating the social cues that evoke endocrine responses is not easy. Nevertheless, this is the major concern of this chapter.

Most of what we know about the social regulation of the reproductive endocrine system of the mammal relates either to the effects of social subordination or to the action of primer pheromones. We will start with the former.

Social Status, Reproductive Success, and Endocrine Stress

The diversity of social organizations and mating systems that exists in mammals has fascinated sociobiologists for decades (e.g., Crook 1977; Eisenberg 1977; Kleiman 1980; Clutton-Brock and Albon 1985). A multitude of principles and hypotheses have emerged from this intense and enduring scrutiny. One of these is that an individual mammal should always try to increase its fitness by suppressing the reproduction of its rivals. This can be done with varying degrees of directness (Wasser and Barash 1983).

Most directly, a mammal can simply kill the rival or the rival's offspring (Hrdy 1979; Hrdy and Hausfater 1984). Less directly, it can harass the rival during sexual encounters, or it can keep the rival away from the resources it needs to reproduce. Still less directly, it can induce emotional stress in the rival, thereby interfering endocrinologically with the rival's potential for reproduction. The context within which all these actions occur relates in one way or another to relative dominance status.

As reviewed in Dewsbury (1982), while there seem to be many behavioral strategies whereby subordinates can increase their productivity, particularly in primates, low dominance status does indeed seem to be associated routinely with lower reproductive success in mammals. Examples of well-documented relations between social rank and productvity in wild populations have been provided for lions (*Panthera leo*; Bertram 1975), elephant seals (*Mirounga leonina*; Reiter, Panken, and Le Boeuf 1981), red deer (Clutton-Brock, Guinness, and Albon 1982), the dwarf mongoose (*Helogale parvula*; Rood 1980), and wolves (*Canis lupus*; Peterson, Woolington, and Bailey 1984). Carefully controlled laboratory experiments with rodents have reached the same conclusions (e.g., Blanchard et al. 1984; Dewsbury 1984).

A particularly detailed example of a strong relation between social rank and productivity is shown in figure 7.2. This figure summarizes the results of a study done on the wild European rabbit (*Oryctolagus cuniculus*) in Australia by Mykytowycz and Fullagar (1973). These workers counted the number of young rabbits produced over a 4-year period by the individual females in several colonies of these animals coexisting in a large pasture. The forty-two socially dominant females in this pasture produced 51 percent of the offspring, while the fifty-six third- and fourth-rank females produced only 7 percent. The difference, 42 percent, was produced by the seventy-five females of the second social rank.

The effective period of reproduction also varied seasonally in relation to social rank in these rabbits (albeit due in part probably to age differences). Dominant females produced offspring throughout the 6-month breeding season (fig. 7.2). In contrast, social subordinates tended to produce their offspring only late in the breeding season, when their survival was lower and when it was too late in the year for the offspring to achieve puberty and produce another generation. All in all, the reproductive contribution of the subordinate females of this population was miniscule indeed.

The precise way in which social status influenced the productiv-

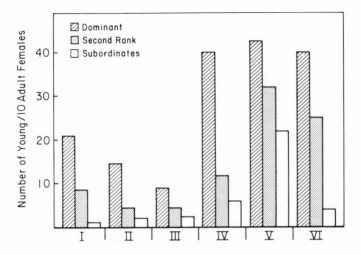

Figure 7.2. Number of young produced by female European rabbits during each of the 6 months of their breeding season in Australia, depending on social rank. Redrawn from Mykytowycz and Fullagar (1973).

ity of these rabbits is unclear. Obviously, the suppression observed by Mykytowycz and Fullagar (1973) might be traced to a host of factors. In all probability, however, the poor performance of the subordinate females in this pasture was a reflection of some combination of four factors: younger age, being forced away from the best food and burrow resources and toward those that were only marginally acceptable (e.g., some burrows are more susceptible to flooding than others), direct behavioral harassment without endocrine mediation, and/or the endocrine ramifications of the constant emotional stress associated with subordination. As in most field studies, one is never quite sure which factors contribute most importantly to such complex phenomena, but our concern in this chapter is with the latter possibility.

Most of what is known about social subordination, endocrine stress, and reproduction stems from laboratory studies with small rodents. As noted earlier in chapter 5, there is no doubt that the kinds of emotional stresses that can be generated in the laboratory can exert potent suppressive effects on gonadotropin secretion and hence on the reproduction of domestic rodents. Indeed, in some cases emotional stressors seem to exert more potent effects than what appear to be exceptionally powerful physical stressors. Blake (1975), for example, showed that simply immobilizing an ovariectomized rat resulted in an immediate loss of LH pulses, but breaking the rat's leg did not.

There is also no doubt that a reciprocal relation between circulat-

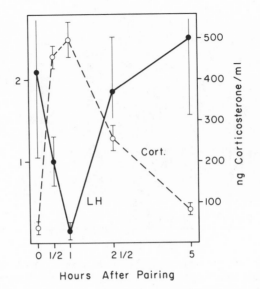

Figure 7.3. Mean (±SE) change in circulating levels of LH and corticosterone after previously isolated adult male mice were placed together in a neutral cage. All these pairs of males began fighting vigorously within 15 min. They were separated and returned to their home cage after 30 min. Thus the measures obtained at 1, 2.5, and 5 hours were all collected as the animals were recovering in isolation (Bronson 1973) and reprinted from Bronson (1979b).

ing levels of LH and adrenocortical activity can be demonstrated in carefully controlled agonistic interactions in the laboratory. As shown in figure 7.3, even a short aggressive encounter between two male laboratory mice results in a dramatic elevation of circulating corticosterone and an equally dramatic drop in circulating LH. At least the corticosterone dimension of this response is conditionable in the classic sense. That is, exposure of a naive male mouse to a trained fighter for a few bouts conditions the nonfighting male to react (secrete corticosterone at a high level) just when placed in the presence of the trained fighter, without any physical contact (Bronson and Eleftheriou 1965).

Presumably, both the enhancement of corticosterone secretion and the inhibition of LH secretion seen in figure 7.3 are secondary reflections of the emotional stress associated with physical defeat and subordination. These responses are somewhat analogous to the nonspecific release of epinephrine seen earlier in relation to sexual arousal in figure 7.1, only carried to a greater extreme.

There are indications that emotional stress and its endocrine and reproductive ramifications might routinely accompany subordination in densely crowded populations of house mice, at least in the laboratory (reviewed in Christian and Davis 1964; Christian 1971, 1980; see also Van Zegeren 1980; Yasukawa et al. 1985). In a typical experiment of this genre, a large and physically complex cage is seeded with a few pairs of mice, and the population is allowed to grow until it regulates itself. This self-regulation often involves a marked inhibition of sexual maturation as well as a cessation of reproduction by most but not all adults. Dense populations are characterized by considerable intermale aggression. The losers of these fights, other social subordinates, and most of the onlookers seem physiologically stressed in the classic Selyean sense. That is, they generally have large adrenals and small reproductive organs. Indeed, some of the effects of crowding on reproduction can be duplicated in mice simply by injecting them with adrenocorticotropin (ACTH) (Christian 1964).

Even more profound effects have been observed in crowded cages of deermice. As shown by Terman and his colleagues (e.g., Terman 1973), young deermice normally become fertile at 5–8 weeks of age when they are paired in small cages with adults of the opposite sex. When born and reared in densely caged, freely growing populations, however, as many as 95 percent of these deermice are still not fertile by 90 days of age, and, indeed, many die at well over a year of age without ever having achieved fertility. While the reproductive development of young male deermice can be delayed markedly by exposure to aggression (Whitsett and Miller 1985), aggression per se does not seem to provide a complete answer for the dramatic effects seen in densely crowded pens of deermice.

Several attempts have failed to document a continuing relation between adrenal activity and gonadotropin secretion in these densely caged populations of deermice. Thus, recent interest here has focused on prolactin and thyroid activity (e.g., Thompson and Bradley 1979; Coppes and Bradley 1984; Pitman and Bradley 1984; Kirkland and Bradley 1986). Much remains to be learned, but it is apparent now that something in addition to subordination and endocrine stress is operating to suppress reproduction in caged populations of deermice.

A few other laboratory studies suggest the importance of emotional stress and its endocrine correlates as a potential regulator of reproductive success in rodents. Huck, Bracken, and Lisk (1983), for example, demonstrated a potent inhibition of implantation in Syrian hamsters that could be traced unequivocally to fighting between females. Observations such as this, along with the house mouse and rat studies noted earlier, pose obvious questions. Could subordination routinely be accompanied by endocrine stress in the wild, and could this combination of factors routinely be a factor of real importance for reproductive success in wild populations of rodents?

The answer to these questions of course is that we do not know, but both seem like reasonable possibilities, depending on the rate at which agonistic interactions actually occur in the wild. A particularly interesting attempt to answer these questions has been provided by Gipps and his coworkers (Gipps et al. 1981; Gipps 1982), who implanted scopalamine in male *Microtus townsendii* to reduce aggressiveness. This was done in some locales and not in others. The result was a significant, albeit not a dramatic, increase in reproduction in the areas where the males were treated with scopalamine.

Obviously, the effect seen by Gipps and his coworkers could have been brought about by direct as well as by indirect (via endocrine stress) actions of decreased aggressiveness (see also Gustafson, Andersson, and Hyholm 1983). All in all, however, it seems reasonable now to assume that subordination can be accompanied by enough emotional stress to interfere with gonadotropin secretion and hence reproduction in some wild populations of rodents at some times. It also seems reasonable, however, to acknowledge that this is only one of many factors that can influence reproduction in wild populations and that determining the relative importance of each of these possiblities presents a particularly difficult challenge.

Beyond studies with rodents, the only reasonably large literature dealing with social status, endocrine stress, and reproduction stems from studies with primates. The complex societies of primates have proved endlessly fascinating to anthropologists and behaviorists, some of whom have concerned themselves with endocrine stress. As noted by Sapolsky (1986), the individuals in a typical group of primates seem to spend much of their time pondering how to deal with limited resources such as the best food source, the best place to rest, and the best sexual partner.

Inherent in the primates' competition for these resources is considerable aggression and emotional tension (e.g., De Waal 1984). Sometimes this results in greater reproductive success for dominant males or females, and sometimes it does not (reviewed in Dewsbury 1982). When reproductive success actually is suppressed in subordinate primates, however, this again is undoubtedly a reflection of many factors, only one of which is classic endocrine stress.

Many attempts to relate low reproductive success to enhanced adrenal activity and the consequent inhibition of gonadotropin secretion have been made now in primates, some successfully and some not. Creating a new social group by housing strange animals together

Table 7.1   Mean Basal Serum Testosterone Titer and Change in This
Titer 1 Hour after Darting and Capture in High- and
Low-ranking Olive Baboons When the Population Was
Socially Stable and Unstable

	Stable		Unstable	
	High Rank	Low Rank	High Rank	Low Rank
Basal titer (ng/ml)	10±3	20±7	8±1	2±1
Change (ng/ml)	+11	−0	+1	−1

Source: Sapolsky 1986.

often results in increased adrenal activity in primates (e.g., Goo and Sassenrath 1980; Perret and Predine 1984). Often the resulting social conflict also yields lower titers of testosterone in the blood of subordinate males (cf. Rose, Holaday, and Bernstein 1971; Rose, Gordon, and Bernstein 1972; Rose, Bernstein, and Gordon 1975; Manogue, Leshner, and Candlace 1975; Yodyingyaud, Eberhart, and Keverne 1982; Eberhardt, Keverne, and Meller 1980, 1983). Sometimes testosterone increases in the blood of the winner of an aggressive encounter, but it does not decrease in the blood of a loser, as in the squirrel monkeys (*Saimiri sciureus*) studied by Coe et al. (1982).

Perhaps typical of the data available for primates are those resulting from Sapolsky's (1983, 1986) studies on wild male olive baboons (*Papio anubis*) in Kenya. Single "looks" at blood levels reveal no relation between social rank and circulating testosterone (table 7.1), regardless of the frequency of agonistic interaction. Obvious in table 7.1, however, is the fact that all these males had low blood levels of this steroid during a period of social disruption when aggression was high. This disruption was caused by the wounding of the alpha male and a consequent disintegration of the group's social structure. Also obvious in table 7.1 is the fact that the reactions of these animals to nonsocial stress (darting and capture) did indeed vary with rank and with group stability. In no case, however, were any of these changes related to circulating levels of corticosterone.

In captive female primates, there is abundant evidence that socially induced emotional stresses can result in reproductive aberration of one kind or another (e.g., Bowman, Dilley, and Keverne 1978; Adams, Kaplan, and Koritnik 1985; Pope, Gordon, and Wilson 1986). Again, however, the expected relation between circulating levels of adrenal hormones and gonadotropins has proved difficult to verify.

In general then, undoubtedly the relation between social subordination, the corticotropin-releasing hormone (CRF)–ACTH–adrenal axis, and the reproductive axis is real but exceptionally complex in primates. Also undoubtedly, we are probably trying to apply the laboratory-generated concept of endocrine stress to social strife in too simplistic a fashion in primates. There probably does indeed exist a strong *potential* for seeing the expected relation between subordination, emotional stress, adrenal activity, gonadotropin, and gonadal steroid secretion and reproductive success in primates. Documenting this relation may be difficult, however, both because of technical problems (single "looks" at blood hormone levels as opposed to sequential blood sampling) and because this potential is buried among many other physiological and behavioral potentials. The primate brain is a wonderfully complex organ, and its many capacities undoubtedly defy making simple generalities about behavior and endocrine physiology.

The Priming Pheromone System of the House Mouse

A particularly interesting mode of socioendocrine regulation in mammals involves the use of primer pheromones. Most mammals are nocturnal in their activity. Correlatively, chemical cues and mediation by primary or accessory olfaction provides the dominant mode of communication for most of them (Brown and MacDonald 1984). One can dichotomize these chemical cues on a purely functional basis. They can act simply as signals conveying information that can be used in one way or another or ignored entirely; alternatively, as shown earlier in figure 7.1, they can elicit a specific endocrine response of some kind. Modeled after earlier work in insects, molecules that act in the latter way have generally become known as primer pheromones (but not without some controversy; cf. Bronson 1968; Beauchamp et al. 1976).

The study of mammalian priming pheromones began in laboratory mice in the 1950s when a series of observations suggested that ovulation in this species was readily susceptible to manipulation by social cues of some unknown kind. The presence of other females decelerated an individual female's ovulatory cycle, the presence of a male accelerated it, and exposure to a strange male prevented implantation in a recently inseminated female, returning her instead to a normal ovulatory cycle (van der Lee and Boot 1956; Whitten 1956, 1959; Bruce 1959). Duplication of the latter two effects using only topical exposure to male urine unequivocally established the primer pheromonal basis for such phenomena in the mid-1960s (Marsden and Bronson 1964; Dominic 1965).

These early papers initiated a rush of endeavors, the landmarks of which are as follows. Rather rapidly, it was determined that the mouse's pubertal ovulation is as amenable to pheromonal manipulation as is the adult cycle and in the same general ways (Vandenbergh 1967, 1969b; Cowley and Wise 1972; Colby and Vandenbergh 1974; McIntosh and Drickamer 1977). Then it was established that in at least some cases the urinary cues act synergistically with tactile cues that seem to exert no effect by themselves (e.g., Drickamer 1977; Bronson and Maruniak 1975). Next the expected gonadotropin/gonadal steroid basis for some of these effects was verified (Bronson and Desjardins 1974; Bronson 1974, 1976).

Next, as shown earlier in figure 7.1, it was discovered that males as well as females react to primers from the opposite sex by releasing LH and testosterone (Macrides, Bartke, and Dalterio 1975; Maruniak and Bronson 1976; Coquelin and Bronson 1979). Then it was shown that the vomeronasal organ rather than the primary olfactory system mediates at least some of these effects (Reynolds and Keverne 1979; Bellringer, Pratt, and Keverne 1980; Kaneko et al. 1980; Coquelin et al. 1984; reviewed in Wysocki, Bean, and Beauchamp 1986). Finally, there have been several attempts recently to ask whether all these laboratory findings have any real meaning in wild habitats (e.g., Massey and Vandenbergh 1980, 1981; Heske and Nelson 1984).

The way that male- and female-originating primers interact to control the pubertal ovulation in mice is illustrative of the way primers function generally in mammals. As shown in figure 7.4, CF-1 female mice weighing 14g respond to 3 days of exposure to an adult male with uterine growth, but they cannot achieve ovulation. Their response to the male's primers is antagonized if other females are present. At 18g most females will ovulate when exposed to an adult male for 3 days. Again, the presence of other females largely overrides the accelerating action of the male, however. By the time they reach 22g, a few females have begun to ovulate spontaneously, even when housed in isolation. A male can rapidly organize a female's pubertal cycle even if other females are also present, his primers overriding theirs.

Given such laboratory observations, one can visualize a condition in the wild in which a young female house mouse is protected by the presence of her sisters and mother from being inseminated too early in her life by her father or another adult male. This protection is gradually lost as the female matures, and it is lost entirely should she disperse from her home environs and find a new home with adequate resources for reproduction. At such a time, a male could rapidly induce her pubertal ovulation and then mate with her (see Vandenbergh 1983).

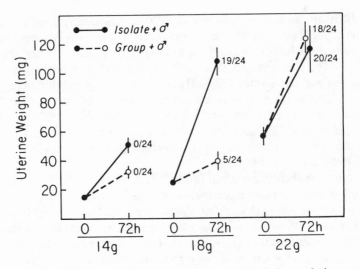

Figure 7.4. Mean (±SE) uterine weight in CF-1 female mice before and after exposure for 72 hours to a male, starting at three different body weights. Females were either otherwise isolated or held in groups of four. The fraction beside each point indicates the proportion of these females that ovulated during the 72-hour test period. From Bronson and Macmillan (1983).

The total variation in time that is encompassed here in the laboratory can be as much as a couple of weeks in the domestic CF-1 mouse and up to 4 or more weeks in wild females (Drickamer 1983b). In view of the fact that house mice often have an average life span of only 10 or 12 weeks in the wild (Berry 1970), this species' pheromonal cuing system obviously confers potent flexibility in the timing of the pubertal ovulation.

The endocrine bases for the effects seen in figure 7.4 are reasonably well understood now. Production of the male's urinary primer is androgen dependent (Bronson and Whitten 1968; Lombardi, Vandenbergh, and Whitsett 1976; see also Gangrade and Dominic 1984). This cue has been partially isolated chemically (Vandenbergh et al. 1976; Nishimura, Utsumi, and Yuhara 1983; see also Jemiolo, Andreolini, and Novotny 1986). As little as one µl of male urine per day is effective in inducing puberty in the laboratory, and only minutes of daily exposure can elicit a detectable uterine response (e.g., Drickamer 1983a, 1984).

Acting synergistically with an undefined tactile facet of the male, the result of exposure to this urinary cue is a rapid release of LH followed by greatly elevated levels of circulating estradiol (fig. 7.5). The only effect of the male on serum levels of FSH is to lower

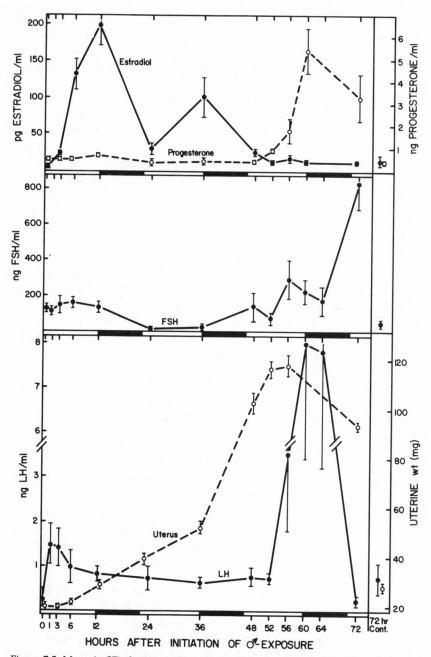

Figure 7.5. Mean (±SE) changes in hormone levels and uterine weight of 17–18g CF-1 females housed alone with males for 2.5 days. The light cycle is indicated at the bottom of the graph. From F. H. Bronson and C. Desjardins, Circulating concentrations of FSH, LH, estradiol, and progesterone associated with acute, male-induced puberty in female mice, *Endocrinology* 94:1658–68, © 1974 by the Endocrine Society.

them on the second day of male exposure while, simultaneously, prolactin levels in the blood begin to rise (Bronson and Maruniak 1976). Both the latter responses probably are secondary reflections of the high estradiol titer because they do not occur in estradiol-implanted, ovariectomized adults that are exposed to males (Bronson 1976).

The endocrine basis for the production of the female's inhibitory primer is decidedly different from the production of the accelerating primer in the male. Ovariectomy is without effect on the production of this primer, but adrenalectomy removes it from a female's urine (e.g., McIntosh and Drickamer 1977; but see Pandey and Pandey 1985; and Clee, Humphreys, and Russell 1975). The urethra acts as some kind of a gate here since the bladder of an intact female always contains the pheromonal factor but voided urine is active only if the females are grouped (McIntosh and Drickamer 1977). Based on experiments with ovariectomized adult females implanted with estradiol, the action of the female's inhibitor apparently is simultaneously to depress LH secretion and increase prolactin secretion (Bronson 1976). Functionally, the first of these actions would be by far the most important for prolonging prepubertal development.

All the actions described so far continue after the pubertal ovulation, albeit sometimes with somewhat different characteristics. Adult females isolated in a cage show prolonged and irregular estrous cycles that can be made short, predictable, and synchronized by exposure to an adult male. Grouping of females in the absence of a male prolongs the ovulatory cycle still more, and it may result in pseudopregnancy. Males can break the pseudopregnancy and return the female to a short ovulatory cycle.

Males can exert the latter act mentioned above even if the female has been recently inseminated. This is the "strange male effect" first described by Hilda Bruce. In this case, exposure of the inseminated female to a male other than her stud prevents implantation and returns her to an ovulatory cycle, whereupon the stranger inseminates her. The first male creates an individual olfactory memory of some kind that inhibits the inseminated female from reacting to him after she is inseminated. Thus, re-exposure to the original stud male has no effect on implantation.

While prolactin probably plays only a minor role in mediating the actions of primers before a young female's pubertal ovulation, the importance of this hormone increases dramatically after puberty. As reviewed in Marchlewska-Koj (1983), both pseudopregnancy and early pregnancy are characterized in mice by prolactin-induced, progestational dominance. Socially induced pseudopregnancy and the breaking of this condition by exposure to a male are both accomplished by the alteration of prolactin secretion, with LH playing a secondary role (Ryan and Schwartz 1980; see Marois 1982; Keverne 1983b; Sahu and Dominic 1983).

Likewise, exposure of a recently inseminated female to a strange male blocks the expected postovulatory rise in circulating levels of prolactin (or at least exogenous prolactin protects the female from such a block; Bruce 1966; Dominic 1966; reviewed in Marchlewska-Koj 1983). A schematic model accounting for all the endocrine interactions underlying the known priming phenomena of mice has been presented in Bronson and Macmillan (1983).

Before leaving the house mouse's pheromonal cuing system, it is perhaps wise to note that, while much has been learned about this system, there are strong hints that many of its dimensions remain still undiscovered. For example, under some social conditions the urine of pregnant and lactating females actually accelerates rather than decelerates the pubertal development of a young female (Drickamer and Hoover 1979). As another example, removal of the vomeronasal organ inhibits the ability of grouped females to void their decelerating primer as well as preventing its reception (Lepri, Wysocki, and Vandenbergh 1985). This suggests a complexity of control mechanisms well beyond those presently visualized.

Finally, two deficiencies that stand out here should be mentioned. First, much confusion remains about whether the female-induced release of LH in a male actually serves any reproductively meaningful function in the male (cf. Vandenbergh 1971; Maruniak, Coquelin, and Bronson 1978; Svare, Bartke, and Macrides 1978; Jean-Faucher et al. 1982). Second, there is the equally confusing issue of the meaning of strangeness and individuality in eliciting primer responses, whether one's concern is the strangeness of the male that is necessary for blocking pregnancy or the so-called Coolidge effect relating to a male's LH response to a female (Coquelin and Bronson 1979). We have little understanding of this interesting facet of the mouse's system. The interested reader should consult Yamazaki et al. (1979, 1982, 1983), Keverne and de la Riva (1982), Lenington and Egid (1985), Egid and Lenington (1985), Halpin (1986), and Beauchamp et al. (1986).

Priming Phenomena in Other Mammals

The study of mammalian pheromones, signaling and priming, has expanded rapidly in the past two decades. Albone (1984) has reviewed what little is known about the chemical character of these molecules. Meredith (1983) and Johns (1986) have reviewed their sensory reception. Komisaruk, Terasawa, and Rodriguez-Sierra (1981) have reviewed what is known about the brain mediation of primer effects. Important, anecdotal evidence is rapidly accumulating that suggests that primer pheromones are indeed broadly used to regulate reproduction in mammals (e.g., Hradecky 1985 reviews the available evidence for carnivores).

In general, as shown in table 7.2, priming phenomena more or less analogous to those described in the house mouse, yet often fascinatingly different, have been documented in the laboratory in many other species. It is important to note, however, that table 7.2 includes many phenomena that at this time can be described only as primerlike because the nature of the mediating cue is unknown. In many cases, a primer pheromone seems probable, but in other cases another type of cue and another sensory modality undoubtedly are involved.

To document the richness of priming phenomena in mammals, one can begin by considering the deermouse. This species exhibits all the diverse kinds of effects seen in the house mouse, plus some more. Chemical primers are known to be involved in all these effects. Female primers suppress ovulation in both prepubertal and adult female deermice, male primers acclerate the ovulatory cycle in both young and adult females, and exposure to a strange male prior to implantation blocks pregnancy. Furthermore, exposure of immature males to an adult female accelerates their maturation (references given in table 7.2).

One of the most interesting phenomena occurring in *Peromyscus* was discovered by Haigh (1987). When a weanling female whitefooted mouse (*P. leucopus*) is housed with an adult male and either her mother or another adult female, the older female produces litter after litter of offspring, but fewer than 2 percent of the younger females produce a litter when observed for up to 300 days. This is a period of time far beyond the average life span of this species in the wild.

Originally thought to be a block to the pubertal ovulation, it is now known that these young females actually suffer a block to implantation (Haigh, Cushing, and Bronson 1988). They routinely ovulate and copulate with the male, but they return to a normal ovulatory cycle in a few days, repeating this process over and over again. The endocrine basis for this dramatic phenomenon has not yet been elucidated, but it can be duplicated just with soiled bedding.

As is easily seen in table 7.2, the microtine rodents, and particularly voles of the genus *Microtus*, have become our most commonly studied mammals in regard to priming phenomena. Many elements of the house mouse's priming system can be seen in voles, but again

Table 7.2 Species in Which the Presence of Conspecific Males or Females Is Known to Influence the Ovulatory Cycle and Species in Which the Strange Male Pregnancy Block Has Been Demonstrated

Species	Effect on Cycle by		Pregnancy Block	References
	Female	Male		
Rodents				
Deermouse (*P. maniculatus*)	X	X	X	Bronson and Eleftheriou (1963), Bronson and Dezell (1968), Bediz and Whitsett (1979), Lombardi and Whitsett (1980)
Prairie vole (*M. ochrogaster*)	X	X	X	Hasler and Nalbandov (1974), Stehn and Richmond (1975), Carter et al. (1980), Carter, Getz, and Cohen-Parsons (1986), Getz, Dluzen, and McDermott (1983)
California vole (*M. californicus*)		X		Batzli, Getz, and Hurley (1977), Rissman and Johnston (1986)
Field vole (*M. agrestis*)	X	X	X	Milligan (1974, 1976, 1979), Clulow and Clarke (1968), Clarke (1977)
Montane vole (*M. montanus*)			X	Stehn and Jannett (1981)
Pine vole (*M. pinetorum*)		X	X	Schadler (1981, 1983), Stehn and Jannett (1981), Lepri and Vandenbergh (1986)
Levant vole (*M. pinetorum*)		X		Benjamini (1987)
Red back vole (*Clethrionomys glareolus*)		X	X	Clarke and Clulow (1973), Clarke (1977), Marchlewska-Koj and Kruczek (1986)
Collared lemming (*Dicrostonyx groenlandicus*)	X	X	X	Hasler and Banks (1975), Mallory and Brooks (1980)
Hopping mouse (*Notomys alexis*)	X	X		Breed (1976)
Mongolian gerbil (*Meriones unguiculatus*)		X	X	Norris and Adams (1979), Payman and Swanson (1980), Rohrbach (1982)

Table 7.2 *continued*

Species	Effect on Cycle by		Pregnancy Block	References
	Female	Male		
Golden hamster (*Mesocricetus auratus*)		X		Handelmann, Ravizza, and Ray (1980)
Djungarian hamster (*Phodopus sungorus*)			X	Wynne-Edwards and Lisk (1984)
Laboratory rat (*Rattus norvegicus*)	X	X		Cooper and Haynes (1967), Vandenbergh (1976), Taleisnik, Caligaris, and Astrada (1966)
Cui (*Galea musteloides*)		X		Weir (1973)
Cotton rat (*Sigmodon hispidus*)	X			Evans and McClure (1986)
Naked mole rat (*Heterocephalus glaber*)		X		Jarvis (1981)
Insectivores:				
Musk shrew (*Suncus murinus*)		X		Rissman (1987b)
Ungulates:				
Sheep (*Ovis aries*)	X			Parsons and Hunter (1967), Knight and Lynch (1980), Atkinson and Williamson (1985), Martin et al. (1985)
Goat (*Capra hircus*)	X			Shelton (1960), Coblentz (1976), Chemineau, Poulin, and Cognie (1984)
Pig (*Sus scrofa*)	X	X		Brooks and Cole (1970), Hughes and Cole (1976), Kirkwood, Forbes, and Hughes (1981), Hemsworth, Winfield, and Chamley (1981)
Cow (*Bos taurus*)	X	X		Weston and Ulberg (1976), Izard and Vandenbergh (1982)
Marsupials:				
Short-tailed opposum (*Monodelphis domestica*)	X			Fadem (1985)
Marsupial mouse (*Antechinus stuartii*)	X			Scott (1986)

Table 7.2 *continued*

Species	Effect on Cycle by		Pregnancy Block	References
	Female	Male		
Primates				
Saddle-backed tamarin (*Saguinus fuscicollis*)	X			Epple (1976)
Marmoset (*Callithrix jacchus*)		X		Abbott and Hearn (1978)
Lesser mouse lemur (*Microcebus murinus*)		X		Perret (1986)
Brown lemur (*Lemur fulvus*)	X			Boskoff (1978)

with interesting variations. Often these variations seem to be associated in some way with the fact that these rodents are induced ovulators.

Thus, a male prairie vole first induces the final stages of reproductive maturation and behavioral estrus in a young female using pheromonal cues to elicit LH and estradiol secretion. Then he induces ovulation via the tactile dimension of copulation (Carter, Getz, and Cohen-Parsons 1986). Interestingly, in some voles the continued presence of the stud is necessary to maintain pregnancy, apparently because of a need for primers (e.g., in the montane vole; Berger and Negus 1982). Inhibition of the reproductive development of young females by urinary primers produced by other females has also been documented in some voles (Getz, Dluzen, and McDermott 1983).

Pregnancy blocking by a strange male is easily demonstrated in some of the microtines in the laboratory. The nature of this block differs fundamentally from that seen in house mice and deermice, however. It is not limited to the preimplantation period. In many microtines, exposure of a pregnant female to a strange male can result in the loss of all her fetuses and a return to an estrous condition, even at mid-pregnancy (e.g., Stehn and Richmond 1975).

The laboratory rat has not proved a good subject to use for primer studies. This species shows some of the same effects seen in house mice, but often less robustly and more erratically (cf. Vandenbergh 1976; Slob, van Es, and van der Werff ten Bosch 1985; reviewed in Aron 1979). In all probability, the wild ancestors of our present domestic stocks of rats had a chemical primer system much like that of the house mouse, but this system has been muted by domestication. Thus, some priming effects can be seen today in some stocks of rats under some conditions, but not in other stocks or in other conditions.

A notable exception to the generality that the laboratory rat is not a good subject for primer studies involves the way individual females in a group synchronize each other's estrous cycles. As shown nicely by McClintock (1978, 1983a), airborne odors emanating from a female in the follicular phase of her cycle shorten the cycles of other females. Odors associated with a female approaching ovulation lengthen the cycles of her neighbors. The result is a statistically detectable degree of synchrony of cycles within a group of females exposed to each other's odors. Similarly, odors from pregnant rats shorten the cycle of nonpregnant individuals, while odors from lactating rats lengthen it (reviewed in McClintock 1983b). It must be emphasized that these odors are airborne and that their reception is presumably not by way of the vomeronasal organ.

One of the most interesting priming phenomena documented in mammals is that seen in the naked mole rat (*Heterocephalus glaber*) by Jarvis (1981). These animals live underground in large colonies in Kenya. Only one female in each colony breeds. The ovaries and reproductive tracts of the other females are repressed somehow. When the one breeding female dies, or when she is experimentally removed from the colony, another female undergoes rapid reproductive development and takes her place; the others remain infertile. A role for chemical cuing has not been documented for this phenomenon, but this seems likely given their underground existence.

Beyond the rodents, most of what we know about priming phenomena comes from studies of domestic ungulates, and most of this relates to the action of a male on ovulation (reviewed in Izard 1983). The observations of Shelton (1960) in Angora goats (*Capra hircus*) typify the kinds of effects that can be seen in livestock. Shelton preexposed one group of females for a week to a vasectomized male before releasing them into a breeding pasture containing intact males. As shown in figure 7.6, these females gave birth later than a control group, apparently because the vasectomized male induced estrus and ovulation, and thus these females had to wait the length of another estrous cycle before being bred by the intact male. This has not been verified as a pheromonal effect, but certainly this seems like a reasonable expectation.

There is a large literature dealing with the effects of rams on ovulation in sheep (reviewed in Martin 1984). Indeed, perhaps the best documentation of the effect of a male on LH secretion in any female mammal has been accomplished with this species (fig. 7.7). A chemical odor associated with the ram's wool seems to be the primary

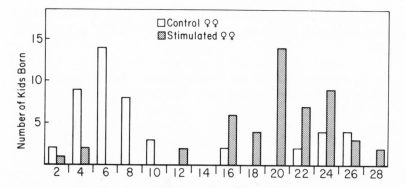

Figure 7.6. Number of kids born, as assessed at 2-day intervals, in two groups of Angora goats. One group was exposed to a vasectomized buck for 1 week before they were pastured with an intact buck. The other group was not pre-exposed to a buck. Redrawn from Shelton (1960).

agent responsible for this effect (Knight, Tervit, and Lynch 1984). It is important to note, however, that, as shown by Cohen-Tannoudji, Locatelli, and Signoret (1986), some kinds of nonpheromonal cues can yield the same response.

Only a few primates have been examined carefully in relation to potential priming effects (see Keverne 1983a). As might be expected given the complexity of primate communication, a high degree of individual tailoring seems destined to be a characteristic of these effects in primates. As shown by Epple (1976), for example, the pubertal ovulation of some young tamarins is suppressed by their mother but not by other females. This particular effect has been duplicated just with glandular secretions. A few reports of pheromonal-like phenomena exist for humans (e.g., Russell, Switz, and Thompson 1980), but the existence of this mode of regulation in the human remains doubtful (see Doty 1981).

Finally, in relation to priming effects in female mammals, it must be emphasized again that, while pheromonal primers obviously are widely used, it is reasonable now to assume that priming can be accomplished routinely in mammals via other sensory modalities also. We know little about nonchemical primers, however.

The one well-documented case of nonchemical priming has been seen in the red deer. McComb (1987) has recently shown how the roaring of a red deer stag can advance the onset of estrus in females. Indeed, recordings of these roars were almost as effective in accelerating estrus as the presence of a vasectomized stag. Undoubtedly, purely visual priming also exists in mammals.

As well as the documentation provided in table 7.2 for wide-

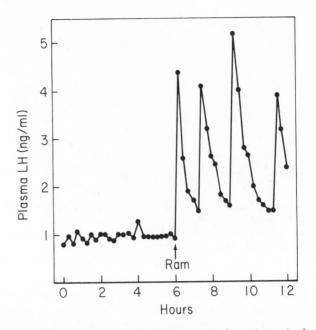

Figure 7.7. Plasma LH levels in a cannulated, estrogenized, ovariectomized ewe before and after being exposed to a ram. Redrawn from Martin (1984).

spread priming effects in female mammals, many such effects have also been seen in males. Specifically, there are many reports of adult males of many species releasing LH acutely in response to the presence of females or their pheromones or in association with copulation itself. Among those species are rats (Taleisnik, Caligaris, and Astrada 1966; Kamel et al. 1977; see also Dessi-Fulgheri and Lupo 1982), rabbits (Saginor and Horton 1968), bulls (Katongole, Naftolin, and Short 1971), field voles (Charlton et al. 1975), pigs (Ellendorf et al. 1975; Hemsworth, Winfield, and Chamley 1981), the tamar wallaby (Catling and Sutherland 1980), guinea pigs (Robert and Pajot 1984), and the rhesus monkey (e.g., Herndon, Turner, and Collins 1981). Interestingly, this is a conditionable response in the male rat (Graham and Desjardins 1980), and it is subject to habituation to individual females in the house mouse (Coquelin and Bronson 1979).

The Adaptive Significance of Priming Phenomena

Whether mediated by chemical cues or not, much has been written about the adaptive significance of priming phenomena in mammals, both in relation to house mice and more generally (e.g., Rogers and

Beauchamp 1976; Bronson 1973, 1983; Bronson and Coquelin 1980; Vandenbergh 1983, 1986; Jannett 1984b; Drickamer 1986; Keverne and Rosser 1986; Storey 1986; Coppola 1986; Vandenbergh and Coppola 1986).

The adaptive significance of these cuing systems seems in some ways straightforward and in other ways confusing. The ability to regulate the occurrence of ovulation in relation to current social conditions would seem to provide an advantage in almost any species under any condition. This is most obvious in relation to the pubertal ovulation of short-lived rodents, who cannot afford to ill time what may be their one chance to reproduce.

Likewise, priming systems can yield a high degree of synchrony in the reproductive effort of a group of mammals, and this undoubtedly would prove advantageous for some species under some conditions. For example, one can easily see how social cuing could yield a high degree of synchrony in a population at the beginning of a breeding season, even when more ecologically relevant factors are changing only slowly. As will be detailed later, combining such socially induced synchrony with photoperiodic control might be the only way a species could use the latter cue in the tropics, where daylength changes only a few seconds each day.

Beyond these two obvious generalities lies mostly confusion and speculation. This is particularly true when one tries to visualize how natural selection might promote each and every known priming phenomenon in its own right in each and every mammal in which these phenomena have been documented. How can one visualize the selective advantage associated with the strange male pregnancy block, for example? While the advantage to the strange male is obvious, what is the advantage to the first male or to the female? Why has natural selection not acted to protect the first male's potential progeny, and why has it not acted to promote the female's first potential litter given her short life span? There is evidence that such blocks do indeed occur in the wild, at least in microtines (e.g., Mallory and Clulow 1977; Heske and Nelson 1984), and thus there must be some kind of advantage associated with this phenomenon.

As reviewed in Storey (1986), the advantages that have been suggested for a female when her pregnancy is interrupted by the appearance of a new male are as follows: this could allow her quickly to gain acceptance in a new social group if she is forced to emigrate; it could save time by avoiding infanticide by the new male should she give birth to the first male's offspring, or it could strengthen the social bond with the second male, if indeed this is an advantage. The selective advantages that have been suggested for such blocks at the population level include preventing inbreeding or, in contrast, preventing gene flow between demes and limiting reproduction at high population density.

Any or all of these possibilities might have been a factor of some selective importance for some mammal under some conditions, but arguing strongly for the universal importance of any one of them is difficult. The same problem arises when one tries too vigorously to justify the suppression of the reproductive effort of one female by another. The advantage for the suppressor is always obvious, but what about the suppressed? Why has natural selection promoted the former's reproductive effort over that of the latter (see Wasser and Barash 1983)?

In general, it is probably well to remember that almost all our knowledge about mammalian priming phenomena has been garnered in the carefully controlled confines of the laboratory or the livestock pen. It is interesting, even enjoyable, to speculate about the adaptive advantages of such phenomena in the wild. These phenomena exist, and thus they must have been promoted by natural selection. In the absence of field observations, however, we will probably never be able to verify our speculations about their specific adaptive advantages, only argue about them.

Conclusions

The social environment is a rich source of cues that can fine-tune a mammal's reproduction. At one level, information exchange is essential for organizing the behavioral interactions that are necessary to initiate and bring the process of reproduction to fruition. At another level, individual mammals often influence either directly or indirectly the potential for another individual's reproductive success, thereby altering their own fitness. The major concern of this chapter is with the way social cues can influence reproduction by altering the endocrine milieu of a mammal. They do this in at least two general ways.

First, social cues can regulate endocrine secretion indirectly in relation to crowding or social status. Agonistic interactions can induce an aversive emotional state that, in turn, secondarily and nonspecifically depresses reproductive success. In carefully controlled laboratory situations, one can easily induce emotional stress and create the expected inverse relation between adrenal activity and LH secretion. This has been done in relation to both fighting and social subordination in both rodents and primates.

Extending these laboratory-generated concepts to wild populations, or even to complex penned populations, has proved difficult, however. This is probably not because the potential for such actions is not present in these situations. Rather our confusion here probably simply reflects the fact that social stress is only one of many potential influences operating simultaneously in complex social situations, and particularly in the wild. The potential for subordination secondarily to influence the secretion of the reproductive hormones and hence modulate reproduction is a real phenomenon, and it must play an important role in some populations under some conditions, even if difficult to detect.

The second way the social environment can endocrinologically influence reproductive success in mammals relates to primer phero-mones or to priming phenomena that involve other sensory modalities. It has been shown in many species that discrete auditory, tactile, and chemical cues can act via specific neuroendocrine pathways to influence particular reproductive events.

The best understood of such actions are those associated with the regulation of ovulation in house mice. Here urinary primers, often acting in conjunction with poorly understood tactile cues, can either potentiate or inhibit the secretion of LH and prolactin in recip-ients. They often do so via vomeronasal rather than primary olfactory mediation. The result is an ongoing modulation of the ovulatory cycle both before and after puberty by both male- and female-originating primers and a block to implantation by exposure to the urinary cues of a strange male. Female primers can influence the release of LH in male mice.

There are often fascinating differences in the ways house mice and other mammals use chemical primers. Pregnancy blocks induced by females as well as by strange males have been documented in some species, for example, as has the ability of groups of females to synchronize each other's ovulatory cycles. The suppression of the maturation of young females by some individual females, but not by others, has been documented in some species and will probably even-tually be shown to be a widespread phenomenon.

In all likelihood, many, and probably most, mammals use prim-ing phenomena of some kind to add flexibility to their reproduction. In many cases, the relevant cues assuredly are pheromonal, but in some they just as assuredly are not. In either case, the major advan-tages of such cuing systems would seem to be twofold: coordinating one's reproduction in relation to existing social conditions and, re-lated to this, enhancing synchrony in a population's reproductive ef-fort under ecologically marginal conditions.

8

The Interaction of Cues and Processes

Most of our detailed knowledge about the way mammals respond reproductively to environmental influences, whether physical, dietary, or social, has been gained by careful experimentation in the laboratory or livestock pen. Only in these situations, and particularly in the former, can one rigorously control for all possible sources of variation except the one of immediate interest. The total amount of variation confronting the experimenter can be reduced still further by employing an inbred stock of mammal that is well adapted to these conditions. Using this combination of approaches, one can truly isolate an environmental cuing system and thereby study its characteristics.

The negative side of all this of course is biological unrealism. Wild mammals in wild habitats are never subjected to one source of variation acting in a vacuum. They are continually bombarded by a diversity of forces, many of which are potential regulators of their reproduction. Mammals have been complexly designed by natural selection for tens of millions of years to live in environmentally complex conditions. As noted earlier in relation to the onset of fertility, this basic design must still exist in our domestic stocks, even if parts of it have been muted by a few hundred to a few thousand years of artificial selection. Inherent in the traditional laboratory approach, then, is a great potential for misleading oversimplification.

The role played by the Syrian hamster in our modern effort to understand the environmental regulation of reproduction is a case in point. Two phrases—"seasonal breeding" and "photoperiodic cuing"—are so closely linked with the name of this species in the endocrine literature that they often seem synonymous. Actually, if one scours the literature on this species, one can find buried among

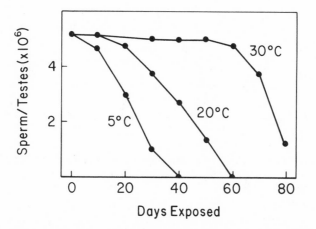

Figure 8.1. Time required for sperm to disappear from the testes of adult golden hamsters maintained on short daylengths at different ambient temperatures. Redrawn from Desjardins and Lopez (1980). For a comparison of the effect of cold on another hibernator, the edible dormouse (*Glis glis*), see Jallageas and Assenmacher (1984).

the myriad of papers dealing with photoperiodic control some examples of equally potent effects of other kinds of regulators.

As expected, for example, both food availability and variation in the quality of a hamster's diet can exert potent effects on the hamster's reproduction, even in long daylengths (Printz and Greenwald 1970; Johnson and Hoffman 1985). Likewise, low temperature can potentiate the effect of short daylengths in this hibernator (Hoffman, Hester, and Towns 1965; Reiter 1968; Hoffman 1968; Desjardins, Ewing, and Johnson 1971; fig. 8.1) Neither of these regulatory factors seems to operate via the pineal (Liu and Frehn 1973; Eskes 1983), suggesting that multiple divergent pathways converge on the final control of gonadotropin secretion in this species.

Furthermore, a primer pheromone produced by a female hamster alters to a significant degree the male's testicular response to short daylengths (Vandenbergh 1977). The use of a running wheel antagonizes this response more strongly (Elliot 1974; Gibbs and Petterborg 1986). Indeed, the use of a running wheel completely reverses the inhibitory effect of short days on the estrous cycle of the adult female (Borer et al. 1983). Thus, as discussed by Brainard, Vaughan, and Reiter (1984) and Johnson and Hoffman (1985), the reproductive system of the hamster can respond simultaneously and in complex ways to many features of its environment. We really have no idea how all these factors interact to regulate the reproduction of this animal in its native Syria, but there obviously must be more kinds of regulation acting there than just a reaction to photoperiod.

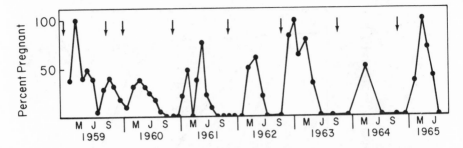

Figure 8.2. Frequency of pregnancy in a population of California voles trapped over a 7-year period in a grassland in California. The arrows indicate the onset of periods of rain. Redrawn from Lidicker (1973).

The ecologist working in wild habitats has long recognized the fact that a mammal's reproduction is subject to regulation simultaneously by many different factors. The normal approach of the field biologist is to measure as many facets of both the environment and a population's reproduction as possible, develop correlations, and then speculate on that basis.

A traditional conceptual framework for the ecologist's speculations is Liebeg's old law of the minimum. Here one asks which of the many factors that could potentially limit a population's reproduction is actually the one in operation in a particular population at a particular time. The assumption here is that all other potential limiting factors are exerting no pressure. According to this law, only one factor can limit at a time. This is a highly questionable approach because it does not allow for synergistic, additive, or antagonistic interactions between potential limiting factors.

The complexity and importance of such interactions can be illustrated in relation to the reproduction of the California vole. This is a relatively well-studied microtine in the San Francisco Bay area. As mentioned earlier in passing, it typically reproduces in the winter and early spring in that locale. As shown in figure 8.2, however, there can actually be considerable year-to-year variation in the time of year that this vole begins to breed. There can also be considerable variation in the length of breeding season, and there can be variation in the proportion of females reproducing at any one moment of time during the breeding season.

In the mild climate of the Bay area, the ultimate factors shaping this vole's seasonal pattern of reproduction are fairly obvious: a winter rainfall pattern and hence profound seasonal variation in the availability of the grasses and forbes on which it must feed in order to reproduce (Lidicker 1973; Ford and Pitelka 1984). On the other hand, laboratory experimentation has established the sensitivity of the reproduction of these animals to the availability of free water, certain minerals, a plant predictor, and a variety of potent primer effects (e.g., Nelson, Dark, and Zuker 1983: Rissman and Johnston 1986; Batzli 1986).

While not well documented, the California vole is undoubtedly also subject to the kinds of energetic constraints expected in mammals of this small size, and undoubtedly their reproduction can be suppressed by the direct and indirect effects of agonistic encounters. To confuse things further, as noted earlier this vole initiates breeding in the laboratory on the long days of summer rather than on the short days of winter, when it breeds in the wild (Nelson, Bamat, and Zucker 1982).

The question of how all these forces actually interact to regulate proximately the California vole's breeding season in the wild and to determine the success enjoyed by different individuals during this season is a difficult one. Obviously, the propensity of this animal to breed on long daylengths evolved at another time, or more probably in another place entirely, and apparently this control mechanism is now overridden routinely in natural populations by other considerations. Beyond these facts lies uncertainty. What is needed is an imaginative and systematic dissection of the precise way all potential environmental regulators interact with each other. This must be done in the laboratory. Unfortunately, only three of the many possible interactions have been studied so far, and none of these has involved food availability.

As shown in figure 8.3, long daylengths and lettuce supplements (that contain 6-MBOA) combine in an additive manner to promote testicular development in young males. In contrast, lettuce supplements completely override the inhibitory action of the opposite sex primer on the development of males. As still another contrast, feeding lettuce to a young female has no effect if that female is simultaneously exposed to opposite-sex primers; the female reacts maximally to the latter.

All in all then, three tests of the way environmental factors interact to shape the reproduction of the California vole have yielded three different patterns of results and no overall picture of how this animal's reproduction is actually regulated environmentally. It is obvious here, however, that environmental factors can interact with each other in complex ways to regulate reproduction in a mammal, and it is also obvious that the law of the minimum provides an inadequate framework within which to view these interactions.

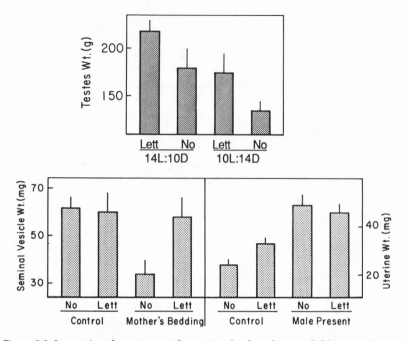

Figure 8.3. Interactions between supplementing the diet of young California voles with lettuce (Lett) and either photoperiodic or pheromonal variation. All reproductive indices are shown as means ± 1 standard error. Redrawn from Nelson, Dark, and Zucker (1983) and Rissman and Johnston (1986).

The thrust of this chapter is to emphasize rather than minimize the complexities involved in the regulation of mammalian reproduction. The approach that will be followed here will be somewhat the reverse of reductionism. That is, we will start with further acknowledgment of the many ways environmental factors can interact to control reproduction, and then we will add two other dimensions to this already complex view. The first dimension will acknowledge the fact that a mammal's sensitivity to environmental forces varies with the stage of its reproductive and life cycle. The second dimension will emphasize that a mammal's reproductive processes must be regulated in synchrony with its survival mechanisms.

It is hoped that the message will be clear: in reality, the environmental regulation of mammalian reproduction is indeed complicated. As will be witnessed shortly by many examples, however, understanding this complexity is clearly possible. It simply requires a good deal of experimental rigor and the acceptance of a particularly fascinating scientific challenge.

Interacting Cues and Endocrine Responses

Figure 8.4 draws on the preceding five chapters to summarize the potential actions of the environment on the neuroendocrine pathways that directly control reproduction in the order Mammalia. The animal under consideration here is largely hypothetical; it is either peripubertal or adult, and it is either a male or a nonpregnant, nonlactating female, but it is of unspecified taxon. The environmental factors of major concern are shown on the outside of the stippled area, and their pathways of action are shown inside.

Food availability is visualized in figure 8.4 as including both the

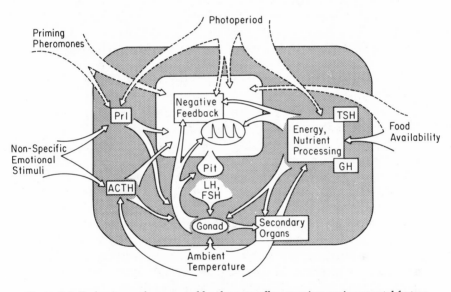

Figure 8.4. Endocrine pathways used by the naturally occurring environmental factors that are known to influence reproduction in mammals. This scheme is discussed in detail in the text. In brief, however, the ambient factors of concern are shown outside the stippled area. Their pathways of action are shown somewhat abstractly by the arrows penetrating the stippled area. Arrows drawn with solid lines indicate pathways of universal importance in mammals. Those drawn with dashed lines indicate pathways that are fully functional in some but not all mammals. The large open box in the upper center of the stippled area indicates two neural controls over gonadotropin secretion: the GnRH pulse generator and its negative feedback control by gonadal steroids (whose paths are shown but not identified specifically in the figure). As indicated, some environmental factors regulate gonadotropin secretion by acting directly on the GnRH pulse generator, some act indirectly by altering negative feedback sensitivity, and some act both ways. In some cases, it is not known how an environmental factor acts. In this scheme, the pathways of action of these factors simply terminate in the general vicinity of the pulse generator and its negative feedback control. From Bronson (1987a).

locomotor costs of finding food and the food actually found and consumed in competition with the other individuals in a population. This factor influences reproduction by way of the competitive energy- and nutrient-partitioning processes discussed earlier. Ultimately, food availability influences gonadotropin secretion, particularly luteinizing hormone (LH) secretion, by acting either directly on the gonadotropin-releasing hormone (GnRH) pulse generator or indirectly by way of enhanced negative feedback sensitivity to the gonadal steroids. Independently of such actions, low food availability may also exert effects downstream on both the gonad and the accessory tissues either directly or by way of altered prolactin, thyroid-stimulating hormone (TSH), or growth hormone (GH) secretion.

A potential action for predictive plant cues is acknowledged in figure 8.4, but it is not known how such cues influence gonadotropin secretion. Given how little we know about how water shortage influences gonadotropin secretion, this variation is simply combined as a nutrient here with food availability. Ambient temperature is shown in figure 8.4 as acting either directly on the testes of some nonburrowing males (high temperature), or as a classic stressor, or by purely energetic pathways in conjunction with food availability.

As suggested in figure 8.4, photoperiod can regulate gonadotropin secretion either directly via the GnRH pulse generator or indirectly by way of any one of three routes: by changing negative feedback sensitivity, by influencing energetic pathways, or by altering prolactin secretion. Finally, as noted in the preceding chapter, the social environment can contribute specific primers that influence LH or prolactin secretion, and it can also elicit nonspecific emotional stresses that can secondarily alter gonadotropin secretion by way of their action on prolactin or the corticotropin-releasing hormone (CRF)–adrenocorticotropin (ACTH)–adrenocortical axis.

In line with our earlier considerations of the Syrian hamster and the California vole then, the impression presented by figure 8.4 is meant to be one wherein gonadotropin secretion can be regulated simultaneously by a variety of external factors via a large number of interacting internal pathways. The assumption here is that natural selection has acted on this entire complement of control mechanisms, altering parts of it routinely to fit the actual challenges facing individuals and thereby a particular species, population, or subset of a population. The first question that can be asked in relation to this figure is which of the several environmental factors and their many pathways of action are of universal importance in mammals and which represent specializations found in some but not all mammals.

There are probably only three environmental factors and their associated sets of neuroendocrine pathways that are of universal importance in mammals: food availability, ambient temperature (acting either in conjunction with food availability or as an acute stressor), and nonspecific emotional stress. The potential for high ambient temperature to influence the gonads directly, the use of primers, and the use of photoperiod and plant predictors are not universal. Some mammals have all the capacities shown in figure 8.4, and some have some combination of one or more of them.

The second question of importance here is whether there are universally important patterns in the way environmental factors interact with each other to control reproduction in mammals. As suggested earlier, there is the potential for great complexity in such interactions. They can combine their actions either additively, synergistically, or antagonistically, and the latter can result in either a complete or a partial override of one cue by another.

Intuitively, one might suspect that mammals as a group should exhibit some kind of hierarchical organization of their reactions to the different kinds of environmental factors that can control their reproduction. That is, intuitively it seems as though the actions of some kinds of factors should always take precedence over the potential actions of other kinds of factors.

For example, it would seem as though energetic and nutrient limitations should always take precedence and that neither predictors nor positively acting social primers should be able to override these limitations. Indeed, intuitively it would seem as though social factors should at best be able only to fine-tune the general result dictated by dietary and physical factors. The latter is more or less true, but the relation between food availability, temperature, and the use of predictors is far more complicated than that suggested above.

As shown by Foster and his coworkers (e.g., Foster, Olster, and Yellon 1985), for example, ewe lambs allowed to grow normally in decreasing daylengths rapidly achieve their pubertal ovulation. Maintaining these lambs at 20kg body weight by restricting food availability totally blocks puberty until ad lib feeding is resumed. In the latter situation, however, ad lib feeding results in rapid pubertal development only if it occurs during decreasing daylengths. Puberty does not occur until the following fall if the lambs are returned to excess feeding when daylength is increasing in the spring.

Thus, as shown in figure 8.5, both a permissive photoperiod and an adequate food supply are required for full reproductive development in the ewe lamb, and the lack of either completely blocks the positive action of the other (see also Hunter and Van Aarde 1975). Interestingly, there are reports that low temperature can advance the

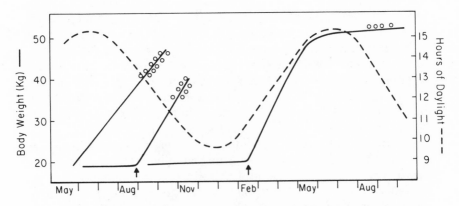

Figure 8.5. Effect of body weight and photoperiod on the time of the pubertal ovulation in ewe lambs. Spring-born lambs were allowed to grow normally, or, conversely, their food was restricted to hold their weight at 20kg. At either of two later times, the lambs were allowed to resume growth by giving them ad lib quantities of food (arrows). Time of ovulation for each individual is noted by a circle. The dotted line represents change in daylength. Redrawn from Foster, Olster, and Yellon (1985).

onset of breeding in some fall-breeding sheep (e.g., Dutt and Bush 1955).

In contrast to what is seen in figure 8.5, the action of a male primer can sometimes override the effect of inadequate food intake in an immature female house mouse, and sometimes it cannot, all depending on the stage of development reached when food restriction is applied. As shown by Hamilton and Bronson (1986), female mice do not exhibit any uterine growth when housed with a male if their growth is stopped at 30 or 45 percent of their expected adult weight by restricting their food intake.

At 60 percent of their expected adult weight, however, house mice apparently can secrete enough LH and estradiol in response to the male to promote considerable uterine growth, even though they are not growing somatically. They do not ovulate in response to 3 days of exposure to the male at this level of food restriction, but they react endocrinologically to his primer pheromones. Unlike what was seen in sheep then, a positively acting factor can sometimes partially override the effect of severe food restriction on gonadotropin secretion (see also Vandenbergh, Drickamer, and Colby 1972; Pennycuik 1972).

An example of a primer partially overriding a physical cue has been found in relation to the photoperiodic control of reproduction in deermice. As shown in figure 8.6, the photoperiodically responsive segment of a population of this species from South Dakota becomes

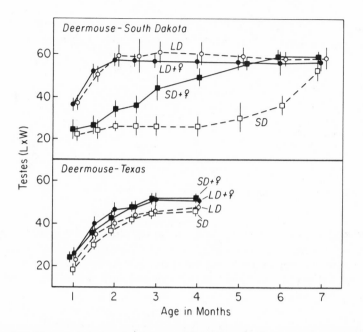

Figure 8.6. Changes in testes size (mean ± SE) in deermice from 1 to 7 months of age while being held on short days (SD, 8 hours of light) versus long days (LD, 16 hours of light), with or without a female of the same age in their cages. Two populations were studied, one whose progenitors had been trapped in South Dakota and another that was descended from animals trapped in Texas. Data collected by C. Desjardins and F. H. Bronson and partially published previously in Bronson (1985).

refractory to the inhibitory effect of short daylengths after about 6 months if the test males are housed in isolation. This is the length of the typical nonbreeding season in this species in that locale. Exposure of the young males to a female, however, cuts that time in half. The female's primer exerts no discernible effect in males held on long days because their reproductive development is already proceeding at its maximum rate anyhow. Also as shown in this figure, exposure to females has no effect on males of this species from Texas, whether maintained on long or short daylengths, because this particular population is not reproductively photoresponsive (Desjardins and Lopez 1980).

The fourth example of interesting interactions involves the two species featured in the previous two examples: house mice and deermice. Blank and Desjardins (1985) maintained males of both species on long daylengths (unimportant in the case of the nonphotoperiodic house mice) and 30 percent food restriction. This level of

Table 8.1 Changes in Body Weight and Reproductive Parameters
in Adult Male House Mice and Deermice Subjected to
30 Percent Food Restriction for 5 Weeks

	House Mice		Deermice	
	Ad Lib	Restricted	Ad Lib	Restricted
Body weight (g)	24.8±0.6	17.1±0.4*	19.5±0.3	17.1±0.7*
Testes weight (mg)	165±6	178±10	378±27	265±14*
Seminal vesicle weight (mg)	26.6±1.9	24.1±1.3	36.2±4.0	21.3±1.4*
Plasma testosterone (ng/ml)	0.30±0.12	0.31±0.07	1.34±0.67	0.46±0.07*

Source: Blank and Desjardins (1985).
* Significant effects of food restriction.

food restriction caused a loss of body weight in both species, but it depressed reproduction only in the deermice (table 8.1). The highly opportunistic house mouse ignored this insult, at least in regard to its reproductive potential (see also Pryor and Bronson 1981; Blank and Desjardins 1986).

As a fifth example, in separate experiments Breed (1975) found significant effects on the length of the estrous cycle of the hopping mouse (*Notomys alexis*) in response to three different kinds of influences: the presence versus the absence of a male; water deprivation versus ad lib watering; and long versus short daylengths. The precise way these factors interacted with each other depended on whether the female under consideration was prepubertal or adult as well as on its reproductive history if it was an adult. It is important to note that in no case did the lack of a male, the lack of water, or short daylength, either alone or in combination, totally eliminate ovulation in these animals.

In the wild, the hopping mouse breeds opportunistically in relation to the unpredictable periods of rain characteristic of the central Australian deserts. Since these animals cease breeding entirely during prolonged drought, some factor other than the three studied by Breed, or some other combination of factors, must play a crucial role. Undoubtedly, food availability is of core importance here. The fact that many cues can interact with each other subtly to modulate the ovulatory cycle of this animal, however, seems like an exceptionally good tactic for an inhabitant of this particular unpredictable environment.

The reader will probably have noticed that, of the several examples of interacting environmental influences discussed so far, only one has involved an animal other than a temperate-zone rodent. This is a reasonably accurate reflection of the available literature. Unfortunately, most of what we know about the way environmental cues interact to regulate reproduction comes from studies done with such animals.

To broaden our perspective, we might for the moment consider how environmental factors *might* interact to regulate reproduction in other kinds of mammals. To provide some focus here, we can concentrate on a question that has intrigued physiologists, ecologists, and behaviorists working with primates for decades now. What factors produce seasonal breeding in tropical primates?

As noted earlier, many primates breed seasonally in the tropics, usually phased in some relation to seasonal rainfall patterns (Vandenbergh 1973; Drickamer 1974). Sometimes the degree of reproductive synchrony seen in these animals can be remarkable. Jolly (1967), for example, observed that all the matings that occurred in a single wild troop of a lemur (*Lemur catta*) took place in a 12-day period. While there was some troop-to-troop variation in time of mating, the neighboring troops of these lemurs all completed their breeding in well less than a month. Breeding was followed a few weeks later by a highly synchronized period of births.

There can be little doubt that the ultimate factor of most concern in such situations is food availability in relation to either lactation or the postweaning period. Either predator pressure or competition could be an important secondary consideration, however. In any case, many primates have long periods of gestation and lactation, and this suggests that whenever possible they should opt to use a predictor of some kind. Only in this way could they ensure that the later, more demanding stages of their reproductive cycle would coincide with the correct phase of the seasonal rainfall pattern.

There is both direct and indirect evidence that some primates are reproductively photoresponsive. Sometimes this literature is weak and confusing, as it is in relation to the rhesus monkey (cf. Birkner 1970; Bielert and Vandenbergh 1981; Wehrenberg and Dyrenfurth 1983; Rawlins and Kessler 1985; Herndon et al. 1985). Nevertheless, at least some tropical primates definitely do have the capacity to respond reproductively to variation in daylength (reviewed in chapter 5; see also Coe, Erla, and Levine 1985). Whether these animals actually use this cue in the wild is a much more difficult question (see Vandenbergh and Vessey 1968).

Could photoperiod be used effectively in the tropics to track the relatively predictable patterns of rainfall that characterize much of this region? Photoperiod could not be used as a predictive cue on the equator for obvious reasons. As noted earlier, however, at about 8° of latitude there is about an hour of annual variation in daylength. As first suggested by Vandenbergh (1969a), some primates might be able to use such slight annual variation in some such physical predictor to produce seasonal breeding if they supplemented it with social synchrony (reviewed in Herndon 1983).

That is, daylength changes by only a few seconds a day at 8° of latitude, and it is difficult to see how such small changes could yield any reasonable degree of reproductive synchrony among the genetically diverse individuals in a population, and certainly not between diverse populations. If the first animals to react to their critical daylength then used primers to activate the other members of the population (e.g., Ruiz de Elvira, Herndon, and Collins 1983), however, the result could be a snowballing effect that indeed could yield a well-synchronized breeding season.

Whether this is what actually happens in some, in many, or in all tropical primates is open to question, but a large number of studies indicate that social synchrony is used by these animals to supplement some kind of predictor.

An alternate possibility to photoperiodic regulation is that some of these animals may have evolved a dependence on plant predictors (e.g., Whitten 1983). Many tropical plants show reasonably predictable cycles that are apparently regulated directly by the rainfall cycle. It is not uncommon, for example, to find some species of plants flowering even in the middle of an intense seasonal drought where there is otherwise little sign of plant reproduction. How truly equatorial primates or those living in reasonably constant environments use proximal cues to obtain seasonal synchrony is a totally unexplored question.

Before leaving the problem of how environmental factors interact to regulate reproduction, it is worth noting a few other outstanding papers dealing with this subject, again of necessity in rodents, however. Excellent examples include the several efforts of Kenagy and his coworkers to understand the environmental regulation of various species of pocket mice (*Perognathus* sp.; e.g., Kenagy and Bartholomew 1981; Kenagy and Barnes 1984; see also Ostwald et al. 1972). Also of importance here is Kenagy's work on ground squirrels and chipmunks (e.g., Kenagy 1981, 1987; Kenagy and Bartholomew 1985) and the several experiments by Desjardins and his coworkers on deermice (e.g., Desjardins and Lopez 1983; Blank and Desjardins 1986; Blank 1986). The latter are particularly important papers because these authors recognized the fact that subsets of a population can differ greatly in their response to environmental factors.

The interested reader might also want to consult papers in which the laboratory rat has been subjected to different combinations of environmental manipulations and different combinations of surgical ablations in an effort to study the internal interactions of some of the pathways used by environmental cues. The ablations include pinealectomies, blinding, olfactory bulbectomy, and hypothalamic lesions (e.g., Piacsek and Meites 1967; Reiter, Sorrentino, and Ellison 1970; Relkin 1971; Walker and Frawley 1977; Blask and Nodelman 1979; Reiter et al. 1980; Blask et al. 1980; Nelson and Zucker 1981; Nelson, Bamat, and Zucker 1982; see also Pieper et al. 1984). Unfortunately, no broadly meaningful conceptual scheme has yet emerged from such studies in rats.

Finally, earlier in this chapter the question was posed as to whether there is a universally important pattern in the way environmental factors interact to regulate reproduction in mammals. The obvious answer to this question is that we do not yet have enough information to see such a pattern if indeed it exists. Social cues can provide a potent fine-tuning of the regulation of gonadotropin secretion by physical and dietary factors, but how the latter factors commonly interact is less obvious. One might guess that there probably is not a universally important pattern of interactions here, however, only a wide variety of solutions to a wide variety of environmental challenges.

Responses in Relation to Phase of Life and Reproductive Cycles

So far we have been considering the way environmental cues might interact to regulate the reproductive effort of peripubertal and adult males and females, with the latter being neither pregnant nor lactating. An entirely new dimension of complexity emerges if we concern ourselves with other phases of the life and reproductive cycles of mammals, particularly in the case of the female.

When a female becomes pregnant, her capacity to react to environmental cues changes, and so do the kinds of response these cues can elicit (e.g., Racey 1981). In general, the female remains sensitive to some but not all kinds of environmental perturbations early in pregnancy. She becomes generally insensitive to most of these factors after the placenta assumes many of the functions of the hypothalamus and pituitary, thereby closing off most of the pathways shown earlier in figure 8.4.

As noted in chapter 4, females of small size with small fat reserves remain sensitive to energetic challenge early in pregnancy, but only extreme and prolonged food shortage or low temperature yields embryo mortality late in pregnancy. These conditions could occur during spring ice storms. Large females with their large fat stores are better buffered against such short-term challenges throughout pregnancy. On the other hand, regardless of body size, a shortage of critical nutrients becomes progressively more important as pregnancy progresses because these nutrients are necessary for the growth and development of the enlarging fetuses.

Switching from a permissive photoperiod to an unpermissive photoperiod in the laboratory seems to have little effect on the pregnant female, but this is an unbiological consideration anyhow; no mammal has evolved in environments characterized by such rapid changes. As a generality, stress becomes less likely to influence the production of offspring as pregnancy progresses, whether it is induced by aversive emotions or by acute temperature change. Likewise, with the exception of the microtine rodents, pregnant females seem not to react to primers after implantation has occurred.

Independent of a concern for the female's ability to produce offspring, an important consideration here is the potential effect of environmental factors on the unborn young of the pregnant female. As noted much earlier in this book, restricting the amount of food available to a pregnant female influences the rate of development of her offspring even after they are born. Also as noted earlier, at least in some species the critical photoperiod to which an individual reacts as an adult is determined in part by the photoperiod its mother experiences when it is in the uterus.

Additionally, in the last decade a large number of papers have established unequivocally that other kinds of variation in the uterine environment can influence the ability of fetuses to reproduce after they have achieved adulthood. Three sources of such variation have been explored with varying degrees of intensity: nutrition, stress, and the proximity of a fetus to other fetuses of the same or the opposite sex.

In the latter regard, a female rat or mouse fetus residing in the uterus between two male fetuses is masculinized to a greater or lesser degree relative to a female located between two female fetuses. Usually, this means that the female located in the uterus next to males will function more or less normally in adulthood while displaying subtle masculinization of a variety of reproductively related characteristics. These include the precise timing of the pubertal ovulation, the duration of the ovulatory cycle immediately after the pubertal ovulation, her attractiveness to males, the propensity to show purely female-typical sexual behavior, her aggressiveness, and the morphological characteristics of her external genitalia (e.g., Clemens, Gladue, and

Coniglio 1978; vom Saal and Bronson 1978, 1980; vom Saal 1981; reviewed in vom Saal, 1983).

The modifying influence of an individual's position in the uterus relative to the sex of its neighbors can extend even to the timing of reproductive senescence (vom Saal and Moyer 1985). Indeed, it can extend even to such seemingly esoteric characteristics as the rate of production of a steroid-dependent epidermal growth factor by an adult's submandibular gland (Brown, Schultz, and Hilton 1984).

As far as maternal nutrition is concerned, there is a strong relation between litter size and later fertility in rodents, and much of this relation is determined in utero and probably nutritionally (e.g., Leamy 1981). There is no doubt that experimentally undernourishing a pregnant female yields a slower rate of growth of her offspring, even after birth, and that this delays the onset of puberty (reviewed in Glass and Swerdloff 1980; Bronson and Rissman 1986). Likewise, this treatment specifically impairs the sexual behavior of the offspring after they mature (e.g., Rhees and Fleming 1981), and it can influence aggressiveness as well (Halas, Hanlon, and Sandstead 1975). Indeed, maternal undernourishment can even alter the sex ratio of the offspring. As shown by McClure (1981) and Austad and Sunquist (1986), imposing food restriction on a pregnant female favors survival of the female offspring in both the wood rat (*Neotoma floridana*) and the opossum (*Didelphis virginianus*), respectively.

A variety of physical stressors, when applied to a pregnant female rodent, can also change the reproductive characteristics of her offspring as adults, often in ways similar to those seen in relation to variation in position in the uterus (e.g., Ward 1972; Dunlap, Zadina, and Gougis 1978; Herrenkohl 1979; Meisel and Ward 1981; Politch and Herrenkohl 1984).

In general, the female's sensitivity to environmental variation that is largely lost during pregnancy returns during lactation, but often in a modified form. Ovulation is routinely suppressed by negative feedback in most lactating mammals, and thus there is no substrate on which primers can act, for example. The major environmental concerns for the lactating female are simply the availability of the food and water needed to sustain her milk production.

A variety of reports now document both the acute and the prolonged effects of stressors on milk production (see chap. 4). Unfortunately, despite the importance of knowledge about lactation to the livestock industry, no systematic studies involving subtle environmental controls have been made. Nor is there much information about the interaction of environmental factors in the control of lactation.

In summary then, to appreciate fully the actions of the environment on a mammal's reproduction, one must recognize the fact that the responses to these factors change constantly during a mammal's life cycle and that their effects cumulate, starting when the mammal is still in the uterus. To schematize the environmental regulation of reproduction accurately then, one would need to take the two-dimensional scheme presented earlier in figure 8.4 and mold a third dimension to it: stage of reproductive or life cycle.

Responses in Relation to Survival Mechanisms

To appreciate fully the way reproduction is regulated in mammals, it is necessary to add still one more dimension to our thinking. This need arises because the process of reproduction does not function independently of other biological processes. A mammal's investment in reproduction must be integrated ecologically, physiologically, and behaviorally with its need to survive.

The interplay between the mechanisms devoted primarily to reproduction and those devoted primarily to survival adds a vast new dimension of complexity to our perspective on reproductive biology. This dimension will be illustrated here by considering just one of its many facets: the way reproduction and a mammal's other needs for energy relate to each other in a seasonally changing environment in the temperate zone.

The way that energy is partitioned competitively between a mammal's need to reproduce and its other demands for calories has been considered in detail in chapter 3. To remind the reader, reproduction often has one of the lowest priorities in this competition in nonpregnant females, while pregnant females and males give it a higher priority. Seldom, however, do the caloric demands of reproduction outweigh those of thermoregulation and cellular maintenance. The first point to be made here, then, is that during a breeding season the reproductive axis, acting through its agents the gonadal steroids, influences the demands that compete with reproduction for energy as well as being influenced by them. This two-way relation is presented schematically in figure 8.7.

At first glance, figure 8.7 may seem to defy rational explanation. Actually, it is only an amalgamation of the first two subjects discussed in this chapter, but with a more detailed concern for energetic pathways. The scheme shown in this figure is specifically designed to emphasize three principles.

First, this figure is meant to note again that there are many interacting pathways linking a mammal's reproductive axis to its environ-

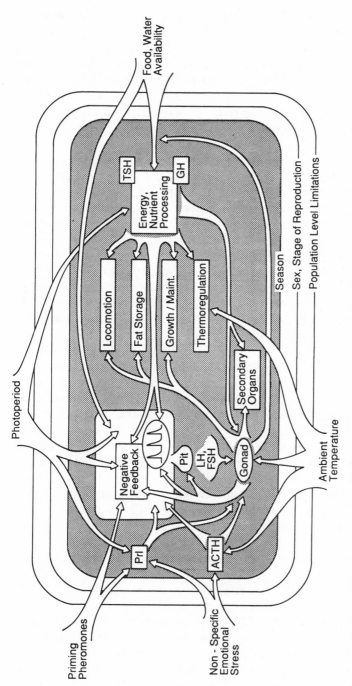

Figure 8.7. The multiple interactions between energetic considerations, other environmental factors, and the reproductive axis of a hypothetical mammal. This figure is discussed in detail in the text. In general, however, its design more or less follows that of figure 8.4. Indeed, this figure is mostly just an expansion of figure 8.4 to include three more elements: a concern for the physiological demands that compete with reproduction for energy and nutrients; a concern for the effect of the gonadal steroids on these other competing demands; and an acknowledgment that a mammal's reactions to environmental cues depend on its species, population, or subpopulation, its sex and stage of reproduction, and, finally, seasonal considerations.

ment. Second, it is meant to emphasize that a mammal's reproductive reaction to environmental variation depends on its species (or population or subset of a population), its sex, and its stage of reproduction and, as will be discussed shortly, on seasonal considerations as well. Third, this figure illustrates the two-way energetic relation noted above, namely that the gonadal steroids can influence food intake and most of the energetic demands that compete directly with reproduction for available calories as well as being influenced indirectly by these same demands.

In the latter regard, most of what we know about the effect of the gonads on a mammal's nonreproductive demands for energy has been learned with laboratory rats. In the cycling female rat, for example, it has been shown repeatedly that the high levels of estradiol associated with proestrus decrease the female's food intake, change her meal patterns, decrease her body weight, decrease fat storage, and increase her spontaneous activity on a running wheel. Some of these effects reflect direct hypothalamic action, and others involve more peripheral mechanisms (reviewed in Wade and Gray 1979). Female rats in the wild need to find food and consume it every day, but as the time of ovulation approaches their use of energy becomes driven as much by the need to find a male as it is by their need to forage.

Testosterone influences these same parameters in male rats, but, not surprisingly, the effects of this steroid in this sex differ somewhat from those of estradiol in the female. The evolutionary and energetic challenges facing the two sexes are different. Testosterone increases food intake and spontaneous activity in male rats while decreasing fat storage and body weight (Wade 1976; Wade and Gray 1979). Again not surprisingly, the specific effects of the gonadal steroids on these parameters can differ both directionally and in potency in males and females of other species (cf. Slusser and Wade 1981; Zucker and Boshes 1982; Dark and Zucker 1984; Kemnitz et al. 1986).

Still not surprisingly, pregnancy and lactation can alter all these relations in complex ways (e.g., Fleming 1976; Wade, Jennings, and Trayhurn 1986). Finally, the gonadal steroids also influence the growth of a young mammal. The well-known effect of these hormones on epiphyseal closure, and hence on the energetic demands of somatic growth, is also indicated in figure 8.7.

In general then, figure 8.7 suggests that all but one of the energetic demands that compete with reproduction for calories are reciprocally influenced by gonadal activity. The one exception here is thermoregulation, and there is some evidence now that even this energetic need may be influenced by gonadal activity as well as competing with it. Wade, Jennings, and Trayhurn (1986) suggest that thermogenesis of brown adipose tissue may change during pregnancy via actions by either progesterone or prolactin.

As a generality then, it seems likely that the gonadal steroids probably routinely influence food intake and all the nonreproductive demands for energy in breeding mammals, but undoubtedly always in ways that will prove adaptive to the particular species, sex, and stage of reproduction of concern.

To continue adding complexity, the interesting two-way relations described above during the breeding season emerge as only a small part of a much larger picture when one also considers the nonbreeding season. Mammals living in seasonally changing environments in the temperate zone must make many metabolic and behavioral adjustments to survive the winter months. As the season of low temperature and food scarcity approaches, the mammals of this region experience a veritable cascade of energy-related changes, only a few of which relate directly to reproduction.

The large number of specific adaptations that have evolved in these mammals to aid winter survival include daily torpor, hibernation, migration, huddling, food hoarding, and choice of habitat as well as more subtle changes associated with nest building, metabolism of energy, daily activity patterns, and, finally, sometimes the photoperiodic synchronization of all such changes (e.g., Cherry and Verner 1975; Lynch and Gendler 1980; Wickler 1981; Dark, Zucker, and Wade 1983; Dark and Zucker 1983; Quay 1984; Wunder 1984; Feist 1984; Feist and Feist 1986; Blank and Desjardins 1986).

Even the set point for defended body weight can change seasonally. Some voles, for example, actually decrease rather than increase their body weight in the winter, apparently to decrease the total amount of food needed and hence foraging time outside the nest (e.g., Dark and Zucker 1983; Ure 1984).

All the adjustments noted above must be made in harmony with a mammal's reproductive needs. Likewise, the mammal's reproductive needs must conform to limitations imposed by survival mechanisms. This is what life-history strategies are all about, and the point here is simply that to approach a mammal's reproductive biology properly one must view it broadly in terms of all the components of its life-history strategy.

The stated objective of this chapter was to emphasize the complexities rather than the simplicities involved in the way reproduction is regulated in mammals. After integrating the different concerns of this chapter, the result—figure 8.7—certainly seems complex. Actually, in reality this particular scheme is still greatly oversimplified. For example, there is no acknowledgment in it of the circadian organization that permeates the reproductive processes of so many mammals.

From a purely endocrine standpoint, there is no concern in figure 8.7 for the manifold roles played by prolactin and the adrenal hormones. Neither is more than a nod given here to the importance of seasonal changes in TSH regulation. From an ecological perspective, visualizing only the sex, stage of reproduction, season, and the population of concern as important sources of variation hides an amazing amount of interesting diversity.

Indeed, the entire scheme shown in figure 8.7 could be reoriented to focus on any of many entirely different facets of reproduction. At the core of figure 8.7 is the regulation of gonadotropin secretion. An alternative choice could have been the regulation of reproductively related behaviors: aggression, maternal, and sexual behavior itself. These are no less important for reproductive success than gonadotropin secretion. The result assuredly would have been even more complex (see McClintock 1984; Mauget, Maurel, and Sempere 1986). This, however, is the reality of mammalian reproduction.

Reproduction is a complicated process, and its external regulation is even more complex. Fortunately, this complexity is readily susceptible to careful dissection using rigorous experimental designs and methods.

Conclusions

Reductionism is at the core of most physiological research. This is the way progress is made, providing that reality is not lost in the process. The thrust of this chapter has been to emphasize that reality. The regulation of a mammal's reproduction is an exceptionally complex process, and inherent in its study is the danger that simple generalities may reflect only gaps in our knowledge or one-dimensional thinking.

Three dimensions of complexity have been emphasized here. First, mammals have evolved in ways that allow them to surmount environmental complexity. Probably seldom in the wild is a mammal's reproduction controlled at any one moment in time by a single environmental variable. Many environmental factors can alter a mammal's reproductive potential, and these factors can interact with each other in complex ways. Furthermore, there probably is no single, universally important pattern in the way these factors interact with each other in the class Mammalia. Rather, many strategies probably have evolved for using environmental factors to regulate reproduction of the many different kinds of mammals that live in many different kinds of environments.

The second dimension of complexity emphasized here relates to the fact that the actions and interactions of environmental factors can vary greatly with the stage of the mammal's life cycle during which they are perceived. Many reactions to environmental factors are lost during early pregnancy, only to reappear during lactation. On the other hand, many of these factors act via the mother to influence her unborn young. Thus, as noted in an earlier chapter, a mammal's reproductive potential during adulthood may be modulated by a variety of earlier experiences, starting even in the uterus.

The final dimension of complexity emphasized here relates to the ongoing interplay between a mammal's need to reproduce and its need to survive. This adds a vast dimension of complexity to our perspective of the way reproduction is regulated. This dimension was illustrated here by considering only one of its many facets: how the energetic demands of survival both influence and are influenced by the activity of the reproductive axis in seasonally changing environments.

Mammals have been complexly designed to reproduce in a complex manner while living in complex environments. Whether the concern is physiological, ecological, or behavioral, to ignore this basic design while searching for simple answers is a mistake. Accepting the reality of the situation, on the other hand, presents a fascinating challenge to the researcher.

9

A Taxonomic Perspective

Most of this book has emphasized general principles that it is hoped cross taxonomic boundaries with some ease. Ecologically, our concern has been with general attributes such as life span and body size and with the general kinds of environmental challenges confronting a population. The framework used to develop physiological principles has been that stemming mostly from detailed studies of domesticated rodents, livestock, and primates.

There is merit to taking a more traditional taxonomic approach to exploring reproductive biology. Taxonomically related mammals tend to have similar life spans, be of similar size, and exploit similar environments. They also tend to share a common physiological organization. Some of these organizations and some of the ways they interface with the environment depart radically from those found in our standard domesticated animals, however, and therein lies a richness that must be acknowledged.

It is beyond the scope of this book to review in detail all that is known about the reproductive biology of all mammalian taxa. This has been done already by Asdell (1964) and by the combined chapters by Griffiths, Tyndale-Biscoe, Rowlands and Weir, and Spies and Chappel in the fourth edition of *Marshall's Physiology of Reproduction* (Lamming 1984). Our interest here is simply to emphasize the kinds of diversity that can be found in the class Mammalia and to document the kinds of information about environmental regulation that are presently available for mammals as a whole. This can be done using a limited number of taxa that represent the most common forms.

Specifically then, this chapter will survey the reproductive biology of ten of the nineteen orders in the class Mammalia. These ten orders contain over 98 percent of all the species known to exist in this class. The classificational scheme followed here is mostly that of

Vaughan (1978), except in regard to the cetaceans and pinnipeds, for which Eisenbergh is followed (1981). Numbers of species where given are those in Vaughan's (1978) classification.

Order Marsupialia

Because of continental drift, the marsupials became physically isolated from the eutherians well over 100 million years ago. Thus, the 242 species of this radiation are of particular interest to students of reproductive biology for three reasons. First, the marsupials have evolved a markedly different mode of reproduction. Second, given the absence of competition from placentals, the marsupials underwent spectacular adaptive radiation in Australia. Within this one order, one can find much of the diversity in reproductive strategies seen elsewhere in all the eutherians, but all conforming to the basic marsupial plan. Third, largely because of the efforts of Australian scientists, we now know a great deal about both the ecology and the reproductive physiology of these animals.

Fortunately, almost everything that is known about the reproductive biology of this interesting order of mammals has been exhaustively reviewed in Tyndale-Biscoe and Renfree (1987). These authors have produced an exceptionally thorough and scholarly book, and it should be read in combination with the more evolutionary perspective provided by Lee and Cockburn (1985). Shorter reviews that should be consulted include those in Sharman (1976) and Parker (1977). Of particular interest are comparisons of the energetics of marsupial and eutherian reproduction provided by McNab (1988) and Nicoll and Thompson (1987). The present abbreviated look at the marsupials relies heavily on all these references and their extensive bibliographies.

Several facets of the marsupial reproductive system differ greatly from those of eutherians. Externally, these include such interesting anatomical features as a prepenal scrotum and bipartite penes and vaginae in most groups and typically, but not always, a pouch over the teats. The major difference, however, involves the marsupial's dramatically abbreviated period of gestation and the functional bases for this phenomenon. Few marsupials have a period of gestation longer than their estrous cycle, and no marsupial weighs more than 1g at birth. Thus, these animals are born in an exceptionally altricial state, and most of their early development takes place while fused to a teat. Pouch life may last for as few as 2 months in some of the smaller, rapidly reproducing forms, or it may extend for over a year in some of the larger marsupials.

All marsupials examined so far are spontaneous ovulators, and

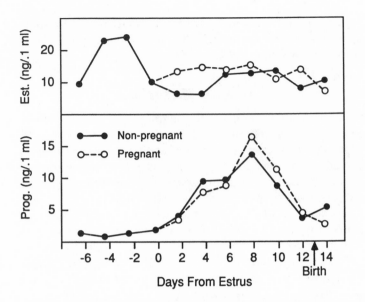

Figure 9.1. Change in circulating levels of estradiol and progesterone during the abbreviated pregnancy of the Virginia opossum (*Didelphis virginianus*). While there are significant changes in both hormones over time, there are no significant differences between pregnant and nonpregnant females. These data are condensed and redrawn from a large set of data published by Harder and Fleming (1981).

most are polyestrous. The marsupial ovum has a shell membrane and some yolk. This yolk, along with the uterine secretions that are elicited independently of mating, sustains the embryo during its short existence in the uterus. A delay in embryonic development—embryonic diapause—is often seen in marsupials. In some seasonally breeding species, the embryo overwinters in this stage, development being reinitiated only in time for birth to occur during the most propitious season.

Marsupials actually do form several types of organs that fit the definition of a placenta. All are short lived, however. Indeed, endocrinologically, it is often difficult to detect the short pregnancy of a marsupial. Figure 9.1, for example, examines the changes in circulating levels of estrogens and progesterone observed during the reproductive cycle of the common opossum (*Didelphis virginianus*) of North America. One can easily see a follicular phase during which estrogens are secreted as well as a luteal phase during which progesterone is secreted, but there is no meaningful difference between the pregnant and the nonpregnant female in the latter case.

The corpus luteum of the marsupial develops largely indepen-

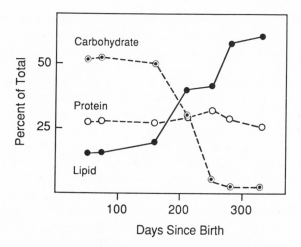

Figure 9.2. Changes in the composition of the milk of the tammar wallaby during lactation. Redrawn from Green (1984).

dently of pituitary control, and its luteolysis likewise seems to be somewhat autonomous. Tyndale-Biscoe and Renfree (1987) offer a detailed classification of the kinds of ovarian cycles that can be found in marsupials.

Lactation in marsupials has been reviewed in Green (1984). As shown in figure 9.2, the composition of milk can vary dramatically during a long period of pouch existence, at least in some of the large kangaroos. Interestingly, some monotocus marsupials routinely suckle two offspring simultaneously, even though the two were produced in different reproductive cycles. When this happens, the different mammary glands show a great deal of autonomous control, each producing milk tailored for the age of the offspring using it.

The kind of annual reproductive strategy shown by a marsupial depends on the interaction of several factors: whether it is monestrous or polyestrous and, if the latter, how quickly it can return to a fertile condition; the duration of gestation and, more important, the length of lactation and pouch life; whether it exhibits embryonic diapause and the factors associated with this delay; and, of course, its feeding strategy and the precise set of environmental challenges facing it.

In the latter regard, the marsupials of the southwestern Pacific live in an area ranging latitudinally from close to the equator to the middle of the temperate zone. Within this broad area, they exploit predictable environments such as those found in monsoonal rain forests, more mesic forests and brushlands, and temperate grasslands. They also exist here in some of the harshest, most unpredictable deserts found anywhere in the world. Within this broad range of climates, some marsupials are omnivorous, and some specialize exclusively on eating foods as diverse as leaves, herbs, seeds, nectar, fruit, insects, and vertebrate flesh. Given all this diversity, one expects to find great variation in the annual reproductive strategies of these animals, and this expectation certainly is borne out.

The majority of marsupials are seasonal breeders, but asynchronous, year-round breeding is not uncommon. Representative annual patterns for some Australian forms can be found in figure 9.3. As an example of a typical seasonal breeder, the sugar glider (*Petaurus breviceps*) lives in the canopy of the forests of eastern Australia, where it eats nectar, gum, and insects. It is polyestrous but without a postpartum estrus. Removal of the young from the pouch results in an immediate return to estrus. Thus, recovery to a fertile condition can be rapid if a litter is lost in the wild.

The female sugar glider's reproductive cycle totals over 110 days, of which pouch time amounts to 70–75 days. One or two litters are produced each year in association with the seasonal peak in available insects. As testimony of a degree of opportunism in this strategy, however, male sugar gliders remain spermatogenic throughout the year. The birthing season shown in figure 9.3 is that seen in a population near Melbourne studied by Suckling (1984). This general pattern seems to be typical of many other polyestrous marsupials, as is its ultimate environmental correlate—food availability.

The brush-tailed possum (*Trichosurus vulpecula*) is a polyestrous, arboreal folivore that is widespread in the eucalyptus forests of Australia. Pouch life is 5–7 months, after which the females return to estrus. In some places, this species reproduces only in the autumn, but the island population studied by Dunnet (1964) showed a decidedly bimodal pattern of births (fig. 9.3). In one of the few studies of South American marsupials, Atramentowicz (1982) reported a similar pattern of bimodal peaks superimposed on a more or less continuous breeding pattern for the wooly opossum (*Caluromys philander*) in equatorial French Guiana. The obvious environmental correlates in this case were rainfall and thus the availability of this species' diet of fruit and insects.

As an example of a potentially year-round breeder, most bandicoots are also polyovular and polyestrous. Indeed, for their size (up to 2.5kg) these animals have a surprisingly high fecundity. They can rapidly produce litter after litter of offspring, and the young can mature and breed rapidly. As shown in figure 9.3, births occurred in all

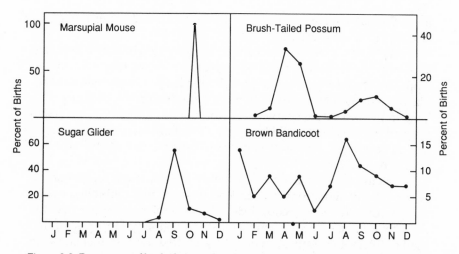

Figure 9.3. Percentage of births by month in four populations of Australian marsupials. Redrawn from Dunnet (1964), Wood (1970), Hall (1983), and Suckling (1984).

months of the year, and males remained fertile all year in the population of northern brown bandicoots (*Isodon macrourus*) near Brisbane studied by Hall (1983). Some other bandicoots in other parts of Australia show strong seasonal tendencies, however, and some show well-defined breeding seasons (see Barnes and Gemmell 1984). Scarlett and Woolley (1980) provide another example of a continuously breeding population of marsupials—the honey possum (*Tarsipes spencerae*) in western Australia.

Perhaps the most fascinating strategy shown in figure 9.3 is that exhibited by one of the monestrous marsupial mice, *Antechinus stuartii*. This small (less than 30g) animal produces only one litter of offspring each year, synchronizing its pouch time with the peak availability of its insect food. The degree of reproductive synchrony exhibited by these animals at the population level is amazing. In the population studied by Wood (1970) in Victoria, for example, all the young were born in less than a 2-week period.

There is another novel feature associated with the strategy of this little marsupial mouse. All the adult males in a population rapidly age, become senile, and die within a 3-week period after they have served their reproductive function. This die-off is associated somehow with a drastically suppressed immune system. Thus, an *Antechinus* population seasonally balances its demand on the resources of its environment, and it does so in a most biologically economical manner; it eliminates males after they have served their purpose. Similar strategies can be seen in other members of this genus (see Dickman 1982; Friend 1985).

The environmental control of the highly synchronized breeding season of *Antechinus* is partly understood now, at least in females. Apparently, this synchrony is brought about by pheromonal synchronization coupled to more crude photoperiodic control, as was postulated in the preceding chapter for some tropical primates. Scott (1986) trapped females in the wild in April and explored the factors required to induce a high degree of synchrony of ovulation at the expected time in early August.

Placing these animals on a constant photoperiod, long or short, failed to yield synchrony, and indeed this treatment inhibited ovulation in some females (Scott, 1986). This could mean either that the *Antechinus* female needs a continuously changing photoperiod or that the light cycles chosen by Scott phase shifted a circannual clock. In either case, as shown in figure 9.4, a high degree of synchrony was seen only when several females were housed in the same animal room in combination with a natural photoperiod. The implication here is that the primers of concern are airborne rather than requiring contact.

As far as the annual patterns of reproduction shown by marsupials as a whole are concerned, the ultimate importance of variation in temperature, rainfall, and hence food availability seems obvious (see Loudon 1987). Tyndale-Biscoe (1984) argues that food conditions at the time of pouch emergence are particularly critical for shaping a marsupial's annual reproductive effort. This seems reasonable. Certainly, the marsupial female's investment of resources in pregnancy is almost as minuscule as the male's direct investment in his offspring. In this regard, it is interesting to emphasize again that males remain capable of breeding year-round in many marsupial populations normally characterized by seasonal breeding. The immediate and evolutionary significance of this opportunistic characteristic is of obvious import, but it is not well conceptualized now.

Whether food availability or food predictors also routinely act as proximal triggers for breeding in marsupials remains to be seen. Long-term photoperiodic prediction would be a decided advantage for species with long pouch times who live in predictable seasonal environments. Unfortunately, only a handful of Australian marsupials have been tested rigorously in the laboratory for reproductive photoresponsiveness. As noted earlier in chapter 6, several have shown some degree of reproductive photoresponsiveness, however, and with interesting variations relative to eutherians.

Females of the seasonally breeding Tammar Wallaby (*Macropus*

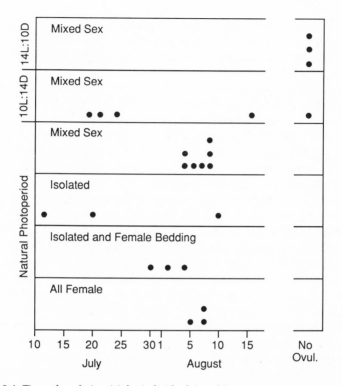

Figure 9.4. Time of ovulation (●) for individual *Antechinus stuartii*, depending on their social environment and whether they were housed on a naturally changing photoperiod, on long daylengths (14 hours of light to 10 hours of dark), or on short daylengths (10 hours of light to 14 hours of dark) after they had been trapped in April. "Mixed Sex" refers to animals held one per cage but with both sexes in the same animal room. "All Female" refers to females held in a group in the same cage. "Isolated" means one female per animal room with no other animals present. "No Ovul" refers to a failure to ovulate during the period of time under study. Redrawn from Scott (1986).

eugenii), for example, shift their time of birth in response to changing variation in daylength in the laboratory (Sadlier and Tyndale-Biscoe 1977). Furthermore, pineal denervation abolishes the seasonal embryonic diapause that determines the time of birth in this animal (Renfree et al. 1981). Males of this species remain fertile year-round.

Many correlational attempts to determine the proximal causes of seasonal breeding have been made in wild populations of Australian marsupials. Some have yielded a good correlation with changing daylength, and some have not (cf. Barnes and Gemmell 1984; Woolley 1984; McAllan and Dickman 1986).

There is good evidence for the use of social primers in marsupials other than *Antechinus* now. Catling and Sutherland (1980), for example, demonstrated a marked increase in circulating levels of testosterone in tammar males in response to the presence of sexually active females.

Finally, as noted earlier in relation to the bandicoots, not all marsupial females are seasonal breeders. Some are pure opportunists. In placentals, one often finds a great degree of opportunism in small, short-lived species, but opportunism is relatively rare in the larger and longer-lived eutherians, at least in the temperate zone. One of the most interesting aspects of the marsupial mode of reproduction is that it can promote a purely opportunistic strategy even in very large, very long-lived animals living in the temperate zone.

The herbivorous red kangaroo (*Macropus rufus*) provides such an example. This large marsupial lives in some of the most arid regions of Australia, where rainfall is unpredictably episodic and droughts may last for well over a year. When food conditions are good, it is normal for the female red kangaroo to have one joey at heel, one suckling in the pouch, and a blastocyst in suspended development in the uterus. Pouch emergence, birth, and postpartum estrus are all highly synchronized; the corpus luteum remains quiescent during lactation, becoming active again when suckling ceases. This, in turn, reinitiates development of the blastocyst. Embryonic diapause may last up to 200 days in this species (Tyndale-Biscoe 1984).

This assembly-line production of single offspring by the red kangaroo can be interrupted by drought. Mild drought causes death of the joey at heel, and more prolonged drought causes death of the young in the pouch, after which the corpus luteum becomes active, and development of the blastocyst proceeds. When drought is prolonged for over a year, the result is a loss of all three stages, and the induction of a true anovulatory anestrus.

When the drought is broken and fresh green growth appears, the female red kangaroo returns to estrus, often within a 2-week period (Newsome 1966, 1975). Whether this is due to a specific plant predictor or to the generally increased availability of energy and nutrients is not known. Male red kangaroos with their longer gametic cycle often remain fertile throughout a drought, largely independent of food availability, but greatly prolonged drought coupled with high temperatures can cause testicular degeneration (Newsome 1973).

The strategy of the red kangaroo represents opportunism in its purest and most interesting form, and, as a result, the annual pattern of realized reproduction seen in a population of these animals can vary immensely from one year to the next. It can also vary between populations from one region to another in the same year, all depending on variation in rainfall (Poole 1983). Another example of this kind of variation was seen by Shield (1964) while studying two populations of another macropod, *Setonix brachyurus*. One population of these animals showed continuous reproduction throughout the year, while another population, only 50 miles away, exhibited distinct seasonality.

Order Insectivora

This is our third largest order of mammals. It includes sixty-nine genera and 406 species, over two-thirds of which are shrews. Most of the rest are moles, tenrecs, or hedgehogs. Representatives of this order are found throughout Europe, Asia, North and Central America, and the northern third of South America. Most are small seasonal breeders. Some hibernate, and some do not. Those facing high rates of mortality (e.g., the true shrews) are mostly polyestrous and polyovulators, producing litters rapidly and repeatedly during a breeding season. Those with low rates of mortality tend to be monestrous (e.g., many of the moles whose fossorial existence offers protection from predation). Both spontaneous and induced ovulation is seen in this order.

It is a tragedy that we know so little about the reproductive biology of these common mammals. The reason for this ignorance is simple: most insectivores have cryptic patterns of activity in the wild, and most do not breed well (or at all) in the laboratory. In the latter regard, stated differently, we have not yet learned which environmental factors are critically important for the reproduction of insectivores, and therefore we have not yet learned how to manipulate these factors in a way that will allow them to reproduce in the laboratory. Thus, our present knowledge about insectivores rests on data obtained from trapped animals and from a few experiments done with the handful of species that can be bred successfully in the laboratory.

At least superficially the organization of the reproductive system of the insectivores, as well as its endocrine bases, appears more or less like what one sees in other eutherians (Rowlands and Weir 1984). Nevertheless, there are tantalizing suggestions here that hidden in this order are some exceptionally interesting, even bizarre adaptations. In some species, for example, it is almost impossible to distinguish the two sexes externally during the nonbreeding season.

As described by Deanesly (1966), the ovaries of the common European mole (*Talpa europaea*) exhibit much more profound seasonal change than that seen normally in noninsectivores. During the winter, the gametogenic cortex of this animal's ovary is reduced to a thin peripheral rind, while the interstitial component enlarges dramatically. The precise steroidogenic result of all this is uncertain, but as one consequence the vagina disappears entirely, not to reappear until the following breeding season.

Studies of the musk shrew (*Suncus murinus*) suggest even more fundamental differences in the roles played by ovarian steroids. This induced ovulator shows absolutely no ovarian or behavioral estrous cycle (Dryden 1969). The female copulates whenever exposed to a male, often within a few minutes of perceiving him, and she will continue to do so day after day throughout early pregnancy and all lactation. Sometimes females will copulate with a male even when ovariectomized, apparently supported in part by the adrenal steroids (Rissman and Bronson 1987). Inexplicably, the uterus of this animal is unresponsive to estradiol, while the cervix is responsive (Dryden and Anderson 1977).

Finally, among the more bizarre adaptations to be noted in this order, some insectivores carry polytocy to an extreme. One tenrec, for example, routinely sheds sixteen to eighteen eggs at a time, and occasionally up to thirty-two. Other insectivores routinely ovulate fifty or sixty ova, producing only four or five offspring at birth, however (Rowlands and Weir 1984). The adaptive advantage (or physiological necessity) for such wastage is unknown.

Classic papers on the reproduction of wild populations of insectivores include those of Pearson (1944) for the short-tailed shrew (*Blarina brevicauda*), Vogel (1972) for the common European shrew (*Sorex araneus*), and Conaway (1959) for the common American mole (*Scalopus aquaticus*). The African elephant shrews (*Elephantulus* sp.) have proved to be of considerable interest to sociobiologists because of their monogamous mating system (e.g., Rathbun 1979; see also Neal 1982).

One species of insectivore that has been studied with reasonable intensity is the European hedgehog (*Erinaceus europaeus*). This is a widely occurring hibernator whose annual pattern of reproduction varies markedly with latitude (e.g., Saurel 1969; see Fowler and Racey 1986). Saboureau and his coworkers have described in great detail the annual cycle of the male of this species in France, with an emphasis on hormonal correlates (e.g., Saboureau and Dutourne 1981; Saboureau, Laurent, and Boissin 1982; Saboureau and Boissin 1983; Saboureau and Castaing 1986; see also Asawa and Mathur 1981; Bidwai and Bawa 1981).

A particularly interesting study was conducted on one of the tenrecs (*Tenrec ecaudatus*) living in the Seychelles Islands (4° S latitude) by Nicoll (1985). These animals were introduced to the Seychelles from the higher latitudes of Madagascar about 100 years ago (Eisenberg and Gould 1970). The annual cycle of moult, reproduction, fattening, and torpor seen in the Madagascar populations of this species still exists in the Seychelles populations, but it is phase shifted in accordance with local rainfall patterns and hence food availability. No other mammal living this close to the equator is known to show seasonal torpor.

One last comment about insectivores seems in order. This group of animals is widely thought to be close to the primitive stem of the mammalian radiation. Thus, our lack of information about the reproductive ecology of the insectivores is doubly unfortunate. It is particularly unfortunate that we know so little about the energetic control of reproduction in these animals because some of them face the most extreme challenges known to mammals (Lindstedt 1978). Along with a few bats, our smallest mammals are shrews. Adult *Microsorex* average well under 5g in body weight. Nevertheless, this and many other genera of shrews penetrate far into the northern part of the temperate zone, where they face a high rate of predation and the need to reproduce at an equally high rate. Their energetic costs of lactation can be staggering. Pearson (1944), for example, observed a *Blarina* female weighing only 11g supporting a litter mass of 55g toward the end of lactation. That such a small mammal can balance its maternal and foraging behaviors in such a way as to nourish successfully five times its own body weight in a cold climate is amazing to say the least. On the other hand, this same species dies of heat stress if exposed to 32°C for only 1 hour (Deavers and Hudson 1981).

Order Lagomorpha

This is a small order that displays little overall diversity among its ten genera and sixty-three-odd species of rabbits, hares, and pikas. One of these species, the domestic form of the European rabbit (*Oryctolagus cuniculus*), has been a standard research animal in reproductive physiology for decades now. Much of the interest in this laboratory animal relates to the fact that it is a reflex ovulator.

Conversely, the major reason for considering the lagomorphs in this chapter is ecological and historical. Rabbits and hares are usually either pests or game animals. For both reasons, the factors governing their reproduction and survival have proved to be of great interest to a great many field biologists (see Swihart 1986). Some of the earlier papers on lagomorphs are classics in the field of reproductive biology, and for this reason they deserve to be highlighted in a book such as this.

The best-studied wild lagomorph is the wild form of the European rabbit. The reproductive biology of this animal was explored extensively in England by Southern (1940) and Brambell (1944). It is a pest in Australia, where it was introduced by colonists in the eighteenth century (Poole 1960; Myers 1970). In a landmark paper, Myers and Poole (1962) compared the reproduction of this animal in different kinds of habitats in England, Australia, and New Zealand. Their summary diagram is presented in figure 9.5.

Without going into detail, Myers and Poole (1962) concluded that no single environmental factor could account for the annual pattern of reproduction seen in these seasonally breeding lagomorphs in any habitat. They conceived of a basic, photoperiodically driven annual cycle in males that was fine-tuned by the availability of green vegetation and social conditions. In females, they postulated an endogenously derived bimodal pattern in fertility that was fine-tuned again by nutritional considerations.

Unfortunately, the reproductive photoresponsiveness of both sexes of this species have not been compared under rigorous conditions; therefore, the nature of the endogenous bimodal rhythm postulated for females by Myers and Poole remains suspect. Neither has the question of green plant predictors (as opposed to simple availability of energy, nutrients, or water) been explored rigorously in these animals. There is no doubt, however, that females of this species cannot reproduce during a drought, regardless of photoperiod or social conditions. Neither is there any doubt that the overall control of this species' reproduction is routinely multifactorial in the wild (e.g., Wheeler and King 1985).

The importance of dietary conditions in shaping the seasonal reproductive patterns of lagomorphs has been emphasized repeatedly by other investigators utilizing other species. Winter food supplements accelerate the onset of breeding in snowshoe hares, for example (Vaughan and Keith 1981; Boutin 1984). Correlatively, warm spring temperatures yield earlier breeding in mountain hares (*Lepus timidus*) in Sweden (Angerbjorn 1986). This effect could be due either to a direct action of temperature or to an indirect action of increased food availability, or to both. Computer modeling has been applied in an interesting fashion to the energy and protein requirements for jackrabbit reproduction (Clark and Innis 1982).

Seasonal changes in hormone titers, as well as tissue-level changes in the reproductive organs, have been studied only cursorily in wild populations of European rabbits (Dahlback and Andersson 1981; Saad and Bayle 1985). On the other hand, the pheromonal biology of this animal has been explored extensively (reviewed in Mykytowycz 1979).

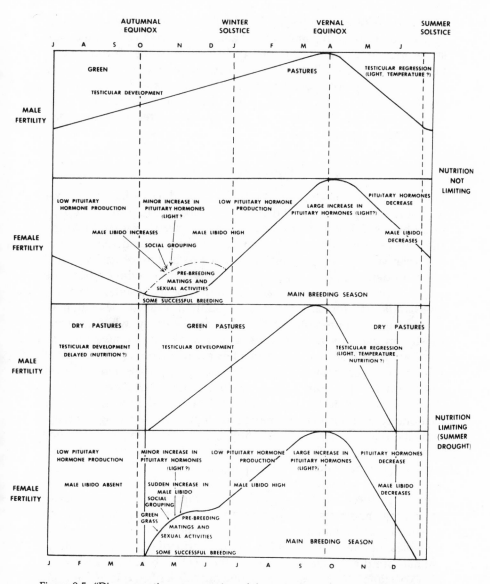

Figure 9.5. "Diagrammatic representation of the main factors which appear to determine the extent of seasonal breeding in the wild rabbit in climates similar to England and parts of New Zealand, where green pastures are present all the year, and southern Australia with its well-defined Mediterranean (summer drought) climate." Both the legend and the figure are reprinted without alteration from Myers and Poole (1962).

A particularly interesting bit of behavioral diversity seen in this species, as well as in some other lagomorphs, has been termed "absentee parental care" by Eisenberg (1981). Many lagomorphs spend little time with their offspring, suckling them perhaps only once every 24 hours (see also Boyd 1985). Finally, Meunier and Martinet (1986) and Caillol et al. (1986) have explored the role of photoperiod in enforcing seasonality and some of the hormonal correlates of seasonality in *Lepus europaeus*.

Order Rodentia

How does one quickly summarize the reproductive biology of our largest (1,690 species), most diverse, and most broadly studied group of eutherians? Two out of every five mammals are rodents. During the Eocene, this order underwent amazingly rapid diversification, and relatively rapid speciation continues to be one of its hallmarks today. Rodents are found throughout the world from the Arctic to the tropics, where they exploit habitats as diverse as deserts, wetlands, grasslands, rainforests, and high mountain valleys. Several have carved out a commensal niche with man. Dietarily, while focusing mostly on plant parts, most rodents are somewhat omnivorous, yet some are truly insectivorous, and a few are carnivorous. The result of this broad diversification is almost 1,700 species classified into over thirty families. There are 137 species just in the genus *Rattus* alone.

The answer to the question posed above, of course, is simply that one cannot quickly summarize the reproductive biology of these animals. What I will do here is simply acknowledge some of the kinds of diversity that can be found in this large order while re-emphasizing some important principles developed earlier.

The best-known rodents are the murids and cricetids of the superfamily Muroidea. This one taxon encompasses about one-quarter of all living mammals. Included here are most of the mammals known generically as rats and mice as well as such well-studied animals as the voles, gerbils, and hamsters. The reproductive strategies of these animals are dominated routinely by the need to balance a very short life expectancy. Rather aptly, someone once described one of the voles as the "potato chip of the prairie." This is a good analogy for most murids. Wherever they are found, they routinely are the preferred food of carnivorous mammals, birds, and reptiles.

Murids counter their exceptionally short life span in two general ways. First, the typical murid matures quickly, after which it has the capacity to produce large litters of offspring rapidly and repeatedly, unless inhibited from doing so by environmental conditions. An occasional montane vole can ovulate and become fertilized at 14 days of age, for example (P.J. Berger, 1983, personal communication). Gestation periods are typically 3 weeks or less, and there is a postpartum estrus.

Second, the reproductive strategies of most murids include a strong element of opportunism (Bronson and Perrigo 1987). As noted earlier in this book, this flexibility takes the form of multiple cuing of gonadotropin secretion, experiential modification of the response to those cues, and great within- and between-population variation in cuing mechanisms. In one of the most interesting examples of the effect of local conditions on the realized reproduction of these flexible animals, Newson (1963) documented marked differences in the annual pattern of reproduction of two populations of bank voles separated in distance by only 1km.

In marked contrast to the murids, some other kinds of rodents suffer little predation. Consequently, they have a long life span and, correlatively, a low reproductive potential. For obvious reasons, the North American porcupine (*Erethizon dorsatum*) is seldom subject to predation. Neither sex of this animal achieves puberty before 15 months of age. On an annual basis, this porcupine is monestrous, and its estrous cycle is a leisurely 29 days in length. Gestation requires 210–230 days, after which it gives birth to one or occasionally two young. Lactation requires only 8 weeks because young porcupines are born in a relatively precocial state (Mossman and Judas 1949; reviewed in Rowlands and Weir 1984).

Another porcupine, the Cape porcupine (*Hystrix africaeaustralis*), shows similar characteristics in South Africa (van Aarde and Skinner 1986). Some information about seasonal changes in circulating hormone levels is available for this species (van Aarde 1986).

The reproductive strategy of the heteromyid rodents are perhaps intermediate between the extremes represented by the murids and the porcupines. Even in the heteromyids, however, one finds great variation in tactics from population to population living in the same locale as well as between populations living in different locales. The former principle is illustrated nicely by Kenagy's (1973) classic study of three heteromyid rodents in a California desert. This desert experiences unpredictable rainfall but a reasonably predictable annual cycle in ambient temperature.

In the desert, the Great Basin kangaroo rat (*Dipodomys microps*) feeds upon the leaves of perennial plants. It reproduces consistently at the same time each year, as do the plants upon which it feeds. A closely related species, the Merriam kangaroo rat (*D. merriami*), reproduces opportunistically in relation to rainfall and the less predictable production of its food: the seeds of annual plants. The little pocket mouse (*Perognathus longimembris*) exhibits the same annual pattern as the Merriam kangaroo rat. It, however, is dormant most of the winter, while the larger kangaroo rat remains active.

In this one complex of animals, one can see many factors shaping reproductive strategies. At the ultimate level, there is the annual cycle in temperature and the action of this cycle in combination with unpredictable rainfall on plant growth. Also of importance is competition between the two closely related kangaroo rats, which may have driven them to rely on different foods. At a more proximate level, there is probably the direct action of photoperiod (all three species moult at the same time), the indirect effect of photoperiod via its regulation of the annual cycle of perennial but not annual plants, day-to-day variation in ambient temperature, possibly green plant predictors, and certainly social cues (see also Kenagy and Bartholomew 1981, 1985). It is important to note that, as discussed in Kenagy (1973), the reproductive strategy of each of these three related rodents is only a small part of the life-history strategy exhibited by each for coexisting without much direct competition in this particular locale.

Perhaps modestly illustrative of the many other kinds of rodents are the forty-six genera of squirrels, chipmunks, and marmots of the family Sciuridae. In size, the members of this family range from the neotropical pygmy squirrel (*Sciurus pusillus*), which weighs only 10g as an adult, to some marmots weighing several kilograms. The sciurids are distributed worldwide, except for Australia, Madagascar, southern South America, and some of the north African deserts.

The annual reproductive strategies of the sciurids are shaped heavily by whether they hibernate. Hibernators typically produce only one litter each season. This must be done early in the year in order to give the offspring time to accumulate fat before they hibernate (e.g., Barnes 1984; Dobson and Kjelgaard 1985). Thus, hibernators typically break their seasonal anestrus while still in hibernation. It is an interesting experience to dig up a hibernating sciurid in the wild, just prior to its expected arousal. All physiological systems in the animal are operating at barely detectable levels, except those related directly to reproduction. These are almost fully functional. As noted earlier, to do this at least some hibernators rely on a circannual clock whose entrainment is poorly understood.

Nonhibernating sciurids are either monestrous or polyestrous, depending on the nature of their seasonal challenges. For example, the palm squirrel (*Fernambulus pennanti*) is reproductively active throughout the year at 13° N latitude in southern India. In contrast, it produces only one or two litters a year during a limited February to September breeding season near Delhi at 28° N (Prasad et al. 1966).

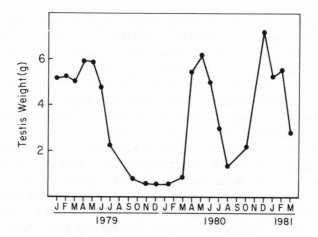

Figure 9.6. Change in average weight of the testes in a population of grey squirrels examined in Great Britain. Only data from adults, as determined by epiphyseal closure, are included here. Redrawn from Webley and Johnson (1983).

The gray squirrel (*Sciurus carolinensis*) was introduced to Britain from North America in the 1920s. On both continents, it seems to have the capacity to produce two litters during its limited breeding season. Weather conditions can vary greatly from year to year at these latitudes, however, and thus, depending on the mast (acorn) crop, this squirrel may or may not realize its capacity to produce both litters. As shown in figure 9.6, the resulting year-to-year variation is not just a matter of survival versus nonsurvival of the offspring. The male's testes reflect this great variation, as do circulating titers of testosterone (Webley, Pope, and Johnson 1985).

How can one visualize the control mechanisms and the evolutionary considerations that could produce the great annual variation seen in figure 9.6? One would certainly suspect photoperiodic regulation in both sexes of this species at this latitude. The prolonged period of testicular suppression characterizing the fall, winter, and spring of 1979 and 1980 in figure 9.6 was not seen in squirrels given supplemental food, however, confirming the overriding importance of food availability (Webley and Johnson 1983; see also Sullivan and Sullivan 1982). It would be wasteful for a female squirrel to attempt to reproduce in times of great food shortage, but why should males react this way?

It would seem genetically most profitable for males to remain reproductively ready whenever there is any chance that an occasional female would turn up in breeding condition. As shown in figure 9.6, the males do not do this, however, possibly because these squirrels feed mostly on mast, an annual crop. There can be no momentary change in food availability within any one year. On the other hand, testicular-induced aggression and territorial defense can be both energetically costly and dangerous. The result of all these considerations then seems to be a strategy in which the two sexes react in the same manner to low food availability rather than reacting rigidly to photoperiod. It would be interesting to try to confirm this hypothesis in the laboratory.

Space does not permit further discussion of the immense literature pertaining to the reproductive biology of rodents. While not on the grand scale of the marsupials, there is great diversity in this one order, only a small part of which has been acknowledged here. A few fascinating tidbits related to the reproductive biology of the many rodents not considered here, however, are as follows.

As was seen in insectivores, some rodents carry egg wastage to an extreme. The plains viscacha (*Lagostomus maximus*) sheds two hundred to four hundred ova each ovulatory cycle. Only 10 percent of these ova are fertilized, and only 10 percent of those that are fertilized actually achieve implantation (Weir 1971). One rodent, the degus (*Octodon degus*), has abdominal testes even during the breeding season. The testicular temperature of this animal is less than 1°C below body temperature, yet obviously these testes are functional (Contreras and Rosenmann 1982). Finally, at least one rodent displays bilateral asymmetry in its reproductive system. The left ovary of the mountain viscacha (*Lagidium peruanum*) is almost always nonfunctional, unless the right ovary is removed (Pearson 1949).

Order Carnivora

This order contains 284 species delegated to seven families: the mustelids (e.g., weasels, skunks, badgers, and the martens); the viverids (mongooses, genets, and civets); the procyonids (racoons, coatamundis, and pandas); the ursids (bears); and the many canids and felids. Most of these animals are carnivorous, but some are insectivorous, herbivorous, or frugivorous, and some are true omnivores. Three domesticated carnivores—the dog, cat, and ferret—have been studied in great detail in the laboratory. Many other representatives of this order are favorites in zoos. Thus, the basic mechanics of reproduction have been described in many carnivores.

A major variable in classifying the reproductive cycles of carnivores is the presence or absence of delayed implantation. This adaptation is superficially similar to the embryonic diapause seen in marsupials. Delayed implantation is common in mustelids, but it occurs sporadically in other families as well. As noted by Rowlands and Weir (1984), the stoat (*Mustela ermina*), a European mustelid, makes the most dramatic use of this adaptation.

This species gives birth only once each year, in the spring, after which it mates. The blastocyst remains unimplanted for up to 9 months. Implantation then occurs early the following spring, just in time for 4 or 5 weeks of true gestation, followed by the predictable birthing season. Thus, there is no true seasonal anestrus in this seasonally monestrous species. Interestingly, young female stoats can conceive before they are weaned, long before they are physiologically mature. Delayed implantation then allows them to give birth on schedule the next spring after they have matured physically (Gulamhusein and Thawley 1972).

A particularly interesting situation involving natural selection and delayed implantation was described by Mead (1968a, 1968b). As shown in figure 9.7, the annual reproductive strategy of the spotted skunk (*Spilogale putorius*) varies dramatically from one side of the continental divide of the United States to the other. East of the Rocky Mountains, this species breeds in March and April, and its litters are born in May and June after a 50–65-day gestation. Mating occurs in September west of the divide, after which the blastocysts overwinter in the uterus, and litters are born in May following a delay of well over 200 days. Spermatogenesis is timed accordingly in the males of the two kinds of populations.

Two comments seem particularly germaine regarding the two strategies seen in figure 9.7. First, as emphasized previously in relation to rodents, the species concept that pervades our conceptualization of reproduction really is not a good concept when applied in its traditionally rigid manner. Natural selection is a dynamically ongoing process, and visualizing the reproductive strategy (and its underlying physiological mechanisms) of a widespread species in static, one-dimensional terms is both unrealistic and misleading.

Selection for reproductive success in different environments leads to different strategies, and these strategies need not be constant within a species. One can argue, as did Mead (1968b), that the two populations considered in figure 9.7 are effectively isolated reproductively, and thus they actually should be considered as two separate species. On the other hand, what happens in the southwestern United States, where these forms meet?

Second, the two strategies shown in figure 9.7 certainly should have an adaptive basis. What it is, however, is not readily apparent. These two environments are not all that different. Why should fall breeding be an advantage west of the continental divide and not east

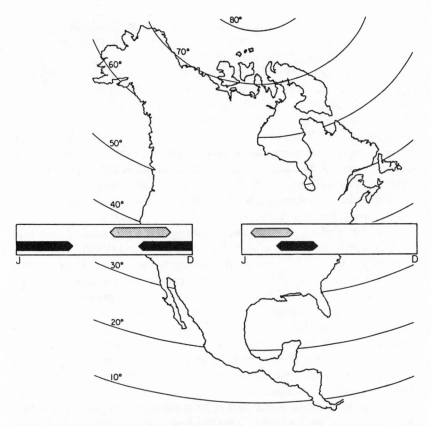

Figure 9.7. A comparison of the annual strategies of spotted skunks east and west of the Continental Divide. The duration of spermatogenesis is shown in the stippled boxes. Mating and pregnancy are shown in black. Redrawn from Mead (1968a, 1968b).

of it? The end result in either case is the production of young during the lush conditions of late spring. It is disturbing to see such radical diversity and not be able to see any obvious reason for it. Speaking teleologically, one could say that these skunks know precisely what they are doing, but we do not, and this is frustrating.

The order Carnivora contains both seasonal and asynchronously continuous breeders. The latter is typically seen only in the tropics, but as shown in figure 9.8 this is not always true. The spotted hyena (*Crocuta crocuta*) is decidedly opportunistic in temperate southern Africa. Females have the capacity to produce two litters a year if food conditions are good. The time at which they do so varies from individual to individual, however, and some females give birth in every month of the year. The pattern shown in figure 9.8 thus varies in other

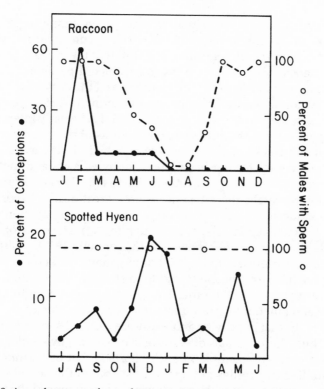

Figure 9.8. Annual patterns of reproduction seen in the racoon in Maryland and in the spotted hyena in southern Africa, both at 35°–40° latitude. Redrawn from Lindeque and Skinner (1982) and Dunn and Chapman (1983).

locales or in other years in the same locale (Skinner, van Aarde, and van Jaarsveld 1984). As should be expected with such an opportunistic strategy, male spotted hyenas remain in reproductive condition throughout the year.

For comparison, at about the same latitude in Maryland the racoon (*Procyon lotor*) routinely produces one litter of offspring a year in the late winter or spring. Correlatively, male racoons show a profound, photoperiodically driven, seasonal cycle in testis function, with peak reproductive condition being attained well in advance of the time mating will take place. The selective advantage of this testicular cycle undoubtedly relates to the avoidance of androgen-dependent searching and aggressive behavior except during the one time of the year when these behaviors are genetically profitable. Like most carnivores, racoons have large canine teeth that can inflict great damage when fighting with conspecifics.

Latitudinal and hemispheric variation in annual reproductive patterns within species is reasonably well documented in the carnivores. Gorman (1976), for example, found that the breeding season of the mongoose (*Herpestes auropunctatus*) differed by almost exactly 6 months in the Fiji Islands at 18° S latitude and the Hawaiian Islands at 21° N. As discussed by Eckstein and Zuckerman (1956), even the domestic cat is subject to some such variation. Particularly interesting in this regard are the strongly seasonal patterns of reproduction shown by domestic stocks of cats that have gone wild in the islands of the subantarctic after having been left there by whalers and meteorologists (e.g., van Aarde 1983; Brothers, Skira, and Copson 1985).

Unfortunately, there has not been a great deal of experimental work conducted on the regulation of carnivore reproduction by specific environmental factors, even though the ferret was one of the first animals shown to be photoperiodic (Bissonnette 1932). A little such effort has been invested in dogs, but in general we know little about use of predictors or the effect that food shortage has on these or any other carnivores. On the other hand, we do know something about the social regulation of reproduction in carnivores. Many large carnivores are diurnal in activity, and many are easily observed even in the wild. Thus, these animals often have been studied by ethologists.

An excellent example of such efforts is that of Bertram (1975), who studied two prides of lions (*Panther leo*) on the Serengeti plains in Tanzania. These animals can reproduce at any time of the year, but births tend to be somewhat synchronized within a given pride. This synchrony is statistical rather than robust; nevertheless, it is real, and it reflects synchronized periods of estrus. This might have a pheromonal basis, but that remains unproved. When a new male takes over a pride, driving the old male away, the result is an increase in the mortality of both unborn and newly born young and some degree of estrous synchrony in the females losing young.

One feature of lion reproduction that is particularly awe inspiring relates to the fact that they are immune from predation. Thus, they can afford to invest a great deal of time in sexual activity. Bertram (1975) calculated that 1,500 copulations were performed for each litter of offspring born.

As far as the endocrinology of carnivores is concerned, an example of the kinds of hormonal data available for these animals is shown in figure 9.9. This figure summarizes the steroidal changes observed during an entire reproductive cycle in the female beagle. The high estrogen titers of early proestrus are important for the production of the pheromones that signal approaching heat. Interestingly, the luteinizing hormone (LH) surge occurs after circulating lev-

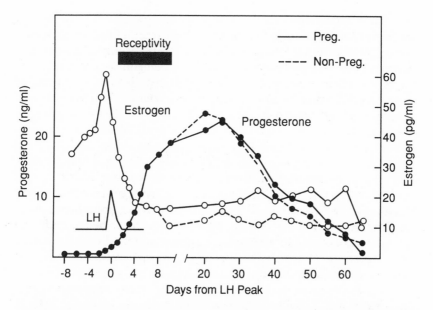

Figure 9.9. Change in circulating levels of estrogen and progesterone during the ovulatory cycle, pregnancy, and pseudopregnancy in the beagle. Estrogen is significantly elevated in the pregnant as opposed to the pseudopregnant bitch, but progesterone is not. Condensed and redrawn from Concannon, Hansel, and Visek (1975).

els of estrogen have begun to fall, and receptivity apparently is triggered by the increasing titers of progesterone set against a background of previously high levels of estrogen (Concannon, Hansel, and McEntee 1977; Chakraborty, Panko, and Fletcher 1980; see Beach, Dunbar, and Buehler 1982).

A particularly interesting facet of the bitch's cycle is the fact that a prolonged pseudopregnancy often follows even an infertile estrus. Thus, as shown in figure 9.9, there is no detectable difference in the titers of progesterone in a pregnant and an unmated bitch (see Hadley 1975). This similarity was noted earlier in relation to the marsupials, of course, but for entirely different reasons.

Milk production is often seen late in pseudopregnancy in the bitch, and it is often copious. Indeed, some pseudopregnant females will display surprisingly zealous maternal behavior toward inanimate objects. Finally, not surprisingly, domestication has yielded differences between the various breeds of dog in such factors as rate of sexual maturity, number of cycles per year, and litter size (see Rowlands 1950; Eckstein and Zuckerman 1956).

A fair amount of effort has been expended in charting seasonal patterns of hormone change in wild populations of carnivores. Recent studies of this type include Soares and Hoffman (1981) on the mongoose, Stellflug et al. (1981) on the coyote, and Maurel, Lacroix, and Boissin (1984) and Mondain-Monval et al. (1986) on the red fox (*Vulpes vulpes*). The European badger (*Meles meles*) has also been the focus of several such studies (Maurel, Laurent, and Boissin 1981; Maurel, Lacroix, and Boissin 1984; Audy et al. 1982).

Order Pinnipedia

This order contains the seals and sea lions as well as the walrus. According to Eisenberg (1981), this order is actually an artificial assemblage of thirty-two species that arose from two separate branches of the Carnivora. All pinnipeds are adapted for a combined aquatic and terrestrial existence, some emphasizing one mode of existence more than the other. They tend to breed, give birth, and lactate on land while feeding aquatically on fish, mollusks, or crustacea.

We have few details about the reproductive physiology of the pinnipeds, and we know even less about their endocrinology. This is because most such information can come only from the autopsy of commercially caught animals. In general, however, all pinnipeds have gestation periods of 9–12 months, and many include a period of delayed implantation that may last up to 5 months. Lactation is short in most seals and sea lions (2–6 weeks), and most have a postpartum estrus (Harrison 1969). Thus, most pinniped females breed once a year if conditions permit, spending most of the intervening time in one or another stage of reproduction (see Sergeant 1973). The walrus, on the other hand, typically reproduces only every third year.

All pinnipeds have markedly restricted breeding seasons, and several papers have appeared now describing the annual cycle of one or another species of these animals in one or another location. The interested reader can obtain a flavor of this literature by reading Davies (1953) on the grey seal (*Halichoerus grypus*), Lugg (1966) on the Weddell seal (*Leptonychotes weddelli*), and Bester (1981) and Kerley (1983) on the fur seal (*Arctocephalus tropicalis*) in two different locations. Clines and the expected regional variation in breeding seasons are well documented in pinnipeds. Bigg (1973) established the genetic basis for some such variation by bringing harbor seals (*Phoca vitulina*) from different populations into a common environment, where they maintained their original seasonal patterns.

Three facets of the reproductive biology of the pinnipeds have received particular attention. The first of these is relatively unique in reproductive biology, namely the role of reproduction in maintaining population size, as determined by computer simulation. The driving force behind this type of research is of course the fact that many pinnipeds are of economic importance. Thus, a large literature has developed in which mortality from commercial harvesting and other causes is estimated from life tables and then compared to known or postulated reproductive indices to predict population trends (e.g., Smith and Polacheck 1981; Eberhardt 1981; DeMaster 1981; Lett, Mohn, and Gray 1981).

The second well-studied facet of pinniped reproductive biology relates to the causes and consequences of polygyny (reviewed in Bartholomew 1970). Polygyny is not characteristic of all pinnipeds, but some show a particularly dramatic mating system involving the maintenance of harems. This system will be illustrated here in relation to the seasonal cycle of the southern elephant seal (*Mirounga leonina*) on Marian Island in the South Indian Ocean at 47° of latitude (Condy 1979; Griffiths 1984).

The elephant seal spends much of the year feeding at sea. It hauls out on land for two reasons: reproduction and moulting. The older males arrive at the breeding beaches first. Those successful in establishing a territory are known as "beachmasters," some of whom accept a single subordinate male in their territory as an "assistant beachmaster." The seasonal testicular cycle associated with this behavior is shown in figure 9.10. Females come ashore within the limits of one territory or another, give birth, experience a postpartum estrus, and mate, usually with the beachmaster.

Since there are few territories and many females, the result of this spatial organization is a harem, but it is the territory rather than the harem that is defended by the bull. Defeated bulls and yearling males haul out in other locales, but some of the former may remain on the periphery of a territory and occasionally mate with a female who wanders away from the territory. Moulting follows the breeding season in these seals, but it is initiated 4 months in advance. As suggested in figure 9.10, photoperiod is the most likely proximate cue for both moulting and reproduction. Air temperature varies little throughout the year, and water temperature (not shown) varies even less.

The third facet of the reproductive biology of the pinnipeds that has attracted considerable attention relates to the energetic costs of territorial maintenance for bulls and the costs of lactation for females. A relatively large literature is devoted to these subjects, including Fedak and Anderson (1982), McCann (1983), Boness (1984), Anderson and Fedak (1985, 1987), and Stewart (1986). A bull usually fasts while defending its territory, yet its body weight in part determines its suc-

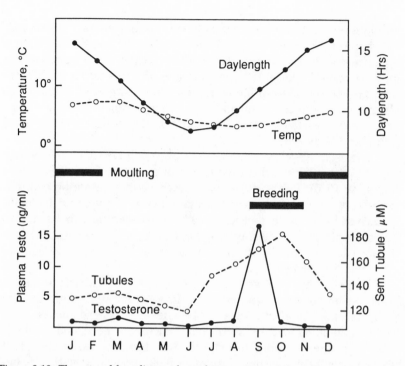

Figure 9.10. The annual breeding and moulting seasons of the bull elephant seal in relation to annual change in daylength and air temperature on Marian Island in the South Indian Ocean. "Tubules" refers to the average diameter of the seminiferous tubules. Compiled and redrawn from Condy (1979) and Griffiths (1984).

cess in defending that territory. This places the bull in an energetic conflict that can be resolved only by storing large amounts of fat ahead of time. The interest in lactational costs in pinnipeds relates to the fact that young pups must gain considerable fat during a very short lactational period, which places exceptional demands on the mother.

Order Chiroptera

There are 853 species of bats, or roughly one-quarter of the total number of species in the class Mammalia. These are long-lived animals. They first appeared in the Eocene already adapted for flight. They probably arose from the same stem line that yielded the primates, flying lemurs and tree shrews. There are two suborders of chiropterans.

The suborder Megachiroptera includes about 150 species of very large bats restricted to the Paleotropics (e.g., the flying foxes). All feed on plant parts, usually fruit, and sometimes nectar and pollen. The suborder Microchiroptera includes a horde of smaller bats that have radiated extensively in both the Old and the New worlds and in both the tropics and the temperate zone. Microchiropterans specialize on foods as diverse as fruit, nectar, pollen, insects, other invertebrates, fish, amphibians, and blood.

Unfortunately, like many members of the order Insectivora, most bats breed poorly, if at all, in the laboratory. Again, this simply means that we have not yet learned how to manipulate the dietary, physical, and emotional needs of these animals in a way that will allow them to reproduce well in captivity. Thus, we have little detailed knowledge about the endocrine bases of reproduction in these animals. On the other hand, bats have fascinated biologists for decades, and the result is an unusually rich knowledge about seasonal cycles.

Bats usually produce only one offspring at a time, but twinning does occur, and occasionally it is the norm. One species produces three or four young routinely. On an annual basis, rigid seasonal monestry is the standard in the temperate latitudes. In the tropics, one can see both monestry and polyestry. The latter may be either continuous or bimodal, sometimes supported by a postpartum estrus and sometimes not. An excellent review of the seasonal cycles of bats, and the environmental correlates of these cycles, has been provided by Racey (1982). This section relies heavily on that review as well as on the summary provided in Rowlands and Weir (1984). Other reviews that should be consulted include Gustafson (1979), Jerrett (1979), Krutzsch (1979), Oxberry (1979), and Wilson (1979).

As in all mammals, the ultimate factors shaping the annual breeding pattern of bats are food availability, rainfall (as it affects food availability), and temperature. Also, like most mammals, the most critical phase of the reproductive cycle in most bats is lactation (e.g., Fleming, Hooper, and Wilson 1972; Bonaccorso 1979; Racey 1982; Thomas and Marshall 1984; Racey and Speakman 1987; cf. Bradbury and Vehrencamp 1977). Sometimes this fact is dramatically apparent. McWilliam (1982), for example, examined the relation between rainfall, food availability, and lactation in several species of insectivorous cave-dwelling bats living in Kenya close to the equator (4° S latitude). In this region, there is a seasonally bimodal pattern of rainfall but little variation in temperature. The excellent correlation between rainfall, the availability of flying insects, and the proportion of adult females lactating is obvious in figure 9.11.

A similar study was done in Kenya by O'Shea and Vaughn (1980). These workers analyzed the annual patterns of reproduction of twenty-five species. Again, few bred during the extended summer

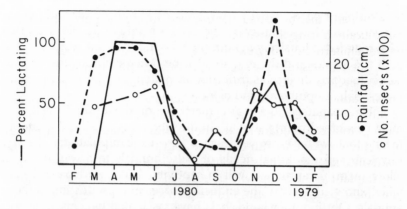

Figure 9.11. Correlation between the annual pattern of rainfall, the number of flying insects available to be eaten, and the percentage of insectivore bats that were lactating in coastal Kenya. Redrawn from McWilliam (1982), which was not seen in its original form but copied from Racey (1982).

dry season. Most reproduced during the heavy rains of November and December. A few reproduced only during the March to June rainy period, however, and some reproduced during both rainy seasons. It is important to note that, where the food supply of bats does not fluctuate on a seasonal basis, they often breed asynchronously, year-round (e.g., the true vampires of the family Desmodontidae that feed on the blood of large ungulates).

Like the marsupials, the bats offer a radical departure from the general picture of mammalian reproduction generated by our study of domestic eutherians. Nowhere is this more apparent than in the microchiropterans that exploit the temperate zone. These small but long-lived animals have evolved a variety of survival and reproductive adaptations that allow them to reproduce in ways characteristic of much larger mammals. That is, even though they are small in size, they produce only one or two young each year. The survival adaptations that allow them to do this include daily torpor, hibernation, and migration. Reproductively, the correlative adaptations here include sperm storage on the part of both males and females, delayed ovulation, delayed implantation, and sometimes even decelerated embryogenesis after implantation.

The way microchiropterans combine these various kinds of survival and reproductive adaptations to exploit the temperate zone is fascinating. In general, the seasonal monestry shown by microchiropterans in this zone is routinely timed in a way to ensure lactation during the late spring. Gametogenesis normally takes place in the summer, and mating usually takes place during the fall or sometimes periodically during the winter, whenever the bats arouse momentarily from hibernation. Beyond these generalities lies great variation.

The females of some species prolong the follicular phase of their estrous cycle and store sperm in their uteri, delaying ovulation and fertilization until after they arouse completely in the spring. Females of other species rely on delayed implantation to lengthen pregnancy enough to accommodate hibernation. These females mate in the fall or winter concurrent with ovulation, but the blastocyst does not implant until after these bats become active in early spring. Finally, some bats implant in the fall or winter, but fetal development proceeds only at a snail's pace until spring. In part, this is a direct reflection of the hibernator's low body temperature and low metabolic rate, but apparently only in part (reviewed in Racey 1982).

The males of the species noted above can also display profound reproductive accommodation for hibernation and migration. Some species can store sperm for up to 7 months before they mate (Racey 1973). Indeed, some species show complete asynchrony between spermatogenesis, steroidogenesis, accessory organ condition, and mating behavior. This has been called a dissociated behavioral strategy by Crews and Moore (1986).

The dissociated behavioral strategy has been studied most intensively in the little brown bat (*Myotis lucifugus*), a common resident in the northeastern United States. In this species, the female's cycle features a delay in ovulation until after spring arousal (Wimsatt and Parks 1966). The seasonal pattern in circulating levels of testosterone, accessory organ weight, and sexual behavior in male little brown bats is shown in figure 9.12.

In New England, these animals hibernate from October until late April or early May. Spermatogenesis is initiated after arousal. It peaks in intensity in the spring and terminates in late summer. Testosterone titers are high at this time, but the male's accessory organs are initially unresponsive to this steroid. Contrary to what is seen in our standard laboratory animals, both maximum function of the accessory organs and mating occur when circulating levels of testosterone are at their seasonal minima. The specific endocrine or receptor bases for this asynchrony remain confusing (Callard, Junz, and Petro 1983; Gustafson and Damassa 1985), as does the role of the pituitary (Anthony and Gustafson 1984).

The various adaptations described above, and their many combinations, make great sense for hibernating mammals of small size in the temperate zone, but these adaptations appear occasionally in the tropics as well. Sperm storage, for example, has been seen in both

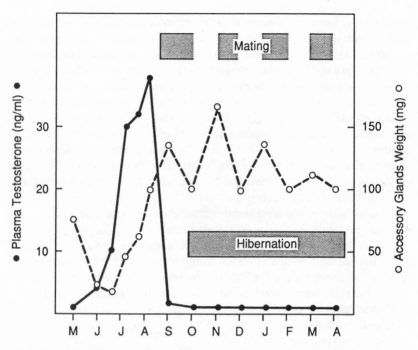

Figure 9.12. The dissociation between the seasonal changes in circulating levels of testosterone and both mating behavior and the mean weight of the accessory gland complex of the hibernating little brown bat in New England. The accessory gland complex includes the ampullary glands, the seminal vesicles, and the prostate gland. Redrawn from Gustafson and Damassa (1985).

males and females in the tropics (e.g., Gopalakrishna and Madhaven 1971), as has delayed implantation and delayed development (e.g., Mutere 1968; Heideman 1987).

Given the broad geographic distribution of bats, one expects to see good latitudinal correlates of reproduction, and these have been documented repeatedly now. A related form of the rigidly monestrous little brown bat noted above, *M. adversus*, experiences three or four cycles a year at 22° S in Queensland (Dwyer 1970), for example. The Indian sheath-tailed bat (*Taphozous longimanus*) breeds continuously in rodent-like fashion in India, while a related species (*T. georgianus*) is seasonally monestrous in western Australia (Gopalakrishna 1955; Kitchener 1973).

In this regard, a particularly interesting paper by Anciaux de Faveaux (1977) attempts to define the biological equator in terms of boreal versus austral patterns of reproduction in bats. These basic annual patterns can vary from cave to cave in the same locale and even within a single cave near the geographic equator. Obviously, there can be strong channeling effects of natural selection in bats.

While the ultimate factors shaping the annual reproductive strategies of bats seem well understood, the proximate cues used by the members of this order are not. The potential for photoperiodic cuing is particularly confusing. Evidence of a circannual clock has been seen in one species (e.g., Haussler, Moller, and Schmidt 1981; see also Beasley, Pelz, and Zucker 1984; Beasley and Zucker 1984). If the use of a circannual clock is common in monestrous or seasonally polyestrous bats, what cue entrains the cycle?

One would expect that photoperiodic cuing might be common in the temperate zone, but in relation to what stage of the female's cycle, and how does this relate to hibernation (see Wimsatt 1960)? As noted by Racey (1982), little evidence of photoperiodic regulation has been seen in bats, possibly in part because no one has looked at the right stage of the female's cycle. To my knowledge, no one has investigated the potential importance of short-term dietary predictors in bats, nor have they looked for evidence of primer potentiation of seasonal synchrony.

Order Primates

The primate line emerged in the Paleocene and then radiated broadly in both the Old and the New worlds during the Eocene. Today, we recognize 166 species of these animals, making them the sixth largest order in the class Mammalia. Our interest in primates far exceeds their abundance, however, because we ourselves are primates. In part to gain a better understanding of ourselves then, the reproductive biology of primates has been studied intensively for decades now both in the laboratory and in the wild.

The reproductive system of the rhesus monkey and its associated neuroendocrine mechanisms was considered briefly in chapter 4. A more detailed look at this system and its counterparts in a few other primates can be found in Norman (1983) and Spies and Chappel (1984). Herndon (1983) has taken a broad look at the reproductive biology of the New World primates, and Graham (1981) has done the same for the great apes.

All primates enjoy a relatively low rate of mortality, and hence they can routinely afford a relatively low reproductive potential (Dunbar 1987). As a group, they exploit only a limited variety of grassland and forested habitats in a limited part of the world. Nevertheless, being mostly tropical, each of these habitats in itself can be quite complex. The result of all this is a limited variety of reproductive strategies in comparison to the marsupials, bats, and rodents but as many as can be found in several other eutherian orders.

As discussed in chapter 8, and as witnessed by many of the collected papers in Smuts et al. (1987), many primates reproduce seasonally in relation to rainfall and hence food availability (and probably influenced sometimes by predator pressures as well). In contrast, some populations of primates breed asynchronously such that every month finds some individuals actively breeding. These populations often (but not always) show a seasonal peak in their reproduction (reviewed in Lancaster and Lee 1965; Butler 1974; and Van Horn 1980).

Indeed, some primates show two seasonal peaks in productivity. For example, the pygmy marmoset (*Cebuella pygmaea*) shows two peaks annually in the Amazon basin, as does the population of Senegalese galagos (*Galago senegalensis*) studied in the Sudan by Butler (1967). Regional variation in the degree of seasonality shown by more or less continuously breeding primates has been documented in several species (e.g., the common langur, *Presbytis entellus*, in northern India by Jay 1965; and the purple-faced langur, *P. senex*, in Ceylon by Rudran 1973; see also Jones 1985).

While the annual reproductive strategies of primates show limited variation, the kinds of mating systems and the social strategies shown by these animals are almost unlimited (Smuts et al. 1987). The advanced brain of the primate allows elegantly complex communication, and it allows a high degree of experiential modulation of behavior. One result is a richness of social organization and a richness of social regulation of reproduction that is seen nowhere else in mammals (Cheney et al. 1987). The ecological and phylogenetic constraints placed on the evolution of primate social organization have been reviewed many times (e.g., Clutton-Brock 1977; Doyle and Martin 1979; Hinde 1983; Box 1984; Taub and King 1986).

Given the fact that the reproductive biology of the nonhuman primates has been reviewed so well and so often recently, perhaps the most interesting (i.e., fun) thing that can be done here is to try to develop a more biological perspective of our own reproduction. This has already been attempted in relation to the adult ovulatory cycle by Short (1976) and for puberty by Bronson and Rissman (1986).

To provide some focus for the present endeavor, we can speculate briefly about the recent evolution of some of our most fundamental reproductive characteristics. A few hundred generations ago, we humans were primitive hunter-gatherers. What was our reproduction like at that time, how was it controlled environmentally, and how has all this changed as we became "culturally domesticated"?

By way of background, our reproductive potential is the lowest of all the primates (relative to actual time, not life span). We usually produce only one infant at a time. Pregnancy is not unduly long relative to some other mammals, but the minimum time required for lactation is quite extended in humans because our young are born in a particularly altricial state. As an aside, altricial newborns are not all that uncommon in primates; some even have a period when the young are confined to a nest (e.g., the Demidoff's galago, *Galago demidovii*, in Africa; Charles-Dominique 1972).

It takes well over a decade for us to achieve functional fertility, and a few hundred generations ago it probably took human females even longer because of their poorer nutrition. This probably was not true for males, with their greater degree of reproductive independence from food shortage. There is a period of adolescent sterility in human females during which ovulation is uncertain. Ford and Beach (1952) have argued that this trait evolved so that the smaller female could gain support and protection from the larger male. In this vein, Ohno (1976) notes that the human female is the only primate in which the breasts develop prior to the first pregnancy, thereby acting as a sexual stimulus.

Once fully mature, adult male humans are capable of breeding anytime, and females show prolonged but recurring ovulatory cycles unless pregnant or lactating. The coincidence between the average length of the human's ovulatory cycle and the lunar cycle is interesting, and probably not unimportant in an evolutionary sense, but little else can be said. While there is some evidence of a cyclic tendency to be sexually receptive in the human female (e.g., Matteo and Rissman 1984), this is at best only a small tendency. Mating can occur throughout the ovulatory cycle as well as during most of pregnancy in humans, independent of steroidal control, and this probably has been true throughout the few hundred generations of concern here.

Socially, we may or may not have been monogamous in earlier times. Monogamy and shared parental duties certainly occur now in other primates, even if they are not the norm (e.g., in many Neotropical ceboids; Eisenberg 1977). Intuitively, it seems as though selection should have enforced monogamy on us in these earlier times for the same reason it might have enforced a period of adolescent sterility in the young female.

Because of adolescent sterility and lactational anestrus, Short (1976) has argued, primitive woman probably experienced no more than a couple of dozen ovulatory cycles during her lifetime. This argument ignores the undoubtedly high rate of infant mortality suffered by our species in earlier times, which would have frequently returned lactating females to a fertile condition. On the other hand, this is somewhat balanced by the fact that our ancestors apparently suffered a much higher rate of adult mortality as primitive hunters and gatherers. Thus, Short (1976) probably is more or less correct. Poor nutrition, selection for adolescent sterility, lactational anestrus, and a short life expectancy probably all combined to make ovulation a much rarer event in primitive woman than it is in modern woman.

Primitive humans were subject to a variety of physical and dietary challenges, many of which changed either seasonally or unpredictably, depending on the geographic region under consideration. As far as the seasonal strategy of our ancestors is concerned, two facts seem of overriding importance. First, our reproductive cycle, including both pregnancy and lactation, is far too long to allow rigidly recurrent seasonality of reproduction based on the energetic needs of lactation. Second, our large size and our large energy reserves offer at least some energetic buffering during lactation (Prentice and Whitehead 1987). Thus, we must have adopted an opportunistic reproductive strategy in which predictors were routinely ignored. We probably also shunned exceptionally unpredictable habitats.

The modern !Kung of the Kalahari desert may provide a model for an annual pattern of reproduction that might have been common in humans several hundred generations ago, when we had little capacity to preserve food. The Kalahari has a seasonally harsh climate, where rainfall is almost unknown during part of the year. Seasonal drought results in great annual variation in both the growth of vegetation and the availability of the animals that feed on vegetation. Both are staple foods for the bush people. Thus, the !Kung show a marked annual cycle in body weight, and, as suggested by birth patterns, ovulation must be relatively uncommon during the dry season, when the body weight and food availability are low (fig. 9.13).

Conceivably, then, copulation was probably frequent in our ancestors, but ovulation was probably dependent on the female's body condition, which, in turn, reflected a summation of recent energetic conditions, mostly food availability. In regions where food supplies were relatively constant, we were undoubtedly continuous reproducers, albeit at a low rate. In strongly seasonal environments, whether temperate or tropical, or in years of low food availability, pregnancy was probably less common.

In any case, once birth occurred, survival of the offspring probably was determined mostly by the reactions of other adults to the female's need to consume enough food to support lactation. A high level of emotionally based parental investment would have promoted success during lactation (see Hoyenga and Hoyenga 1982). On the other hand, we have no idea if infanticide was practiced, particularly in less predictable environments (Hrdy and Hausfater 1984).

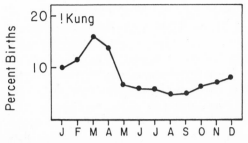

Figure 9.13. Frequency of births at monthly intervals in the !Kung of the Kalahari desert. Redrawn from L. A. Van der Walt, E. N. Wilmsen, and, T. Jenkins, Unusual sex hormone patterns among desert dwelling hunter-gatherers, *J. Clin. Endocrinol. Metab.* 46:658–63, © 1978 by the Endocrine Society.

Was early man's opportunism ever reinforced in predictable seasonal environments by photoperiodic regulation? As argued earlier, the answer is probably not. It would have been a waste of time, particularly for females whose offspring died. There is no good evidence that reproduction is regulated seasonally by photoperiod now in any human population. Seasonal reproductive tendencies can be strong in some Eskimo tribes (e.g., Ehrenkranz 1983), and it would be interesting to see if there is any degree of photoperiodic responsiveness in these people. In general, however, our earlier nomadic existence and our long reproductive cycle would seem to have yielded little advantage for rigid seasonal prediction. All-out opportunism would have been a far better strategy.

In this vein, there have been many attempts now to manipulate the human's vestigial photoperiodic pathway by administering melatonin, and all have failed (reviewed in Tamarkin, Baird, and Almeida 1985). What about short-term plant prediction? Humans do react to plant products such as gossypol, but there is no evidence that we are responsive to true plant predictors. On the other hand, neither has anyone seriously considered this possibility.

As time progressed, and as humans developed the capacity to produce and store food, our seasonal tendencies would have disappeared. One can still see seasonal trends in some urban humans, but these appear to be related to the suppression of copulation either by high temperatures or purely culturally derived phenomena (e.g., Chang et al. 1963; Cowgill 1966). The energetic or nutrient regulation of ovulation can still be seen in modern woman in relation to three conditions, however: frank famine (e.g., Chakravarty et al. 1982; Kulin et al. 1984); intense athletic training (e.g., Frisch et al. 1981; Bullen et al. 1985); and anorexia nervosa (e.g., Falk et al. 1983; Gardiner, Martin, and Jikier 1983).

There is no doubt that severe mental stress, such as that experienced in prisons, can depress ovulation in human females (Warren 1982). The degree to which less severe emotional stress can interfere with ovulation, spermatogenesis, or steroid production on a day-by-day basis is unknown and largely unexplored, however, at least to my knowledge (see Kreuz, Rose, and Jennings 1972).

Whether priming pheromones occur and act in humans is also controversial. There is no doubt that humans respond behaviorally to social odors per se (e.g., Doty 1981). There are also several reports now demonstrating how particular housing and sleeping arrangements can modulate ovulation in humans. These studies sometimes conflict with each other, however (cf. McClintock 1971; Veith et al. 1983). Furthermore, positive results always seem to be of a decidedly statistical nature rather than robustly obvious (Russell, Switz, and Thompson 1980).

In general then, early man was probably a pure opportunist, divorced from photoperiodic control. We probably reproduced asynchronously and continuously, with or without seasonal tendencies, depending on existing energetic and nutrient conditions and our emerging capacity to store food. Interference because of aversive emotional states undoubtedly occurred, but regulation by primer pheromones seems doubtful. How much have we changed genetically since those early times? Probably not much.

Selection pressure on our reproduction would have relaxed greatly as we moved indoors and developed a stable food supply. Traits that are truly selectively neutral remain in a gene pool forever unless lost by chance, however. Thus, today we probably retain about the same genetically fixed regulatory mechanisms that we possessed in early times. The exception here might relate to adolescent sterility, which no longer seems to serve any adaptive function and which presumably is now selectively disadvantageous, at least where adequate medical care is available.

In general, however, as noted earlier by Short (1976), genetically we probably are not much different now from our hunter-and-gatherer ancestors, at least as far as our reproduction is concerned. We probably have the fundamental mechanisms of an opportunist but the environment of a domestic mammal. Thus, most of our genetically fixed inhibitory mechanisms seldom show themselves.

Order Cetacea

This is a modestly populated order containing the whales, dolphins, and porpoises. All cetaceans are adapted for an exclusively underwater existence, where they prey mostly on crustaceans or fish. Unfortunately, as noted by Rowlands and Weir (1984), our information about cetacean reproduction is fragmentary, anecdotal, or nonexistent. As in the case of the pinnipeds, most of our relevant knowledge stems from the autopsy of specimens caught for commercial reasons (see Harrison 1969).

In general, most cetaceans breed seasonally, sometimes in relation to long migrations from one feeding area to another. As an example, some of the common porpoises (*Phocaena phocaena*) that winter in the open North Atlantic migrate close to shore to breed and give birth in the summer. The population studied by Fisher and Harrison (1970) bred from June to August in the Gulf of Saint Lawrence and the Bay of Fundy, returning after a 9-month gestation period to give birth and then repeat the cycle. Males of this species show an annual cycle of testicular activity.

Likewise, many whales that feed in the Antarctic during its short summer migrate to the warmer waters of the South Atlantic or the Indian Ocean to breed and give birth, often after a gestation period of about 1 year. Populations of the same species in the northern hemisphere often show the same pattern of migration, stopping short of the equator on the southern leg of their migration. Thus, there probably is a high degree of reproductive isolation between such hemispherically separated populations. Interestingly, many whales and indeed many other cetaceans are bilaterally asymmetrical in ovarian function. As reviewed in Ohsumi (1964), usually the left ovary is more active, sometimes impressively so.

One of the few insights that we have into the environmental control of cetacean reproduction relates to the impact of man on whale populations. The history of whaling is one of tragic overexploitation of one species of whale after another. The most economically desirable species available at any one moment in time is pursued until its numbers are reduced to the point where further effort is uneconomical. Then concentration shifts to the next most desirable species. This cycle has been repeated many times.

Gambell (1973) summarized the effect of overexploitation on the Antarctic population of blue and finback whales (*Balaenoptera musculus* and *B. physalus*, respectively). Individual reproduction improved markedly as populations of these animals declined (fig. 9.14). Pregnancy rates doubled, more individuals began experiencing postpartum ovulation, and there was a greater incidence of conception at estrus in declining populations. The age of sexual maturity in the finback decreased from about 10 years to 4–6 years as the population density of these animals declined, for example. Gambell (1973) con-

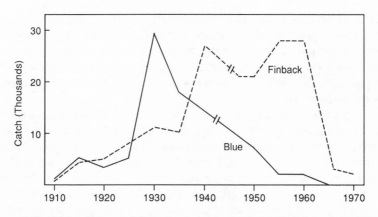

Figure 9.14. Catch of blue and finback whales in the Antarctic fishery from 1910 to 1970. Condensed and redrawn from Gambell (1973).

cluded that these changes reflected not a relaxation of direct behavioral competition but rather an increase in food availability. As an aside, Laws (1973) has provided us with a broad look at the effects of man's activities on the reproduction of many kinds of wild mammals.

Finally, two new areas of research of concern to reproductive biologists seem to be emerging rapidly in cetacean biology. The first of these relates to underwater observation of aggression and sexual activity and promises to add much to our knowledge about the reproductive behavior of these animals (e.g., Baker and Herman 1984). The second involves the same kinds of computer simulations relating mortality to reproduction discussed previously in relation to the pinnipeds (e.g., Allen 1981).

Order Artiodactyla

This is a relatively large group of large-sized ungulates, all with an even number of toes (as opposed to the odd-toed horses, tapirs, and rhinos of the order Perissodactyla). The order Artiodactyla contains 171 species, including our domestic livestock, their wild ancestors, and their many close relatives, the deer- and antelope-like mammals, and such species as the hippopotamus and giraffe. Most are strictly herbivores. Both ruminant and nonruminant digestion occurs in this order.

Most artiodactyls are monovular, but twinning can occur, and a few species are routinely polyovular. Being born in the open, where they are immediately subject to predation, the young of these animals are always relatively precocial at birth. Delayed implantation has been observed in a few species (e.g., the roe deer, *Capriolus capriolus;* Short and Hay 1966), as has bilateral asymmetry of ovarian function (e.g., the alpaca, *Lama pacos;* Fernandez-Baca et al. 1979).

Artiodactyls are distributed worldwide. The wild forms inhabiting the higher latitudes of the temperate zone are always rigidly seasonal in their reproduction. Lactation during spring and early summer is the norm, with the timing of the previous breeding season being dictated by the length of gestation, which varies from species to species. Photoperiod is undoubtedly the proximal cue of most importance in most such cases. Tropical artiodactyls breed either seasonally or continuously and asynchronously.

Examples of tropical artiodactyls exhibiting the continuous/ asynchronous pattern of reproduction include the giraffe (*Giraffa camelopardalis*) (Nje 1983) and pygmy antelope (*Neotragus batesi*) in Cameroon (Feer 1982) and the nyala (*Tragelaphus angasi*) in Natal (Anderson 1984). This pattern has been observed occasionally in artiodactyls even in the lower latitudes of the temperate zone (e.g., the collared peccary, *Tayassu tajaca*, in Arizona; Sowls 1966).

In contrast, all the births in a population of wildebeest (*Connochaetes taurinus*) occur in a 3-week period on the Serengeti plains of equatorial Tanzania. The timing of this birthing period varies somewhat from year to year, however, depending on temporal variation in these animals' annual migration between feeding areas (Watson 1969). As noted earlier, an example of an exceptionally high degree of seasonality in a tropical artiodactyl relates to the breeding season of the impala in Rhodesia (now Zimbabwe). As with the primates, nothing is known about the proximate regulation of reproduction in tropical artiodactyls.

Much of our interest in the order Artiodactyla stems from the fact that many of its representatives have been domesticated and many others are game animals. The former include the buffalo (*Bubalus bubalus*), reindeer (*Rangifer tarandus*), yak (*Bos grunniens*), and several of the South American camelids of the genus *Llama* (the alpaca, vicuna, quanaco, and llama) as well as the more familiar cattle, sheep, goats, and pigs. The correlate of domestication, namely to accelerate and otherwise increase the production of offspring, has been documented in many of these species.

Our domestic pig, for example, is a descendant of one of five species of *Sus*, probably the European wild boar (*S. scrofa*). The latter still exists in robust numbers in parts of Asia and North Africa, where it displays a strongly seasonal pattern of breeding (Eckstein and Zuckerman 1956).

As reviewed in Perry (1960) and Hagen and Kephart (1980), domestication of the modern pig has resulted in an acceleration of pubertal development, a 10 percent shorter period of gestation, a doubling of the number of offspring, and a loss of seasonality. If the ancestral European wild boar was photoperiodic, which seems likely, this trait has been masked in the domestic form. Our modern pig breeds nonseasonally, independently of photoperiod. The same is largely true of cattle also, where only a slight degree of reproductive photoresponsiveness is seen now (see Rowlands and Weir 1984). Most sheep and goats, on the other hand, have retained their reproductive photoresponsiveness and hence their seasonality, despite domestication.

The application of modern cannulation techniques and hormone radioimmunoassay to domestic animals has greatly increased our knowledge of the endocrinology of reproduction in mammals as a whole. Recent reviews that compare the endocrine bases of reproduction in our common domestic livestock include Amaun and Schanbacher (1983), whose focus is on the male, and Hansel and Convey (1983) and Bazer and First (1983), whose concern is with the estrous cycle and pregnancy and parturition, respectively. A particularly outstanding review is that of Martin (1984), who takes an exceptionally broad view of the regulation of LH secretion in sheep.

Blood collection and radioimmunoassay also have been applied many times to cervids that are either game animals or of other economic interest to man. An example of these kinds of studies is shown in figure 9.15. The data in this figure were collected on white-tailed deer held in outdoor pens in Ontario at about 43° N latitude. The annual endocrine cycle that leads to the November rut is easily seen in this figure, as is the asynchrony of the various relevant hormones. While testosterone titers peak routinely in November, folliclestimulating hormone (FSH) titers peak in September or October, and blood levels of prolactin peak in June. LH levels are more variable, but generally they reach their highest blood concentrations well before the rut in August (see also Lincoln 1971).

In a somewhat similar study, Sempere and Lacroix (1982) explored the seasonal relation between LH, testosterone, and antler growth in roe deer. Van Mourik, Stelmasiak, and Outch (1986) have documented the seasonal rise in circulating testosterone associated with the rut in male Rusa deer (*Cervus rusa*), and these authors also established the fact that this species' pituitary response to gonadotropin-releasing hormone (GnRH) is enhanced in the fall (see Van Mourik and Stelmasiak 1986).

As far as environmental factors are concerned, Webster and Barrell (1985) demonstrated that puberty could be accelerated in red deer females either by exposing them to short daylengths or with injections of melatonin (see also Chao and Brown 1984). Ryg (1984) demonstrated the depressing effect of food restriction on the expected annual peak in testosterone secretion in reindeer in Norway. Some of the recent research on the environmental regulation of reproduction

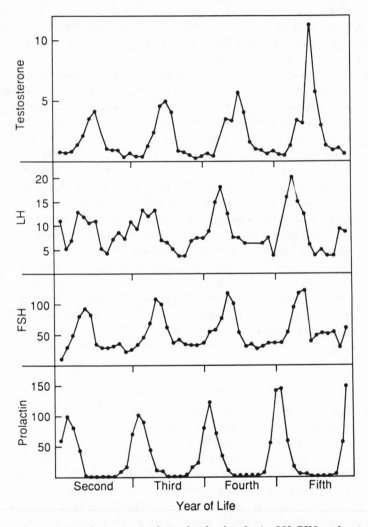

Figure 9.15. Average change in circulating levels of prolactin, LH, FSH, and testosterone at monthly intervals in anesthetized white-tailed deer during their second to fifth year of life. All hormone values are presented as ng/ml. Redrawn from Bubenik and Schams (1986).

in cervids has achieved a high degree of conceptual elegance as witnessed by the attempt by Loudon, McNeilly, and Milne (1983) to separate the relative importance of photoperiod, suckling frequency, and quality of diet in determining when a lactating female red deer returns to estrus.

As with carnivores, the artiodactyls' preference for grasslands, their diurnal habits, and their larger size have allowed detailed investigation of a dimension of reproduction that is hidden in most wild mammals—the behavioral dimension. In a classic study, for example, Clutton-Brock, Guinness, and Albon (1982) explored in great depth the fundamentally different behavioral strategies exhibited by the two sexes of red deer. Female red deer are markedly resource oriented in their behavior, while males are socially oriented. Reproductive success for a stag red deer is in direct proportion to its physical dominance of other stags (see Albon, Mitchell, and Staines 1983; Clutton-Brock, Albon, and Guinness 1986).

In the same manner, Buechner, Morrison, and Leuthold (1966) examined the highly stylized social system seen in the Uganda kob (*Adenoto kob*). This medium-sized antelope breeds throughout the year in western Uganda. Mating takes place on leks, or breeding grounds, that have been in existence for decades. Each lek consists of thirty or forty individual territories, each of which is occupied by a male. Spermatogenesis begins at 1 year of age, but successful breeding is delayed another couple of years until a male has the physical size and experience to hold a territory. Males do not defend females (unlike the red deer); they defend territories. Territorial defense is so ritualized, however, that encounters seldom result in an actual fight. Females wander from territory to territory, eventually selecting a male for mating. The courting ritual is also highly stereotyped in kobs.

Conclusions

This chapter attempts to acknowledge the wonderful diversity of reproductive strategies that exist in mammals by viewing them from a taxonomic perspective. In reality, however, much more diversity was ignored here than was acknowledged. Of concern in this chapter were the marsupials and only about half the orders of eutherians. While these combined taxa account for over 98 percent of all mammalian species, they ignore such interesting mammals as the egg-laying Prototherians (whose reproduction has been reviewed in great detail in Griffiths 1984), the armadillos, the anteaters, the tree shrews, the flying lemurs, the elephants, and the odd-toed ungulates as well as the pangolin, the aardvark, the hyrax, the dugong, and the manatee.

Nevertheless, even given the present limited effort, one is struck by the way three interrelated forces shape the reproductive strategies of mammals as a whole. The first of these is the precise set of physical and dietary challenges presented by a mammal's environment. Mammals exploit about every conceivable kind of habitat on this planet from the tropics to the polar regions, including underwater. Furthermore, most of these habitats change seasonally, sometimes drastically so, even in the tropics. The result may be either rigid seasonal breeding or continuous but asynchronous breeding, with or without seasonal tendencies. Which of these options is chosen depends in part on the other two forces.

The second force concerns the other life forms exploiting the same habitat. A mammal must compete with all these other life forms for energy, nutrients, and space. Two closely related mammals exploiting the same habitat will evolve strategies for reproducing successfully in spite of this competition (or one will become locally extinct). Conversely, many mammals are preyed on by other mammals. This in part determines their average life span, which in turn shapes their reproductive potential.

The third force is the channeling effect of past selection, which establishes a mammal's maximum body size, influences its life span, and limits both the kinds of habitats it can exploit and its reproductive reactions to the challenges presented by those habitats. A primate and a rodent exploiting the same habitat do so in greatly different ways. Indeed, a muroid rodent and a heteromyid rodent exploiting the same habitat employ greatly different strategies while doing so.

The interactions of these three forces with each other and with the diversity of mammals that exist on this planet yield a rich array of reproductive strategies. This chapter has only nodded in the direction of that richness.

10

Some Avenues for Future Research

The thrust of this book has been to develop a broader, more integrative, more truly biological perspective of mammalian reproduction. One of the values of developing a broad perspective is that it allows us to see gaps in our knowledge that escape detection when employing a more limited perspective.

For example, it is obvious now that a question of fundamental importance in reproductive biology is, How do genes actually translate into *complex* neural and hormonal mechanisms? The molecular pathway between a gene and a steroid receptor is easily visualized, as is the way genes can block or promote the synthesis of the steroid. How does natural selection act on the gene pool to promote or block the use of a circannual clock, however?

Genetically, molecularly, and then physiologically, how does natural selection act to determine whether luteinizing hormone (LH) secretion will be influenced by an environmental cue directly, by altering negative feedback sensitivity, or by way of both control mechanisms simultaneously? How does natural selection promote or block particular behavioral components of a mammal's reproductive cycle? At this time, we have no good concepts, either genetic or physiological, with which to deal with such large questions.

From a comparative standpoint, there are a great many gaps in our knowledge, some of which are truly monumental. We can never know everything there is to know about the reproductive biology of all mammals. If we take as a final goal here, however, the development of a reasonably large series of animal models, each of which encompasses a solid linkage between ecological and physiological concerns, and which are representative of all mammals, then there are many profitable avenues for future research.

First, at the most basic level, it is obvious that we have not studied enough wild mammals in sufficient detail both in the laboratory and in their natural habitats to provide a truly meaningful overview of the environmental control of reproduction in this class of animals as a whole. Is it life span or body size that best predicts a mammal's reproductive potential? The former was favored in this book, but is this really true?

Also important, but largely missing, are good hormonal data obtained from wild populations. How does one collect such data given the episodic nature of the secretion of many of these hormones and the interfering stress of capture? Some truly imaginative thinking will be required to solve this problem.

Particularly important from a comparative standpoint is the lack of good information about tropical mammals. It is humbling indeed to realize that we have so much information about a few highly domesticated animals, yet so little information about the annual breeding patterns and the factors responsible for these patterns in the most common mammals on this planet: the small to average-sized mammals living in the tropics. Most reproductive biologists live and work in the temperate zone, and most of the mammals we study evolved here also. Had the science of reproductive biology developed in the tropics, where most mammals live, our current view of the environmental control of mammalian reproduction might be quite different.

In this vein, there are several kinds of very common mammals, tropical and otherwise, about which we know little. The insectivores and the bats provide ready examples. We need to develop a better understanding of the environmental control of the reproduction of these mammals so that more of them can be bred and studied in the laboratory. While our information about marsupial reproduction is increasing rapidly, this is a particularly fascinating group of mammals, and it deserves much more effort. Because of its importance to human reproductive biology, we also need much more ecological, behavioral, and physiological information about nonhuman primates other than the rhesus monkey.

Still thinking comparatively, conspicuously absent in reproductive biology are routine side-by-side comparisons of males and females, whether the concern is energetics, nutrients, predictors, or the neuroendocrine pathways through which these factors act to modulate reproduction. As noted often in this book, the reproductive efforts of the two sexes have been shaped by fundamentally different evolutionary forces, and there is every reason to suspect that the environmental control of their reproduction will often differ either quantitatively or qualitatively. This implies a routinely different neural organization for the two sexes. A broad exploration of this possibility could add a great richness to our perception of the reproductive strategies employed by mammals as well as of the neuroendocrine underpinnings of these strategies.

Likewise, reproductive biology needs to move away from the species concept and routinely compare populations that are closely related genetically. It is not surprising that laboratory physiologists remain wedded to the importance of the taxon we call a species. On the other hand, it is indeed surprising that many reproductively oriented ecologists remain uninterested in the variation in control mechanisms that can be found within a single species. A hopeful prediction is that the future will see many attempts to use artificial selection to develop closely related lines of mammals that differ only in one basic control mechanism. This approach could yield a dramatically improved set of research tools.

With regard to the specific environmental factors known to influence mammalian reproduction, each seems to present its own unique set of ignorances and hence its own unique research opportunities. Of core concern here is food availability. The argument presented in chapter 4 was that food shortage probably routinely depresses the reproduction of some mammals in some populations all the time and that it may routinely suppress the reproduction of most mammals in most populations some of the time. Whether the concern is ultimate or proximate, we need to know if this is really true. Food supplementation studies have been conducted several times now in wild populations of rodents but seldom in other kinds of mammals. Whether food shortage routinely regulates reproduction proximately in wild populations is a question of key importance.

Also as detailed in chapter 4, we know very little about the neuroendocrine reactions of pregnant or lactating females to food shortage. This near vacuum of information represents an immense gap in our knowledge of mammalian reproductive biology. We have some facts about the effect of food shortage on ovulation and spermatogenesis, but even here there exist some monumental ignorances.

For example, which dimension of food is of most importance most of the time for most populations: energy or nutrients? If the latter, which particular nutrients are usually most important in depressing reproduction? What is the route of communication between the metabolic processing of food and the activity of the gonadotropin-releasing hormone (GnRH) pulse generator? Do growth hormone (GH), thyroid-stimulating hormone (TSH), and prolactin routinely play important regulatory roles when reproduction is suppressed by food shortage? There is much to be learned here.

Surprisingly, as detailed in chapter 5, we actually know very little about the action of aversive ambient temperature on reproduction. Indeed, in the past there has been a total absence of a rational overview for the way this factor controls reproduction neuroendocrinologically. This absence, in turn, reflects the simple fact that this problem has never been attacked systematically in the laboratory in either sex of any mammal. The speculative overview presented here may or may not be useful. Only time will tell.

The concept of nonspecific stress was first addressed in this book in relation to temperature insult. This concept has proved useful for decades now in both physiology and ecology, perhaps unrealistically and simplistically so. I was once asked by a neuroendocrinologist why one should be interested in the effects of low temperature and food shortage on reproduction "since these were just stressors like so many other environmental factors, and thus most of the important questions had already been answered." This is a rather narrow view of the way that the environment regulates mammalian reproduction.

To my mind, we still do not have a good perspective of the adaptive significance of the collective set of mechanisms we refer to as *stress*. These mechanisms exist, and they must have evolved in relation to the need to both survive and reproduce. Beyond this obvious truism lies great uncertainty. Employing the stress construct to conceptualize the reproductive responses of mammals to all kinds of environmental perturbations not only is unrealistic, it obscures the fundamental issues. The lack of a biologically rational perspective of stress represents one of the greatest gaps in our knowledge of reproductive biology.

A major effort was made in this book to combine the actions of low temperature and food shortage within the unifying framework of energetic theory. Our knowledge here is limited in two major ways. First, while this theoretical approach makes great physiological sense, at least superficially and particularly for small mammals, we have no real idea if it is functionally useful for understanding the ultimate and proximate regulation of mammalian reproduction in wild populations. Is this construct as presented here too oversimplified to reflect accurately what is actually happening in wild populations? Imaginative research will be required to answer that question.

Second, at this time we have no detailed theoretical framework for visualizing the way the energy partitioning process relates to the endocrine system in its entirety and specifically to the neuroendocrine control of reproduction. We have only pieces of the puzzle. The development of such a framework could go a long way toward unifying our knowledge of the reactions of mammals to such diverse manipulations as food restriction, protein or fat restriction, enforced locomotion, and temperature variation. All these manipulations are related energetically. How are they linked physiologically?

Regarding potential predictors of seasonal change, we may not have thought about this problem in sufficiently broad scope. There may be other potential predictors used by mammals in addition to photoperiod and the one secondary plant compound identified so far. Reasonable possibilities here include ground temperature, a physical dimension of rainfall, the chemical composition of insects, and some facet of the energetic cost/gain ratio of foraging.

A physical facet of rainfall could have evolved as a predictive cue in some animals living in deserts or dry grasslands, and a chemical component of an insect could provide an important trigger for the breeding of insectivores or omnivores, while a foraging parameter could be useful for small mammals generally. Could a small mammal use the energetic cost/gain ratio of the foraging conditions it encounters before ovulation to predict whether it will later be able to support the much greater cost of lactation?

Despite a great amount of experimental interest, several gaps remain in our knowledge about the way photoperiod controls reproduction in mammals. There probably are many ways that critical daylength, short-term endogenous programming, and circannual rhythms act and interact to regulate reproduction in different mammals living in different environments. This remains a poorly researched subject. What is the nature of the interval timer postulated out of ignorance in chapter 6? How is melatonin secretion coupled to GnRH secretion? Do all photoperiodic mammals rely on the critical daylength model so well elucidated in the hamster? Probably not.

Can photoperiod be used to track rainfall patterns and vegetation cycles in the tropics, where most mammals live, particularly near the equator? If so, is there a selective advantage for such prediction over pure opportunism? How does this choice relate to body size, life span, and a population's social organization? Of particular interest here would be studies directed toward understanding the physiological and genetic bases of population heterogeneity in reproductive photoresponsiveness and a determination of how common this phenomenon actually is in mammals.

Documentation of the ability of one mammal to use a secondary plant compound to predict an oncoming period of high food availability certainly opens the door for further explorations that could be quite rewarding. There is indirect evidence now for the existence of other potential plant predictors—for example, the phytoestrogens.

Critical in all such work, however, will be the experimental separation of the direct from the predictive effects of a cue. This is the problem that has proved so difficult in visualizing the use of ambient temperature as a predictor.

The social regulation of mammalian reproduction remains a poorly conceptualized subject. Field studies often document the importance of social cues of some kind in fine-tuning the reproductive effort of many populations of mammals. Laboratory studies have emphasized mostly the use of primer pheromones (or the priming action of other unknown factors) and the aversive effects of the emotional stress associated with chronic subordination. There must be other cuing dimensions of equally great importance here.

The biggest lack of knowledge about the social priming systems of mammals concerns our continuing inability to relate this type of regulation in a meaningful way to the evolution of a mammal's social organization and to visualize the adaptive advantages of these systems in natural populations. This field of interest began as a laboratory science, and, unfortunately, it largely remains so today. In another vein, could one expect to find within-population heterogeneity in primer mechanisms? Probably so, but no one has yet looked for such variation.

The emotional control of reproduction, aversive and beneficial, offers a host of research opportunities. This is one of the few factors that probably influences the reproduction of all mammals. Indeed, given the nutritional and energetic buffering offered by large body size, emotional controls may be the only meaningful ones operating on a short-term basis in large mammals. Our understanding of the relevant emotional states, the endocrine responses to them, and how all this relates to specific reproductive processes is rudimentary to say the least. Particularly interesting here might be experiments involving subtle stimulation and fine-grained hormonal assessments in large mammals generally and in primates in particular.

Probably the most important question relating to the environmental regulation of mammalian reproduction concerns the interaction of cues rather than reactions to specific cues. How are the brain and the endocrine system organized adaptively to accommodate multiple environmental cuing? This is a big question, and it has great conceptual import.

Probably seldom in the wild is a mammal subjected to one environmental influence at a time. It is subjected to many. It is not from this viewpoint that we normally study the effects of environmental factors in the laboratory, however. In the laboratory, we take great care to stabilize all sources of variation in order to isolate and study the actions of the one in which we are interested. While this is a necessary *first* approach, it leads to oversimplified concepts.

In evolutionary, energetic, neural, and endocrine terms, why does the presence of a running wheel override inhibitory daylengths in female hamsters? What happens to LH secretion if an animal is subjected to a permissive photoperiod while living in threshold energetic conditions? Can specific social cues override specific nutrient deficiencies, and can they potentiate the effect of plant predictors?

We rarely ask such questions, but real appreciation of the ecological and neuroendocrine organization of the mammal's reproductive effort awaits such efforts. These are the kinds of complexities that have been faced by mammals during their evolution, and handling such complexities adaptively probably is what they are designed to do best. Understanding this complexity is absolutely crucial if we are to develop a truly broad perspective of mammalian reproduction.

References

Abbott, D. H., and J. P. Hearn. 1978. Physical, hormonal and behavioural aspects of sexual development in the marmoset monkey *Callithrix jacchus*. *J. Reprod. Fert.* 53:155–66.

Adams, L. 1959. An analysis of a population of snowshoe hares in northwestern Montana. *Ecol. Monogr.* 29:141–70.

Adams, M. R., J. R. Kaplan, and D. R. Koritnik. 1985. Psychosocial influences on ovarian endocrine and ovulatory function in *Macaca fascicularis*. *Physiol. Behav.* 35:935–40.

Adams, W. J., Jr. 1960. Population ecology of white-tailed deer in northeastern Alabama. *Ecology* 41:706–15.

Aguilar, E., L. Pinilla, R. Guisado, D. Gonzalez, and F. Lopez. 1984. Relation between body weight, growth rate, chronological age and puberty in male and female rats. *Rev. Esp. Fisiol.* 40:83–86.

Aidara, D., C. Tahiri-Zagret, and C. Robyn. 1981. Serum prolactin concentrations in *Mangabey, Cercocebus aterrimus* and *patas, Erythrocebus patas*, monkeys in response to stress: Ketamine thyrotropin releasing hormone, supliride and L dopa. *J. Reprod. Fert.* 62:165–72.

Albon, S. D., B. Mitchell, and B. W. Staines. 1983. Fertility and body weight in female red deer: A density dependent relationship. *J. Anim. Ecol.* 52:969–80.

Albone, E. S. 1984. *Mammalian semiochemistry.* Chichester: John Wiley.

Alibhai, S. K. 1985. Effects of diet on reproductive performance in the bank vole (*Clethrionomys glareolus*). *J. Zool.* (Lond.) 205:445–52.

Alkass, J. E., M. J. Bryant, and J. S. Walton. 1982. Some effects of level of feeding and body condition upon sperm production and gonadotropin concentrations in the ram. *Anim. Prod.* 34:265–78.

Allen, D. M., and G. B. Lamming. 1961. Nutrition and reproduction in the ewe. *J. Agric. Sci. Camb.* 56:69–79.

Allen, K. R. 1981. Application of population models to large whales. In *Dynamics of large mammal populations*, ed. C. Fowler and T. Smith, 263–76. New York: John Wiley.

Almeida, O. F. X., and G. A. Lincoln. 1984. Reproductive photorefractoriness in rams and accompanying changes in the patterns of melatonin and prolactin secretion. *Biol. Reprod.* 30:143–58.

Almquist, J. O. 1982. Effect of long-term ejaculation at high frequency on output of sperm, sexual behavior and fertility of Holstein bulls: Relation of reproductive capacity to high nutrient allowance. *J. Dairy Sci.* 65:814–23.

Amaun, R. P., and B. D. Schanbacher. 1983. Physiology of male reproduction. *J. Anim. Sci.* 57:380–403.

Anciaux de Faveaux, M. 1977. Definition de l'equateur biologique en fonction de la reproduction de chiropteres d'Afrique centrale. *Ann. Soc. Roy. Zool. Belg.* 107:79–89.

Andelt, W. F. 1985. Behavioral ecology of coyotes, *Canis latrans* in S. Texas, USA. *Wildl. Monogr.* 94:1–45.

Anderson, J. 1964. Reproduction of imported British breeds of sheep on a tropical plateau. *Proc. Vth Int. Congr. Anim. Reprod.* (Trento) 3:465–69.

———. 1984. Reproduction in the Nyala (*Tragelaphus angasi*) (Mammalia:Ungulata). *J. Zool.* (Lond.) 204:129–42.

Anderson, S. S., and M. A. Fedak. 1985. Gray seal males *Halichoerus grypus*: Energetic and behavioral links between size and sexual success. *Anim. Behav.* 33:829–38.

———. 1987. The energetics of sexual success of grey seals and comparison with the costs of reproduction in other pinnipeds. In *Reproductive energetics in mammals*, ed. A. S. I. Loudon and P. A. Racey, 319–41. Oxford: Clarendon.

Andersson, M., and S. Jonasson. 1986. Rodent cycles in relation to food resources on an Alpine heath. *Oikos* 46:93–106.

Andrzejewski, R. 1975. Supplementary food and the winter dynamics of bank vole populations. *Acta Theriol.* 20:23–40.

Angerbjorn, A. 1986. Reproduction of mountain hares (*Lepus timidus*) in relation to density and physical condition. *J. Zool.* (Lond.), ser. A, 208:559–68.

Anthony, E. L. P., and A. W. Gustafson. 1984. Seasonal variations in pituitary LH-gonadotropes of the hibernating bat *Myotis lucifugus lucifugus*: An immunohistochemical study. *Am. J. Anat.* 170:101–15.

Arendt, J., A. M. Symons, J. English, A. L. Poulton, and I. Tobler. 1988. How does melatonin control seasonal reproductive cycles? *Reprod. Nutr. Dév.* 28:387–98.

Armario, A., and J. M. Castellanos. 1984. Effect of acute and chronic stress on testosterone secretion in male rats. *J. Endocrinol. Invest.* 7:659–61.

Armstrong, D. T. 1986. Environmental stress and ovarian function. *Biol. Reprod.* 34:29–39.

Aron, C. 1979. Mechanisms of control of the reproductive function by olfactory stimuli in female mammals. *Physiol. Rev.* 59:229–84.

Asawa, S. C., and R. S. Mathur. 1981. Quantitative evaluation of the interrelationship of certain endocrine glands of *Hemiechinus auritus collaris* (Gray) during the reproductive cycle. *Acta Anat.* 111:259–67.

Asdell, S. A. 1964. *Patterns of mammalian reproduction.* Ithaca, N.Y.: Cornell University Press.

Atkinson, S., and P. Williamson. 1985. Ram-induced growth of ovarian follicles and gonadotropin inhibition in anestrous ewes. *J. Reprod. Fert.* 73:185–90.

Atramentowicz, M. 1982. Influence du milieu sur l'activite locomotrice et la reproduction de *Caleromys philander. Rev. Ecol. (Terre et Vie)* 36:373–95.

Audy, M. C., B. Martin, G. Charron, and M. Bonnin. 1982. Steroid binding proteins and testosterone level in the badger *Meles meles* plasma during the annual cycle. *Gen. Comp.Endocrinol.* 48(2): 239–46.

Austad, S. N., and M. Sunquist. 1986. Sex-ratio manipulation in the common opossum. *Nature* 324:58–60.

Austin, C. R., and R. V. Short. 1982–86. *Reproduction in mammals.* 2d ed. 5 vols. New York: Cambridge University Press.

Badinga, L., R. J. Collier, W. W. Thatcher, and C. J. Wilcox. 1985. Effects of climatic and management factors on conception rate of dairy cattle in subtropical environment. *J. Dairy Sci.* 68:78–85.

Baird, D. T. 1984. The ovary. In *Reproduction in mammals,* vol. 3, *Hormonal control of reproduction,* ed. C. R. Austin and R. V. Short, 91–114. Cambridge: Cambridge University Press.

Baishya, N., S. V. Morant, G. S. Pope, and J. D. Leaver. 1982. Rearing of dairy cattle: 8. Relationships of dietary energy intake changes in live weight, body condition and fertility. *Anim. Prod.* 34:63–70.

Baker, C. S., and L. M. Herman. 1984. Aggressive behavior between humpback whales *Megaptera novaeangliae* wintering in Hawaiian water USA. *Can. J. Zool.* 62:1922–37.

Baker, J. R. 1938. The evolution of breeding seasons. In *Evolution: Essays on aspects of evolutionary biology,* ed. G. R. de Beer, 161–77. London: Oxford University Press.

Baker, J. R., and Z. Baker. 1936. The seasons in a tropical rainforest (New Hebrides): 3. Fruit bats (*Pteropidae*). *J. Linn. Soc.* 40:123–41.

Baker, J. R., and T. F. Bird. 1936. The seasons in a tropical rainforest (New Hebrides): 4. Insectivorous bats (*Vespertilionidae* and *Rhinolophidae*). *J. Linn. Soc.* 40:143–61.

Baker, J. R., and R. M. Ransom. 1932. Factors affecting the breeding of the field mouse (*Microtus agrestis*): 1. Light. *Proc. Roy. Soc. (Lond.),* ser. B, 110:313–22.

Baker, R. H. 1956. Mammals of Coahuila, Mexico. *Univ. Kans. Publ., Mus. Nat. Hist.* 9:125–335.

Baker, T. G. 1982. Oogenesis and ovulation. In *Reproduction in mammals,* vol. 1., *Germ cells and fertilization,* ed. C. R. Austin and R. V. Short, 17–45. Cambridge: Cambridge University Press.

Bakker, H., J. Nagai, and E. J. Eisen. 1977. Genetic differences in age and weight at sexual maturation in female mice selected for rapid growth rate. *J. Anim. Sci.* 44:203–12.

Banai, Y., and U. A. Sod-Moriah. 1976. Effect of high ambient temperature on cell division rate of fertilized ova in heat-acclimatized rats. *Isr. J. Med. Sci.* 12:881–83.

Banasiak, C. F. 1961. Deer in Maine. *Maine Game Div. Bull.* 6:1–168.

Barb, C. R., R. R. Kraeling, G. B. Rampacek, E. S. Fonda, and T. E. Kiser. 1982. Inhibition of ovulation and LH secretion in the gilt after treatment with ACTH or hydrocortisone. *J. Reprod. Fert.* 64:85–92.

Bardin C. W. 1986. Pituitary-testicular axis. In *Reproductive endocrinology,* ed. S. S. C. Yen and R. B. Jaffe, 177–99. Philadelphia: W. B. Saunders.

Barenton, B., and J. Pelletier. 1980. Prolactin testicular growth and LH receptors in the ram following light and 2-Br-alpha-ergocryptine (CB-154) treatments. *Biol. Reprod.* 22:781–90.

———. 1983. Seasonal changes in testicular gonadrotropin receptors and steroid content in the ram. *Endocrinology* 112:1441–46.

Barnes, A., and R. T. Gemmell. 1984. Correlations between breeding activity in the marsupial bandicoots and some environmental variables. *Austr. J. Zool.* 32:219–26.

Barnes, B. M. 1984. Influence of energy stores on activation of reproductive function in male golden-mantled ground squirrels. *J. Comp. Physiol.,* ser. B, 154:421–25.

Barnes, M. A., J. V. Longnecker, J. W. Riesen, and C. O. Woody. 1980. Influence of unilateral castration and increased plane of nutrition on sexual development of Holstein bulls: 3. Endocrine responses. *Theriogenology* 14:67–81.

Barnett, S. A. 1965. Adaptation of mice to cold. *Biol. Rev.* 40:5–51.

———. 1973. Maternal processes in the cold adaptation of mice. *Biol. Rev.* 48:477–508.

Barnett, S. A., and R. G. Dickson. 1984. Changes among wild house mice *Mus musculus* bred for 10 generations in a cold environment and their evolutionary implications. *J. Zool.* (Lond.) 203:163–80.

Barnett, S. A., K. M. H. Munro, J. L. Smart, and R. C. Stoddart. 1975. House mice bred for many generations in two environments. *J. Zool.* (Lond.) 177:153–69.

Barnett, S. A., G. Rhondda, G. Dickson, and W. E. Hocking. 1979. Genotype and environment in the social interactions of wild and domestic "Norway" rats. *Aggr. Behav.* 5:105–19.

Barraclough, C. A., and P. M. Wise. 1982. The role of catacholamines in the regulation of pituitary luteinizing hormone and follicle-stimulating hormone secretion. *Endocrinol. Rev.* 3:91–119.

Bartholomew, G. A. 1970. A model for the evolution of pinniped polygyny. *Evolution* 24:546–59.

———. 1977. Energy metabolism. In *Animal physiology: Principles and adaptations,* ed. M. S. Gordon, G. A. Bartholomew, A. D. Grinnel, C. B. Jorgensen, and F. N. White, 57–110. New York: Macmillan.

Bartke, A., K. S. Matt, T. M. Siler-Khodr, M. J. Soares, F. Talamantes, B. D. Goldman, M. P. Hogan, and A. Hebert. 1984. Does prolactin modify testosterone feedback in the hamster pituitary? Grafts alter the ability of testosterone to suppress luteinizing hormone and FSH release in castrated male hamsters. *Endocrinology* 115:1506–10.

Bartke, A., and T. A. Parkening. 1981. Effects of short photoperiod on pituitary and testicular function in the Chinese hamster (*Cricetus griseus*). *Biol. Reprod.* 25:958–62.

Batzli, G. O. 1986. Nutritional ecology of the California vole: Effects of food quality on reproduction. *Ecology* 67:406–12.

Batzli, G. O., L. L. Getz, and S. S. Hurley. 1977. Suppression of growth and reproduction in microtine rodents by social factors. *J. Mammal.* 58:583–91.

Baum, M. J., A. K. Slob, F. H. de Jong, and D. L. Westbrock. 1978. Persistence of sexual behavior in ovariectomized stumptail macaques following dexamethasone treatment or adrenalectomy. *Horm. Behav.* 11:323–47.

Bazer, F. W., and N. L. First. 1983. Pregnancy and parturition. *J. Anim. Sci.* 57:425–60.

Bazzarre, T. L. 1984. The effects of diet and exercise on food intake, body weight, body fat and growth hormone in male weanling rats. *Nutr. Rept. Int.* 29:997–1007.

Beach, F. A. 1976. Sexual attractivity, proceptivity and receptivity in female mammals. *Horm. Behav.* 7:105–38.

Beach, F. A., I. F. Dunbar, and M. G. Buehler. 1982. Sexual characteristics of female dogs during successive phases of the ovarian cycle. *Horm. Behav.* 16:414–42.

Beasley, L. J., K. M. Pelz, and I. Zucker. 1984. Circannual rhythms of body weight in pallid bats. *Am. J. Physiol.* 246:R955–R958.

Beasley, L. J., and I. Zucker. 1984. Photoperiod influences the annual reproductive cycle of the male pallid bat (*Antrozous pallidus*). *J. Reprod. Fert.* 70:567–73.

Beatley, J. C. 1969. Dependence of desert rodents on winter annuals and precipitation. *Ecology* 50:721–23.

———. 1976. Rainfall and fluctuating plant populations in relation to distributions and numbers of desert rodents in southern Nevada. *Oecologia* (Berl.) 24:21–42.

Beauchamp, G. K., R. L. Doty, D. G. Moulton, and R. A. Mugford. 1976. The pheromone concept in mammalian chemical communication: A critique. In *Mammalian olfaction, reproductive processes and behavior*, ed. R. L. Doty, 143–60. New York: Academic Press.

Beauchamp, G. K., A. Gilbert, K. Yamazaki, and E. A. Boyse. 1986. Genetic basis for individual discriminations: The major histocompatibility complex of the mouse. In *Chemical signals in vertebrates*, vol. 4, ed. D. Duvall, D. Muller Schwarze, and R. M. Silverstein, 413–32. New York: Plenum.

Bedford, the duke of, and F. H. A. Marshall. 1942. On the incidence of the breeding season in mammals after transference to a new latitude. *Proc. Roy. Soc.* (Lond.), ser. B, 130:396–99.

Bedford, J. M. 1982. Fertilization. In *Reproduction in mammals*, vol. 1, *Germ cells and fertilization*, ed. C. R. Austin and R. V. Short, 128–63. Cambridge: Cambridge University Press.

Bediz, G. M., and J. M. Whitsett. 1979. Social inhibition of sexual maturation in male prairie deermice. *J. Comp. Physiol. Psychol.* 93:493–500.

Bedrak, E., Z. Chap, and K. Fried. 1979. Relationship between serum concentrations of gonadotropins and testosterone in heat-exposed aging male rats. *Exp. Geront.* 14:193–99.

Beeby, J. M., and H. Swan. 1983. Hormone and metabolite concentrations of beef steers of two maturity types under two systems of production. *Anim. Prod.* 37:345–52.

Beer, J. R., and C. F. MacLeod. 1966. Seasonal population changes in the prairie deer mouse. *Am. Midl. Nat.* 76:277–89.

Begon, M. 1985. A general theory of life history variation. In *Behavioral ecology,* ed. R. M. Sibley and R. H. Smith, 91–97. Oxford: Blackwell Scientific.

Bekoff, M., and M. C. Wells. 1982. Behavioral ecology of coyotes: Social organization, rearing patterns, space use and resource defense. *Z. Tierpsychol.* 60:281–305.

Bellringer, J. F., H. P. M. Pratt, and E. B. Keverne. 1980. Involvement of the vomeronasal organ and prolactin in pheromonal induction of delayed implantation in mice. *J. Reprod. Fert.* 59:223–28.

Benjamini, L. 1987. Primer pheromones in the Levant vole (*Microtus guentheri*): Activation of reproduction in the female by male-related stimuli. *Phytoparasitica* 14:3–14.

Benson, G. K., and L. R. Morris. 1971. Fetal growth and lactation in rats exposed to high temperatures during pregnancy. *J. Reprod. Fert.* 27:369–84.

Berg, B. N. 1965. Dietary restriction and reproduction in the rat. *J. Nutr.* 87:344–48.

Berger, P. J., and N. C. Negus. 1982. Stud male maintenance of pregnancy in *Microtus montanus. J. Mammal.* 63:148–51.

Berger, P., N. Negus, and C. N. Rowsemitt. 1987. Effect of 6-methoxybenzoxazolinone on sex ratio and breeding performance in *Microtus montanus. Biol. Reprod.* 35:255–60.

Berndtson, W. E., and C. Desjardins. 1974. Circulating LH and FSH levels and testicular function in hamsters during light deprivation and subsequent photoperiodic stimulation. *Endocrinology* 95:195–205.

Berry, R. J. 1969. The genetical implications of domestication in animals. In *The domestication and exploitation of plants and animals,* ed. P. J. Ucko and G. W. Dimbleby, 207–17. Chicago: Aldine.

———. 1970. The natural history of the house mouse. *Field Stud.* 3:219–62.

Bertram, B. 1975. Social factors influencing reproduction in wild lions. *J. Zool.* 177:463–82.

Bester, M. N. 1981. Seasonal changes in the population composition of the fur seal *Arctocephalus tropicalis* at Gough Island. *S. Afr. Wildl. Res.* 11:49–55.

Bex, F., A. Bartke, B. D. Goldman, and S. Dalterio. 1978. Prolactin, growth hormone, luteinizing hormone receptors, and seasonal changes in testicular actvitiy in the golden hamster. *Endocrinology* 103:2069–80.

Bidwai, P. P., and S. R. Bawa. 1981. Correlative study of the ultrastructure and the physiology of the seasonal regression of the epididymal epithelium in the hedgehog *Paraechinus micropus. Andrologia* 13:20–32.

Bielert, C., and J. G. Vandenbergh. 1981. Seasonal influences on births and male sex skin coloration in rhesus monkeys *Macaca mulatta* in the southern hemisphere. *J. Reprod. Fert.* 62:229–34.

Bigg, M. A. 1973. Adaptation in the breeding of the harbour seal, *Phoca vitulina. J. Reprod. Fert.* 19, suppl., pp. 131–42.

Biggers, J. D., M. R. Ashroub, A. McLaren, and D. Michie. 1958. The growth and development of mice in three climatic environments. *J. Exp. Biol.* 35:144–55.

Bigham, S. R. 1966. Breeding season of the cottontail rabbit in north central Oklahoma. *Proc. Okla. Acad. Sci.* 46:217–19.

Binkley, S. 1988. *The pineal.* Englewood Cliffs, N.J.: Prentice-Hall.

Birkner, F. E. 1970. Photic infuences on primate (*Macaca mulatta*) reproduction. *Lab. Anim. Care* 20:181–85.

Bissonnette, T. H. 1932. Modifications of mammalian sexual cycles: Reactions of ferret (*Putoris vulgaris*) of both sexes to electric light added in November and December. *Proc. Roy. Soc.* (Lond.), ser. B, 110:332–36.

Bissonnette, T. H., and A. G. Csech. 1937. Modifications of mammalian sexual cycles: 7. Fertile matings of raccoons in December instead of February induced by increasing daily periods of light. *Proc. Roy. Soc.* (Lond.), ser. B, 122:246–54.

———. 1939. Modified sexual photoperiodicity in cottontail rabbits. *Biol. Bull.* 77:364–67.

Bittman, E. L. 1984. Melatonin and photoperiodic time measurement evidence from rodents and ruminants. In *Comprehensive endocrinology: The pineal gland,* ed. R. J. Reiter, 155–92. New York: Raven.

———. 1985. The role of rhythms in the response to melatonin. In *Photoperiodism, melatonin and the pineal,* CIBA Foundation Symposium no. 117, pp. 149–69. London: Pittman.

Bittman, E. L., and I. Zucker. 1981. Photoperiodic termination of hamster refractoriness: Participation of the pineal gland. *Biol. Reprod.* 24:568–72.

Blackshaw, A. W. 1977. Temperature and seasonal influences. In *The testes,* vol. 4, ed. A. D. Johnson and W. R. Gomes, 517–45. New York: Academic Press.

Blair, W. F. 1958. Effects of X-irradiation of a natural population of the deer mouse. *Ecology* 39:113–18.

Blake, C. 1975. Effects of "stress" on pulsatile luteinizing hormone release in ovariectomized rats. *Proc. Soc. Exp. Biol. Med.* 148:813–15.

Blanchard, D. C., C. Fukunaga-Stinson, L. K. Takahashi, K. J. Flannelly, and R. J. Blanchard. 1984. Dominance and aggression in social groups of male and female rats, *Rattus norvegicus. Behav. Proc.* 9:31–48.

Blank, J. 1986. Combined influence of photoperiod and temperature on metabolism and reproduction in deer mice (*Peromyscus maniculatus*). In *Endocrine regulations as adaptive mechanisms to the environment,* ed. I. Assenmacher and J. Boissin, 185–90. Paris: Centre National de la Recherche Scientifique.

Blank, J., and C. Desjardins. 1984. Spermatogenesis is modified by food intake in mice. *Biol. Reprod.* 30:410–15.

———. 1985. Differential effects of food restriction on pituitary-testicular function in mice. *Am. J. Physiol.* 248:R181–R189.

————. 1986. Metabolic and reproductive strategies in the cold. In *Living in the cold: Physiological and biochemical adaptations*, ed. C. H. Heller, X. J. Musacchia, and L. C. H. Wang, 373–82. New York: Elsevier.

Blask, E. D., and J. L. Nodelman. 1979. Anti-gonadotrophic and prolactin-inhibitory effects of melatonin in anosmic male rats. *Neuroendocrinology* 29:406–12.

Blask, E. D., J. L. Nodelman, C. A. Leadem, and B. A. Richardson. 1980. Influence of exogenously administered melatonin on the reproductive system and prolactin levels in underfed male rats. *Biol. Reprod.* 22:507–12.

Bobek, B., R. Kunelius, and J. Weiner. 1983. Energy balance and population structure of elk *Cervus elaphus nelsoni* (Nelson, 1902) in Banff National Park. *Acta Theriol.* 28:259–72.

Böckler, H., and G. Heldmaier. 1983. Interaction of shivering and non-shivering thermogenesis during cold exposure in seasonally-acclimatized Djungarian hamsters (*Phodopus sungorus*). *J. Therm. Biol.* 8:87–98.

Boinski, S. 1987. Mating patterns in squirrel monkeys. *Behav. Ecol. Sociobiol.* 21:13–21.

Boissin-Agasse, L., and J. Boissin. 1985. Incidence of a circadian cycle of photosensitivity in the regulation of the annual testis cycle in the mink, a short day mammal. *Gen. Comp. Endocrinol.* 60:109–15.

Boissin-Agasse, L., R. Ortavant, and J. Boissin. 1986. Circadian rhythm of photosensitivity and control of the annual testicular cycle in long-day (ferret) and short day (mink) breeding animals. In *Endocrine regulations as adaptive mechanisms to the environment*, ed. I. Assenmacher and J. Boissin, 131–42. Paris: Centre National de la Recherche Scientifique.

Bomford, M. 1985. Food quality, diet, and reproduction of house mice on irrigated cereal farms. Ph.D. diss., Australian National University.

————. 1987a. Food and reproduction of wild house mice: 2. A field experiment to examine the effect of food availability and food quality on breeding in spring. *Austr. Wildl. Res.* 14:197–206.

————. 1987b. Food and reproduction in wild house mice: 1. Diet and breeding seasons in various habitats on irrigated cereal farms in N. S. Wales. *Austr. Wildl. Res.* 14:183–96.

Bonaccorso, F. J. 1979. Foraging and reproductive ecology in a Panamanian bat community. *Bull. Fla. St. Mus., Biol. Ser.* 24:359–408.

Boness, D. J. 1984. Activity budget of male gray seals, *Halichoerus grypus*. *J. Mammal.* 56:291–97.

Bookhout, T. A. 1965. Breeding biology of snowshoe hares in Michigan's upper peninsula. *J. Wildl. Mgmt.* 29:296–303.

Borer, K., C. S. Campbell, J. Tabor, K. Jorgenson, S. Kandarian, and L. Gordon. 1983. Exercise reverses photoperiodic anestrus in golden hamsters. *Biol. Reprod.* 29:38–47.

Boskoff, K. J. 1978. Estrus cycles of brown lemur *Lemur fulvus*. *J. Reprod. Fert.* 54:313–18.

Bothma, J., and J. G. Tern. 1977. Reproduction and productivity of south Texas cottontail rabbits. *Mammalia* 41:253–81.

Boutin, S. 1984. Effect of late winter food addition on numbers and movements of snowshoe hares. *Oecologia* 62:393–400.

Bowman, L. A., S. R. Dilley, and E. B. Keverne. 1978. Suppression of estrogen induced LH surges by social subordination in talapoin monkeys. *Nature* (Lond.) 275:56–58.

Box, H. O. 1984. *Primate behaviour and social ecology.* London: Chapman & Hall.

Boyd, I. L. 1985. Investment in growth by pregnant wild rabbits in relation to litter size and sex of the offspring. *J. Anim. Ecol.* 54:137–47.

Bradbury, J. W., and S. L. Vehrencamp. 1977. Social organization and foraging in emballonurid bats: 1. Field studies: Parental investment patterns. *Behav. Ecol. Sociobiol.* 1:337–81.

Braden, A. W. H., and P. E. Mattner. 1970. The effects of scrotal heating in the ram on semen characteristics, fecundity and embryonic mortality. *Austr. J. Agric. Res.* 21:509.

Brainard, G. C., M. K. Vaughan, and R. J. Reiter. 1984. The influence of artificial and natural short photoperiods on male Syrian hamsters: Reproductive effects. *Int. J. Biometeor.* 28:317–25.

Brambell, F. W. R. 1944. The reproduction of the wild rabbit, *Oryctolagus cuniculus. Proc. Zool. Soc. Lond.* 114:1–45.

Brambell, M. R. 1972. Mammals: Their nutrition and habitat. In *Biology of nutrition,* ed. R. N. T-W-Fiennes, 613–48. Oxford: Pergamon.

Breed, W. G. 1975. Environmental factors and reproduction in the female hopping mouse, *Notomys alexis. J. Reprod. Fert.* 45:273–81.

———. 1976. Effect of environment on ovarian activity of wild hopping mice (*Notomys alexis*). *J. Reprod. Fert.* 47:395–97.

Brien, F. D., G. L. Sharp, W. G. Hill, and A. Robertson. 1984. Effects of selection on growth, body composition and food intake in mice: 2. Correlated responses in reproduction. *Genet. Res.* 44:73–86.

Brokx, P. A. J. 1972. Ovarian composition and aspects of reproductive physiology of Venezuelan white-tailed deer. *J. Mammal.* 53:760–73.

Bronson, F. H. 1968. Pheromonal influences on mammalian reproduction. In *Reproduction and sexual behavior,* ed. M. Diamond, 344–65. Bloomington: Indiana University Press.

———. 1973. Establishment of social rank among grouped male mice: Relative effects on circulating FSH, LH and corticosterone. *Physiol. Behav.* 10:947–51.

———. 1974. Pheromonal influence on reproductive activities in rodents. In *Pheromones,* ed. M. Birch, 344–65. Amsterdam: North Holland.

———. 1976. Serum FSH, LH and prolactin in adult ovariectomized mice bearing silastic implants of estradiol: Responses to social cues. *Biol. Reprod.* 15:147–52.

———. 1979a. Light intensity and reproduction in wild and domestic house mice. *Biol. Reprod.* 21:235–39.

———. 1979b. The reproductive ecology of the house mouse. *Q. Rev. Biol.* 54:265–99.

———. 1983. Chemical communication in house mice and deermice: Functional roles in the reproduction of natural populations. In *Recent ad-*

vances in the study of mammalian behavior, ed. J. F. Eisenberg and D. Kleiman, Special Publication no. 7, 198:229. Shippensburg, Pa.: American Society of Mammologists.

———. 1984. Energy allocation and reproductive development in wild and domestic house mice. *Biol. Reprod.* 31:83–88.

———. 1985. Mammalian reproduction: An ecological perspective. *Biol. Reprod.* 32:1–26.

———. 1986. Food-restricted, prepubertal female rats: Rapid recovery of luteinizing hormone pulsing with excess food, and full recovery of pubertal development with gonadotropin-releasing hormone. *Endocrinology* 118:2483–87.

———. 1987a. Contraception: Potential manipulation of pathways normally used by environmental cues. In *Contraception in the year 2001,* ed. T. A. van Keep, K. Ellison Davis, and D. de Wied, 165–80. Amsterdam: Elsevier.

———. 1987b. Susceptibility of fat reserves to natural challenges in mice. *J. Comp. Physiol.,* ser. B, 157:551–54.

———. 1988a. Effect of food manipulation on the gonadrotropin releasing hormone-luteinizing hormone-estradiol axis of the young female rat. *Am. J. Physiol.* 254:R616–R621.

———. 1988b. Seasonal regulation of reproduction in mammals. In *The physiology of reproduction,* ed. E. Knobil and J. D. Neill, 1831–72. New York: Raven.

———. 1988c. Mammalian reproductive strategies: Genes, photoperiod and latitude. *Reprod. Nutr. Develop.* 28:335–47.

Bronson, F. H., and A. Coquelin. 1980. The modulation of reproduction by priming pheromones in house mice: Speculations on adaptive function. In *Chemical signals,* ed. D. Muller Schwarze and R. M. Silverstein, 243–65. New York: Plenum.

Bronson, F. H., and C. Desjardins. 1974. Circulating concentrations of FSH, LH, estradiol and progesterone associated with acute, male-induced puberty in female mice. *Endocrinology* 94:1658–68.

———. 1982. Endocrine responses to sexual arousal in male mice. *Endocrinology* 111:1286–91.

Bronson, F. H., and H. E. Dezell. 1968. Studies on the estrus-inducing (pheromonal) action of male deermouse urine. *Gen. Comp. Endocrinol.* 10:339–43.

Bronson, F. H., and B. E. Eleftheriou. 1963. Influences of strange males on implantation in the deermouse. *Gen. Comp. Endocrinol.* 3:515–18.

———. 1965. Adrenal response to fighting in mice: Separation of physical and psychological causes. *Science* 147:627–28.

Bronson, F. H., and B. Macmillan. 1983. Hormonal responses to primer pheromones. In *Pheromones and reproduction in mammals,* ed. J. G. Vandenbergh, 175–97. New York: Academic Press.

Bronson, F. H., and F. A. Marsteller. 1985. Effect of short-term food deprivation on reproduction in female mice. *Biol. Reprod.* 33:660–67.

Bronson, F. H., and J. A. Maruniak. 1975. Male-induced puberty in female mice: Evidence for a synergistic action of social cues. *Biol. Reprod.* 13:94–98.

———. 1976. Differential effects of female stimulation on follicle stimulating hormone, luteinizing hormone and prolactin secretion in prepubertal female mice. *Endocrinology* 98:1101–8.

Bronson, F. H., and G. Perrigo. 1987. Seasonal regulation of reproduction in muroid rodents. *Am. Zool.* 27:929–40.

Bronson, F. H., and S. Pryor. 1983. Ambient temperature and reproductive success in rodents living at different latitudes. *Biol. Reprod.* 29:72–80.

Bronson, F. H., and E. Rissman. 1986. Biology of puberty. *Biol. Rev.* 61:157–95.

Bronson, F. H., and O. W. Tiemeier. 1958. Reproduction and age distribution of black-tailed jack rabbits in Kansas. *J. Wildl. Mgmt.* 22:409–14.

———. 1959. The relationship of precipitation and black-tailed jack rabbit populations in Kansas. *Ecology* 40:194–98.

Bronson, F. H., and W. Whitten. 1968. Oestrus-accelerating pheromone of mice: Androgen-dependency and presence in bladder urine. *J. Reprod. Fert.* 15:131–34.

Brooks, P. H., and D. J. A. Cole. 1970. The effect of the presence of a boar on the attainment of puberty in gilts. *J. Reprod. Fert.* 23:435–40.

Brothers, N. P., I. J. Skira, and G. R. Copson. 1985. Biology of the feral cat, *Felis catus* (L) on Macquarie Island. *Austr. Wildl. Res.* 12:425–36.

Brown, L. N. 1964. Reproduction of the brush mouse and white-footed mouse in the central United States. *Am. Midl. Nat.* 72:226–40.

———. 1966. Reproduction of *Peromyscus maniculatus* in the Laramie Basin of Wyoming. *Am. Midl. Nat.* 76:183–89.

Brown, M., G. Schults, and F. Hilton. 1984. Intra-uterine proximity of male fetuses predetermines levels of epidermal growth factor in submandibular glands of adult female mice. *Endocrinology* 115:2318–23.

Brown, R. E., and D. W. Macdonald, eds. 1984. *Mammalian social odours*. Oxford: Oxford University Press.

Bruce, H. M. 1959. An exteroceptive block to pregnancy in the mouse. *Nature* (Lond.) 184:105.

———. 1963. A comparison of olfactory stimulation and nutritional stress as pregnancy blocking agents in mice. *J. Reprod. Fert.* 6:221–27.

———. 1966. Smell as an exteroceptive factor. *J. Anim. Sci.* 25:83–89.

Bubenik, G. A. 1983. Shift of seasonal cycle in white-tailed deer by oral administration of melatonin. *J. Exp. Zool.* 225:155–56.

Bubenik, G. A., and D. Schams. 1986. Relationship of age to seasonal levels of LH, FSH, prolactin and testosterone in male, white-tailed deer. *Comp. Biochem. Physiol.*, ser. A, 83:179–83.

Budde, W. S. 1983. Effects of photoperiod on puberty attainment of female white-tailed deer. *J. Wildl. Mgmt.* 47:595–604.

Buechner, H. K., J. A. Morrison, and W. Leuthold. 1966. Reproduction in Uganda kob with special reference to behavior. *Symp. Zool. Soc. Lond.* 15:68–88.

Bullen, B. A., G. S. Skrinar, I. Z. Beitins, G. von Mering, B. A. Turnbull, and

J. W. McArthur. 1985. Induction of menstrual disorders by strenuous exercise in untrained women. *N.E. J. Med.* 312:1349–53.

Butler, H. 1967. Seasonal breeding of the Senegal galago (*Galago senegalensis*) in the Nuba mountains, Republic of the Sudan. *Folia Primatol.* 5:165–75.

———. 1974. Evolutionary trends in primate sex cycles. *Con. Primatol.* 3:2–35.

Cahill, L. P., C. M. Oldham, Y. Cognie, J. P. Ravault, and P. Mauleon. 1984. Season and photoperiod effects on follicles and atresia in the sheep ovary. *Austr. J. Biol.* 37:71–78.

Caillol, M., M. Meunier, M. Mondain-Monval, and P. Simon. 1986. Seasonal variations of pituitary sensitivity to LH-RH in the brown hare (*Lepus europaeus*). In *Endocrine regulations as adaptive mechanisms to the environment*, ed. I. Assenmacher and J. Boissin, 177–84. Paris: Centre National de la Recherche Scientifique.

Callard, G. V., T. H. Junz, and Z. Petro. 1983. Identification of androgen metabolic pathways in the brain of the little brown bat *Myotis lucifugus:* Sex and seasonal differences. *Biol. Reprod.* 28:1155–62.

Calow, P. 1979. The cost of reproduction—a physiological approach. *Biol. Rev.* 54:23–40.

Cameron, J. L., P. D. Hansen, T. H. McNeill, D. J. Koerker, D. K. Clifton, K. V. Rogers, W. J. Bremner, and R. A. Steiner. 1985. Metabolic cues for the onset of puberty in primate species. In *Adolescence in females*, ed. C. Flamigni, S. Venturali, and J. R. Givens, 59–78. Chicago: Yearbook Medical.

Campbell, G. A., M. Kurcz, S. Marshall, and J. Meites. 1977. Effects of starvation in rats on serum levels of follicle stimulating hormone, luteinizing hormone, thyrotropin, growth hormone and prolactin: Response to LH-releasing hormone and thyrotropin-releasing hormone. *Endocrinology* 100:580–87.

Canivenc, R., and M. Bonnin. 1979. Delayed implantation is under environmental control in the badger (*Meles meles L.*). *Nature* 278:849–50.

Cannon, B., and J. Nedergaard. 1983. Biochemical aspects of acclimation to cold. *J. Therm. Biol.* 8:85–90.

Carter, C. S., L. L. Getz, and M. Cohen-Parsons. 1986. Relationship between social organization and behavioral endocrinology in a monogamous mammal. *Adv. Stud. Behav.* 16:110–46.

Carter, C. S., L. L. Getz, L. Gavish, J. L. McDermott, and P. Arnold. 1980. Male-related pheromones and the activation of female reproduction in the prairie vole *Microtus ochrogaster. Biol. Reprod.* 23:1038–45.

Carter, D. S., and B. D. Goldman. 1983. Progonadal role of the pineal in the Djungarian hamster (*Phodopus sungorus sungorus*): Mediation by melatonin. *Endocrinology* 113:1268–73.

Carter, K. K., P. K. Chakraborty, M. Bush, and D. E. Wildt. 1984. Effects of electroejaculation and ketamine-hydrochloride on serum cortisol progesterone and testosterone in the male cat. *J. Androl.* 5:431–37.

Catling, P. C., and R. L. Sutherland. 1980. Effect of gonadectomy, season, and the presence of females on plasma testosterone, luteinizing hormone, and follicle stimulating hormone levels in male tammar wallabies (*Macropus eugenii*). *J. Endocrinol.* 86:25–33.

Catt, K. J., and J. G. Pierce. 1986. Gonadotropic hormones of the adenohypophysis. In *Reproductive endocrinology*, ed. S. C. Yen and R. B. Jaffe, 75–114. Philadelphia: W. B. Saunders.

Caughley, G., and C. J. Krebs. 1983. Are big mammals simply little mammals writ large? *Oecologia* (Berl.) 59:7–17.

Chakraborty, P. R., W. B. Panko, and W. S. Fletcher. 1980. Serum hormone concentrations and their relationships to sexual behavior in the first and second estrous cycles of the Labrador bitch. *Biol. Reprod.* 22:227–32.

Chakravarty, I., R. Sreedhar, and K. Gosh. 1984. Circulating gonadotropin profiles in various stages of protein-energy malnutrition in children. In *Hormone receptors in growth and reproduction*, Serono Symposia Publications vol. 9, pp. 367–88. New York: Raven.

Chakravarty, I., R. Sreedhar, K. K. Gosh, and S. Bulusu. 1982. Circulating gonadotropin profile in severe cases of protein calorie malnutrition. *Fert. Steril.* 37:650–54.

Challis, J. R. G. 1980. Endocrinology of late pregnancy and parturition. *Int. Rev. Physiol.* 22:277–324.

Chang, K. S. F., S. T. Chan, W. D. Low, and C. K. Ng. 1963. Climate and conception rates in Hong Kong. *Hum. Biol.* 35:366–76.

Chang, M. C., and L. Fernandez-Cano. 1959. Effects of short changes of environmental influence and low atmospheric pressure on the ovulation of rats. *Am. J. Physiol.* 196:653–55.

Channing, C. P., F. W. Schaerf, L. D. Anderson, and A. Tsafriri. 1980. Ovarian follicular and luteal physiology. *Int. Rev. Physiol.* 22:117–202.

Chao, C. C., and R. D. Brown. 1984. Seasonal relationships of thyroid, sexual and adrenocortical hormones to nutritional parameters and climatic factors in white-tailed deer (*Odocoileus virginianus*) of south Texas. *Comp. Biochem. Physiol.*, ser. A, 77:299–306.

Chapman, J. A., and A. L. Harman. 1972. The breeding biology of a brush rabbit population. *J. Wildl. Mgmt.* 36:816–23.

Charles-Dominique, P. 1972. Ecologie et vie sociale de *Galago demidovii* (Fischer, 1808, Prosimii). *Z. Tierpsychol.* 9:7–41.

Charlton, H. M., F. Naftolin, M. C. Sood, and R. W. Worth. 1975. The effect of mating upon LH release in male and female voles of the species *Microtis agrestis*. *J. Reprod. Fert.* 42:167–70.

Charpenet, G., Y. Tache, M. G. Forest, F. Haour, J. M. Saez, M. Bernier, J. R. Ducharme, and R. Collu. 1981. Effects of chronic intermittent immobilization stress on rat testicular androgenic function. *Endocrinology* 109:1254–58.

Chatonnet, J. 1983. Some general characteristics of temperature regulation. *J. Therm. Biol.* 8:33–36.

Cheatham, E. L., and G. H. Morton. 1946. Breeding season of white-tailed deer in New York. *J. Wildl. Mgmt.* 10:249–63.

Chemineau, P., J. Pelletier, Y. Guerin, G. Colas, J. P. Ravault, G. Toure, G. Almeida, J. Thimonier, and R. Ortavant. 1988. Photoperiodic and melatonin treatments for the control of seasonal reproduction in sheep and goats. *Reprod. Nutr. Dév.* 28:409–22.

Chemineau, P., N. Poulin, and Y. Cognie. 1984. Progesterone secretion in the

Creole goat during male-induced ovarian cycles: Seasonal effects. *Reprod. Nutr. Dév.* 24:557–62.

Chen, H. J. 1983. LHRH prevents testicular atrophy in golden hamsters exposed to a short photoperiod: Temporal difference in effectiveness of administration of LHRH. *J. Endocrinol.* 96:147–54.

Cheney, D. L., R. M. Seyfarth, B. B. Smuts, and R. W. Wrangham. 1987. The study of primate societies. In *Primate societies*, ed. B. B. Smuts, D. L. Cheney, R. M. Seyfarth, R. W. Wrangham, and T. T. Struhsaker, 1–10. Chicago: University of Chicago Press.

Cherry, R. H., and L. Verner. 1975. Seasonal acclimatization to temperature in the prairie vole, *Microtus ochrogaster*. *Am. Midl. Nat.* 94:354–60.

Christian, D. P. 1979. Comparative demography of three Namib Desert rodents: Responses to the provision of supplementary water. *J. Mammal.* 60:679–90.

Christian, J. J. 1964. Effect of chronic ACTH treatment on maturation of intact female mice. *Endocrinology* 74:669–98.

———. 1971. Population density and reproductive efficiency. *Biol. Reprod.* 4:248–94.

———. 1980. Regulation of annual rhythms of reproduction in temperate small rodents. In *Testicular development, structure and function*, ed. A. Steinberger and E. Steinberger, 367–80. New York: Raven.

Christian, J. J., and D. E. Davis. 1964. Endocrines, behavior and population. *Science* 145:1550–60.

Clark, B. R., and E. O. Price. 1981. Sexual maturation and fecundity of wild and domestic Norway rats (*Rattus norvegicus*). *J. Reprod. Fert.* 63:215–20.

Clark, J. H., and B. M. Markaverich. 1988. Actions of ovarian steroid hormones. In *The physiology of reproduction*, ed. E. Knobil and J. D. Neill, 675–725. New York: Raven.

Clark, M. M., and B. G. Galef, Jr. 1980. Effects of rearing environment on adrenal weights, sexual development, and behavior in gerbils: An examination of Richter's domestication hypothesis. *J. Comp. Physiol. Psychol.* 94:857–63.

———. 1981. Environmental influence on development, behavior and endocrine morphology of gerbils. *Physiol. Behav.* 27:761–65.

Clark, W. R., and G. S. Innis. 1982. Forage interactions and black-tailed jack rabbit population dynamics: A simulation model. *J. Wildl. Mgmt.* 46:1018–35.

Clarke, I. J. 1987. GnRH and ovarian hormone feedback. *Ox. Rev. Reprod. Biol.* 9:54–95.

Clarke, J. R. 1972. Seasonal breeding in female mammals. *Mammal Rev.* 1:217–30.

———. 1977. Long and short term changes in gonadal activity of field voles and bank voles. *Oikos* 29:457–67.

———. 1981. Physiological problems of seasonal breeding in eutherian mammals. *Ox. Rev. Reprod. Biol.* 3:244–312.

Clarke, J. R., and F. V. Clulow. 1973. The effect of success matings upon bank vole (*Clethrionomys glareolus*) and vole (*Microtus agrestis*) ovaries. In *The development and maturation of the ovary and its functions*. Excerpta Medica

International Congress Series, vol. 267, pp. 160–70. Amsterdam: Excerpta Medica.

Clee, M. D., E. M. Humphreys, and J. A. Russell. 1975. The suppression of ovarian cyclical activity in groups of mice, and its dependence on ovarian hormones. *J. Reprod. Fert.* 45:395–98.

Clemens, L., B. Gladue, and L. Coniglio. 1978. Prenatal endogenous androgenic influences on masculine sexual behavior and genital morphology in male and female rats. *Horm. Behav.* 10:40–53.

Clulow, F. V., and J. R. Clarke. 1968. Pregnancy-block in *Microtus agrestis:* An induced ovulator. *Nature* (Lond.) 219:511.

Clutton-Brock, T. H., ed. 1977. *Primate ecology.* London: Academic Press.

Clutton-Brock, T. H., and S. D. Albon. 1985. Competition and population regulation in social mammals. In *Behavioural ecology,* ed. R. M. Sibly and R. H. Smith, 557–75. Oxford: Blackwell Scientific.

Clutton-Brock, T. H., S. D. Albon, and F. E. Guinness. 1986. Great expectations: Dominance breeding success and offspring sex ratios in red deer, *Cervus elaphus. Anim. Behav.* 34:460–71.

Clutton-Brock, T. H., F. E. Guinness, and S. D. Albon. 1982. *Red deer: Behavior and ecology of two sexes.* Wildlife Behavior and Ecology Series. Chicago: University of Chicago Press.

Coblentz, B. E. 1976. Functions of scent-urination in ungulates with special reference to feral goats (*Capra hircus* L.). *Am. Nat.* 110:549–57.

Cockburn, A. 1981. Population processes of the silky desert mouse *Pseudomys apodemoides* (Rodentia) in mature heathlands. *Austr. J. Zool.* 8:499–514.

Coe, C. L., R. S. Erla, and S. Levine. 1985. The endocrine system of the squirrel monkey. In *Handbook of squirrel monkey research,* 191–218. New York: Plenum.

Coe, C. L., D. Franklin, E. R. Smith, and S. Levine. 1982. Hormonal responses accompanying fear and agitation in the squirrel monkey *Samiri sciureus. Physiol. Behav.* 29:1051–58.

Coffey, D. S. 1988. Androgen action and the sex-accessory tissues. In *The physiology of reproduction,* ed. E. Knobil and J. D. Neill, 1081–1120. New York: Raven.

Cohen, I. R., and D. R. Mann. 1979. Seasonal changes associated with puberty in female rats: Effect of photoperiod and ACTH administration. *Biol. Reprod.* 20:757–62.

Coen-Tannoudji, J., A. Locatelli, and J. P. Signoret. 1986. Non-pheromonal stimulation by the male of luteinizing hormone in the anestrous ewe. *Physiol. Behav.* 36:921–24.

Colby, D. R., and J. G. Vandenbergh. 1974. Regulatory effects of urinary pheromones on puberty in the mouse. *Biol. Reprod.* 11:268–79.

Cole, L. D. 1954. The population consequences of life history phenomena. *Q. Rev. Biol.* 29:103–37.

Collier, R. J., S. G. Doelger, H. H. Head, W. W. Thatcher, and C. J. Wilcox. 1982. Effects of heat stress during pregnancy on maternal hormone concentrations, calf birth weight and postpartum milk yield of Holstein cows. *J. Anim. Sci.* 54:309–19.

Collins, V. R., and M. H. Smith. 1976. Field determination of energy flow in a small nocturnal mammal. *J. Mammal.* 57:149–58.

Conaway, C. H. 1959. The reproductive cycle of the eastern mole. *J. Mammal.* 40:180–94.

———. 1971. Ecological adaptation and mammalian reproduction. *Biol. Reprod.* 4:239–47.

Conaway, C. H., and H. M. Wight. 1962. Onset of reproductive season and first pregnancy of the season in cottontails. *J. Wildl. Mgmt.* 26:278–90.

Conaway, C. H., H. M. Wight, and K. C. Sadler. 1963. Annual productivity by a cottontail population. *J. Wildl. Mgmt.* 27:171–75.

Concannon, P., W. Hansel, and K. McEntee. 1977. Changes in LH, progesterone and sexual behavior associated with preovulatory luteinization in the bitch. *Biol. Reprod.* 17:604–13.

Concannon, P. W., W. Hansel, and W. J. Visek. 1975. The ovarian cycle of the bitch: Plasma estrogen, LH and progesterone. *Biol. Reprod.* 13:112–21.

Condy, P. R. 1979. Annual cycle of the southern elephant seal *Mirounga leonina* (Linn) at Marion Island. *S. Afr. J. Zool.* 14:95–102.

Contreras, L. C., and M. Rosenmann. 1982. Thermoregulation in the testes of *Octodon degus:* A nonscrotal rodent. *Physiol. Zool.* 55:144–47.

Coop, I. E. 1966. Effect of flushing on reproductive performance of ewes. *J. Agric. Sci. Camb.* 67:305–23.

Cooper, K. J. and N. B. Haynes. 1967. Modification of the oestrous cycle in the under-fed rat associated with the presence of the male. *J. Reprod. Fert.* 14:317–20.

Coppes, J. C., and E. L. Bradley. 1984. Serum ACTH and adrenal histology in reproductively inhibited male prairie deermice (*Peromyscus maniculatus bairdii*). *Comp. Biochem. Physiol.*, ser. A, 78:297–306.

Coppola, D. M. 1986. The puberty delaying pheromone of the house mouse: Field data and a new evolutionary perspective. In *Chemical signals in vertebrates*, vol. 4, ed. D. Duvall, D. Muller Schwarze, and R. M. Silverstein, 457–61. New York: Plenum.

Coquelin, A., and F. H. Bronson. 1979. Release of luteinizing hormone in male mice during epxosure to females: Habituation of the response. *Science* 206:1099–1101.

Coquelin, A., A. N. Clancy, F. Macrides, E. P. Noble, and R. A. Gorski. 1984. Phermonally induced release of luteinizing hormone in male mice: Involvement of the vomeronasal system. *J. Neurosci.* 4:2230–36.

Coquelin, A., and C. Desjardins. 1982. Luteinizing hormone and testosterone secretion in young and old male mice. *Am. J. Physiol.* 243:E257–E263.

Corbet, H. J., R. G. Dyer, and S. Mansfield. 1982. Inhibition of oestrogen-stimulated secretion of luteinizing hormone (LH) in fasted rats is reversed by naloxone. *J. Physiol.* 327:37P.

Cornish, L. M., and W. N. Bradshaw. 1978. Patterns in twelve reproductive parameters for the white-footed mouse (*Peromyscus leucopus*). *J. Mammal.* 59:731–39.

Cowgill, U. M. 1966. Historical study of the season of birth in the city of York, England. *Nature* (Lond.) 209:1067–70.

Cowie, A. T. 1984. Lactation. In *Reproduction in mammals*, vol. 3, *Hormonal control of reproduction*, ed. C. R. Austin and R. V. Short, 195–231. Cambridge: Cambridge University Press.

Cowley, J. J., and D. R. Wise. 1972. Some effects of mouse urine on neonatal growth and reproduction. *Anim. Behav.* 20:499–506.

Cox, C. R., and B. J. LeBoeuf. 1977. Female incitation of male competition: A mechanism of mate selection. *Am. Nat.* 111:317–35.

Craigen, W., and F. H. Bronson. 1982. Deterioration of the capacity for sexual arousal in aged male mice. *Biol. Reprod.* 26:869–74.

Crane, D. S. D., A. C. Warnick, M. Koger, and R. E. Rodriguez. 1972. Relation of age and weight at puberty to reproductive performance in two lines of mice selected for 42-day weight. *J. Anim. Sci.* 34:596–600.

Cranford, J. 1983. Ecological strategies of a small hibernator, the western jumping mouse *Zapus princeps*. *Can. J. Zool.* 61:232–40.

Cranford, J. A., and J. O. Wolff. 1986. Stimulation of reproduction in *Peromyscus leucopus* and *Peromyscus maniculatus* with 6-MBOA in the field. *Va. J. Sci.* 37:240–47.

Crews, D., and M. C. Moore. 1986. Evolution of mechanisms controlling mating behavior. *Science* 231:121–25.

Crichton, J. A., J. N. Aitken, and A. W. Boyne. 1959. The effect of plane of nutrition during rearing on growth, production, reproduction and health of dairy cattle. *Anim. Prod.* 1:145–62.

Cripps, A. W., and V. J. Williams. 1975. The effect of pregnancy and lactation on food intake, gastrointestinal anatomy and the absorptive capacity of the small intestine in the albino rat. *Br. J. Nutr.* 33:17–32.

Crook, J. H. 1977. On the integration of gender strategies in mammalian social systems. In *Reproductive behavior and evolution*, ed. J. S. Rosenblatt and B. R. Komisaruk, 17–38. New York: Plenum.

Crowley, W. R., and F. P. Zemlan. 1981. The neurochemical control of mating behavior. In *Neuroendocrinology of reproduction*, ed. N. T. Adler, 451–76. New York: Plenum.

Crump, A. D., R. G. Rodway, and M. A. Lomax. 1985. A note on the relationship between undernutrition and luteinizing hormone release in the ewe. *Anim. Prod.* 40:359–62.

Cutler, G. B., Jr., and D. L. Loriaux. 1980. Recent studies on adrenarche and its relationship to puberty. *Fed. Proc.* 39:2384–90.

Czyba, J. C., C. Girod, and N. Durand. 1964. Sur l'antagonisme epiphysohypophysaire et les variations saisonnieres de la spermatogenese chez le hamster dore (*Mesocricetus auratus*). *C.R. Soc. Biol.* (Paris) 158:742–45.

Dahlback, M., and M. Andersson. 1981. Biology of the wild rabbit *Oryctolagus cuniculus*, in southern Sweden: 4. Leydig cell activity and seasonal development of two male accessory organs of reproduction. *Acta Zool.* 62:113–20.

Daly, M. 1973. Early stimulation of rodents: A critical review of present interpretations. *Br. J. Psychol.* 64:435–60.

Darbeida, H., L. Boulfekhar, N. E. Salahouelhadj, O. Akchiche, F. Ammar-

Khodja, and R. Brudieux. 1986. Variations saisonnieres de l'activite endocrine du testicule et de l'ovaire chez quelques races algeriennes de moutons. In *Endocrine regulations as adaptive mechanisms to the environment*, ed. I. Assenmacher and J. Boissin, 43–48. Paris: Centre National de la Recherche Scientifique.

Dark, J., and I. Zucker. 1983. Short photoperiods reduce winter energy requirements of the meadow vole *Microtus pennsylvanicus*. *Physiol. Behav.* 31:699–702.

———. 1984. Gonadal and photo-periodic control of seasonal body weight changes in male voles. *Am. J. Physiol.* 247:R84–R88.

Dark, J., I. Zucker, and G. N. Wade. 1983. Photo-periodic regulation of body mass, food intake and reproduction in meadow voles. *Am. J. Physiol.* 245:R334–R338.

———. 1984. Short photoperiods counteract the effects of ovariectomy on energy balance of voles. *Am. J. Physiol.* 246:R31–R34.

Darrow, J. M., F. C. Davis, J. A. Elliott, M. H. Stetson, F. W. Turek, and M. Menaker. 1980. Influence of photoperiod on reproductive development in the golden hamster. *Biol. Reprod.* 22:443–50.

Dasmann, R. F., and A. S. Mossman. 1962. Reproduction in some ungulates in southern Rhodesia. *J. Mammal.* 43:533–37.

Dauphine, T. C., Jr. 1976. Growth, reproduction and energy reserves: 4. In Biology of the Kaminuriak population of barren-ground caribou. *Can. Wildl. Ser. Rpt.* 38:1–71.

Davenport, L. B., Jr. 1964. Structure of two *Peromyscus polionotus* populations in old-field ecosystems at the AEC Savannah River Plant. *J. Mammal.* 45:95–113.

Davies, J. L. 1953. Colony size and reproduction in the grey seal. *Proc. Zool. Soc. Lond.* 123:327–32.

Davis, D. E. 1953. The characteristics of rat populations. *Q. Rev. Biol.* 28:373–401.

———. 1976. Hibernation and circannual rhythms of food consumption in marmots and ground squirrels. *Q. Rev. Biol.* 51:477–514.

Davis, G. J., and R. K. Meyer. 1972. The effect of daylength on pituitary FSH and LH and gonadal development of snowshoe hares. *Biol. Reprod.* 6:264–69.

Day, M. L., K. Imakawa, D. D. Zalesky, R. J. Kittok, and J. E. Kinder. 1986. Effects of restriction of dietary energy intake during the prepubertal period on secretion of luteinizing hormone and responsiveness of the pituitary to luteinizing hormone-releasing hormone in heifers. *J. Anim. Sci.* 62:1641–48.

Deanesly, R. 1966. Observations on reproduction in the mole, *Talpa europaea*. *Symp. Zool. Soc. Lond.* 15:387–402.

Deavers, D. R., and J. W. Hudson. 1981. Temperature regulation in two rodents (*Clethrionomys gapperi* and *Peromyscus leucopus*) and a shrew (*Blarina brevicauda*) inhabiting the same environment. *Physiol. Zool.* 54:94–108.

Deevey, E. S., Jr. 1947. Life tables for natural populations of animals. *Q. Rev. Biol.* 22:283–314.

de Kretser, D. M. 1984. The testis. In *Reproduction in mammals*, vol. 3, *Hormonal control of reproduction*, ed. C. R. Austin and R. V. Short, 76–90. Cambridge: Cambridge University Press.

de Kretser, D. M., and J. B. Kerr. 1988. The cytology of the testes. In *The physiology of reproduction*, ed. E. Knobil and J. D. Neill, 837–932. New York: Raven.

Delaney, M. J., and B. R. Neal. 1969. Breeding seasons in rodents in Uganda. *J. Reprod. Fert.* 6, suppl. pp. 229–35.

Delong, K. T. 1967. Population ecology of feral house mice. *Ecology* 48:611–34.

DeMaster, D. P. 1981. Incorporation of density dependence and harvest into a general population model for seals. In *Dynamics of large mammal populations*, ed. C. Fowler and T. Smith, 389–402. New York: John Wiley.

Denenberg, V. H., D. R. Ottinger, and M. W. Stephens. 1962. Effects of maternal factors upon growth and behavior of the rat. *Child Dev.* 33:65–71.

Den Hartog, L. A., and G. J. M. Van Kempen. 1980. Relation between nutrition and fertility in pigs. *Neth. J. Agric. Sci.* 28:211–27.

Desjardins, C. 1981. Latitudinal gradients in the responsiveness of the rodent reproductive system to photic stimuli. *Biol. Reprod.* 24:23A.

Desjardins, C., F. H. Bronson, and J. Blank. 1986. Genetic selection for reproductive photoresponsiveness in deermice. *Nature* 322:172–73.

Desjardins, C., L. L. Ewing, and B. H. Johnson. 1971. Effects of light deprivation upon the spermatogenic and steroidogenic elements of the hamster testis. *Endocrinology* 89:791–800.

Desjardins, C., and M. J. Lopez. 1980. Sensory and nonsensory modulation of testis function. In *Testicular development, structure and function*, ed. A. Steinberger and E. Steinberger, 381–88. New York: Raven.

———. 1983. Environmental cues evoke differential responses in pituitary-testicular function in deer mice. *Endocrinology* 112:1398–1406.

Dessi-Fulgheri, F., and C. Lupo. 1982. Odor of male and female rats changes hypothalamic aromatase and 5-alpha reductase activity and plasma sex steroid levels in unisexually reared male rats. *Physiol. Behav.* 28:231–36.

De Waal, F. B. M. 1984. Coping with social tension: Sex differences in the effect of food provision to small rhesus monkey *Macaca mulatta* groups. *Anim. Behav.* 32:765–73.

Dewsbury, D. A. 1982. Dominance rank, copulatory behavior and differential reproduction. *Q. Rev. Biol.* 57:135–60.

———. 1984. Aggression, copulation and differential reproduction of deermice *Peromyscus maniculatus* in a semi-natural enclosure. *Behaviour* 91:1–23.

Dickerson, J. W. T., G. A. Gresham, and R. A. McCance. 1964. The effect of undernutrition and rehabilitation on the development of the reproductive organs: Pigs. *J. Endocrinol.* 29:111–18.

Dickman, C. R. 1982. Some ecological aspects of seasonal breeding in *Antechinus* (*Dasyuridae, Marsupialia*). In *Carnivorous marsupials*, ed. M. Archer, 139–50. Chipping Norton, N.S.W.: Surrey Beatty.

———. 1985. Effects of photoperiod and endogenous control on timing of reproduction in the marsupial genus *Antechinus*. *J. Zool.* 206:509–24.

Dieterlen, F. von. 1985a. Beziehungen zwischen umweltfaktoren und fort-pflanzungsperiodik myomorphen nager eines afrikanischen tieflandre-genwaldes (Ost-Zaire). Z. Saeug. 50:152–66.

———. 1985b. Daten zur fortpflanzung und populationsstruktur der my-omorphen nager eines afrikanischen tieflandregenwaldes (Ost-Zaire). Z. Saeug. 50:68–88.

Dobrowolska, A., and J. Gromadzka-Ostrowska. 1983. Influence of photo-period on morphological parameters, androgen concentration, haema-tological indices and serum protein fractions in the common vole (Mi-crotus arvalis, Pall.). Com. Biochem. Physiol. ser. A, 74:427–33.

Dobson, F. S., and J. D. Kjelgaard. 1985. The influence of food resources on population dynamics of Columbian ground squirrels. Can. J. Zool. 63:2095–2104.

D'Occhio, M. J., B. D. Schanbacher, and J. E. Kinder. 1984. Profiles of lutein-izing hormone, FSH, testosterone and prolactin in rams of diverse breeds: Effects of contrasting short 8 hours light:16 hours darkness and long 16 hours light:8 hours darkness photoperiods. Biol. Reprod. 30:1039–54.

Dodds, D. G. 1965. Reproduction and productivity of snowshoe hares in Newfoundland. J. Wildl. Mgmt. 29:303–15.

Dolbeer, R. A., and W. R. Clark. 1975. Population biology of snowshoe hares in central Rocky Mountains. J. Wildl. Mgmt. 39:535–49.

Dominic, C. J. 1965. The origin of the pheromones causing pregnancy block in mice. J. Reprod. Fert. 10:469–72.

———. 1966. Observations on the reproductive pheromones in mice: 2. Neu-roendocrine mechanisms involved in the olfactory block to pregnancy. J. Reprod. Fert. 11:415–21.

Donovan, B. T., and J. J. van der Werff ten Bosch. 1965. Physiology of puberty. Monographs of the Physiological Society, no. 15. London: Edward Ar-nold.

Doty, R. L. 1981. Olfactory communication in humans. Chem. Senses 6:351–75.

Doyle, G. A., and R. D. Martin, eds. 1979. The study of prosimian behavior. New York: Academic Press.

Drickamer, L. C. 1974. A ten-year summary of reproductive data for free-ranging Macaca mulatta. Folia Primatol. 21:61–80.

———. 1977. Delay of sexual maturation in female house mice by exposure to grouped females or urine from grouped females. J. Reprod. Fert. 51:77–81.

———. 1978. Annual reproduction patterns in populations of two sympatric species of Peromyscus. Behav. Biol. 23:405–8.

———. 1981a. Acceleration and delay of sexual maturation in female house mice previously selected for early and late first vaginal oestrus. J. Re-prod. Fert. 63:325–29.

———. 1981b. Selection for age of sexual maturation in mice and the conse-quences for population regulation. Behav. Neur. Biol. 31:82–89.

———. 1983a. Effect of period of grouping of donors and duration of stimulus exposure on delay of puberty in female mice by a urinary chemosignal from grouped females. J. Reprod. Fert. 69:723–27.

———. 1983b. Male acceleration of puberty in female mice (*Mus musculus*). *J. Comp. Psychol.* 97:191–200.

———. 1984 Acceleration of puberty in female mice by a chemosignal from pregnant and lactating females: Circadian rhythm effects. *Biol. Reprod.* 31:104–8.

———. 1986. Puberty-influencing chemosignals in house mice: Ecological and evolutionary considerations. In *Chemical signals in vertebrates*, vol. 4, ed. D. Duvall, D. Muller Schwarze, and R. M. Silverstein, 441–55. New York: Plenum.

Drickamer, L. C., and J. E. Hoover. 1979. Effects of urine from pregnant and lactating female house mice on sexual maturation of juvenile females. *Dev. Psychobiol.* 12:545–51.

Dryden, G. L. 1969. Reproduction in *Suncus murinus*. In *Biology of reproduction in mammals*, 376–96. Oxford: Blackwell.

Dryden, G. L., and J. N. Anderson. 1977. Ovarian hormones: Lack of effect on reproductive structures of female Asian musk shrews. *Science* 197:782–84.

Dubey, A. K., J. L. Cameron, R. A. Steiner, and T. M. Plant. 1986. Inhibition of gonadotropin secretion in castrated male rhesus monkeys *Macaca mulatta* induced by dietary restriction analogy with the prepubertal hiatus of gonadotropin release. *Endocrinology* 118:518–25.

Ducker, M. J., J. C. Bowman, and A. Temple. 1973. The effect of constant photoperiod on the expression of oestrus in the ewe. *J. Reprod. Fert.* 19, suppl., pp. 143–50.

Ducker, M. J., N. Yarrow, and S. V. Morant. 1982. The effect of change and level of nutrition on the reproductive performance of group fed dairy heifers. *Anim. Prod.* 34:203–12.

Dufour, J. J., V. Adelakoun, and P. Matton. 1981. Limited multiple ovulation in heifers fed high plane of nutrition before pregnant mares serum gonadotropin stimulation and steroid hormone concentrations in single twin and multiple ovulators. *Theriogenology* 15:433–42.

Dunbar, R. I. M. 1987. Demography and reproduction. In *Primate societies*, ed. B. B. Smuts, D. L. Cheney, R. M. Seyfarth, R. W. Wrangham, and T. T. Struhsaker, 240–49. Chicago: University of Chicago Press.

Duncan, M. J., B. D. Goldman, M. N. Di Pinto, and M. H. Stetson. 1985. Testicular function and pelage color have different critical daylengths in the Djungarian hamster *Phodopus sungorus sungorus*. *Endocrinology* 116:424–30.

Dunlap, J., J. Zadina, and G. Gougis. 1978. Prenatal stress interacts with prepubertal social isolation to reduce male copulatory behavior. *Physiol. Behav.* 21:873–75.

Dunn, J. P., and J. A. Chapman. 1983. Reproduction, physiological responses, age structure and food habits of racoons in Maryland, USA. *Z. Saeug.* 48:161–75.

Dunnet, G. M. 1964. A field study of local populations of the brush-tailed possum *Trichosurus vulpeca* in eastern Australia. *Proc. Zool. Soc. Lond.* 142:665–95.

Dutt, R. H., and L. F. Bush. 1955. The effect of low environmental temperature on initiation of the breeding season and fertility in sheep. *J. Anim. Sci.* 14:885–96.

Dwyer, P. D. 1970. Latitude and breeding season in a polyestrus species of Myotis. *J. Mammal.* 51:405–10.

Dyer, R. G., and T. J. McClure. 1981. Fasting inhibits oestrogen-stimulated secretion of luteinizing hormone in female rats. *J. Physiol.* 319:91P.

Dyer, R. G., H. C. Mansfield, and A. D. P. Dean. 1985. Fasting impairs LH secretion in female rats by activating an inhibitory opioid pathway. *J. Endocrinol.* 105:91–97.

Dyrmundsson, O. R. 1978. Studies on the breeding season of Icelandic ewes and ewe lambs. *J. Agric. Sci.* 90:275–82.

Earnest, D. J., and F. W. Turek. 1983a. Effect of one second light pulses on testicular function and locomotor activity in the golden hamster *Mesocricetus auratus. Biol. Reprod.* 28:557–65.

———. 1983b. Role for acetylcholine in mediating effects of light on reproduction. *Science* 219:77–79.

Easdon, M. P., J. M. Chesworth, M. B. E. Aboul-ela, and G. D. Henderson. 1985. The effect of undernutrition of beef cows on blood hormone and metabolite concentrations post-partum. *Reprod. Nutr. Dév.* 25:113–26.

Eberhardt, L. L. 1981. Population dynamics of the Pribilof fur seals. In *Dynamics of large mammal populations*, ed. C. Fowler and T. Smith, 197–220. New York: John Wiley.

Eberhart, J. A., E. B. Keverne, and R. E. Meller. 1980. Social influences on plasma testosterone levels in male talapoin monkeys *Miopithecus talapoin. Horm. Behav.* 14:247–66.

———. 1983. Social influences on circulating levels of cortisol and prolactin in male talapoin monkeys *Miopithecus talapoin. Phsysiol. Behav.* 30:361–70.

Echternkamp, S. E. 1984. Relationship between LH and cortisol in acutely-stressed beef cows. *Theriogenology* 22:305–11.

Echternkamp, S. E., C. L. Ferrell, and J. D. Rone. 1982. Influence of prepartum and postpartum nutrition on luteinizing hormone secretion in suckled post-partum beef heifers. *Theriogenology* 18:283–96.

Eckstein, P., and S. Zuckerman. 1956. The oestrus cycle in the Mammalia. In *Marshall's physiology of reproduction*, ed. A. S. Parkes, 226–396. London: Longmans, Green.

Egid, K., and S. Lenington. 1985. Responses of male mice to odors of females: Effect of T- and H-2-locus genotype. *Behav. Genet.* 15:287–95.

Ehrenkranz, J. R. L. 1983. Seasonal breeding in humans: Birth records of the Laborador Eskimo. *Fert. Steril.* 40:485–89.

Eisenberg, J. F. 1977. The evolution of the reproductive unit in the class Mammalia. In *Reproductive behavior and evolution*, ed. J. S. Rosenblatt and B. Komisaruk, 39–71. New York: Plenum.

———. 1978. Evolution of arborial herbivores in the class Mammalia. In *The ecology of arboreal folivores*, ed. G. G. Montgomery, 135–52. Washington, D.C.: Smithsonian Institution Press.

———. 1981. *The mammalian radiations.* Chicago: University of Chicago Press.

Eisenberg, J. F., and E. Gould. 1970. The tenrecs: A study in mammalian behavior and evolution. *Smithson. Contr. Zool.* 27:1–127.

Ellendorf, F., N. Parvizi, D. K. Pomerantz, A. Hartjen, A. Konig, D. Smidt, and F. Elsaesser. 1975. Plasma luteinizing hormone and testosterone in the adult male pig: 24 hour fluctuations and the effect of copulation. *J. Endocrinol.* 67:403–10.

Elliott, J. A. 1974. Photoperiodic regulation of testis function in the golden hamster: Relation to the circadian system. Ph.D. diss., University of Texas, Austin.

———. 1976. Circadian rhythms and photoperiodic time measurement in mammals. *Fed. Proc.* 35:2339–46.

———. 1981. Circadian rhythms entrainment and photoperiodism in the Syrian hamster. In *Biological clocks in seasonal reproductive cycles*, ed. B. K. Follett and D. E. Follett, 203–17. Bristol: Wright.

Elliott, J. A., and B. D. Goldman. 1981. Seasonal reproduction: Photoperiodism and biological clocks. In *Neuroendocrinology of reproduction*, ed. N. T. Adler, 377–423. New York: Plenum.

Ellis, G. B., and F. W. Turek. 1979. Time course of the photoperiod-induced change in sensitivity of the hypothalamic-pituitary axis to testosterone feedback in castrated male hamsters. *Endocrinology* 104:625–30.

Ensthaler, G., and W. Holtz. 1986. The effect of flushing on fertility and body weight of sows. *Zuchthygiene* (Berl.) 21:86–89.

Epple, G. 1976. Chemical communication and reproductive processes in nonhuman primates. In *Mammalian olfaction, reproductive processes and behavior*, ed. R. L. Doty, 257–82. New York: Academic Press.

Epstein, W. W., C. N. Rowsemitt, P. J. Berger, and N. C. Negus. 1986. Dynamics of 6-methoxybenzoxazolinone in winter wheat. *J. Chem. Ecol.* 12:2011–20.

Erasmus, J. A., and H. H. Barnard. 1985. Supplementary winter feeding and reproduction of beef heifers on Dohne sour veld. *S. Afr. Tydskr. Veekd* 15:162–64.

Eskes, G. A. 1983. Gonadal responses to food restriction in intact and pinealectomized male golden hamsters. *J. Reprod. Fert.* 68:85–90.

Eskes, G. A., and I. Zucker. 1978. Photoperiodic control of hamster testis: Dependence on circadian rhythms. *Proc. Natl. Acad. Sci.* 75:1034–38.

Etienne, M., S. Camous, and A. Cuvillier. 1983. Effect of feed restriction during growth on puberty and reproductive performance in gilts. *Reprod. Nutr. Dév.* 23:309–19.

Euker, J. S., J. Meites, and G. D. Riegle. 1975. Effects of acute stress on serum LH and prolactin in intact, castrate and dexamethasone-treated male rats. *Endocrinology* 96:85–92.

Evans, A. M., and P. A. McClure. 1986. Effects of social environment on sexual maturation in female cotton rats (*Sigmodon hispidus*). *Biol. Reprod.* 35:1081–87.

Evans, R. D., K. C. Sadler, C. H. Conaway, and T. S. Baskett. 1965. Regional comparisons of cottontail reproduction in Missouri. *Am. Midl. Nat.* 74:176–84.

Everett, J. W. 1988. Pituitary and hypothalamus: Perspectives and overview.

In *The physiology of reproduction*, ed. E. Knobil and J. D. Neill, 1143–60. New York: Raven.

Ewing, L. L., J. C. Davis, and B. R. Zirkin. 1980. Regulation of testicular function: A spatial and temporal view. *Int. Rev. Physiol.* 22:41–116.

Fadem, B. H. 1985. Evidence for the activation of female reproduction by males in a marsupial *Monodelphis domestica*. *Biol. Reprod.* 33:112–16.

Fahmy, M. H., T. M. MacIntyre, and H. W. R. Chancey. 1980. Date of lambing and reproductive performance of New Foundland and "DLS" breeds of sheep raised under extensive management in Nova Scotia. *J. Anim. Sci.* 51:1078–86.

Fahrbach, S. E., and D. W. Pfaff. 1982. Hormonal and neural mechanisms underlying maternal behavior of the rat. In *The physiological mechanisms of motivation*, ed. D. W. Pfaff, 253–86. New York: Springer.

Falconer, D. S. 1984. Weight and age at puberty in female and male mice of strains selected for large and small body size. *Genet. Res.* 44:47–72.

Falk, J. R., K. A. Halmi, E. Eckert, and R. Casper. 1983. Primary and secondary amenorrhea in anorexia nervosa. In *Menarche*, ed. S. Golub, 287–95. Lexington, Mass.: Lexington.

Farris, E. J. 1950. The oppossum. In *The care and breeding of lab animals*, ed. E. J. Farris, 256–67. New York: John Wiley.

Fedak, M. A., and S. S. Anderson. 1982. The energetics of lactation: Accurate measurements from a large wild mammal, the grey seal, *Halichoerus grypus*. *J. Zool.* (Lond.) 198:473–79.

Feder, H. H. 1981a. Estrous cyclicity in mammals. In *Neuroendocrinology of reproduction*, ed. N. T. Adler, 279–329. New York: Plenum.

———. 1981b. Experimental analysis of hormone actions on the hypothalamus, anterior pituitary and ovary. In *Neuroendocrinology of reproduction*, ed. N. T. Adler, 243–68. New York: Plenum.

———. 1985. Peripheral plasma levels of gonadal steroids in adult male and adult, nonpregnant female mammals. In *Handbook of behavioral neurobiology*, vol. 7, ed. N. T. Adler, D. W. Pfaff, and R. W. Goy, 299–370. New York: Plenum.

Feder, H. H., and B. L. Marrone. 1977. Progesterone: Its role in the central nervous system as a facilitator and inhibitor of sexual behavior and gonadotropin release. *Ann. N.Y. Acad. Sci.* 286:331–54.

Feer, F. 1982. Sexual maturity and annual cycle of reproduction in *Neotragus batesi*, an African forest bovid. *Mammalia* 46:65–74.

Feist, D. D. 1984. Metabolic and thermogenic adjustments in winter acclimatization of subarctic Alaskan red-backed voles. *Spec. Publ. Carn. Mus. Nat. Hist.* 10:131–37.

Feist, D. D., and C. F. Feist. 1986. Effects of cold, short day and melatonin on thermogenesis, body weight and reproductive organs in Alaskan red-backed voles. *J. Comp. Physiol.*, ser. B., 156:741–46.

Ferin, M., D. Van Vugt, and S. Wardlaw. 1984. The hypothalamic control of the menstrual cycle and the role of endogenous opioid peptides. *Rec. Prog. Horm. Res.* 40:441–80.

Fernandez-Baca, S., W. Hansel, R. Saatman, J. Sumar, and C. Novoa. 1979.

Differential luteolytic effects of right and left uterine horns in the alpaca. *Biol. Reprod.* 20:586–95.

Ferns, P. N. 1980. Energy flow through small mammal populations. *Mammal. Rev.* 10:165–88.

Finger, S. E., I. L. Brisbin, Jr., and M. H. Smith. 1981. Kidney fat as a predictor of body condition in white-tailed deer. *J. Wildl. Mgmt.* 45:964–68.

Fink, G. 1988. Gonadotropin secretion and its control. In *The physiology of reproduction*, ed. E. Knobil and J. D. Neill, 1349–78. New York: Raven.

Fisher, H. D., and R. J. Harrison. 1970. Reproduction in the common porpoise (*Phocaena phocaena*) of the North Atlantic. *J. Zool.* (Lond.) 161:471–86.

Fitch, H. S. 1947. Ecology of a cottontail rabbit population in central California. *Cal. Fish Game* 33:159–84.

Fitzgerald, J., F. Michel, and W. R. Butler. 1982. Growth and sexual maturation in ewes: Dietary and seasonal effects modulating luteinizing hormone secretion and first ovulation. *Biol. Reprod.* 27:864–70.

Flamigni, C., S. Venturoli, and J. R. Givens, eds. 1985. *Adolescence in females.* Chicago: Yearbook Medical.

Fleischer, S. F., and G. Turkewitz. 1977. Effect of neonatal stunting on development of rats: Large litter rearing. *Dev. Psychobiol.* 12:137–49.

Fleming, A. 1976. Control of food intake in the lactating rat: Role of suckling and hormones. *Physiol. Behav.* 17:969–78.

Fleming, T. H., E. T. Hooper, and D. E. Wilson. 1972. Three Central American bat communities: Structure, reproductive cycles and movement patterns. *Ecology* 53:555–69.

Fletcher, T. J. 1974. The timing of reproduction in red deer (*Cervus elaphus*) in relation to latitude. *J. Zool.* 127:363–67.

Florant, G. L., and L. Tamarkin. 1984. Plasma melatonin rhythms in euthermic marmots *Marmota flaviventris*. *Biol. Reprod.* 30:332–37.

Flowerdew, J. R. 1973. The effect of natural and artificial changes in food supply on breeding in woodland mice and voles. *J. Reprod. Fert.* 19, suppl. pp. 259–69.

Follett, B. K., and D. E. Follett, eds. 1981. *Biological clocks in seasonal reproductive cycles.* Proceedings of the Thirty-second Symposium of the Colston Research Society. New York: John Wiley.

Follett, B. K., T. J. Nicholls, S. M. Simpson, and D. H. Ellis. 1981. Photoperiodic clocks in birds and mammals: Whither Bünning's hypothesis? In *Photoperiodism and reproduction*, ed. R. Ortavant, J. Pelletier, and J. P. Ravault, Les Colloques de INRA, vol. 6, pp. 1–18. Nouzilly: INRA.

Fonda, E. S., G. B. Rampacek, and R. R. Kraeling. 1984. The effect of ACTH or hydrocortisone on serum LH concentration after adrenalectomy and/or ovariectomy in the prepubertal gilt. *Endocrinology* 114:268–73.

Ford, C. S., and F. A. Beach. 1952. *Patterns of sexual behaviour.* London: Eyre & Spottiswoode.

Ford, R. G., and F. A. Pitelka. 1984. Resource limitation in populations of the California vole *Microtus californicus*. *Ecology* 65:122–36.

Fordham, R. A. 1971. Field populations of deermice with supplemental food. *Ecology* 52:138–46.

Forrest, P. K., R. C. Rhodes III, and R. D. Randel. 1980. Effect of bleeding stress and variable suckling intensity upon serum luteinizing hormone in Brangus heifers. *Theriogenology* 13:321–32.

Foster, D. L. 1980. Comparative development of mammalian females: Proposed analogies among patterns of LH secretion in various species. In *Problems in pediatric endocrinology,* vol. 32, *Proceedings of the Serono Symposium,* ed. C. la Cauza and A. W. Root, 193–210. New York: Academic Press.

———. 1988. Puberty in the female sheep. In *The physiology of reproduction,* ed. E. Knobil and J. D. Neill, 1739–62. New York: Raven.

Foster, D. L., F. J. P. Ebling, and L. E. Claypool. 1988. Timing of puberty by photoperiod. *Reprod. Nutr. Dév.* 28:349–64.

Foster, D. L., F. J. Karsch, D. H. Olster, K. D. Ryan, and S. M. Yellon. 1986. Determinants of puberty in a seasonal breeder. *Rec. Prog. Horm. Res.* 42:331–83.

Foster, D. L., and D. H. Olster. 1985. Effect of restricted nutrition on puberty in the lamb: Patterns of tonic luteinizing hormone (LH) secretion and competency of the LH surge system. *Endocrinology* 116:375–81.

Foster, D. L., D. H. Olster, and S. M. Yellon. 1985. Neuroendocrine regulation of puberty by nutrition and photoperiod. In *Adolescence in females,* ed. S. Venturoli, C. Flamigni, and J. Givens, 1–21. Chicago: Yearbook Medical.

Fowler, P. A., and P. A. Racey. 1986. Correlations between reproductive activity and seasonal endocrine cycles in the hedgehog, *Erinaceus europaeus* at 57°N. In *Endocrine regulations as adaptive mechanisms to the environment,* ed. I. Assenmacher and J. Boissin, 297–302. Paris: Centre National de la Recherche Scientifique.

Foxcroft, G. R. 1978. The development of pituitary gland function. In *Control of ovulation,* ed. D. B. Crighton, G. R. Foxcroft, N. B. Haynes, and G. E. Lamming, 117–38. London: Butterworth.

Francos, G., and E. Mayer. 1983. Observations on some environmental factors connected with fertility in heat stressed cows. *Theriogenology* 19:625–34.

Freeman, M. E. 1988. The ovarian cycle of the rat. In *The physiology of reproduction,* ed. E. Knobil and J. D. Neill, 1893–1928. New York: Raven.

Frehn, J. L., and C. C. Liu. 1970. Effects of temperature, photoperiod, and hibernation on the testes of golden hamsters. *J. Exp. Zool.* 174:317–23.

French, C. E., L. C. McEwen, N. D. Magruder, T. Rader, T. A. Long, and R. W. Swift. 1960. Responses of white-tailed bucks to added artificial light. *J. Mammal.* 41:23–29.

Friend, G. R. 1985. Ecological studies of a population of *Antechinus bellus* (Marsupialia:Dasyuridae) in tropical northern Australia. *Austr. Wildl. Res.* 12:151–62.

Frisch, R. E. 1980. Pubertal adipose tissue: Is it necessary for normal sexual maturation? Evidence from the rat and human female. *Fed. Proc.* 39:2395–2400.

————. 1984. Body fat, puberty and fertility. *Biol. Rev.* 59:161–88.

————. 1987. Body fat, menarche, fitness and fertility. *Hum. Reprod.* 2:521–33.

Frisch, R. E., A. V. Gotz-Welbergen, J. W. McArthur, T. Albright, J. Witschi, B. Bullen, J. Birnholz, R. B. Reed, and H. Hermann. 1981. Delayed menarche and amenorrhea of college athletes in relation to age of onset of training. *J. Am. Med. Assoc.* 246:1559–63.

Frisch, R. E., D. M. Hegsted, and K. Yoshinaga. 1975. Body weight and food intake at early estrus of rats on a high fat diet. *Proc. Natl. Acad. Sci.* 72:4172–76.

————. 1977. Carcass components of first estrus of rats on high fat and low fat diets, body water, protein and fat. *Proc. Natl. Acad. Sci.* 74:379–83.

Frith, H. J., and G. B. Sharman. 1964. Breeding in wild populations of the red kangaroo, *Megaleia rufa. CSIRO Wildl. Res.* 9:86–114.

Frost, D., and I. Zucker. 1983. Photoperiod and melatonin influence seasonal gonadal cycles in the grasshopper mouse (*Onychomys leucogaster*). *J. Reprod. Fert.* 69:237–44.

Fuller, G. B., W. C. Hobson, F. I. Reyes, J. S. D. Winter, and C. Faiman. 1984. Influence of restraint and ketamine anesthesia on adrenal steroids, progesterone and gonadotropins in rhesus monkeys. *Proc. Soc. Exp. Biol. Med.* 175:487–90.

Fuller, W. A. 1969. Changes in numbers of three species of small rodents near Great Slave Lake, N.W.T. Canada, 1964–1967, and their significance for general population theory. *Ann. Zool. Fenn.* 6:113–44.

Gaines, M. S., and R. K. Rose. 1976. Population dynamics of *Microtus ochrogaster* in eastern Kansas. *Ecology* 56:1145–61.

Gallo, R. V. 1981a. Pulsatile LH release during periods of low level LH secretion in the rat estrous cycle. *Biol. Reprod.* 24:771–77.

————. 1981b. Pulsatile LH release during the ovulatory LH surge on proestrus in the rat. *Biol. Reprod.* 24:100–104.

Gambell, R. 1973. Some effects of exploitation on reproduction in whales. *J. Reprod. Fert.* 19, suppl., pp. 533–53.

Gangrade, B. K., and C. J. Dominic. 1984. Studies of the male originating pheromones involved in the Whitten effect and Bruce effect in mice. *Biol. Reprod.* 31:89–96.

Ganong, W. F. 1977. *Review of medical physiology.* 8th ed. Los Altos, Calif.: Lange Medical.

Gardiner, R. J., F. Martin, and L. Jikier. 1983. Anorexia nervosa: Endocrine studies of two distinct clinical subgroups. In *Anorexia nervosa: Recent developments in research,* ed. P. L. Darby, P. E. Garfinkel, D. M. Garner, and D. V. Coscina, 285–89. New York: Alan R. Liss.

Garland, T., Jr. 1983. Scaling the ecological cost of transport to body mass in terrestrial mammals. *Am. Nat.* 121:571–87.

Garnier, D. H., M. T. Hochereau de Reviers, J. Pelletier, J. P. Ravault, M. Courot, and M. Terqui. 1981. LH, prolactin, testosterone, testis weight and Leydig cells in the adult normal ram during non breeding season. *Int. J. Androl.* 3, Suppl., p. 44.

Garrard, G., G. A. Harrison, and J. S. Weiner. 1974. Reproduction and survival of mice at 23° and 32°C. *J. Reprod. Fert.* 37:287–98.

Gashwiler, J. S. 1979. Deer mouse reproduction and its relationship to the tree seed crop. *Am. Midl. Nat.* 102:95–104.

Gates, A. H., and J. L. Bozarth. 1978. Ovulation in the pregnant mares serum gonadotropin treated immature mouse: Effect of dose, age, weight, puberty season and strain, Balb-C, 129 and C129F-1 hybrid. *Biol. Reprod.* 18:497–505.

Gauthier, D., M. Terqui, and P. Mauleon. 1983. Influence of nutrition on plasma levels of progesterone and total estrogens and post-partum plasma levels on luteinizing hormone and FSH in suckling cows. *Anim. Prod.* 37:89–96.

Gebczynski, M., and Z. Gebczynska. 1984. The energy cost of nesting and growth in the European pine vole. *Acta Theriol.* 29:231–41.

Georgiadis, N. 1985. Growth patterns, sexual dimorphism and reproduction in African ruminants. *Afr. J. Ecol.* 23:75–87.

Getz, L. L., D. Dluzen, and J. L. McDermott. 1983. Suppression of female reproductive maturation in *Microtus* by a female urine pheromone. *Behav. Proc.* 8:59–64.

Gherardi, P. B., and D. R. Lindsay. 1982. Response of ewes to lupin supplementation at different times of the breeding season. *Austr. J. Exp. Anim. Husb.* 22:264–67.

Gibbs, F. P., and L. J. Petterborg. 1986. Exercise reduces gonadal atrophy caused by short photoperiod or blinding of hamsters. *Physiol. Behav.* 37:159–62.

Gier, H. T. 1957. *Coyotes in Kansas.* Agriculture Experimental Station Bulletin no. 393. Manhatten: Kansas State College of Agriculture and Applied Science.

Gipps, J. H. W. 1982. The effects of testosterone and scopalamine hydrobromide on the aggressive behavior of male voles *Microtus townsendii*. *Can. J. Zool.* 60:946–50.

Gipps, J. H. W., J. M. Taitt, C. J. Krebs, and Z. Dundjerski. 1981. Male aggression and the population dynamics of the vole *Microtus townsendii*. *Can. J. Zool.* 59:147–57.

Gittleman, J. L., and S. D. Thompson. 1988. Energy allocation in mammalian reproduction. *Am. Zool.* 28:863–75.

Glass, A. R., J. Anderson, D. Herbert, and R. A. Vigersky. 1984. Relationship between pubertal timing and body size in underfed male rats. *Endocrinology* 115:19–24.

Glass, A. R., W. T. Dahms, and R. S. Swerdloff. 1979. Body fat at puberty in rats: Alteration by changes in diet. *Pediat. Res.* 13:7–9.

Glass, A. R., R. Harrison, and R. S. Swerdloff. 1976. Effect of undernutrition and amino acid deficiency on the timing of puberty in rats. *Pediat. Res.* 10:951–55.

Glass, R. A., R. Mallitt, R. A. Vigersky, and R. S. Swerdloff. 1979. Hypoandrogenism and abnormal regulation of gonadotropin secretion in rats fed a low protein diet. *Endocrinology* 104:438–42.

Glass, A. R., and R. S. Swerdloff. 1977. Serum gonadotropins in rats fed a low-valine diet. *Endocrinology* 101:702–7.

————. 1980. Nutritional influences on sexual maturation in the rat. *Fed. Proc.* 39:2360–64.

Godfrey, G. K. 1969. Influence of increased photoperiod on reproduction in the dasyurid marsupial, *Sminthopsis crassicaudata*. *J. Mammal.* 50:132–33.

Goldberg, M., N. R. Tabroff, and R. M. Tamarin. 1980. Nutrient variation in beach grass in relation to beach vole feeding. *Ecology* 61:1029–33.

Goldfoot, D. A., S. J. Wiegand, and G. Scheffler. 1978. Continued copulation in ovariectomized adrenal-suppressed stumptail macaques (*Macaca arctoides*). *Horm. Behav.* 11:89–99.

Goncharov, N. P., D. S. Tavadyan, J. E. Powell, and V. C. Stevens. 1984. Levels of adrenal and gonadal hormones in rhesus monkeys during chronic hypokenesia. *Endocrinology* 115:129–35.

Goo, G. P., and E. N. Sassenrath. 1980. Persistent adrenocortical activation in female rhesus monkeys after new breeding group formation. *J. Med. Primatol.* 9:325–34.

Goodman, R. L. 1988. Neuroendocrine control of the ovine estrous cycle. In *The physiology of reproduction*, ed. E. Knobil and J. D. Neill, 1929–70. New York: Raven.

Goodman, R. L., E. L. Bittman, D. L. Foster, and F. J. Karsch. 1982. Alterations in the control of luteinizing hormone pulse frequency underlie the seasonal variation in estradiol negative feedback in the ewe. *Biol. Reprod.* 27:580–89.

Goodman, R. L., and S. L. Meyer. 1984. Effects of pentobarbital anesthesia on tonic luteinizing hormone secretion in the ewe: Evidence for active inhibition of luteinizing hormone in anestrus. *Biol. Reprod.* 30:374–81.

Gopalakrishna, A. 1955. Observations on the breeding habits and ovarian cycle in the Indian sheath-tailed bat, *Taphozous longimanus* (Hardwicke). *Proc. Nat. Inst. Sci. Ind.*, ser. B, 21:29–41.

Gopalakrishna, A., and A. Madhavan. 1971. Survival of spermatoza in the female genital tract of the Indian vespertilionid bat, *Pipestrellus ceylonicus chrysothrix* (Wroughton). *Proc. Ind. Acad. Sci.*, ser. B, 73:43–49.

Gore-Langton, R. E., and D. T. Armstrong. 1988. Follicular steroidogenesis and its control. In *The physiology of reproduction*, ed. E. Knobil and J. D. Neill, 331–86. New York: Raven.

Gorman, M. L. 1976. Seasonal changes in the reproductive pattern of feral *Herpestes auropunctatus* (Carnivora:Viverriadae) in the Fijian Islands. *J. Zool.* (Lond.) 178:237–46.

Goss, R. J. 1983. *Deer antlers: Regeneration, function and evolution.* New York: Academic Press.

Graham, C. E. 1981. *Reproductive biology of the great apes.* New York: Academic Press.

Graham, J. M., and C. Desjardins. 1980. Classical conditioning: Induction of luteinizing hormone and testosterone secretion in anticipation of sexual activity. *Science* 210:1039–41.

Gray, G. D., E. R. Smith, D. A. Damassa, J. E. L. Ehrenkranz, and J. M. Davidson. 1978. Neuroendocrine mechanisms mediating the suppression of circulating testosterone levels associated with chronic stress in male rats. *Neuroendocrinology* 25:247–56.

Green, B. 1984. Composition of milk and energetics of growth in marsupials. *Symp. Zool. Soc. Lond.* 51:369–87.

Greenwald, G. S., and P. F. Terranova. 1988. Follicular selection and its control. In *The Physiology of reproduction*, ed. E. Knobil and J. D. Neill, 387–446. New York: Raven.

Griffiths, D. J. 1984. The annual cycle of the testis of the elephant seal (*Mirounga leonina*) at Macquarie Island. *J. Zool.* (Lond.) 203:193–204.

Grimsdell, J. J. R. 1973. Reproduction in the western buffalo, *Syncerus caffer*, in western Uganda. *J. Reprod. Fert.* 19, suppl., pp. 303–18.

Grodzinski, W., and N. R. French. 1983. Production efficiency in small mammal populations. *Oecologia* (Berl.) 56:41–49.

Grodzinski, W., and B. A. Wunder. 1975. Ecological energetics of small mammals. In *Small mammals: Their productivity and population dynamics*, ed. F. B. Golley, K. Petrusewicz, and L. Ryszkowski, 173–204. Cambridge: Cambridge University Press.

Grosvenor, C. E., and F. Mena. 1983. Effect of underfeeding upon the rate of milk ejection in the lactating rat. *J. Endocrinol.* 96:215–22.

Grumbach, M. M. 1980. The neuroendocrinology of puberty. In *Neuroendocrinology*, ed. D. T. Krieger and J. C. Hughes. Sunderland, Mass.: Sinauer.

Gulamhusein, A. P., and A. R. Thawley. 1972. Ovarian cycle and plasma progesterone levels in the stoat, *Mustela erminea*. *J. Reprod. Fert.* 31:492–93.

Gustafson, A. W. 1979. Male reproductive patterns in hibernating bats. *J. Reprod. Fert.* 56:317–31.

Gustafson, A. W., and D. A. Damassa. 1985. Annual variations in plasma sex steroid-binding protein and testosterone concentrations in the adult male little brown bat: Relation to the asynchronous recrudescence of the testis and accessory reproductive organs. *Biol. Reprod.* 33:1126–37.

Gustafson, T. O., C. B. Andersson, and N. E. I. Hyholm. 1983. Comparison of sensitivity to social suppression of sexual maturation in captive male bank voles *Clethrionomys glareolus* originating from populations with different degrees of cyclicity. *Oikos* 41:250–54.

Gwazdauskas, F. C., W. W. Thatcher, C. A. Kiddy, M. J. Paape, and C. J. Wilcox. 1981. Hormonal patterns during heat stress following prostaglandin F-2-alpha tris hydroxymethylamino methane salt induced luteal regression in heifers. *Theriogenology* 16:271–86.

Gwinner, E. 1981. Circannual sytems. In *Behavioral neurobiology*, vol. 4, *Biological rhythms*, ed. J. Aschoff, 391–410. New York: Plenum.

———. 1986. *Circannual rhythms: Endogenous annual clocks in the organization of seasonal processes*. Berlin: Springer.

Gwinner, E., and J. Dittami. 1986. Adaptive functions of circannual clocks. In *Endocrine regulations as adaptive mechanisms to the environment*, ed. I. Assenmacher and J. Boissin, 115–24. Paris: Centre National de la Recherche Scientifique.

Hackett, A. J. and M. S. Wolynetz. 1982. Effectiveness of photoperiod stimulation on reproductive performance of sheep housed continuously indoors on an accelerated breeding schedule. *Can. J. Comp. Med.* 46:400–404.

Hadley, J. C. 1975. Total unconjugated oestrogen and progesterone concentrations in peripheral blood during the oestrous cycle of the dog. *J. Reprod. Fert.* 44:445–51.

Hafez, E. S. E. 1952. Studies on the breeding season and reproduction in the ewe. *J. Agric. Sci.* 42:189–265.

———. 1964. Effects of high temperature on reproduction. *Int. J. Biometeor.* 7:223–30.

Hagen, D. R., and K. B. Kephart. 1980. Reproduction in domestic and feral swine: 1. Comparison of ovulatory rate and litter size. *Biol. Reprod.* 22:550–52.

Haigh, G. 1987. Reproductive inhibition of female *Peromyscus leucopus:* Female competition and behavioral regulation. *Am. Zool.* 27:867–78.

Haigh, G., B. S. Cushing, and F. H. Bronson. 1988. A novel post-copulatory block of reproduction in white-footed mice. *Biol. Reprod.* 38:623–26.

Halas, E. S., M. J. Hanlon, and H. H. Sandstead. 1975. Intrauterine nutrition and aggression. *Nature* 257:221–22.

Halfpenny, J. C. 1980. Reproductive strategies: Intra and interspecific comparisons within the genus *Peromyscus.* Ph.D. diss., University of Colorado, Boulder.

Hall, E. S., G. T. Makoul, G. R. Lynch, and G. Anderson. 1985. Effects of timed melatonin injections on reproduction in pinealectomized *Peromyscus leucopus. Gen. Comp. Endocrinol.* 58:407–14.

Hall, L. S. 1983. Observations on body weight and breeding of the northern brown bandicoot, *Isodon macrourus,* trapped in south-east Queensland. *Austr. Wildl. Res.* 10:467–76.

Hall, P. F. 1988. Testicular steroid synthesis: Organization and regulation. In *The physiology of reproduction,* ed. E. Knobil and J. D.Neill, 975–98. New York: Raven.

Hall, V., and B. Goldman. 1980. Effects of gonadal steroid hormones on hibernation in the Turkish hamster (*Mesocricetus brandti*). *J. Comp. Physiol.* 135:107–14.

Halpin, Z. T. 1986. Individual odors among mammals: Origins and functioning. *Adv. Stud. Behav.* 16:40–70.

Hamilton, G. D., and F. H. Bronson. 1985. Food restriction and reproductive development in wild house mice. *Biol. Reprod.* 32:773–78.

———. 1986. Food restriction and reproductive development: Male and female mice and male rats. *Am. J. Physiol.* 250:R370–R376.

Hamilton, W. J., Jr. 1940. Breeding habits of the cottontail rabbit in New York State. *J. Mammal.* 28:8–11.

Hammel, H. T. 1983. Phylogeny of regulatory mechanisms in temperature regulation. *J. Therm. Biol.* 8:37–42.

Handelmann, G., R. Ravizza, and W. J. Ray. 1980. Social dominance determines estrous entrainment among female hamsters. *Horm. Behav.* 14:107–15.

Hansel, W., and E. M. Convey. 1983. Physiology of the estrous cycle. *J. Anim. Sci.* 57:404–24.

Hansen, P. J., K. K. Schillo, M. M. Hinshelwood, and E. R. Hauser. 1983. Body composition at vaginal opening in mice as influenced by food intake and photoperiod: Tests of critical body weight and composition hypothesis for puberty onset. *Biol. Reprod.* 29:924–31.

Hansson, L. 1984. Composition of cyclic and non-cyclic vole populations on the causes of variation in individual quality among *Clethrionomys glareolus* in Sweden. *Oecologia* (Berl.) 63:199–206.

Harder, J. D., and M. W. Fleming. 1981. Estradiol and progesterone profiles indicate a lack of endocrine recognition of pregnancy in the oppossum. *Science* 212:1400–1402.

Haresign, W. 1981a. Influence of nutrition on reproduction in the ewe: 1. Effects of ovulation rate, follicle development and luteinizing hormone release. *Anim. Prod.* 32:197–202.

———. 1981b. The influence of nutrition on reproduction in the ewe: 2. Effects of undernutrition on pituitary responsiveness to LHRH stimulation. *Anim. Prod.* 32:257–60.

Harland, R. M., P. J. Blancher, and J. S. Millar. 1979. Demography of a population of *Peromyscus leucopus. Can. J. Zool.* 57:323–28.

Harland, R. M., and J. S. Millar. 1980. Activity of breeding *Peromyscus leucopus. Can. J. Zool.* 58:313–16.

Harper, M. J. K. 1982. Sperm and egg transport. In *Reproduction in mammals,* vol. 1, *Germ cells and fertilization,* ed. C. R. Austin and R. V. Short, 102–27. Cambridge: Cambridge University Press.

Harrison, J. L. 1952. Breeding rhythms of Selangor rodents. *Bull. Raffles Mus.* 24:109–15.

Harrison, R. J. 1969. Reproduction and reproductive organs. In *Biology of marine mammals,* ed. H. T. Anderson, 253–348. New York: Academic Press.

Hart, J. S. 1971. Rodents. In *Comparative physiology of thermoregulation,* ed. G. C. Whittow, 1–49. New York: Academic Press.

Harvey, P. H., and R. M. Zammuto. 1985. Patterns of mortality and age at first reproduction in natural populations of mammals. *Nature* 315:319–20.

Hasler, J. F., and E. M. Banks. 1975. The influence of mature males on sexual maturation in female collared lemmings *Dicrostonyx groenlandicus. J. Reprod. Fert.* 42:583–86.

Hasler, J. F., A. E. Buhl, and E. M. Banks. 1976. The influence of photoperiod on growth and sexual function in male and female collared lemmings. *J. Reprod. Fert.* 46:323–29.

Hasler, M. J., and A. V. Nalbandov. 1974. The effect of weanling and adult males on sexual maturation in female voles *Microtus ochrogaster. Gen. Comp. Endocrinol.* 23:237–38.

Hastings, M. H., J. Herbert, N. D. Martensz, and A. C. Roberts. 1985. Melatonin and the brain in photoperiodic mammals. In *Photoperiodism, melatonin and the pineal,* CIBA Foundation Symposium no. 117, pp. 57–77. London: Pittman.

Haugen, A. O. 1975. Reproductive performance of white-tailed deer in Iowa. *J. Mammal.* 56:151–59.

Haussler, U., E. Moller, and U. Schmidt. 1981. Zur haltung und jugend-twicklung von Molossus molossus (Chiroptera). Z. Saug. 46:337–51.

Havera, S. P. 1979. Energy and nutrient cost of lactation in fox squirrels. J. Wildl. Mgmt. 43:958–65.

Heap, R. B., and A. P. F. Flint. 1984. Pregnancy. In Reproduction in mammals, vol. 3, Hormonal control of reproduction, ed. C. R. Austin and R. V. Short, 153–94. Cambridge: Cambridge University Press.

Heidman, P. 1987. The reproductive ecology of a community of Philippine fruit bats. Ph.D. diss., University of Michigan, Ann Arbor.

Hemsworth, P. H., C. G. Winfield, and W. A. Chamley. 1981. The influence of the presence of the female on the sexual behaviour and plasma testosterone levels of the mature male pig. Anim. Prod. 32:61–65.

Hennemann, W. W., III. 1983. Relationship among body mass, metabolic rate and the intrinsic rate of natural increase in mammals. Oecologia (Berl.) 56:104–8.

Hennesey, D. P., and P. E. Williamson. 1984. Stress and summer infertility in pigs. Austr. Vet. J. 61:212–15.

Hensleigh, P. A., and D. C. Johnson. 1971. Heat stress during pregnancy: 2. Pituitary gonadotrophins in intact, adrenalectomized and ovariectomized rats. Fert. Steril. 22:522–27.

Herndon, J. G. 1983. Seasonal breeding in rhesus monkeys: Influence of the behavioral environment. Am. J. Primatol. 5:197–204.

Herndon, J. G., M. S. Blank, D. R. Mann, D. C. Collins, and J. J. Turner. 1985. Negative feedback effects of estradiol-17 beta on luteinizing hormone in female rhesus monkeys under different seasonal conditions. Acta Endocrinol. 108:31–35.

Herndon, J. G., J. J. Turner, and D. C. Collins. 1981. Ejaculation is important for mating induced testosterone increases in male rhesus monkeys. Physiol. Behav. 27:873–78.

Herrenkohl, L. 1979. Prenatal stress reduces fertility and fecundity in female offspring. Science 206:1097–99.

Heske, E. J., and R. J. Nelson. 1984. Pregnancy interruption in Microtus ochrogaster: Laboratory artifact or field phenomenon? Biol. Reprod. 31:97–103.

Heske, E. J., R. S. Ostfeld, and W. Z. Lidicker, Jr. 1984. Competitive interractions between Microtus californicus and Reithrodontomys megalotis during two peaks of Microtus abundance. J. Mammal. 65:271–80.

Hill, E. P. 1972. Litter size in Alabama cottontails as influenced by soil fertility. J. Wildl. Mgmt. 36:1199–1209.

Hill, R. W. 1976. Comparative physiology of animals: An environmental approach. New York: Harper & Row.

———. 1983. Thermal physiology and energetics of Peromyscus: Ontogeny, body temperature, metabolism, insulation and microclimatology. J. Mammal. 64:19–37.

Hill, T. G., and C. W. Alliston. 1981. Effects of thermal stress on plasma concentrations of luteinizing hormone, progesterone, prolactin and testosterone in the cycling ewe. Theriogenology 15:201–10.

Hinde, R. A., ed. 1983. *Primate social relationships*. Sunderland, Mass.: Sinauer.

Hixon, D. L., G. C. Gahey, Jr., D. J. Kesler, and A. L. Neumann. 1982. Effects of energy level and monensin on reproductive performance and lactation of beef cows. *Theriogenology* 17:515–26.

Hoagland, T. A., and R. P. Wettemann. 1984. Influence of elevated ambient temperature after breeding on plasma corticoids, estradiol and progesterone in gilts. *Theriogenology* 22:15–24.

Hodgen, G. D., and J. Itskovitz. 1988. Recognition and maintenance of pregnancy. In *The physiology of reproduction*, ed. E. Knobil and J. D. Neill, 1995–2022. New York: Raven.

Hodgson, Y., D. M. Robertson, and D. M. de Kretser. 1983. The regulation of testicular function. *Int. Rev. Physiol.* 27:275–327.

Hoffmann, J. C. 1968. Effect of photoperiod on estrous cycle length in the rat. *Endocrinology* 83:1355–57.

Hoffmann, K. 1973. The influence of photoperiod and melatonin on testis size, body weight, and pelage colour in the Djungarian hamster (*Phodopus sungorus*). *J. Comp. Physiol.* 85:267–82.

———. 1978. Effects of short photoperiods on puberty, growth and molt in the Djungarian hamster *Phodopus sungorus*. *J. Reprod. Fert.* 54:29–36.

———. 1981. Photoperiodism in vertebrates. In *Handbook of behavioral neurobiology*, 449–73. New York: Plenum.

———. 1984. Photoperiodic reaction in the Djungarian hamster is influenced by previous light history. *Biol. Reprod.* 30, suppl. 1, pp. 55.

———. 1985. Interaction between photoperiod, pineal and seasonal adaption in mammals. In *The pineal gland: Current state of pineal research*, ed. B. Mess, Cs. Ruzsas, L. Tima, and P. Pevet, 212–27. Amsterdam: Elsevier.

Hoffman, R. A., R. J. Hester, and C. Towns. 1965. Effect of light and temperature on the endocrine system of the golden hamster (*Mesocricetus auratus*). *Comp. Biochem. Physiol.* 15:525–34.

Hoffman, R. A., and R. J. Reiter. 1965. Pineal gland: Influence on gonads of male hamsters. *Science* 148:1609–15.

Holler, N. R., and C. H. Conaway. 1979. Reproduction of the marsh rabbit in south Florida. *J. Mammal.* 60:769–77.

Hooley, R. D., J. K. Findlay, and R. G. A. Stephenson. 1979. Effect of heat stress on plasma concentrations of prolactin and luteinizing hormone in ewes. *Austr. J. Biol. Sci.* 32:231–35.

Horton, T. 1984. Growth and maturation in *Microtus montanus*: Effects of photoperiods before and after weaning. *Can. J. Zool.* 62:1741–46.

———. 1985. Cross-fostering of voles demonstrates in utero effect of photoperiod. *Biol. Reprod.* 33:934–39.

Howard, W. E. 1949. Dispersal, amount of inbreeding, and longevity in a local population of prairie deermice on the George Reserve, southern Michigan. *Contr. Lab. Vert. Biol. Univ. Mich.* 43:1–50.

———. 1951. Relation between low temperature and available food to survival of small rodents. *J. Mammal.* 32:300–312.

Howland, B. E. 1971. Gonadotropin levels in female rats subjected to restricted feed intake. *J. Reprod. Fert.* 27:467–70.

———. 1975. The influence of food restriction and subsequent re-feeding on gonadotropin secretion and serum testosterone levels in the male rat. *J. Reprod. Fert.* 44:429–36.

Howland, B. E., and E. A. Ibrahim. 1973. Increased LH-suppressing effect of oestrogen in ovariectomized rats as a result of underfeeding. *J. Reprod. Fert.* 35:545–48.

Howland, B. E., and K. R. Skinner. 1973. Effect of starvation on gonadotropin secretion in intact and castrated male rats. *Can. J. Physiol. Pharmacol.* 51:759–62.

Howles, C. M., J. Craigon, and N. B. Haynes. 1982. Long-term rhythms of testicular volume and plasma prolactin concentrations in rams reared for 3 years in constant photoperiod. *J. Reprod. Fert.* 65:439–46.

Howles, C. M., G. M. Webster, and N. B. Haynes. 1980. The effect of rearing under a long or short photoperiod on testis growth, plasma testosterone, and prolactin concentrations and the development of sexual behavior in rams. *J. Reprod. Fert.* 60:437–48.

Hoyenga, K. B., and K. T. Hoyenga. 1982. Gender and energy balance: Sex differences in adaptations for feast and famine. *Physiol. Behav.* 28:545–63.

Hradecky, P. 1985. Possible pheromonal regulation of reproduction in wild carnivores. *J. Chem. Ecol.* 11:241–50.

Hrdy, S. B. 1979. Infanticide among animals: A review, classification, and examination of the implications for the reproductive strategy of females. *Ethol. Sociobiol.* 1:13–40.

Hrdy, S. B., and G. Hausfater. 1984. Comparative and evolutionary perspectives on infanticide: An introduction and overview. In *Comparative and evolutionary perspectives,* ed. G. Hausfater and S. B. Hrdy, xiii–xxxv. Hawthorne, N.Y.: Aldine.

Hsueh, A. M., M. Simonson, B. F. Chow, and H. M. Hanson. 1974. The importance of the period of dietary restriction of the dam on behavior and growth in the rat. *J. Nutr.* 104:37–46.

Hubert, B. 1982. Population dynamics of two species of rodents of Senegal, *Mastomys erythroleucus* and *Taterillus gracillis,* Rodentia Muridae and Berbillidae: 1. Demographic study. *Mammalian* 46:137–66.

Huck, U. W., A. C. Bracken, and R. D. Lisk. 1983. Female-induced pregnancy block in the golden hamster. *Behav. Neur. Biol.* 38:190–93.

Hudson, R. J., and R. G. White, eds. 1985. *Bioenergetics of wild herbivores.* Boca Raton, Fla.: CRC.

Hughes, P. E., and D. J. A. Cole. 1976. Reproduction in the gilt. *Anim. Prod.* 23:89–94.

Hunter, G. L., and I. M. R. Van Aarde. 1975. Influence of age of ewe and photoperiod on the intervals between paturition and first oestrus in lactating and non-lactating ewes at different nutritional levels. *J. Reprod. Fert.* 42:205–12.

Illige, D. 1951. An analysis of the reproductive pattern of whitetail deer in south Texas. *J. Mammal.* 32:411–21.

Illnerova, H., and J. Vanecek. 1988. Entrainment of the rat pineal rhythm in melatonin production by light. *Reprod. Nutr. Dév.* 28:515–26.

Ingles, L. G. 1941. Natural history observations on the Audubon cottontail. *J. Mammal.* 22:227–50.

Innami, S., M. G. Yang, O. Mickelsen, and H. D. Hafs. 1973. The influence of high fat diets on estrous cycles, sperm production and fertility of rats. *Proc. Soc. Exp. Biol. Med.* 143:63–68.

Innes, D. G. L., and J. S. Millar. 1981. Body weight, litter size and energetics of reproduction in *Clethrionomys gapperi* and *Microtus pennsylvanicus*. *Can. J. Zool.* 59:785–89.

Izard, M. K. 1983. Pheromones and reproduction in domestic animals. In *Pheromones and reproduction in mammals*, ed. J. G. Vandenbergh, 253–85. New York: Academic Press.

Izard, M. K. and J. Vandenbergh. 1982. Priming pheromones from oestrus cows increase synchronization of oestrus in dairy heifers after PGF-2 injections. *J. Reprod. Fert.* 66:189–96.

Jackson, G. L., and S. L. Davis. 1979. Comparison of luteinizing hormone and prolactin levels in cycling and anestrous ewes. *Neuroendocrinology* 28:256–63.

Jaffe, R. B. 1986. Integrative maternal-fetal endocrine control systems. In *Reproductive endocrinology*, ed. S. S. C. Yen and R. B. Jaffe, 770–88. Philadelphia: W. B. Saunders.

Jallageas, M., and I. Assenmacher. 1984. External factors controlling annual testosterone and thyroxine cycles in the edible dormouse *Glis glis*. *Comp. Biochem. Physiol.: A. Comp. Physiol.* 77:161–68.

Jameson, E. W., Jr. 1953. Reproduction of deer mice *P. maniculatus* and *P. boylei* in the Sierra Nevada, California. *J. Mammal.* 34:44–58.

Jannett, P. J., Jr. 1984a. Reproduction of the montane vole, *Microtus montanus* in subnivean populations. *Spec. Publ. Carn. Mus. Nat. Hist.* 10:215–24.

———. 1984b. Scent communication in social dynamics of mammals. *Acta Zool. Fenn.* 171:43–48.

Jansky, L., G. Haddad, Z. Kahlerova, and J. Nedoma. 1984. Effect of external factors on hibernation of golden hamsters. *J. Comp. Physiol.*, ser. B, 154:427–33.

Jarvis, J. U. M. 1981. Eusociality in a mammal: Cooperative breeding in naked mole-rat colonies. *Science* 212:571–73.

Jay, P. 1965. The common langur of north India. In *Primate behavior*, ed. I. Devore, 197–249. New York: Holt, Rinehart & Winston.

Jean-Faucher, C., M. Berger, M. de Turckheim, G. Veyssiere, and C. Jean. 1982. The effect of preweaning undernutrition upon the sexual development of male mice. *Biol. Neonate* 41:45–51.

Jeffcoate, I. A., N. C. Rawlings, and W. E. Howell. 1984. Duration of the breeding season and response to reproductive manipultions in five breeds of sheep under northern prairie conditions. *Theriogeneology* 22:279–90.

Jemiolo, B., F Andreolini, and M. Novotny. 1986. Chemical and biological investigations of female mouse pheromones. In *Chemical signals in ver-*

tebrates, vol. 4, ed. D. Duvall, D. Muller Schwarze, and R. M. Silverstein, 79–85. New York: Plenum.

Jensen, T. X. 1982. Seed producton and outbreaks of noncyclic rodent populations in deciduous forests. *Oecologia* 54:184–92.

Jerrett, D. P. 1979. Female reproductive patterns in nonhibernating bats. *J. Reprod. Fert.* 56:369–78.

Jewell, P. A. 1976. Selection for reproductive success. In *The evolution of reproduction*, ed. C. R. Austin and R. V. Short, 71–109. Cambridge: Cambridge University Press.

Johns, M. A. 1986. The role of the vomeronasal organ in behavioral control of reproduction. *Ann. N.Y. Acad. Sci.* 474:148–57.

Johnson, K. G., and M. Cabanac. 1982. Homeostatic competition in rats fed at varying distances from a thermoneutral refuge. *Physiol. Behav.* 29:715–20.

Johnson, L. B., and R. A. Hoffman. 1985. Interaction of diet and photoperiod on growth and reproduction in male golden hamsters *Mesocricetus auratus*. *Growth* 49:380–99.

Johnson, M. L., and M. S. Gaines. 1988. Demography of the western harvest mouse, *Reithrodontomys megalotis*, in eastern Kansas. *Oecologia* (Berl.) 75:405–11.

Johnsson, I. E., and J. M. Obst. 1984. The effects of level of nutrition before and after eight months of age on subsequent milk and calf production of beef heifers over 3 lactations. *Anim. Prod.* 38:57–68.

Johnston, P. G., and I. Zucker. 1979. Photoperiodic influences on gonadal development and maintenance in the cotton rat, *Sigmodon hispidus*. *Biol. Reprod.* 21:1–8.

———. 1980. Photoperiodic regulation of reproductive development in white-footed mice (*Peromyscus leucopus*). *Biol. Reprod.* 22:983–89.

Jolly, A. 1967. Breeding synchrony in wild *Lemur catta*. In *Social communication among primates*, ed. S. A. Altmann, 3–14. Chicago: University of Chicago Press.

Jones, C. B. 1985. Reproductive patterns in mantled howler monkeys: Estrus, mate choice and copulation. *Primates* 26:130–42.

Joubert, D. M. 1963. Puberty in female farm animals. *Anim. Breed. Abst.* 31:295–306.

Joy, J., R. B. Melnyk, and N. Mrosovsky. 1980. Reproductive cycles in the male dormouse (*Glis glis*). *Comp. Biochem. Physiol.*, ser. A, 67:219–21.

Judd, F. W., J. Herrera, and M. Wagner. 1978. The relationship between lipid and reproductive cycles of a subtropical population of *Peromyscus leucopus*. *J. Mammal.* 59:669–76.

Kaczmarski, F. 1966. Bioenergetics of pregnancy and lactation in the bank vole. *Acta Theriol.* 11:409–17.

Kaikusalo, A., and J. Tast. 1984. Winter breeding of microtine rodents at Kilpisjarvi, Finnish Lapland. *Spec. Publ. Carn. Mus. Nat. Hist.* 10:243–50.

Kalra, S. P. 1986. Neural circuitry involved in the control of LHRH secretion: A model for preovulatory LH release. In *Frontiers in neuroendocrinology*, vol. 9, ed. W. F. Ganong and L. Martini, 31–75. New York: Raven.

Kalra, S. P., and P. S. Kalra. 1983. Neural regulation of luteinizing hormone secretion in the rat. *Endocrinol. Rev.* 4:311–51.

Kalra, S. P., and C. A. Leadem. 1984. Control of luteinizing hormone secretion by endogenous opioid peptides. In *Opioid modulation of endocrine function*, ed. G. Delitala, M. Motta, and M. Serio, 171–84. New York: Raven.

Kamel, F., W. W. Wright, E. J. Mock, and A. I. Frankel. 1977. The influence of mating and related stimuli on plasma levels of luteinizing hormone, follicle stimulating hormone, prolactin and testosterone in the male rat. *Endocrinology* 101:421–29.

Kanerek, R. B., P. M. Schoenfeld, and P. J. Morgane. 1986. Maternal malnutrition in the rat: Effects on food intake and body weight. *Physiol. Behav.* 38:509–15.

Kaneko, N., E. A. Debski, M. C. Wilson, and W. K. Whitten. 1980. Puberty acceleration in mice: 2. Evidence that the vomeronasal organ is a receptor for the primer pheromone in male mouse urine. *Biol. Reprod.* 22:873–78.

Kaplanski, J., E. Magal, U. A. Sod-Moriah, N. Hirschmann, and I. Nir. 1983. The pineal and endocrine changes in heat exposed male hamsters, *Mesocricetus auratus*. *J. Neur. Trans.* 58:261–70.

Karsch, F. J. 1984. The hypothalamus and anterior pituitary gland. In *Reproduction in mammals*, vol. 3, *Hormonal control of reproduction*, ed. C. R. Austin and R. V. Short, 1–20. Cambridge: Cambridge University Press.

Karsch, F. J. 1986. A role for melatonin as a timekeeping hormone in the ewe. *J. Neur. Transm.* 21, suppl., pp. 109–24.

———. 1987. Central actions of ovarian steroids in the feedback regulation of pulsatile secretion of luteinizing hormone. *Ann. Rev. Physiol.* 49:365–82.

Karsch, F. J., E. L. Bittman, D. L. Foster, R. L. Goodman, S. J. Legan, and J. E. Robinson. 1984. Neuroendocrine basis of seasonal reproduction. *Rec. Prog. Horm. Res.* 40:185–232.

Karsch, F. J., and D. L. Foster. 1981. Environmental control of seasonal breeding: A common final mechanism governing seasonal breeding and sexual maturation. In *Environmental factors in mammal reproduction*, ed. D. Gilmore and B. Cook, 30–53. Hong Kong: Macmillan.

Katongole, C. B., F. Naftolin, and R. V. Short. 1971. Relationship between blood levels of luteinizing hormone and testosterone in bulls, and the effects of sexual stimulation. *J. Endocrinol.* 50:457–66.

Kaur, H., and S. P. Arora. 1982. Influence of level of nutrition and season on the oestrus cycle rhythm and on fertility in buffaloes. *Trop. Agric.* 59:274–78.

Kazmer, G. W., M. A. Barnes, and R. W. Canfield. 1985. Reproductive and metabolic hormones during estrus after fasting in Holstein heifers. *Theriogenology* 24:619–20.

Keefe, D. L., and F. W. Turek. 1986. Circadian time keeping processes in mammalian reproduction. *Ox. Rev. Reprod. Biol.* 7:347–400.

Keith, L. B., J. R. Cary, O. J. Rongstad, and M. C. Brittingham. 1984. Demography and ecology of a declining snowshoe hare population. *Wildl. Monogr.* 90:1–43.

Keith, L. B., and L. A. Windberg. 1978. A demographic analysis of the snowshoe hare cycle. *Wildl. Monogr.* 58:5–70.

Kemnitz, J. W., J. R. Gibber, S. G. Eisele, and K. A. Lindsay. 1986. Relationship of reproductive condition to food intake and sucrose consumption of female rhesus monkeys. In *Current perspectives in primate social dynamics*, ed. D. M. Taub and F. A. King, 274–86. New York: Van Nostrand Reinhold.

Kemper, C. M. 1980. Reproduction in *Pseudomys novaehollandaiae* (Muridae) in the wild. *Austr. Wildl. Res.* 7:385–402.

Kenagy, G. J. 1973. Daily and seasonal patterns of activity and energetics in a heteromyid rodent community. *Ecology* 54:1201–19.

———. 1980. Interrelation of endogenous annual rhythms of reproduction and hibernation in the golden-mantled ground squirrel. *J. Comp. Physiol.* 135:333–39.

———. 1981. Endogenous annual rhythm of reproductive function in the non-hibernating desert ground-squirrel *Ammospermophilus leucurus*. *J. Comp. Physiol.* 142:251–58.

Kenagy, G. J. 1987. Energy allocation for reproduction in the golden-mantled ground squirrel. In *Reproductive energetics in mammals*, ed. A. S. I. Loudon and P. A. Racey, 259–74. Oxford: Clarendon.

Kenagy, G. J., and B. M. Barnes. 1984. Environmental and endogenous control of reproductive function in the Great Basin pocket mouse *Perognathus parvus*. *Biol. Reprod.* 31:637–45.

Kengay, G. J., and G. A. Bartholomew. 1981. Effects of daylength, temperature and green food on testicular development in a desert pocket mouse *Perognathus formosus*. *Physiol. Zool.* 54:62–73.

———. 1985. Seasonal reproductive patterns in five coexisting California desert rodent species. *Ecol. Monogr.* 55:371–97.

Kenagy, G. J., and S. C. Trombulak. 1986. Size and function of mammalian testes in relation to body size. *J. Mammal.* 67:1–22.

Kennaway, D. J. 1988. Short- and long-term effects of manipulation of the pineal/melatonin axis in ewes. *Reprod. Nutr. Dév.* 28:399–408.

Kennaway, D. J., T. A. Gilmore. 1984. Effects of melatonin implants in ewe lambs. *J. Reprod. Fert.* 70:39–46.

Kennaway, D. J., L. M. Snaford, B. Godfrey, and H. G. Friesen. 1983. Patterns of progesterone, melatonin and prolactin secretion in ewes maintained in four different photoperiods. *J. Endocrinol.* 97:229–42.

Kennedy, G. C., and J. Mitra. 1963a. Body weight and food intake as initiating factors for puberty in the rat. *J. Physiol.* 166:408–18.

———. 1963b. Hypothalamic control of energy balance and the reproductive cycle in the rat. *J. Physiol.* 166:395–407.

Kerley, G. I. H. 1983. Comparison of seasonal haul-out patterns of fur seals *Arctocephalus tropicalis* and *A. gazella* on subantarctic Marion Island. *S. Afr. J. Wildl. Res.* 13:71–77.

Keverne, E. B. 1983a. Chemical communication in primate reproduction. In

Pheromones and reproduction in mammals, ed. J. G. Vandenbergh, 79–92. New York: Academic Press.

————. 1983b. Phermonal influences on the endocrine regulation of repro-duction. *Trends Neurosci.* 6:381–84.

Kerverne, E. B., and C. de la Riva. 1982. Pheromones in mice: Reciprocal interaction between the nose and the brain. *Nature* 296:148–50.

Keverne, E. B., and A. E. Rosser. 1986. The evolutionary significance of the olfactory block to pregnancy. In *Chemical signals in vertebrates,* vol. 4, ed. D. Duvall, D. Muller Schwarze, and R. M. Silverstein, 433–39. New York: Plenum.

Keyes, P. L., J. E. Gadsby, M. Y. Khe-Ching, and C. H. Bill III. 1983. The corpus luteum, *Int. Rev. Physiol.* 27:57–98.

King, H. D. 1939. Life processes in gray Norway rats during fourteen years of captivity. *Am. Anat. Memoirs* 17:1–72.

Kirkland, L. E., and E. L. Bradley. 1986. Reproductive inhibiton and serum prolactin concentrations in laboratory populations of the prairie deer-mouse. *Biol. Reprod.* 35:579–86.

Kirkwood, R. N., J. M. Forbes, and P. E. Hughes. 1981. Influence of boars on attainment of puberty in gilts after removal of the olfactory bulbs. *J. Reprod. Fert.* 61:193–96.

Kirtley, D., and R. Maher. 1979. Effect of an isocaloric high fat diet on initia-tion of puberty in Osborne-Mendel rats. *Biol Reprod.* 21:331–38.

Kitchener, D. J. 1973. Reproduction in the common sheath-tailed bat *Tapho-zous georgianus* (Thomas) (Microchiroptera:Emballonuridae) in western Australia. *Austr. J. Zool.* 21:375–89.

Kleiber, M.1975. *The fire of life: An introduction to animal energetics.* Huntington, N.Y.: Krieger.

Kleiman, D. 1980. The sociobiology of captive propagation. In *Conservation biology,* ed. M. E. Soule and B. A. Wilcox, 243–61. Sunderland, Mass.: Sinauer.

Knight, T. W., and P. R. Lynch. 1980. Source of ram pheromones that stimu-late ovulation in the ewe. *Anim. Reprod. Sci.* 3:133–36.

Knight, T. W., H. R. Tervit, and P. R. Lynch. 1984. Effects of boar phero-mones, ram's wool, and presence of bucks on ovarian activity in ano-vular ewes early in the breeding season. *Anim. Reprod. Sci.* 6:129–34.

Knobil, E., and J. D. Neill, ed. 1988. *The physiology of reproduction.* 2 vols. New York: Raven.

Komisaruk, B. R., E. Terasawa, and J. F. Rodriguez-Sierra. 1981. How the brain mediates ovarian responses to environmental stimuli: Neuroana-tomy and neurophysiology. In *Neuroendocrinology of reproduction,* ed. N. T. Adler, 349–76. New York: Plenum.

Koritnik, D. R., W. D. Humphrey, C. C. Kaltenback, and T. Dunn. 1981. Ef-fects of maternal undernutrition on the development of the ovine fetus and the associated changes in growth hormone and prolactin. *Biol. Re-prod.* 24:125–38.

Krebs, C. J., and I. Wingate. 1985. Population fluctuations in the small mam-mals of the Kluane region, Yukon Territory, Canada. *Can. Field Nat.* 99:51–61.

Kreuz, L. E., R. M. Rose, and J. R. Jennings. 1972. Suppression of plasma testosterone levels and psychological stress. *Arch. Gen. Psychiat.* 26:479–82.

Krulich, L., E. Hefco, P. Illner, and C. B. Read. 1974. The effects of acute stress on the secretion of LH, FSH, prolactin, and GH in the normal male rat, with comments on their statistical evaluation. *Neuroendocrinology* 16:293–311.

Krutzsch, P. H. 1979. Male reproductive patterns in nonhibernating bats. *J. Reprod. Fert.* 56:333–44.

Kucera, T. E. 1978. Social behavior and breeding system of the desert mule deer. *J. Mammal.* 59:463–76.

Kulin, H. E., N. Bwibo, D. Mutie, and S. J. Santner. 1984. Gonadotropin excretion during puberty in malnourished children. *J. Pediat.* 105:325–28.

Kuvlesky, W. P., Jr., and L. B. Keith. 1983. Demography of snowshoe hare populations in Wisconsin. *J. Mammal.* 64:233–44.

Lam, Y. L. 1983. Reproduction in the rice field rat *Rattus argentiventer*. *Malay Nat. J.* 36:249–82.

Lamming, G. E. 1966. Nutrition and the endocrine system. *Nutr. Abst. Rev.* 36:1–11.

———, ed. 1984. *Marshall's physiology of reproduction*, fourth edition, vol. 1, *Reproductive cycles of vertebrates*. Edinburgh: Churchill Livingstone.

Lancaster, J. B., and R. B. Lee. 1965. The annual reproductive cycle in monkeys and apes. In *Primate behaviour: Field studies of monkeys and apes*, ed. I. de Vore, 484–513. New York: Holt, Rinehart & Winston.

Lang, U., M. L. Aubert, B. S. Conne, J. C. Bradtke, and P. C. Sizonenko. 1983. Influence of exogenous melatonin on melatonin secretion and the neuroendocrine reproductive axis of intact male rats during sexual maturation. *Endocrinology* 112:1578–84.

Langham, N. 1983. Distribution and ecology of small mammals in three rain forest localities of Peninsula Malaysia with particular references to Keday Peak. *Biotropica* 15:199–206.

Larsson, K., S. G. Carlsson, P. Sourander, B. Forsstrom, S. Hansen, B. Henriksson, and A. Lindquist. 1974. Delayed onset of sexual activity of male rats subjected to pre- and post-natal undernutrition. *Physiol. Behav.* 13:307–11.

Larsson, K., S. Einarsson, K. Lundstrom, and J. Hakkarainen. 1983. Endocrine effects of heat stress in boars. *Acta Vet. Scand.* 24:305–14.

Laws, R. M. 1973. Effects of human activities on reproduction in the wild. *J. Reprod. Fert.* 19, suppl., pp. 523–32.

Laws, R. M., and G. Clough. 1966. Observations on reproduction in the hippopotamus, *Hippopotamus amphibius* L. *Symp. Zool. Soc. Lond.* 15:117–40.

Layne, J. N. 1966. Postnatal development and growth of *Peromyscus floridanus*. *Growth* 30:23–45.

Leamy, L. 1981. The effect of litter size on fertility in *Peromyscus leucopus*. *J. Mammal.* 62:692–97.

Leatham, J. H. 1975. Nutritional influences on testicular composition and function in mammals. In *Handbook of physiology*, sec. 7, *Endocrinology,* vol. 5, *Male reproductive system*, ed. R. O. Greep and E. Astwood, 225–31. Bethesda, Md.: American Physiological Society.

Lecyk, M. 1962. Dependence of breeding in the field vole *Microtus arvalis* on light intensity and wavelength. *Zool. Biol.* 12:255–68.

Lederman, S. A., and P. Rosso. 1980. Effects of food restriction on fetal and placental growth and maternal body composition. *Growth* 44:77–88.

Lee, A. K., and A. Cockburn. 1985. *The evolutionary ecology of marsupials*. Cambridge: Cambridge University Press.

Lee, R. 1970. Latitude and photoperiodism. *Arch. Meteor. Geophys. Bioklimatol.*, ser. B, 18:325–32.

Legan, S. J., and S. S. Winans. 1981. Photo-neuro-endocrine control of seasonal breeding in the ewe. *Gen. Comp. Endocrinol.* 45:317–28.

Lehman, M. N., E. L. Bittman, and S. W. Newman. 1984. Role of the hypothalamic paraventricular nucleus neuroendocrine responses to daylength in the golden hamster *Mesocricetus auratus*. *Brain Res.* 308:25–32.

Le Magnen, J. 1983. Body energy balance and food intake: A neuroendocrine regulatory mechanism. *Physiol. Rev.* 63:314–86.

Lenington, S., and K. Egid. 1985. Female discrimination of male odors correlated with male genotype at the T locus: A response to T-locus or H-2 locus variability? *Behav. Genet.* 15:53–67.

Leon, M., L. Adels, and R. Coopersmith. 1985. Thermal limitation of mother-young contact in Norway rats. *Dev. Psychobiol.* 18:85–105.

Leon, M., and B. Woodside. 1983. Energetic limits on reproduction and maternal food intake. *Physiol. Behav.* 30:945–58.

Leopold, A. S. 1959. *Wildlife of Mexico: The game birds and mammals*. Berkeley: University of California Press.

Lepri, J. J., and J. G. Vandenbergh. 1986. Puberty in pine voles, *Microtus pinetorum*, and the influence of chemosignals on female reproduction. *Biol. Reprod.* 34:370–77.

Lepri, J. J., C. J. Wysocki, and J. G. Vandenbergh. 1985. Mouse vomeronasal organ: Effects on chemosignal production and maternal behavior. *Physiol. Behav.* 35:809–14.

Lett, P. F., R. K. Mohn, and D. F. Gray. 1981. Density dependent processes and management strategy for the Northwest Atlantic harp seal populations. In *Dynamics of large mammal populations*, ed. C. Fowler and T. Smith, 135–58. New York: John Wiley.

Levasseur, M. C. 1977. Thoughts on puberty: Initiation of the gonadotropic function. *Ann. Biol. Anim. Biochem. Biophys.* 17:345–50.

Levasseur, M. C., and C. Thibault. 1980. Reproductive life cycles. In *Reproduction in farm animals*, ed. E. S. E. Hafez, 130–49. Philadelphia: Lea & Febiger.

Leyva, H., L. Addiego, and G. Stabenfeldt. 1984. The effect of different photoperiods on plasma concentrations of melatonin, prolactin and cortisol in the domestic cat. *Endocrinology* 115:1729–36.

Lidicker, W. Z., Jr. 1973. Regulation of numbers in an island population of the California vole: A problem in community dynamics. *Ecol. Monogr.* 43:271–302.

————. 1975. The role of dispersal in the demography of small mammals. In *Small mammals: Their productivity: Population dynamics*, ed. F. B. Golley, K. Petrusewicz, and L. Ryszkowski, 103–28. Cambridge: Cambridge University Press.

Liggins, G. C. 1982. The fetus and birth. In *Reproduction in mammals*, vol. 2, *Embryonic and fetal development*, ed. C. R. Austin and R. V. Short, 114–41. Cambridge: Cambridge University Press.

Liggins, G. C., R. J. Fairclough, and S. A. Grieves. 1973. The mechanism of initiation of parturition in the ewe. *Rec. Prog. Horm. Res.* 29:111.

Lincoln, G. A. 1971. Puberty in a seasonally breeding male, the red deer stag (*Cervus elaphus* L.). *J. Reprod. Fert.* 25:41–54.

————. 1978. Induction of testicular growth and sexual activity in rams by a "skeleton" short day period. *J. Reprod. Fert.* 52:179–81.

————. 1979. Photoperiodic control of seasonal breeding in the ram: Participation of the cranial sympathetic nervous system. *J. Endocrinol.* 82:135–47.

————. 1981. Seasonal aspects of testicular function. In *The testis*, ed. H. Burger and D. de Kretser, 255–305. New York: Raven.

————. 1984. The pineal gland. In *Reproduction in mammals*, vol. 3, *Hormonal control of reproduction*, ed. C. R. Austin and R. V. Short, 52–75. Cambridge: Cambridge University Press.

————. 1988. Endogenous opioids and the control of LH secretion during the reproductive cycle in the ram induced by treatment with melatonin. *Reprod. Nutr. Dév.* 28:527–39.

Lincoln, G. A., F. J. P. Ebling, and O. F. X. Almeida. 1985. Generation of melatonin rhythms. In *Photoperiodism, melatonin and the pineal*, CIBA Foundation Symposium no. 117, pp. 129–48. London: Pittman.

Lincoln, G. A., and P. C. B. MacKinnon. 1976. A study of seasonally delayed puberty in the male hare. *J. Reprod. Fert.* 46:123–28.

Lincoln, G. A., and R. V. Short. 1980. Seasonal breeding: Nature's contraceptive. *Rec. Prog. Horm. Res.* 36:1–52.

Lindeque, M., and J. D. Skinner. 1982. A seasonal breeding in the spotted hyena *Crocuta crocuta* in southern Africa. *Afr. J. Ecol.* 20:271–78.

Lindsay, D. R., J. Pelletier, C. Pisselet, and M. Courot. 1984. Changes in photoperiod and nutrition and their effect on testicular growth of rams. *J. Reprod. Fert.* 71:351–56.

Lindstedt, S. L. 1978. The smallest insectivores: Coping with scarcities of energy and water. In *Comparative physiology: Primitive mammals*, ed. K. Schmidt-Nielson, L. Bolis, and C. R. Taylor, 163–69. Cambridge: Cambridge University Press.

Lindstedt, S. L., and M. S. Boyce. 1985. Seasonality, fasting endurance and body size in mammals. *Am. Nat.* 125:873–78.

Linduska, J. P. 1942. Winter rodent populations in field-shocked corn. *J. Wildl. Mgmt.* 6:353–63.

Lintern-Moore, S., and A. V. Everitt. 1978. The effect of restricted food intake on the size and composition of the ovarian follicle population in the Wistar rat. *Biol. Reprod.* 19:688–91.

Lipner, H. 1988. Mechanisms of mammalian ovulation. In *The physiology of reproduction*, ed. E. Knobil and J. D. Neill, 447–88. New York: Raven.

Lipsett, M. B. 1986. Steroid hormones. In *Reproductive endocrinology*, ed. S. S. C. Yen and R. B. Jaffe, 140–53. Philadelphia: W. B. Saunders.

Liu, C.-C., and J. L. Frehn. 1973. Failure of pineal removal to prevent some cold-induced testicular changes in golden hamsters. *Experientia* 29: 1507–9.

Lloyd, H. G. 1970. Variation and adaptation in reproductive performance. *Symp. Zool. Soc. Lond.* 26:165–88.

Lochmiller, R. L., E. C. Hellgren, L. W. Varner, L. W. Greene, M. S. Amoss, S. W. J. Seager, and W. E. Grant. 1985. Physiological responses of the adult male collared peccary, *Tayassu tajacu* (Tayassuidae) to severe dietary restriction. *Comp Biochem. Physiol.*, ser. A, 82:49–58.

Lombardi, J. R., J. G. Vandenbergh, and J. M. Whitsett. 1976. Androgen control of the sexual maturation pheromone in house mouse urine. *Biol. Reprod.* 15:179–86.

Lombardi, J. R., and J. M. Whitsett. 1980. Effects of urine from conspecifics on sexual maturation in female prairie deermice, *Peromyscus maniculatus bairdii. J. Mammal.* 61:766–68.

Long, C. A. 1973. Reproduction in the white-footed mouse at the northern limits of its geographical range. *Southwestern Nat.* 18:11–20.

Long, C. R. 1980. Cross breeding for beef production: Experimental results. *J. Anim. Sci.* 51:1197–1223.

———. 1981. Effects of breed and heterosis on growth and production characters of cattle. *Tex. Agric. Exp. Stn. Prog. Rept.* 0(3758–3830):90–94.

Lord, R. D., Jr. 1961. Magnitudes of reproduction in cottontail rabbits. *J. Wildl. Mgmt.* 25:28–33.

Loubser, P. G., C. H. Van Niekerk, and L. J. J. Botha. 1983. Seasonal changes in sexual activity and semen quality in the angora ram: 1. Libido and male hormone concentrations. *S. Afr. Tydskr. Veekd.* 13:131–33.

Loudon, A. S. I. 1987. The reproductive energetics of lactation in a seasonal macropodid marsupial: Comparison of marsupial and eutherian herbivores. In *Reproductive energetics in mammals*, ed. A. S. I. Loudon and P. A. Racey, 127–48. Oxford: Clarendon.

Loudon, A. S. I., J. D. Curlewis, and J. English. 1985. The effect of melatonin on the seasonal embryonic diapause of the Bennets wallaby *Macropus rufogriseus rufogriseus. J. Zool.* (Lond.) 206:35–40.

Loudon, A. S. I., A. S. McNeilly, and J. A. Milne. 1983. Nutrition and lactational control of fertility in red deer. *Nature* (Lond.) 302:145–47.

Loudon, A. S. I., and P. A. Racey, eds. 1987. *Reproductive energetics in mammals.* Oxford: Clarendon.

Loveless, C. M. 1959. The Everglades deer herd, life history and management. *Fla. Game Fresh Water Fish Comm. Tech. Bull.* no. 6. Gainesville, Fla.: University Press of Florida.

Lugg, D. J. 1966. Annual cycle of the Weddell seal in the Vestfold hills, Antarctica. *J. Mammal.* 47:317–22.

Lynch, G. R., and S. L. Gendler. 1980. Multiple responses to a short day photoperiod occur in the mouse, *Peromyscus leucopus. Oecologia* 45:318–21.

Lynch, G. R., H. W. Heath, and C. M. Johnston. 1981. Effect of geographical origin on the photoperiodic control of reproduction in the white-footed mouse *Peromyscus leucopus*. *Biol. Reprod.* 25:475–80.

Lynch, G. R., J. K. Sullivan, H. W. Heath, and L. Tamarkin. 1982. Daily melatonin rhythms in photoperiod sensitive and insensitive white-footed mice *Peromyscus leucopus*. In *Progress in clinical and biological research,* ed. R. J. Reiter, vol. 92 of *The pineal and its hormones: Proceedings of an international symposium, 67–74.* New York: Alan R. Liss.

McAllan, B. M., and C. R. Dickman. 1986. The role of photoperiod in the timing of reproduction in the dasyurid marsupial *Antechinus stuartii.* *Oecologia* (Berl.) 68:259–64.

MacArthur, R. H. 1972. *Geographical ecology: Patterns in the distribution of species.* New York: Harper & Row.

McCann, T. S. 1983. Activity budgets of southern elephant seals *Mirounga leonina* during the breeding season. *Z. Tierpsychol.* 61:111–26.

McCartor, M. M., R. D. Randel, and L. H. Carroll. 1979. Dietary alteration of ruminal fermentation on efficiency of growth and onset of puberty in Brangus heifers. *J. Anim. Sci.* 48:488–94.

McClintock, M. K. 1971. Menstrual synchrony and suppression. *Nature* 229:244–45.

———. 1978. Estrous synchrony in the rat and its mediation by airborne chemical communication (*Rattus norvegicus*). *Horm. Behav.* 10:264–76.

———. 1983a. Modulation of the estrous cycle by pheromones from pregnant and lactating rats. *Biol. Reprod.* 28:823–29.

———. 1983b. Pheromonal suppression of the ovarian cycle: Enhancement, suppression and synchrony. In *Phermones and reproduction in mammals,* ed. J. G. Vandenberg, 113–50. New York: Academic Press.

———. 1984. Group mating in the domestic rat as a context for sexual selection: Consequences for the analysis of sexual behavior and neuroendocrine responses. In *Advances in the study of behavior,* ed. J. Rosenblatt, C. Beer, and R. Hinde, 1–15. New York: Academic Press.

McClure, P. A. 1981. Sex-biased litter reduction in food-restricted wood rats (*Neotoma floridana*). *Science* 211:1058–60.

———. 1987. The energetics of reproduction and life histories of cricetine rodents (*Neotoma floridana* and *Sigmodon hispidus*). In *Reproductive energetics in mammals,* ed. A. S. I. Loudon and P. A. Racey, 241–58. Oxford: Clarendon.

McClure, P. A., and J. C. Randolph. 1980. Relative allocation of energy to growth and development of homeothermy in the eastern wood rat *Sigmodon hispidus* and cotton rat *Neotoma floridana. Ecol. Monogr.* 50:199–219.

McClure, T. J. 1962. Infertility in female rodents caused by temporary inanition at or about the time of implantation. *J. Reprod. Fert.* 4:241.

———. 1966. Infertility in mice caused by fasting at about the time of mating. *J. Reprod. Fert.* 12:243–48.

McComb, K. 1987. Roaring by red deer stags advances the date of oestrus in hinids. *Nature* 330:648–49.

McConnell, S. J., and L. A. Hinds. 1985. Effect of pinealectomy on plasma melatonin, prolactin and progesterone concentrations during seasonal reproductive quiescence in the Tamar *Macropus eugenii. J. Reprod. Fert.* 75:433–40.

McEwen, B. S. 1983. Gonadal steriod influence in brain development and sexual differentiation. *Int. Rev. Physiol.* 27:99–146.

McGinnes, B. S., and R. L. Downing. 1977. Factors affecting the peak of white-tailed deer fawning in Virginia. *J. Wildl. Mgmt.* 41:715–19.

McIntosh, T. K., and L. C. Drickamer. 1977. Excreted urine, bladder urine and the delay of sexual maturation in female house mice. *Anim. Behav.* 25:999–1004.

MacKinnon, P. C. B., J. M. Mattock, and M. B. ter Haar. 1976. Serum gonadotropin levels during development in male, female, and androgenized female rats and the effect of general disturbance on high luteinizing hormone levels. *J. Endocrinol.* 70:361–71.

MacKinnon, P. C. B., E. Puig-Duran, and R. Laynes. 1978. Reflections on the attainment of puberty in the rat: Have circadian signals a role to play in its onset? *J. Reprod. Fet.* 52:401–12.

McNab, B. K. 1963. A model of the energy budget of a wild mouse. *Ecology* 44:521–32.

———. 1980. Food habits, energetics and population biology of mammals. *Am. Nat.* 116:106–24.

———. 1984. Physiological convergence amongst ant-eating and termite-eating mammals. *J. Zool.* (Lond.) 203:485–510.

———. 1988. The reproduction of marsupial and eutherian mammals in relation to energy expenditure. In *Reproductive energetics in mammals*, ed. A. S. I. Loudon and P. A. Racey, 29–40. Oxford: Clarendon.

McNatty, K. P., N. L. Hudson, K. M. Henderson, S. Lun, D. A. Heath, M. Gibb, K. Ball, J. M. McDiarmid, and D. C. Thurley. 1984. Changes in gonadotrophin secretion and ovarian antral follicular activity in seasonally breeding sheep throughout the year. *J. Reprod. Fert.* 70:309–21.

McNeilly, A. S., R. M. Sharpe, and H. M. Fraser. 1983. Increased sensitivity to the negative feedback effects of testosterone induced by hyperprolactinemia in the adult male rat. *Endocrinology* 112:22–28.

Macrides, F., A. Bartke, and S. Dalterio. 1975. Strange females increase plasma testosterone levels in male mice. *Science* 189:1104–5.

McWilliam, A. N. 1982. Adaptive responses to seasonality in four species of Microchiroptera in coastal Kenya. Ph.D. diss., University of Aberdeen.

Madan, M. L., and H. D. Johnson. 1973. Environmental heat effects on bovine luteinizing hormone. *J. Dairy Sci.* 56:1420–23.

Magal, E., J. Kaplanski, U. A. Sod-Moriah, N. Hirschmann, and I. Nir. 1981. Role of the pineal gland in male rats chronically exposed to increased temperature. *J. Neur. Transm.* 50:267–73.

Makhmudov, E. S., and E. R. Khaibullina. 1977. Growth and heat resistance of rats subjected to repeated exposure to heat in early ontogeny. *Byul. Eksperim. Biol. Medit.* 83:537–39.

Mallory, F. F., and R. Brooks. 1980. Infanticide and pregnancy failure: Reproductive strategies in the female collared lemming (*Dicrostonyx groenlandicus*). *Biol. Reprod.* 22:192–96.

Mallory, F. F., and F. V. Clulow. 1977. Evidence of pregnancy failure in the wild meadow vole *Microtus pennsylvanicus*. *Can. J. Zool.* 55:1–17.

Mann, T. 1974. Effects of nutrition on male accessory organs. In *Male accessory sex organs*, ed. D. Brandes, 173–81. New York: Academic Press.

Manogue, K. R., A. I. Leshner, and D. K. Candland. 1975. Dominance status and adrenocortical reactivity to stress in squirrel monkeys (*Saimiri sciureus*). *Primates* 16:457–63.

Mansell, W. D. 1974. Productivity of white-tailed deer on the Bruce Peninsula, Ontario. *J. Wildl. Mgmt.* 38:808–14.

Marchlewska-Koj, A. 1983. Pregnancy blocking by pheromones. In *Pheromones and reproduction in mammals*, ed. J. G. Vandenbergh, 151–74. New York: Academic Press.

Marchlewska-Koj, A., and M. Kruczek. 1986. Female-induced delay of puberty in bank vole and European pine voles females. In *Chemical signals in vertebrates*, vol. 4, ed. D. Duvall, D. Muller-Schwarze, and R. M. Silverstein, 551–54. New York: Plenum.

Marois, G. 1982. Ova implantation block in the mouse caused by environmental changes or pheromones: Prevention by prolactin or thio-properazine. *Ann. Endocrinol.* 43:41–52.

Marsden, H. M., and F. H. Bronson. 1964. Estrous synchrony in mice: Alteration by exposure to male urine. *Science* 144:3625.

Marshall, A. J., and O. Wilkinson. 1957. Reproduction of the Orkney vole (*Microtus orcadensis*) under a six hour day-length and other conditions. *Proc. Zool. Soc. Lond.* 126:391–95.

Marsteller, F. A., and C. B. Lynch. 1983. Reproductive consequences of food restriction at low temperature in lines of mice divergently selected for thermoregulatory nesting. *Behav. Genet.* 13:397–410.

Martin, G. B. 1984. Factors affecting the secretion of luteinizing hormone in the ewe. *Biol. Rev.* 59:1–87.

Martin, G. B., Y. Cognie, A. Schirar, A. Nunes-Ribeiro, C. Fabre-Nys, and J.-C. Thiery. 1985. Diurnal variation in the response of anestrous ewes to the ram effect. *J. Reprod. Fert.* 75:275–84.

Martin, G. B., C. M. Oldham, and D. R. Lindsay. 1981. Effect of stress due to laparoscopy on plasma cortisol levels the pre-ovulatory surge of luteinizing hormone and ovulation in the ewe. *Theriogenology* 16:39–44.

Martin, R. D. 1972. A laboratory breeding colony of the lesser mouse lemur. In *Breeding primates*, ed. W. I. B. Beveridge, 161–71. Basel: Karger.

Martinet, L., D. Allain, and M. Meunier. 1983. Regulation in pregnant mink *Mustela vison* of plasma progesterone and prolactin concentrations and regulation of the onset of the spring molt by daylight ratio and melatonin injections. *Can. J. Zool.* 61:1959–63.

Maruniak, J. A., and F. H. Bronson. 1976. Gonadotropic response of male mice to female urine. *Endocrinology* 99:963–69.

Maruniak, J. A., A. Coquelin, and F. H. Bronson. 1978. The release of LH in male mice in response to female urinary odors: Characteristics of the response in young males. *Biol. Reprod.* 18:251–55.

Massaro, T. F., D. A. Levitsky, and R. H. Barnes. 1974. Protein malnutrition in the rat: Its effects on maternal behavior and pup development. *Dev. Psychobiol.* 7:551–61.

Massey, A., and J. G. Vandenbergh. 1980. Puberty delay by a urinary cue from female house mice in feral populations. *Science* 209:821–22.

———. 1981. Puberty acceleration by a urinary cue from male mice *Mus musculus* in feral populations. *Biol. Reprod.* 24:523–27.

Mather, J. G. 1981. Wheel-running activity: A new interpretation. *Mammal. Rev.* 11:41–51.

Matteo, S., and E. F. Rissman. 1984. Increased sexual activity during the midcycle portion of the human menstrual cycle. *Horm. Behav.* 18:249–55.

Matteri, R. L., J. G. Watson, and G. P. Moberg. 1984. Stress or acute ACTH treatment suppresses LHRH-induced luteinizing hormone release in the ram. *J. Reprod. Fert.* 72:385–94.

Mattingly, D. K., and P. A. McClure. 1982. Energetics of reproduction in large-littered cotton rats. *Ecology* 63:183–95.

Mauget, R., D. Maurel, and A. Sempere. 1986. Seasonal aspects of endocrine control of space-time utilization in wild mammals. In *Endocrine regulations as adaptive mechanisms to the environment*, ed. I. Assenmacher and J. Boissin, 497–507. Paris: Centre National de la Recherche Scientifique.

Maurel, D., A. Lacroix, and J. Boissin. 1984. Seasonal reproduction endocrine profiles in 2 wild mammals: The red fox *Vulpes vulpes* and the European badger *Meles meles* considered as short day mammals. *Acta Endocrinol.* 105:130–38.

Maurel, D., A. M. Laurent, and J. Boissin. 1981. Short-term variations of plasma testosterone concentrations in the European badger (*Meles meles*). *J. Reprod. Fert.* 61:53–58.

Mautz, W. W. 1978. Sledding on a bushy hillside: The fat cycle in deer. *Wildl. Soc. Bull.* 6:88–90.

May, R. M., and D. I. Rubenstein. 1984. Reproductive strategies. In *Reproduction in Mammals*, vol. 4, *Reproductive fitness*, ed. C. R. Austin and R. V. Short, 1–23. Cambridge: Cambridge University Press.

Mead, R. A. 1968a. Reproduction in eastern forms of the spotted skunk (genus *Spilogale*). *J. Zool.* (Lond.) 156:119–36.

———. 1968b. Reproduction in western forms of the spotted skunk (genus *Spilogale*). *J. Mammal.* 49:373–89.

———. 1971. Effects of light and blinding upon delayed implantation in the spotted skunk. *Biol. Reprod.* 5:214–20.

Meisel, R., and I. Ward. 1981. Fetal female rats are masculinized by male littermates located caudally in the uterus. *Science* 213:239–42.

Mena, F., D. Aguayo, G. Martinez-Escalera, and C. E. Grosvenor. 1981. Effect of short-term food deprivation and prolactin on milk yield in the lactating rabbit. *Physiol. Behav.* 27:529–32.

Menaker, M. 1985. Eyes—the second (and third) pineal glands? In *Photoperiodism, melatonin and the pineal*, CIBA Foundation Symposium no. 117, 78–92. London: Pittman.

Menendez-Patterson, A., S. Fernandez, J. Florez-Lozano, and B. Marin. 1982. Effect of early pre-natal and post-natal acquired malnutrition on development and sexual behavior in the rat. *Pharmacol, Biochem. Behav.* 17:659–64.

Meredith, M. 1983. Sensory physiology of pheromone communication. In *Pheromones and reproduction in mammals,* ed. J. G. Vandenbergh, 200– 252. New York: Academic Press.

Meredith, S., D. Kirkpatrick-Keller, and R. L. Butcher. 1986. The effects of food restriction and hypophysectomy on numbers of primordial follicles and concentrations of hormones in rats. *Biol. Reprod.* 35:68–73.

Merritt, J. F., and J. M. Merritt. 1980. Population ecology of the deer mouse *Peromyscus maniculatus* on the front range of Colorado, USA. *Ann. Carn. Mus.* 49:113–30.

Merry, B. J., and A. M. Holehan. 1981. Serum profiles of LH, FSH, testosterone and 5α-DHT from 21 to 1000 days of age in *ad libitum* fed and dietary restricted rats. *Exp. Geront.* 16:431–44.

Merson, M. H., and R. L. Kirkpatrick. 1981. Relative sensitivity of reproductive activity and body-fat level to food restriction in white-footed mice. *Am. Midl. Nat.* 106:305–12.

———. 1983. Role of energy intake in the maintanence of reproduction in female white-footed mice *Peromyscus leucopus. Am. Midl. Nat.* 109:206– 8.

Merson, M. H., R. L. Kirkpatrick, P. F. Scanlon, and F. C. Gwazdauskas. 1983. Influence of restricted food intake on reproductive characteristics and carcass fat of male white-footed mice *Peromyscus leucopus. J. Mammal.* 64:353–55.

Mess, B., and C. Ruzsas. 1986. Relationship between suprachiasmatic nuclei and rhythmic activity of the pineal gland. In *Advances in pineal research,* vol. 1, ed. R. J. Reiter and M. Karasek, 149–58. London: John Libbey.

Mess, B., C. Ruzsas, and G. P. Trentini. 1984. Pineal mechanisms regulating reproduction in seasonal and nonseasonal breeders: A comparative survey. *Neuroendocrinol. Lett.* 6:253–59.

Metcalfe, J., M. K. Stock, and D. H. Barron. 1988. Maternal physiology during gestation. In *The physiology of reproduction,* ed. E. Knobil and J. D. Neill, 2145–76. New York: Raven.

Meunier, M., and L. Martinet. 1986. Role of different photoperiodic treatments on the growth of the testis in juvenile and adult brown hares (*Lepus europaeus* Pallas). In *Endocrine regulations as adaptive mechanisms to the environment,* ed. I. Assenmacher and J. Boissin, 155–60. Paris: Centre National de la Recherche Scientifique.

Meyer, S., and R. L. Goodman. 1985. Neurotransmitters involved in mediating the steroid-dependent suppression of pulsatile luteinizing hormone secretion in anestrous ewes: Effects of receptor antagonists. *Endocrinology* 116:2054–61.

———. 1986. Separate neural systems mediate the steroid-dependent and steroid-independent suppression of tonic luteinizing hormone secretion in the anestrous ewe. *Biol. Reprod.* 35:562–71.

Migula, P. 1969. Bioenergetics of pregnancy and lactation in European common voles. *Acta Theriol.* 13:167–79.

Mihok, S., B. N. Turner, and S. L. Iverson. 1985. The characterization of vole *Microtus pennsylvanicus* population dynamics. *Ecol. Monogr.* 55:399–420.

Millar, J. S. 1975. Tactics of energy partitioning in breeding *Peromyscus. Can. J. Zool.* 53:967–76.

———. 1977. Adaptive features of mammalian reproduction. *Evolution* 31:370–86.

———. 1979. Energetics of lactation in *Peromyscus maniculatus. Can. J. Zool.* 57:1015–19.

———. 1984. Reproduction and survival of *Peromyscus* in seasonal environments. *Spec. Publ. Carn. Mus. Nat. Hist.* 10:253–66.

———. 1988. Energy reserves in breeding small rodents. In *Reproductive energetics in mammals,* ed. A. S. I. Loudon and P. A. Racey, 231–40. Oxford: Clarendon.

Millar, J. S., and L. W. Gyug. 1981. Initiation of breeding by northern *Peromyscus* in relation to temperature. *Can. J. Zool.* 59:1094–98.

Millar, J. S., and D. G. L. Innes. 1983. Demographic and life cycle characteristics of montane deer mice *Peromyscus maniculatus borealis. Can. J. Zool.* 61:574–85.

———. 1985. Breeding by *Peromyscus maniculatus* over an elevation gradient. *Can. J. Zool.* 63:124–29.

Millar, J. S., F. B. Wille, and S. L. Iverson. 1979. Breeding by *Peromyscus* in seasonal environments. *Can. J. Zool.* 54:719–27.

Milligan, S. R. 1974. Social environment and ovulation in the vole, *Microtus agrestis. J. Reprod. Fert.* 41:35–47.

———. 1976. Pregnancy blocking in the vole (*Microtus agrestis*): Effect of social environment. *J. Reprod. Fert.* 46:91–95.

———. 1979. Pregnancy blockage and the memory of the stud male in the vole (*Microtus agrestis*). *J. Reprod. Fert.* 57:223–25.

———. 1980. Pheromones and rodent reproductive physiology. *Symp. Zool. Soc. Lond.* 45:251–76.

Minton, J. E., R. P. Wetteman, D. C. Meyerhoeffer, R. L. Hintz, and E. J. Turman. 1981. Serum luteinizing hormone and testosterone in bulls during exposure to elevated ambient temperature. *J. Anim. Sci.* 53:1551–58.

Moen, A. N., and S. Scholtz. 1981. Nomographic estimation of forage intake by white-tailed deer. *J. Range Mgmt.* 34:74–76.

Moline, M. L., H. E. Albers, R. B. Todd, and M. C. Moore-Ede. 1981. Light dark entrainment of proestrous luteinizing hormone surges and circadian locomotor activity in female hamsters. *Horm. Behav.* 15:451–58.

Mondain-Monval, M., M. C. Audy, E. Lamy, P. Simon, R. Schooler, and M. Bonnin. 1986. Seasonal changes in gonadotropic and gonadal functions in red fox females (*Vulpes vulpes*). In *Endocrine regulations as adaptive mechanisms to the environment,* ed. I. Assenmacher and J. Boissin, 57–62. Paris: Centre National de la Recherche Scientifique.

Montgomery, G. W., G. B. Martin, and J. Pelletier. 1985. Changes in pulsatile luteinizing hormone secretion after ovariectomy in Ile-de-France ewes in two seasons. *J. Reprod. Fert.* 73:173–84.

Moos, A. B., D. F. Treagust, and G. E. Folk, Jr. 1979. Photoperiodic changes in the testes of the gerbil, *Meriones unguiculatus. Acta Theriol.* 24:424–27.

Morin, L. P. 1986a. A concept of physiological time: Rhythms in behavior and reproductive physiology. *Ann. N.Y. Acad. Sci.* 474:331–51.

————. 1986b. Environment and hamster reproduction: Responses to phase-specific starvation during estrous cycle. *Am.J. Physiol.* 251:R663–R669.

Morris, J. G. and S. C. Kendeigh. 1981. Energetics of the prairie deer mouse *Peromyscus maniculatus bairdii. Am. Midl. Nat.* 105:368–76.

Morrison, S. R. 1983. Ruminant heat stress: Effect on production and means of alleviation. *J. Anim. Sci.* 57:1594–1600.

Morriss, F. H., Jr., and R. D. H. Boyd. 1988. Placental transport. In *The physiolog of reproduction,* ed. E. Knobil and J. D. Neill, 2043–84. New York: Raven.

Morton, J. R. C., V. H. Denenberg, and M. X. Zarrow. 1963. Modification of sexual development through stimulation in infancy. *Endocrinology* 72:439–42.

Mossman, H. W., and I. Judas. 1949. Accessory corpora lutea, lutein cell origin and the ovarian cycle in the Canadian porcupine. *Am. J. Anat.* 85:1–39.

Mount, L. E. 1979. *Adaptation to thermal environment: Man and his productive animals.* Baltimore: University Park Press.

Mrosovsky, N. 1978. Circannual cycles in hibernators. In *Strategies in cold: Natural torpidity and thermogenesis,* ed. L. Wang and J. W. Hudson, 21–66. New York: Academic Press.

Mueller, C. C., and R. M. F. S. Sadleir. 1979. Age at first conception of black-tailed deer. *Biol. Reprod.* 21:1099–1104.

Mundinger, J. G. 1981. White-tailed deer reproductive biology in the Swan Valley, Montana. *J. Wildl. Mgmt.* 45:132–39.

Murie, J. O., and G. R. Michener, eds. 1984. *The biology of ground-dwelling squirrels.* Lincoln: University of Nebraska Press.

Murua, R., L. A. Gonzalez, and P. L. Meserve. 1986. Population ecology of *Oryzomys longicaudatus philippi,* Rodentia, Cricetidae, in southern Chile. *J. Anim. Ecol.* 55:281–94.

Mutere, F. A. 1968. The breeding biology of equatorial vertebrates: Reproduction in the fruit bat, *Eidolon helvum,* at latitude 0°20'. *J. Zool.* (Lond.) 153:153–61.

Muul, I. 1969. Photoperiod and reproduction in flying squirrels *Glaucomys volans. J. Mammal.* 50:542–49.

Myers K. 1970. The rabbit in Australia. *Proc. Adv. Stud. Inst. Dynamics Numbers Pop.* (Oosterbeek), 478–506.

Myers K., and W. E. Poole. 1962. A study of the biology of the wild rabbit, *Oryctolagus cuniculus* (L) in confined populations: 3. Reproduction. *Austr. J. Zool.* 10:225–67.

Mykytowycz, R. 1979. Some difficulties in the study of the function and composition of semiochemicals in mammals, particularly wild rabbits, *Oryctolagus cuniculus.* In *Chemical ecology: Odour communication in animals,* ed. F. J. Ritter, 105–15. Amsterdam: Elsevier, North Holland.

Mykytowycz, R., and P. J. Fullagar. 1973. Effect of social environment on reproduction in the rabbit *Oryctolagus cuniculus. J. Reprod. Fert.* 19, suppl. pp. 503–22.

Myrcha, A., L. Ryszkowski, and W. Walkowa. 1969. Bioenergetics of pregnancy and lactation in the white mouse. *Acta Theriol.* 14:161–66.

Nadel, E. R. 1983. Factors affecting the regulation of body temperature during exercise. *J. Therm. Biol.* 8:165–69.

Nakashima, A., K. Koshiyama, T. Uozumi, Y. Monden, Y. Hamanaka, K. Kurachi, T. Aono, S. Mizutani, and K. Matsumoto. 1975. Effects of general anesthesia and severity of surgical stress on serum LH and testosterone in males. *Acta Endocrinol.* 78:258–69.

Nazarenko, Y. I. 1975. Sexual maturation, reproductive rate, and missed pregnancy, in female harp seals. *Rapp. P.-V. Reun. Cons. Int. Explor. Mer.* 169:413–15.

Nazian, S. J., and B. E. Piacsek. 1977. Maturation of the reproductive system in male rats raised at low ambient temperature. *Biol. Reprod.* 17:668–75.

Nduka, E. U., O. A. Dada, and D. T. Okpako. 1983. The effect of malnutrition on some aspects of gonadal development and function in rats. *Nutr. Rept. Int.* 28:31–38.

Neal, B. R. 1982. Reproductive ecology of the rufous elephant shrew, *Elephantus rufescens* (Macroscelididae), in Kenya. *Z. Saug.* 47:65–71.

———. 1984. Relationship between feeding habits, climate and reproduction of small mammals in Meru National Park, Kenya. *Afr. J. Ecol.* 22:195–206.

Negus, N. C., and P. J. Berger. 1972. Environmental factors and reproductive processes in mammalian populations. In *Biology of reproduction: Basic and clinical studies,* ed. J. T. Velardo and B. A. Kasprow, Third Pan American Congress on Anatomy, 89–98. New Orleans: Pan American Association of Anatomy.

———. 1977. Experimental triggering of reproduction in a natural population of *Microtus montanus. Science* 196:1230–31.

———. 1987. Mammalian reproductive physiology. In *Current mammalogy,* ed. H. H. Genoways, 149–73. New York. Plenum.

Negus, N. C., P. J. Berger, and B. W. Brown. 1986. Microtine population dynamics in a predictable environment. *Can. J. Zool.* 64:785–92.

Negus, N. C., P. J. Berger, and L. G. Forslund. 1977. Reproductive strategy of *Microtus montanus. J. Mammal.* 58:347–53.

Neill, J. D. 1988. Prolactin secretion and its control. In *The physiology of reproduction,* ed. E. Knobil and J. D. Neill, 1379–90. New York: Raven.

Nelson, R. J. 1985. Photoperiodic regulation of reproductive development in male prairie voles: Influence of laboratory breeding. *Biol. Reprod.* 33:418–22.

Nelson, R. J., M. K. Bamat, and I. Zucker. 1982. Photoperiodic regulation of testis function in rats: Mediation by a circadian mechanism. *Biol. Reprod.* 26:329–35.

Nelson, R. J., J. Dark, and I. Zucker. 1983. Influence of photoperiod, nutrition and water availability on reproduction of male California voles (*Microtus californicus*). *J. Reprod. Fert.* 69:473–77.

Nelson, R. J., and I. Zucker. 1981. Photoperiodic control of reproduction in olfactory-bulbectomized rats. *Neuroendocrinology* 32:266–71.

Nequin, L. G., J. A. Alvarez, and C. S. Campbell. 1975. Alteration in steroid and gonadotropin release resulting from surgical stress during the morning of proestrus in 5-day cyclic rats. *Endocrinology* 97:718–24.

Nett, T. M., and G. D. Niswender. 1982. Influence of exogenous melatonin on seasonality of reproduction in sheep. *Theriogenology* 17:645–54.

Neville, W. E., Jr., and M. W. Neathery. 1974. Effect of temperature under field conditions on the reproductive performance of ewes. *J. Reprod. Fert.* 36:423–26.

Newsome, A. E. 1966. The influence of food on breeding in the red kangaroo in central Australia. *CSIRO Wildl. Res.* 11:187–96.

———. 1970. An experimental attempt to produce a mouse plague. *J. Anim. Ecol.* 39:299–311.

———. 1973. Cellular degeneration in the testis of red kangaroos during hot weather and drought in central Australia. *J. Reprod. Fert.* 19, suppl., pp. 191–201.

———. 1975. An ecological comparison of the two arid zone kangaroos of Australia, and their anomalous prosperity since the introduction of ruminant stock to their environment. *Q. Rev. Biol.* 50:389–424.

Newsome, A. E., R. C. Stendell, and J. H. Myers. 1976. Free-watering a wild population of house mice: A test of an Australian hypothesis in California. *J. Mammal.* 57:677–86.

Newson, R. 1963. Differences in numbers, reproduction and survival between two neighboring populations of bank voles (*Clethrionomys glareolus*). *Ecology* 44:110–20.

Nicholls, T. J., B. K. Follett, A. R. Goldsmith, and H. Pearson. 1988. Possible homologies between photorefractoriness in sheep and birds: The effect of thyroidectomy on the length of the ewe's breeding season. *Reprod. Nutr. Dev.* 28:375–86.

Nicoll, M. E. 1985. Responses to Seychelles tropical forest seasons by a litter-foraging mammalian insectivore, *Tenrec ecaudatus*, native to Madagascar. *J. Anim. Ecol.* 54:71–88.

Nicoll, M. E., and S. D. Thompson, 1987. Basal metabolic rates and energetics of reproduction in therian mammals: Marsupials and placentals compared. In *Reproductive energetics in mammals*, ed. A. S. I. Loudon and P. A. Racey, 7–28. Oxford: Clarendon.

Nishimura, K., K. Utsumi, and M. Yuhara. 1983. Isolation of puberty accelerating pheromone from male mouse urine. *Jap. J. Anim. Reprod.* 29:24–31.

Niswender, G. D., and T. M. Nett. 1988. The corpus luteum and its control. In *The physiology of reproduction*, ed. E. Knobil and J. D. Neill, 489–526. New York: Raven.

Nixon, C. M. 1971. Productivity of white-tailed deer in Ohio. *Ohio J. Sci.* 71:217–25.

Nje, J. N. 1983. Structure et dynamique de la population de girafes du parc national de Waza, Cameroun. *Rev. Ecol. (Terre et Vie)* 37:3–20.

Norman, R. L. 1983. *Neuroendocrine aspects of reproduction.* New York: Academic Press.

Norman, R. L., and H. G. Spies. 1981. Brain lesions in infant female rhesus monkeys: Effects on menarche and first ovulation and on diurnal rhythms of prolactin and cortisol. *Endocrinology* 108:1723–29.

Norris, M. L., and C. E. Adams. 1979. Exteroceptive factors and pregnancy block in the Mongolian gerbil, *Meriones unguiculatus. J. Reprod. Fert.* 57:401–4.

Numan, M. 1988. Maternal behavior. In *The physiology of reproduction,* ed. E. Knobil and J. D. Neill, 1569–1646. New York: Raven.

Nunez, A. A., M. H. Brown, and T. G. Youngstrom. 1985. Hypothalamic circuits involved in the regulation of seasonal and circadian rhythms in male golden hamsters *Mesocricetus auratus. Brain Res. Bull.* 15:149–54.

O'Connell, M. A. 1979. Ecology of didelphid marsupials from northern Venezuela. In *Vertebrate ecology in the northern neotropics,* ed. J. F. Eisenberg, 73–87. Washington, D.C.: Smithsonian Institution Press.

———. 1981. Population ecology of small mammals from northern Venezuela. Ph.D. diss., Texas Tech University.

———. 1982. Population ecology of North and South American grassland rodents: A comparative review. In *Mammalian biology in South America,* ed. M. A. Mares and H. H. Genoways, 167–85. Pittsburgh: University of Pittsburgh Press.

O'Farrell, T. P. 1965. Home range and ecology of snowshoe hares in interior Alaska. *J. Mammal.* 46:406–18.

Oftedal, O. T. 1984. Milk composition, milk yield and energy output at peak lactation: A comparative review. In *Physiological strategies of lactation,* ed. M. Peaker, R. G. Vernon, and C. H. Knight, Symposia of the Zoological Society of London, no. 51, pp. 33–86. London: Academic Press.

Ohno, S. 1976. The development of sexual reproduction. In *The evolution of reproduction,* ed. C. R. Austin and R. V. Short, 1–31. Cambridge: Cambridge University Press.

Ohsumi, S. 1964. Comparison of maturity and accumulation rate of corpora albicantia between the left and right ovaries in Cetacea. *Sci. Rept. of Whale Res. Insti.* 18:123–49.

Ojeda, C., M. Magaly, and L. B. Keith. 1982. Sex and age composition and breeding biology of cottontail rabbit populations in Venezuela. *Biotropics* 14:99–107.

Ojeda, S. R., L. I. Aguado, and S. Smith. 1983. Neuroendocrine mechanisms controlling the onset of female puberty: The rat as a model. *Neuroendocrinology* 37:306–13.

Ojeda, S. R., W. W. Andrews, J. P. Advis, and S. Smith White. 1980. Recent advances in the endocrinology of puberty. *Endocrinol. Rev.* 1:228–57.

Ojeda, S. R., S. Smith White, J. P. Advis, and W. W. Andrews. 1981. Current studies on the mechanisms underlying the onset of female puberty. In *Physiopathology of endocrine diseases and mechanisms of hormone action,* 199–218. New York: Alan R. Liss.

Ojeda, S. R., and H. F. Urbanski. 1988. Puberty in the rat. In *The physiology of reproduction*, ed. E. Knobil and J. D. Neill, 1699–1738. New York: Raven.

Ortavant, R., A. Daveau, D. H. Garnier, J. Pelletier, M. M. de Reviers, and M. Terqui. 1982. Diurnal variation in release of LH and testosterone in the ram. *J. Reprod. Fert.* 64:347–53.

O'Shea, T. J., and T. A. Vaughn. 1980. Ecological observations on an east African bat community. *Mammalia* 44:485–96.

Ostwald, R., K. Wilken, J. Simons, H. Highstone, S. Cimino, and S. Shimondle. 1972. Influence of photoperiod and partial contact on estrus in the desert pocket mouse *Perognathus pencillatus. Biol. Reprod.* 7:1–8.

Oxberry, B. A. 1979. Female reproductive patterns in hibernating bats. *J. Reprod. Fert.* 56:359–67.

Oyedipe, E. O., D. I. K. Osori, O. Akerejola, and D. Saror. 1982. Effect of level of nutrition on onset of puberty and conception rates of Zebu heifers. *Theriogenology* 17:525–40.

Padge, R. B. 1988. The anatomy of the hypothalamo-hypophyseal complex. In *The physiology of reproduction*, ed. E. Knobil and J. D. Neill, 1161–1234. New York: Raven.

Padmanabhan, V., C. Keech, and E. M. Convey. 1983. Cortisol inhibits and ACTH has no effect on LHRH-induced release of LH from bovine pituitary cells in vitro. *Endocrinology* 112:1782–87.

Pandey, S. D., and S. C. Pandey. 1985. Regulation of estrus-suppressing pheromone in wild mice by ovarian hormones. *Ind. J. Exp. Biol.* 23:188–90.

Panke, E. S., R. J. Reiter, M. D. Rollag, and T. W. Panke. 1978. Pineal serotonin N-acetyltransferase activity and melatonin concentrations in prepubertal and adult Syrian hamsters exposed to short daily photoperiods. *Endocrine Res. Comm.* 5:311–24.

Paris, A., P. Kelly, and J. A. Ramaley. 1973. Effects of short-term stress upon fertility: 2. After puberty. *Fert. Steril.* 24:546–52.

Paris, A. L., and J. A. Ramaley. 1973. Effects of short-term stress upon fertility: 1. Before puberty. *Fert. Steril.* 24:540–45.

Parker, G. R. 1977. Morphology, reproduction, diet and behavior of the arctic hare (*Lepus arcticus*) on Axel Heiberg Island, Northwest Territories. *Can. Field Nat.* 91:8–18.

Parsons, S. D., and G. L. Hunter. 1967. Effect of the ram on duration of oestrus in the ewe. *J. Reprod. Fert.* 14:61–70.

Pau, K-Y. F., D. E. Kuehl, and G. L. Jackson. 1982. Effect of frontal hypothalamic deafferation on luteinizing hormone secretion and seasonal breeding in the ewe. *Biol. Reprod.* 27:999–1010.

Pau, M-Y., and J. A. Milner. 1984. Dietary arginine deprivation and delayed puberty in the female rat. *J. Nutr.* 114:112–18.

Payman, B. C., and H. H. Swanson. 1980. Social influence on sexual maturation and breeding in the female Mongolian gerbil (*Meriones unguiculatus*). *Anim. Behav.* 28:528–35.

Peaker, M., R. G. Vernon, and C. H. Knight, eds. 1984. *Physiological strategies of lactation*. Symposia of the Zoological Society of London, no. 51. London: Academic Press.

Pearson, O. P. 1944. Reproduction in the shrew (*Blarina brevicauda* Say). *Am. J. Anat.* 75:39–93.

——. 1949. Reproduction of a South American rodent, the mountain vicacha. *Am. J. Anat.* 84:143–74.

Pelikan, J. 1981. Patterns of reproduction in the house mouse. In *Biology of the house mouse*, ed. R. J. Berry, Symposia of the Zoological Society of London, no. 47, pp. 205–29. London: Academic Press.

Pelletier, J., J. P. Ravault, J. Thomonier, P. Volland-Nail, and R. Ortavant. 1986. Annual cycle of gonadotropic activity and photostimulation in the ram. In *Endocrine regulations as adaptive mechanisms to the environment*, ed. I. Assenmacher and J. Boissin, 237–52. Paris: Centre National de la Recherche Scientifique.

Pengelley, E. T., and S. J. Asmundson. 1974. Circannual rhythmicity in hibernating mammals. In *Circannual clocks*, ed. E. T. Pengelley, 95–160. New York: Academic Press.

Pengelley, E. T., and K. C. Fisher. 1963. The effect of temperature and photoperiod on the yearly hibernating behavior of the captive golden-mantled ground squirrels (*Citellus lateralis tescorum*). *Can. J. Zool.* 41:1103–20.

Pennycuik, P. R. 1967. A comparison of the effects of a range of high environmental temperatures and of two different periods of acclimatization on the reproductive performance of male and female mice. *Austr. J. Exp. Biol. Med. Sci.* 45:527–32.

——. 1969. Reproductive performance and body weights of mice maintained for twelve generations at 34°C. *Austr. J. Biol. Sci.* 22:667–75.

——. 1971. Effect of acclimatization at 33°C on the oxygen uptake, growth rate, and reproductive productivity of hairless and naked mice. *Austr. J. Biol Sci.* 24:301–10.

——. 1972. Seasonal changes in reproductive productivity, growth rate, and food intake in mice exposed to different regimes of day length and environmental temperature. *Austr. J. Biol. Sci.* 25:627–35.

Pennycuik, P. R., P. G. Johnston, N. H. Westwood, and A. H. Reisner. 1986. Variation in numbers in a house mouse population housed in a large outdoor enclosure: Seasonal fluctuations. *J. Anim. Ecol.* 55:371–91.

Perret, M. 1986. Social influences on estrous cycle length and plasma progesterone concentrations in the female lesser mouse lemur *Microcebus murinus. J. Reprod. Fert.* 77:303–11.

Perret, M., and J. Predine. 1984. Effects of long-term grouping on serum cortisol levels in *Microcebus murinus. Horm. Behav.* 18:346–58.

Perrigo, G. 1987. Breeding and feeding strategies in deer mice and house mice when females are challenged to work for their food. *Anim. Behav.* 35:1298–1316.

Perrigo, G., and F. H. Bronson. 1983. Foraging effort, food intake, fat deposition and puberty in female mice. *Biol. Reprod.* 29:455–63.

——. 1985. Sex differences in the energy allocation strategies of house mice. *Behav. Ecol. Sociobiol.* 17:297–302.

——. 1985. Behavioral and physiological responses of female house mice to foraging variation. *Physiol. Behav.* 34:437–40.

Perry, J. S. 1960. The incidence of embryonic mortality as a characteristic of the individual sow. *J. Reprod. Fert.* 1:71–83.

Peterson, R. O., J. D. Woolington, and T. N. Bailey. 1984. Wolves *Canis lupus* of the Kenai Peninsula, Alaska, USA. *Wildl. Monogr.* 88:1–52.

Petitclerc, D., R. R. Peters, L. T. Chapin, W. D. Oxender, K. R. Refsal, R. K. Braun, and H. A. Tucker. 1983. Effect of blinding and pinealectomy on photoperiod and seasonal variations in secretion of prolactin in cattle. *Proc. Soc. Exp. Biol. Med.* 174:205–11.

Petter-Rousseaux, A. 1970. Observations sur l'influence de la photoperiode sur l'activité sexuelle chez *Microcebus murinus* en captivité. *Ann. Biol. Anim. Biochem. Biophys.* 10:203–8.

———. 1972. Application d'un système semestriel de variation de la photo-periode chez *Microcebus murinus* (Miller, 1777). *Ann. Biol. Anim. Biochem. Biophys.* 12:367–75.

Pevet, P. 1988. The role of the pineal gland in the photoperiodic control of reproduction in different hamster species. *Reprod. Nutr. Dév.* 28:443–58.

Pfaff, D. W. 1980. *Estrogens and brain function.* New York: Springer.

———. 1982. Neurobiological mechanisms of sexual motivation. In *The physiological mechanisms of motivation,* ed. D. W. Pfaff, 287–318. New York: Springer.

Pfaff, D. W., and S. Schwartz-Giblin. 1988. Cellular mechanisms of female reproductive behaviors. In *The physiology of reproduction,* ed. E. Knobil and J. D. Neill, 1393–1486. New York: Raven.

Philipp, E., and K.-M. Pirke. 1987. Effect of starvation on hypothalamic tyrosine hydroxylase activity in adult male rats. *Brain Res.* 413:53–59.

Phillips, D., E. A. Dunstan, S. K. Waler, and A. W. Singh. 1984. A definition of the breeding season of poll Dorset ewes. *Theriogenology* 21:561–68.

Piacsek, B. E. 1984. Reduced caloric intake alters the feedback response to testosterone in prepubertal male rats. *Biol. Reprod.* 30:163–68.

———. 1985. Altered negative feedback response due to ovariectomy and estrogen in prepubertal restricted-diet rats. *Biol. Reprod.* 32:1062–68.

———. 1987. Effects of nutrition on reproductive endocrine function. In *Handbook of endocrinology,* ed. G. H. Gass and H. M. Kaplan, 143–51. Boca Raton, Fla.: CRC.

Piacsek, B. E., and J. Meites. 1967. Reinitiation of gonadotropin release in underfed rats by constant light or epinephrine. *Endocrinology* 81:535–41.

Piacsek, B. E., and S. J. Nazian. 1981. Thermal influences on sexual maturation in the rat. In *Environmental factors in mammal reproduction,* ed. D. Gilmore and B. Cook, 215–31. London: Macmillan.

Pianka, E. 1976. Natural selection of optimal reproductive strategies. *Am. Zool.* 16:775–87.

Pieper, D. R., Y.-K. Tang, T. P. Lipski, M. G. Subramanian, and S. W. Newman. 1984. Olfactory bulbectomy prevents the gonadal regression associated with short photoperiod in male golden hamsters. *Brain Res.* 321:183–86.

Pinter, A. J., and N. C. Negus. 1965. Effects of nutrition and photoperiod on reproductive physiology of *Microtus montanus*. *Am. J. Physiol.* 208:633–38.

Pirke, K. M., and B. Spyra. 1981. Influence of starvation on testosterone-luteinizing hormone feedback in the rat. *Acta Endocrinol.* 96:413.

Pitman, J. M., III, and E. L. Bradley. 1984. Hypothyroidism in reproductively inhibited prairie deermice (*Peromyscus maniculatus bairdii*) from laboratory populations. *Biol. Reprod.* 31:895–904.

Pittendrigh, C. S. 1981. Circadian organization and the photoperiodic phenomena. In *Biological clocks in seasonal cycles*, ed. B. K. Follett and D. E. Follett, 1–36. Bristol: Scientechnica.

Plant, T. M. 1988. Puberty in primates. In *The physiology of reproduction*, ed. E. Knobil and J. D. Neill, 1763–88. New York: Raven.

Plas-Roser, S., and C. Aron. 1981. Stress related effects in the control of sexual receptivity and in the secretion of progesterone by the adrenals in cyclic female rats. *Physiol. Behav.* 27:261–64.

Platt, B. S., and R. J. C. Stewart. 1971. Reversible and irreversible effects of protein-calorie deficiency on the central nervous system of animals and man. *World Rev. Nutr. Diet* 13:43–85.

Pohl, C. R., and J. Hotchkiss. 1983. Neural control of reproduction function in primates. *Int. Rev. Physiol.* 27:147–76.

Politch, J. A., and L. R. Herrenkohl. 1984. Effects of pre-natal stress on reproduction in male and female mice. *Physiol. Behav.* 32(1): 95–99.

Pond, C. M. 1978. Morphological aspects and the ecological and mechanical consequences of fat deposition in wild vertebrates. *Ann. Rev. Ecol. Syst.* 9:519–70.

———. 1981. Storage. In *Physiological Ecology*, ed. C. R. Townsend and P. Calow, 190–219. Sunderland, Mass.: Sinauer.

Poole, W. E. 1960. Breeding of the wild rabbit *Oryctolagus cuniculus* (L.) in relation to the environment. *CSIRO Wildl. Res.* 5:21–43.

———. 1983. Breeding in the grey kangaroo *Macropus giganteus* from widespread locations in eastern Australia. *Austr. Wildl. Res.* 10(3): 453–66.

Pope, N. S., T. P. Gordon, and M. E. Wilson. 1986. Age, social rank and lactational status influence ovulatory patterns in seasonally breeding rhesus monkeys. *Biol. Reprod.* 35:353–59.

Porter, W. P., and P. A. McClure. 1984. Climate effects on growth and reproductive potential in *Sigmodon hispidus* and *Peromyscus maniculatus*. *Spec. Publ. Carn. Mus. Nat. Hist.* 10:173–81.

Poulet, A. R., G. Courturier, B. Hubert, and F. Adam. 1981. Consequences of supplementary feeding on the population dynamics of rodents in Senegal. *Rev. Ecol. (Terre et Vie)* 35:195–215.

Powell, R. A., and R. D. Leonard. 1983. Sexual dimorphism and energy expenditure for reproduction in female fisher *Martes pennanti*. *Oikos* 40:166–74.

Powers, R. A., and B. Verts. 1971. Reproduction in the mountain cottontail rabbit in Oregon. *J. Wildl. Mgmt.* 35:605–13.

Prakash, I., and P. K. Gosh, eds. 1975. *Rodents in desert environments*. The Hague: Dr. W. Junk.

Prasad, M. R. N., G. K. Dhaliwal, P. Seth, A. H. Reddi, A. K. Sivashankar, and N. K. Uberoi. 1966. Biology of reproduction in the Indian palm squirrel *Funambulus pennanti* (Wroughton). *Symp. Zool. Soc. Lond.* 15:353–85.

Prentice, A. M., and R. G. Whitehead. 1987. The energetics of human reproduction. In *Reproductive energetics,* ed. A. S. I. Loudon and P. A. Racey, 275–304. Oxford: Clarendon.

Pretorius, P., and G. Marincowitz. 1968. Post-natal penis development, testes descent and puberty in merino ram lambs on different planes of nutrition. *S. Afr. J. Agric. Sci.* 11:319–34.

Price, E. O. 1984. Behavioral aspects of animal domestication. *Q. Rev. Biol.* 59:1–32.

———. 1985. Sexual behavior of large domestic farm animals: An overview. *J. Anim. Sci.* 6:62–74.

Printz, R. H., and G. S. Greenwald. 1970. Effects of starvation on follicular development in the cyclic hamster. *Endocrinology* 86:290–95.

Pryor, S., and F. H. Bronson. 1981. Relative and combined effects of low temperature, poor diet and short daylength on the productivity of wild house mice. *Biol. Reprod.* 25:734–43.

Quay, W. B. 1984. Winter tissue change and regulatory mechanisms in non-hibernating small mammals: A survey and evaluation of adaptive and non-adaptive features. *Spec. Publ. Carn. Mus. Nat. Hist.* 10:149–64.

Racey, P. A. 1973. The viability of spermatazoa after prolonged storage by male and female European bats. *Period. Biol.* 75:201–5.

———. 1978. The effect of photoperiod on the initiation of spermatogenesis in pipistrelle bats, *Pipistrellis pipistrellus.* In *Proceedings of the 4th International Bat Research Conference,* ed. R. J. Olembo, J. B. Castelino, and F. A. Mutere, 255–58. Nairobi: Kenya Literature Bureau.

———. 1981. Environmental factors affecting the length of gestation in mammals. In *Environmental factors in mammalian reproduction,* ed. D. Gilmore and B. Cook, 199–213. London: Macmillan.

———. 1982. Ecology of bat reproduction. In *Ecology of bats,* ed. Thomas H. Kunz, 57–104. New York: Plenum.

Racey, P. A., and J. R. Speakman. 1987. The energy costs of pregnancy and lactation in heterothermic bats. In *Reproductive energetics in mammals,* ed. A. S. I. Loudon and P. A. Racey, 107–26. Oxford: Clarendon.

Radford, H. M. 1961. Photoperiodism and sexual maturity in Merino ewes: 1. The effect of continuous light on the development of sexual activity. *Austr. J. Agric. Res.* 12:139–53.

Ralph, C. L. 1975. The pineal gland and geographical distribution of animals. *Int. J. Biometeor.* 19:189–303.

Ramaley, J. A. 1978. The adrenal rhythm and puberty onset in the female rat. *Life Sci.* 23:2079–88.

———. 1979. Development of gonadrotropin regulation in the prepubertal mammal. *Biol. Reprod.* 20:1–31.

———. 1980. Biological clocks and puberty onset. *Fed. Proc.* 29:2355–59.

———. 1981a. Puberty onset in males and females fed a high fat diet. *Proc. Soc. Exp. Biol. Med.* 166:294–96.

————. 1981b. Stress and fertility. In *Environmental factors in mammalian reproduction*, ed. D. Gilmore and B. Cook, 127–42. London: Macmillan.

Ramaley, J. A., and N. B. Schwartz. 1980. The pubertal process in the rat. *Neuroendocrinology* 30:213–19.

Ramirez, V. D. 1973. Endocrinology of puberty. In *Handbook of physiology*, sect. 7, *Endocrinology*, vol. 2, *Female Reproduction*, pt. 1, R. O. Greep and E. B. Astwood, 1–28. Bethesda, Md.: American Physiological Society.

Ramirez, V. D., H. H. Feder, and C. H. Sawyer. 1984. The role of brain catecholamines in the regulation of LH secretion: A critical inquiry. In *Frontiers in neuroendocrinology*, vol. 8, ed. L. Martini and W. F. Ganong, 27–84. New York: Raven.

Randolph, J. C. 1980. Daily energy metabolism of two rodents (*Peromyscus leucopus* and *Tamias striatus*) in their natural environment. *Physiol. Zool.* 53:70–81.

Randolph, P. A., J. C. Randolph, K. Mattingly, and M. M. Foster. 1977. Energy costs of reproduction in the cotton rat *Sigmodon hispidus*. *Ecology* 58:31–45.

Ransom, A. B. 1966. Breeding seasons of white-tailed deer in Manitoba. *Can. J. Zool.* 44:59–62.

Rao, P. B. R., V. Chalam Metta, and C. J. Johnson. 1959. The amino acid composition and the nutritive value of proteins: 1. Essential amino acid requirements of the growing rat. *J. Nutr.* 69:387–91.

Rasmussen, D. D., and P. V. Malven. 1983. Effects of confinement stress on episodic secretion of luteinizing hormone in ovariectomized sheep. *Neuroendocrinology* 36:392–96.

Rathbun, G. B. 1979. The social structure and ecology of elephant-shrews. *Z. Tierpsychol.* 20, suppl., pp. 1–76.

Ravault, J. P. 1976. Prolaction in the ram: Seasonal variations in the concentration of blood plasma from birth until three years old. *Acta Endocrinol.* 83:720.

Rawlins, R. G., and M. J. Kessler. 1985. Climate and seasonal reproduction in the Cayo-Santiago Puerto Rico macaques *Macaca mulatta*. *Am. J. Primatol.* 9:87–100.

Redfield, J. A., C. J. Krebs, and M. J. Taitt. 1977. Competition between *Peromyscus maniculatus* and *Microtus townsendii* in grasslands of coastal British Columbia. *Anim. Ecol.* 46:607–16.

Reimov, R., K. Adamczyk, and R. Andrzejewski. 1968. Some indices of the behaviour of wild and laboratory house mice in a mixed population. *Acta Theriol.* 13:129–50.

Reiss, M. J. 1985. The allometry of reproduction: Why larger species invest relatively less in their offspring. *J. Theor. Biol.* 113:529–44.

Reiter, E. O., and M. M. Grumbach. 1982. Neuroendocrine control mechanisms and the onset of puberty. *Annual Rev. Physiol.* 44:595.

Reiter, J.,. K. J. Panken, and B. J. LeBoeuf. 1981. Female competition and success in northern elephant seals. *Anim. Behav.* 29:670–87.

Reiter, R. J. 1968. Changes in the reproductive organs of cold-exposed and light-deprived female hamsters (*Mesocricetus auratus*). *J. Reprod. Fert.* 16:217–22.

————. 1980. The pineal and its hormones in the control of reproduction in mammals. *Endocrinol. Rev.* 1:109–31.

————. 1982. Neuroendocrine effects of the pineal gland and melatonin. In *Frontiers in neuroendocrinology,* vol. 7, ed. W. F. Ganong and L. Martini, 287:316. New York: Raven.

————. 1986. Pineal melatonin production: Photoperiodic and hormonal influences. In *Advances in pineal research,* vol. 1, ed. R. J. Reiter and M. Karasek, 77–87. London: John Libbey.

Reiter, R. J., and B. K. Follett. 1980. *Seasonal reproduction in higher vertebrates.* Vol. 5 of *Progress in reproductive biology.* Basel: Karger.

Reiter, R. J., L. J. Petterborg, C. Trakulrungsi, and W. K. Trakulrungsi. 1980. Surgical removal of the olfactory bulbs increases sensitivity of the reproductive system of female rats to the inhibitory effects of late afternoon melatonin injections. *J. Exp. Zool.* 212:47–52.

Reiter, R. J., S. Sorrentino, and N. M. Ellison. 1970. Interaction of photic and olfactory stimuli in mediating pineal-induced gonadal regression in adult female rats. *Gen. Comp. Endocrinol.* 15:326–33.

Relkin, R. J. 1971. Relative efficacy of pinealectomy, hypothalamic and amygdaloid lesions in advancing puberty. *Endocrinology* 88:415–18.

Renfree, M. B. 1982. Implantation and placentation. In *Reproduction in mammals, 2, Embryonic and fetal development,* ed. C. R. Austin and R. V. Short, 26–69. Cambridge: Cambridge University Press.

Renfree, M. B., D. W. Lincoln, O. F. X. Almeida, and R. V. Short. 1981. Abolition of seasonal embryonic diapause in a wallaby *Macropus eugenii* by pineal denervation. *Nature* 293:138–39.

Rennels, E. E., and D. C. Herbert. 1980. Functional correlates of anterior pituitary cytology. *Int. Rev. Physiol.* 22:1–40.

Reppert, S. M., M. J. Duncan, and B. D. Goldman. 1985. Photic influences on the developing mammal. In *Photoperiodism, melatonin and the pineal,* CIBA Foundation Symposium no. 117, 116–28. London: Pittman.

Reynolds, J., and E. B. Keverne. 1979. Accessory olfactory system and its role in pheromonally mediated suppression of oestrus in grouped mice. *J. Reprod. Fert.* 57:31–35.

Rhees, R. W., and D. E. Fleming. 1981. Effects of malnutrition, maternal stress, or ACTH injections during pregnancy on sexual behavior of male offspring. *Physiol. Behav.* 27:879–83.

Rhind, S. M., J. M. Doney, R. G. Gunn, and I. D. Leslie. 1984. Effect of body condition and environmental stress on ovulation rate, embryo survival and associated plasma FSH, luteinizing hormone, prolactin and progeterone profiles in Scottish blackface ewes. *Anim. Prod.* 38:201–10.

Richter, C. P. 1954. The effects of domestication and selection on the behavior of the Norway rat. *J. Natl. Canc. Insti.* 15:727–38.

Rintamaa, D. L., P. A. Mazur, and S. H. Vessey. 1976. Reproduction during two annual cycles in a population of *Peromyscus leucopus noveboracensis. J. Mammal.* 57:593–95.

Rissman, E. F. 1987a. Gonadal influences on sexual behavior in the male musk shrew (*Suncus murinus*). *Horm. Behav.* 21:132–39.

———. 1987b. Social variables influence female sexual behavior in the musk shrew (Suncus murinus). *J. Comp. Psychol.* 101:3–10.

Rissman, E. F., and F. H. Bronson. 1987. Role of the ovary and adrenal gland in the sexual behavior of the musk shrew (Suncus murinus). *Biol. Reprod.* 36:664–68.

Rissman, E., and R. E. Johnston. 1986. Nutritional and social cues influence the onset of puberty in California voles. *Physiol. Behav.* 36:343–47.

Rissman, E., R. Nelson, J. Blank, and F. H. Bronson. 1987. Reproductive response of a tropical mammal to photoperiod. *J. Reprod. Fert.* 81:563–66.

Rivier, C., J. Rivier, and W. Vale. 1986. Stress-induced inhibition of reproductive functions: Role of endogenous corticotropin-releasing factor. *Science* 231:607–9.

Rivier, C., and W. Vale. 1984. Influence of corticotropin-releasing factor on reproductive functions in the rat. *Endocrinology* 114:914–21.

Robbins, C. T. 1983. *Wildlife feeding and nutrition.* New York: Academic Press.

Robert, A., and J. Pajot. 1984. Effect of the presence of females on the concentration of androgens in the male guinea-pig at puberty. *Physiol. Behav.* 33:69–72.

Roberts, A. C., N. D. Martensz, M. H. Hastings, and J. Herbert. 1985. Changes in photoperoid alter the daily rhythms of pineal melatonin content and hypothalamic beta endorphin content and the luteinizing hormone response to naloxone in the male Syrian hamster. *Endocrinology* 117:141–48.

Roberts, J. C., and R. J. Chaffee. 1976. Metabolic and biochemical aspects of heat acclimation in the deer mouse, *Peromyscus maniculatus sonoriensis. Comp. Biochem. Physiol.*, ser. A, 53:367–73.

Robertshaw, D. 1977. Role of the adrenal medulla in thermoregulation. *Int. Rev. Physiol.* 15:189–215.

Robertson, P. B. 1975. Reproduction and community structure of rodents over a transect in southern Mexico. Ph.D. diss., University of Kansas.

Robinson, J. E., and F. J. Karsch. 1984. Refractoriness to inductive day lengths terminates the breeding season of the Suffolk ewe. *Biol. Reprod.* 31:656–63.

———. 1988. Timing the breeding season of the ewe: What is the role of daylength? *Reprod. Nutr. Dév.* 28:365–74.

Robinson, J. E., N. L. Wayne, and F. J. Karsch. 1985. Refractoriness to inhibitory day lengths initiates the breeding season of the Suffolk ewe. *Biol. Reprod.* 32:1024–30.

Robinson, R. M., J. W. Thomas, and R. G. Marburger. 1965. The reproductive cycle of male white-tailed deer in central Texas. *J. Wildl. Mgmt.* 29:53–59.

Rogers, J. G., and G. K. Beauchamp. 1976. Some ecological implications of primer chemical stimuli in rodents. In *Mammalian olfaction, reproductive processes and behavior*, ed. R. Doty, 181–95. New York: Academic Press.

Rohrbach, C. 1982. Investigation of the Bruce effect in the Mongolian gerbil *Meriones unguiculatus. J. Reprod. Fert.* 65:411–17.

Ronnekleiv, O. K., S. R. Ojeda, and S. M. McCann. 1978. Undernutrition, puberty and the development of estrogen positive feedback in the female rat. *Biol. Reprod.* 19:414–24.

Rood, J. P. 1980. Mating relationships and breeding suppression in the dwarf mongoose *Helogale parvula*. *Anim. Behav.* 23:143–50.

Root, A. W., and R. D. Russ. 1972. Short-term effects of castration and starvation upon pituitary and serum levels of luteinizing hormone and follicle stimulating hormone in male rats. *Acta Endocrinol.* 70:665–75.

Rose, R. K., and M. S. Gaines. 1978. The reproductive cycle of *Microtus ochrogaster* in eastern Kansas. *Ecol. Monogr.* 48:21–42.

Rose, R. M., I. Bernstein, and T. Gordon. 1975. Consequences of social conflict on plasma testosterone levels in rhesus monkeys. *Psychosom. Med.* 37:50–61.

Rose, R. M., J. Holaday, and I. Bernstein. 1971. Plasma testosterone, rank, and aggressive behavior in male rhesus monkeys. *Nature* (Lond.) 231:366–68.

Rose, R. M., T. P. Gordon, and I. S. Bernstein. 1972. Plasma testosterone levels in the male rhesus: Influences of sexual and social stimuli. *Science* 178:643–45.

Roseberry, J. L., and W. D. Klimstra. 1970. Productivity of white-tailed deer on Crab Orchard National Wildlife Refuge. *J. Wildl. Mgmt.* 34:23–28.

Rosenblatt, J. S., H. I. Siegel, and A. D. Mayer. 1979. Progress in the study of maternal behavior in the rat: Hormonal, nonhormonal, sensory, and developmental aspects. In *Advances in the study of behavior*, vol. 10, ed. J. S. Rosenblatt, R. A. Hinde, C. Beer, and M.-C Busnel, 226–312. New York: Academic Press.

Rosmos, D. R., H. J. Palmer, K. L. Muiruri, and M. R. Bennink. 1981. Influence of a low carbohydrate diet on performance of pregnant and lactating dogs. *J. Nutr.* 111:678–89.

Ross, G. T., and J. R. Schreiber. 1986. The ovary. In *Reproductive endocrinology*, ed. S. S. C. Yen and R. B. Jaffe, 115–39. Philadelphia: W. B. Saunders.

Roux, M., J. P. Richoux, and J. L. Cordonnier. 1977. Influence of the photoperiod on the ultrastructure of the pineal gland before and during the seasonal genital cycle in the female garden dormouse (*Eliomys quercinus* L.). *J. Neur. Trans.* 41:209–23.

Rowlands, I. W. 1950. Some observations on the breeding of dogs. *Proc. Soc. Stud. Fert.* 2:40–55.

Rowlands, I. W., and B. J. Weir. 1984. Mammals: Non-primate eutherians. In *Marshall's physiology of reproduction*, ed. G. E. Lamming, 455–658. New York: Churchill Livingston.

Rudran, R. 1973. The reproductive cycles of two subspecies of purple-faced langurs (*Presbytis senex*) with relation to environmental factors. *Folia Primatol.* 19:41–60.

Ruiz de Elvira, M. C., J. G. Herndon, and D. C. Collins. 1983. Effect of estradiol-treated females on all-female groups of rhesus monkeys during the transition between the nonbreeding and breeding seasons. *Folia Primatol.* 41:191–203.

Rusak, B., and L. P. Morin. 1976. Testicular responses to photoperiod are blocked by lesions of the suprachiasmatic nuclei in golden hamsters. *Biol. Reprod.* 15:366–74.

Rusak, B., and I. Zucker. 1979. Neural regulation of circadian rhythms. *Physiol. Rev.* 59–449–526.

Russell, J. K. 1982. Timing of reproduction in coatis (*Nasua narica*) in relation to fluctuations in food resources. In *The ecology of a tropical forest: Seasonal rhythms and longterm changes*, ed. E. G. Leigh, Jr., A. S. Rand, and D. M. Windsor, 413–31. Washington, D.C.: Smithsonian Institution Press.

Russell, M. J., G. M. Switz, and K. Thompson. 1980. Olfactory influences on the human menstrual cycle. *Pharmacol. Biochem. Behav.* 13:737–39.

Ryan, K. D., and N. B. Schwartz. 1980. Changes in serum hormone levels associated with male-induced ovulation in adult female mice. *Endocrinology* 106:959–66.

Rychnovsky, B. 1985. The reproduction of *Microtus arvalis* under various temperature and lighting conditions. *Acta Sc. Nat. Brno.* 19:1–37.

Ryg, M. 1984. Effect of nutrition on seasonal changes in testosterone levels in young male reindeer *Rangifer tarandus tarandus*. *Comp. Biochem. Physiol*, ser. A, 77:619–22.

Saad, M. ben, and J-D. Bayle, 1985. Seasonal changes in plasma testosterone, thyroxine and cortisol levels in wild rabbits (*Oryctolagus cuniculus algirus*) of Zembra Island. *Gen. Comp. Endocrinol.* 57:383–88.

Saboureau, M. 1981. Environmental factors and regulation of the annual testicular cycle in a hibernating mammal: The hedge hog. In *Photoperiodism and reproduction in vertebrates*, ed. R. Ortavant, J. Pelletier, and J.-P. Ravault, 319–37. Paris: INRA.

Saboureau, M., and J. Boissin. 1983. Peripheral metabolism of testosterone during the annual reproductive cycle in the male hedgehog, a hibernating mammal. *Can. J. Zool.* 61:2849–55.

Saboureau, M., and L. Castaing. 1986. Hibernation and reproduction in the female hedgehog. In *Endocrine regulations as adaptive mechanisms to the environment*, ed. I. Assenmacher and J. Boissin, 191–200. Paris: Centre National de la Recherche Scientifique.

Saboureau, M., and B. Dutourne. 1981. The reproductive cycle in the male hedgehog (*Erinaceus europaeus* L.): A study of endocrine and exocrine testicular functions. *Reprod. Nutr. Dév.* 21:109–26.

Saboureau, M., A. M. Laurent, and J. Boissin. 1982. Plasma testosterone binding protein capacity in relation to the annual testicular cycle in a hibernating mammal, the hedgehog (*Erinaceus europaeus* L). *Gen. Comp. Endocrinol.* 47:59–63.

Sachs, B. D. 1965. Sexual behavior of male rats after one to nine days without food. *J. Comp. Physiol. Psychol.* 60:144–46.

Sachs, B. D., and R. L. Meisel. 1988. The physiology of male sexual behavior. In *The physiology of reproduction*, ed. E. Knobil and J. D. Neill, 1393–1486. New York: Raven.

Sadleir, R. M. F. S. 1969. *The ecology of reproduction in wild and domestic mammals*. London: Methuen.

———. 1974. The ecology of the deermouse *Peromyscus maniculatus* in a coastal coniferous forest: 2. Reproduction. *Can. J. Zool.* 52:119–31.

———. 1982. Energy consumption and subsequent partitioning in lactating black-tailed deer. *Can. J. Zool.* 60:382–86.

Sadleir, R. M. F. S., and C. H. Tyndale-Biscoe. 1977. Photoperiod and the termination of embryonic diapause in the marsupial *Macropus eugenii*. *Biol. Reprod.* 16:605–8.

Saginor, M., and R. Horton. 1968. Reflex release of gonadotropin and increased plasma testosterone concentration in male rabbits during copulation. *Endocrinology* 82:626–30.

Sahu, S. C., and C. J. Dominic. 1983. Effect of serotonin precursor tryptophane on the pheromonal block to pregnancy: The Bruce effect in mice. *J. Adv. Zool.* 4:1–6.

Sanders, E. H., P. D. Gardner, P. J. Berger, and N. C. Negus. 1981. 6-methoxybenzoxazolinone: A plant derivative that stimulates reproduction in *Microtus montanus*. *Science* 214:67.

Sanford, L. M., and T. A. Yarney. 1983. Circannual changes in serum levels of pituitary hormones and testosterone and in testis size of sexually active and inactive adult rams. *Can. J. Anim. Sci.* 63:811–21.

Sapolsky, R. M. 1983. Endocrine aspects of social instability in the olive baboon (*Papio anubis*). *Am. J. Primatol.* 5:365–79.

———. 1986. Stress, social status and reproductive physiology in free-living baboons. In *Psychobiology of reproductive behavior*, ed. D. Crews, 291–322. Englewood Cliffs, N.J.: Prentice-Hall.

Sarkar, D. K., S. A. Chiappa, G. Fink, and N. M. Sherwood. 1976. Gonadotropin releasing hormone surge in pro-oestrus rats. *Nature* 264:461–63.

Saurel, J. 1969. Histological studies on the sexual cycle of the male hedgehog, *Erinaceus europaeus*. *Aquilo* 9:1–43.

Scales, G. H., R. N. Burton, and R. A. Moss. 1986. Lamb mortality, birthweight and nutrition in late pregnancy. *N.Z. J. Agric. Res.* 29:75–82.

Scarlett, G., and P. A. Woolley. 1980. The honey possum *Tarsipes spenserae* Marsupialia Tarsipedidae, a non seasonal breeder. *Austr. Mammal.* 3:97–104.

Schadler, M. H. 1981. Postimplantation abortion in pine voles (*Microtus pinetorum*) induced by strange males and pheromones of strange males. *Biol. Reprod.* 25:295–97.

———. 1983. Male siblings inhibit reproductive activity in female pine voles, *Microtus pinetorum*. *Biol. Reprod.* 28:1137–39.

Schams, D., E. Stephan, and R. D. Hooley. 1980. The effect of heat exposure on blood serum levels of anterior pituitary hormones in calves, heifers and bulls. *Acta Endocrinol.* 94:309–14.

Schanbacher, B. D. 1988. Responses of market lambs and Suffolk rams to a stimulatory skeleton photoperiod. *Reprod. Nutr. Dév.* 28:431–42.

Schanbacher, B. D., W. Wu, J. A. Nienaber, and G. L. Hahn. 1985. 24-hour profiles of prolactin and testosterone in ram lambs exposed to skeleton photoperiods consisting of various light pulses. *J. Reprod. Fert.* 73:37–44.

Scheffer, T. H. 1924. Notes on the breeding of *Peromyscus*. *J. Mammal.* 5:258–60.

Schenck, P. E., A. Koos Slob, J. Th. J. Uilenbroek, and J. J. van der Werff ten Bosch. 1980. Effect of neonatal under nutrition on serum follicle stimulating hormone levels and ovarian development in the female rat. *Br. J. Nutr.* 44:179–82.

Schiller, E. L. 1956. Ecology and health of *Rattus* at Nome, Alaska. *J. Mammal.* 37:181–88.

Schillo, K. K., C. W. Alliston, and P. V. Malven. 1978. Plasma concentrations of luteinizing hormone and prolactin in the ovariectomized ewe during induced hypothermia. *Biol Reprod.* 19:309–13.

Schillo, K. K., D. Kuehl, and G. L. Jackson. 1985. Do endogenous opioid peptides mediate the photoperiodic release of luteinizing hormone and prolactin in overiectomized ewes? *Biol. Reprod.* 32:779–87.

Schinckel, P. G. 1954. The effect of the ram on the incidence and occurrence of oestrus in ewes. *Austr. vet. J.* 30:189.

Schmidt-Nielsen, K. 1964. *Desert animals.* London: Oxford University Press.

Schoffeniels, E. 1986. Adaptation and finality or "a Boeing is not a submarine." In *Endocrine regulations as adaptive mechanisms to the environment*, ed. I. Assenmacher and J. Boissin, 19–28. Paris: Centre National de la Recherche Scientifique.

Schuler, L. von, and P. M. Borodin. 1976. The time of sexual maturation in female mice: A genetic analysis with diallel crossing. *Z. Versuchstierkd.* 18:296–302.

Schweiger, U., M. Warnhoff, and K.-M. Pirke. 1985a. Brain tyrosine availability and the depression of central nervous norepinephrine turnover in acute and chronic starvation in adult male rats. *Brain Res.* 335:207–12.

———. 1985b. Norepinephrine turnover in the hypothalamus of adult male rats: Alteration of circadian patterns by semistarvation. *J. Neurochem.* 45:706–9.

Scott, M. P. 1986. The timing and synchrony of seasonal breeding in the marsupial, *Antechinus stuartii*: Interaction of environmental and social cues. *J. Mammal.* 67:551–60.

Selwood, L. 1985. Synchronization of oestrus, ovulation and birth in female *Antechinus stuartii* (Marsupialia:Dasyuridae). *Austr. Mammal.* 8:91–96.

Selye, H. 1936. A syndrome produced by diverse noxious agents. *Nature* (Lond.) 158:32–43.

———. 1980. *A guide to stress research.* Vol. 1. New York: Van Nostrand Reinhold.

Sempere, A. J., and A. Lacroix. 1982. Temporal and seasonal relationships between luteinizing hormone, testosterone and antlers in fawn, and adult male roe deer *Capreolus capreolus*: A longitudinal study from birth to four years of age. *Acta Endocrinol.* 99:295–301.

Sergeant, D. E. 1973. Environment and reproduction in seals. *J. Reprod. Fert.* 19, suppl., pp. 555–61.

Sergent, D., P. Berbigier, G. Kann, and J. Fevre. 1985. The effect of sudden solar exposure on thermophysiological parameters and on plasma prolactin and cortisol concentrations in male creole goats. *Reprod. Nutr. Dév.* 25:629–40.

Setchell, B. P. 1982. Spermatogenesis and spermatozoa. In *Reproduction in mammals,* vol. 1, *Germ cells and fertilization,* ed. C. R. Austin and R. V. Short, 63–101. Cambridge: Cambridge University Press.

Shailaja, K., and G. L. Kumari. 1984. Effect of seasonal variations on hormone levels of follicular fluid of sheep ovarian follicles. *Ind. J. Exp. Biol.* 22:357–62.

Sharman, G B. 1976. Evolution of viviparity in mammals. In *The evolution of reproduction,* ed. C. R. Austin and R. V. Short, 32–70. Cambridge: Cambridge University Press.

Shelton, M. 1960. Influence of the presence of a male goat on the initiation of estrous cycling and ovulation of angora does. *J. Anim. Sci.* 19:368–75.

Shield, J. W. 1964. A breeding season difference in two populations of the Australian macropod marsupial *Setonix brachyurus. J. Mammal.* 45:616–25.

Shin-ichi, T. I., and F. W. Turek. 1986. Horizontal knife cuts either ventral or dorsal to the hypothalamic paraventricular nucleus block testicular regression in golden hamsters maintained in short days. *Brain Res.* 370:102–7.

Shipp, E., K. Keith, R. L. Hughes, and K. Myers. 1963. Reproduction in a free-living population of domestic rabbits *Oryctolagus cuniculus* L. on a sub-Antarctic island. *Nature* (Lond.) 200:858–60.

Short, R. V. 1976. The evolution of human reproduction. *Proc. Roy. Soc.* (Lond.), ser. B, 195:3–24.

———. 1984. Oestrus and menstrual cycles. In *Reproduction in mammals,* vol. 3, *Hormonal control of reproduction,* ed. C. R. Austin and R. V. Short, 115–52. Cambridge: Cambridge University Press.

Short, R. V., and M. F. Hay. 1966. Delayed implantation in the roe deer *Capreolus capreolus. Symp. Zool. Soc. Lond.* 15:173–94.

Sibley, R., and P. Calow. 1985. Classification of habitats by selection pressures: A synthesis of life-cycle and r/K theory. In *Behavioural ecology,* ed. R. M. Sibley and R. H. Smith, 75–90. Oxford: Blackwell Scientific.

Sicard, B., D. Maurel, J.-C. Gautun, and J. Boissin. 1988. Activation ou inhibition testiculaire par la photoperiode chez plusieurs espèces de rongeurs saheliens: Première mise en evidence d'une variation circadienne de la photogonadosensibilite. *C.R. Acad. Sci.* (Paris) 307:11–17.

Sides, G., T. Dunn, and C. Kaltenbach. 1986. Luteinizing hormone response to gonadotropin-releasing hormone infusion in postpartum fall-lambing ewes subjected to prepartum energy restrictions. *Theriogenology* 25:537–50.

Silver, R., and E. L. Bittman. 1984. Reproductive mechanisms: Interaction of circadian and interval timing. *Ann. N.Y. Acad. Sci.* 423:488–514.

Silverman, A.-J. 1988. The gonadotropin-releasing hormone (GnRH) neuronal systems: Immunocytochemistry. In *The physiology of reproduction,* ed. E. Knobil and J. D. Neill, 1283–1304. New York: Raven.

Simpson, S. M., B. K. Follett, and D. H. Ellis. 1982. Modulation by photoperiod of gonadotropin secretion in intact and castrated Djungarian hamsters, *Phodopus sungorus*. *J. Reprod. Fert.* 66:243–50.

Sisk, C., and F. H. Bronson. 1986. Effects of food restriction and restoration on gonadotropin and growth hormone secretion in immature male rats. *Biol. Reprod.* 35:554–61.

Sisk, C. L., and F. W. Turek. 1983. Gonadal growth and gonadal hormones do not participate in the development of responsiveness to photoperiod in the golden hamster *Mesocricetus auratus*. *Biol. Reprod.* 29:439–45.

Skinner, J. D., R. J. van Aarde, and A. S. van Jaarsveld. 1984. Adaptation in three species of large mammals (*Antidorcas marsupialis, Hystrix africaeaustralis, Hyaena brunnea*) to arid environments. *S. Afr. J. Zool.* 19:82–86.

Skinner, J. D., R. J. van Aarde, and A. S. van Jaarsveld. 1986. Annual reproductive cycles in selected African mammals in response to environmental cues. In *Endocrine regulations as adaptive mechanisms to the environment*, ed. I. Assenmacher and J. Boissin, 31–36. Paris: Centre National de la Recherche Scientifique.

Slob, A. K., G. van Es, and J. J. van der Werff ten Bosch. 1985. Social factors and puberty in female rats. *J. Endocrinol.* 104:309–13.

Slob, A. K., J. T. M. Vreeburg, and J. J. van der Werff ten Bosch. 1979. Body growth, puberty and undernutrition in the male guinea-pig. *Br. J. Nutr.* 41:231–37.

Slob, A. K., S. J. Wiegand, R. W. Goy, and J. A. Robinson. 1978. Heterosexual interactions in laboratory-housed stumptail macaques (*Macaca arctoides*): Observations during the menstrual cycle and after ovariectomy. *Horm. Behav.* 10:193–211.

Slusser, W. N., and G. N. Wade. 1981. Testicular effects on food intake, body weight, and body composition in male hamsters. *Physiol. Behav.* 27:637–40.

Slyter, A. L., R. D. Roigen, and B. D. Schanbacher. 1986. Use of controlled photoperiod to induce out-of-season breeding in ewes. *Theriogenology* 25:609–16.

Smith, G. M., H. A. Fitzhugh, Jr., L. V. Cundiff, T. C. Cartwright, and K. E. Gregory. 1976a. A genetic analysis of maturing patterns in straight bred and cross bred Hereford, Angus and shorthorn cattle. *J. Anim. Sci.* 43:389–95.

———. 1976b. Heterosis for maturing patterns in Hereford, Angus and shorthorn cattle. *J. Anim. Sci.* 43:380–88.

Smith, I. D. 1967. The effect of constant long daily photoperiod upon the onset of puberty in ewes. *J. Agric. Sci.* 69:43–45.

Smith, M. F., L. D. Shipp, W. N. Songster, J. N. Wiltbank, and L. H. Carroll. 1980. Effect of monensin energy level and cow body condition on pregnancy rate in nonlactating beef cows. *Theriogenology* 14:91–104.

Smith, M. H. 1971. Food as a limiting factor in the population ecology of *Peromyscus polionotus* (Wagner). *Ann. Zool. Fenn.* 8:109–12.

Smith, M. H., and J. T. McGinnis. 1968. Relationships of latitude, altitude, and body size to litter size and mean annual production of offspring in *Peromyscus*. *Res. Pop. Ecol.* 10:115–26.

Smith, M. J., J. H. Bennett, and C. M. Chesson. 1978. Photoperiod and some other factors affecting reproduction in female *Sminthopsis crassicaudata*, Marsupialia Dasyuridae in captivity. *Austr. J. Zool.* 26:449–64.

Smith, M. S., M. E. Freeman, and J. D. Neill. 1975. Control of progesterone secretion during the estrous cycle and early pseudopregnancy in the rat: Prolactin, gonadotropin and steroid levels associated with rescue of the corpus luteum of pseudopregnancy. *Endocrinology* 96:219–26.

Smith, R., and T. Polacheck. Reexamination of the life table for northern fur seals with implications about population regulatory mechanisms. In *Dynamics of large mammal populations*, ed. C. W. Fowler and T. D. Smith, 99–120. New York: John Wiley.

Smith, V. H., R. R. Hacker, and R. G. Brown. 1977. Effect of alterations in ambient temperature on serum prolactin concentration in steers. *J. Anim. Sci.* 44:645–49.

Smuts, B. B., D. L. Cheney, R. M. Seyfarth, R. W. Wrangham, and T. T. Struhsaker, eds. 1987. *Primate societies.* Chicago: University of Chicago Press.

Smyth, M. 1966. Winter breeding in woodland mice, *Apodemus sylvaticus* and voles, *Clethrionomys glareolus* and *Microtus agrestis* near Oxford. *J. Anim. Ecol.* 35:471–85.

Soares, M. J., and J. C. Hoffman. 1981. Seasonal reproduction in the mongoose *Herpestes auropunctatus:* 1. Androgen, luteinizing hormone and follicle stimulating hormone in the male. *Gen. Comp. Endocrinol.* 44:350–58.

———. 1982. Role of daylength in the regulation of reproductive function in the male mongoose, *Herpestes auropunctatus. J. Exp. Zool.* 224:365–69.

Sod-Moriah, U. A., G. M. Goldberg, and E. Bedrak. 1974. Intrascrotal temperature, testicular histology and fertility of heat-acclimatized rats. *J. Reprod. Fert.* 37:263–68.

Solomon, S. 1988. The placenta as an endocrine organ: Steroids. In *The physiology of reproduction*, ed. E. Knobil and J. D. Neill, 2085–92. New York: Raven.

Southern, H. N. 1940. The ecology and population dynamics of the wild rabbit *Oryctolagus cuniculus. Ann. Appl. Biol.* 27:509–26.

Southwood, T. R. E. 1977. Habitat, the templet for ecological strategies? *J. Anim. Ecol.* 46:337–65.

Sowls, L. K. 1966. Reproduction in the collared peccary *Tayassu tajacu. Symp. Zool. Soc. Lond.* 15:155–72.

Spears, N., and J. R. Clarke. 1988. Selection in field voles (*Microtis agrestis*) for gonadal growth under short photoperiods. *J. Anim. Ecol.* 57:61–70.

Spencer, A. W. 1984. Food habits, grazing activities, and reproductive development on long-tailed voles, *Microtus longicaudus* (Merriam) in relation to snow cover in the mountains of Colorado. *Spec. Publ. Carn. Mus. Nat. Hist.* 10:67–90.

Spies, H. G., and S. C. Chappel. 1984. Mammals: Nonhuman primates. In *Marhsall's physiology of reproduction*, vol. 1, ed. G. E. Lamming, 659–712. New York: Churchill Livingstone.

Srebnik, H., W. Fletcher, and G. Campbell. 1978. Neuroendocrine aspects of reproduction in experimental malnutrition. In *Environmental endocrinology*, ed. I Assenmacher and D. Farmer, 306–12. New York: Springer.

Stanton-Hicks, C. 1972. The nutritional requirements of living things. In *Biology of nutrition*, ed. R. N. T-W-Fiennes, 375–438. Oxford: Pergamon.

Stearns, S. C. 1976. Life-history tactics: A review of the ideas. *Q. Rev. Biol.* 51:3–47.

———. 1983. The influence of size and phylogeny on patterns of covariation among life history traits in the mammals. *Oikos* 41:173–87.

Stebbins, L. L. 1977. Energy requirements during reproduction of *Peromyscus maniculatus*. *Can. J. Zool.* 55:1701–4.

Steger, R. W., A. Bartke, K. S. Matt, M. J. Soares, and F. Talamantes. 1984. Neuroendocrine changes in male hamsters following photostimulation. *J. Exp. Zool.* 229:467–74.

Steger, R. W., K. S. Matt, and A. Bartke. 1985. Neuroendocrine reglation of seasonal reproductive activity in the male golden hamster. *Neurosci. Biobehav. Rev.* 9:191–201.

———. 1986. Interactions of testosterone and short-photoperiod exposure on the neuroendocrine axis of the male Syrian hamster. *Neuroendocrinology* 43:69–74.

Stehn, R. A., and F. J. Jannett. 1981. Male-induced abortion in various microtine rodents. *J. Mammal.* 62:369–72.

Stehn, R. A., and M. E. Richmond. 1975. Male-induced pregnancy termination in the prairie vole, *Microtus ochrogaster. Science* 187:1211–13.

Steinberger, A., and D. N. Ward. 1988. Inhibin. In *The physiology of reproduction*, ed. E. Knobil and J. D. Neill, 567–83. New York: Raven.

Steiner, R. A., J. L. Cameron, T. H. McNeill, D. K. Clifton, and W. J. Bremner. 1983. Metabolic signals for the onset of puberty. In *Neuroendocrine aspects of reproduction*, ed. R. L. Norman, 183–227. New York: Academic Press.

Stellflug. J. N., P. D. Muse, D. O. Everson, and T. M. Louis. 1981. Changes in serum progesterone and estrogen of the non-pregnant coyote during the breeding season. *Proc. Soc. Exp. Biol. Med.* 167:220–23.

Stenseth, N. C., T. O. Gustafsson, L. Hansson, and K. I. Ugland. 1985. On the evolution of reproductive rates in microtine rodents. *Ecology* 66:1795–1808.

Stetson, M. H., and B. Tate-Ostroff. 1981. Hormonal regulation of the annual reproductive cycle of golden hamsters *Mesocricetus auratus. Gen. Comp. Endocrinol.* 45:329–44.

Stetson, M. H., and M. Watson-Whitmyer. 1976. Nucleus suprachiasmaticus: The biological clock in the hamster? *Science* 191:197–99.

Stevens, V. C. 1962. Regional variations in productivity and reproductive physiology of the cottontail rabbit in Ohio. *N. Am. Wildl. Conf., Trans.* 27:243–54.

Stewart, R. E. A. 1986. Energetics of age-specific reproductive effort in female harp seals (*Phoca groenlandica*). *J. Zool.* (Lond.) 208:503–17.

Stewart, R. J. C. 1973. A marginally malnourished rat colony. *Nutr. Rept. Int.* 7:487–93.

Stewart, T. S., C. R. Long, and T. C. Cartwright. 1980. Characterization of cattle of a five-breed diallel: 3. Puberty in bulls and heifers. *J. Anim. Sci.* 50:808–20.

Stoddart, R. C. 1970. Breeding and growth of laboratory mice in darkness. *Lab. Anim.* 4:13–16.

Stoebel, D. P., and G. P. Moberg. 1982. Effect of ACTH and cortisol on luteinizing hormone surge and estrous behavior of cows. *J. Dairy Sci.* 65:1016–24.

Storey, A. 1986. Advantages to female rodents of male-induced pregnancy disruptions. *Ann. N.Y. Acad. Sci.* 474:135–47.

Stout, G. G. 1970. Breeding biology of desert cottontail in the Phoenix region. *Ariz. J. Wildl. Mgmt.* 34:47–51.

Studier, E. H. 1979. Bioenergetics of growth, pregnancy and lactation in the laboratory mouse, *Mus musculus. Comp. Biochem. Physiol.*, ser. A, 64: 473–81.

Suckling, G. C. 1984. Population ecology of the sugar glider, *Petaurus breviceps*, in a system of fragmented habitats. *Austr. Wildl. Res.* 11:49–75.

Sullivan, J. K., and G. R. Lynch. 1986. Photoperiod time measurement for activity, torpor, molt and reproduction in mice. *Physiol. Behav.* 36:167–74.

Sullivan, T. P., and D. S. Sullivan. 1982. Population dynamics and regulation of the Douglas squirrel (*Tamiasciurus douglasii*) with supplemental food. *Oecologia* (Berl.) 53:264–70.

Svare, B., A. Bartke, and F. Macrides. 1978. Juvenile male mice: An attempt to accelerate testis function by exposure to adult female stimuli. *Physiol. Behav.* 21:1009–13.

Svendson, G. 1964. Comparative reproduction and development in two species of mice in the genus *Peromyscus. Trans. Kans. Acad. Sci.* 67:527–38.

Swan, J. F., and F. W. Turek. 1985. Multiple circadian oscillators regulate the timing of behavioral and endocrine rhythms in female golden hamsters. *Science* 228:898–900.

Swanepoel, C. M. 1980. Some factors influencing the breeding season of *Praomys natalensis. S. Afr. J. Zool.* 15:95–98.

Swihart, R. K. 1986. Body size, breeding season length, and life history tactics of lagomorphs. *Oikos* 43:282–90.

Tache, Y., P. du Ruisseau, J. R. Ducharme, and R. Collu. 1978. Pattern of adenohypophyseal hormone change in male rats following chronic stress. *Neuroendocrinology* 26:208–19.

Tähkä, K. M., A. Ruokonen, H. Wallgren, and T. Teravainen. 1983. Temporal changes in testicular histology and steroidogenesis in juvenile bank voles (*Clethrionomys glareolus*, Schreber) subjected to different photoperiods. *Endocrinology* 112:1420–26.

Taitt, M. J., and C. J. Krebs. 1981. The effect of extra food on small rodent populations: 2. Voles. (*Microtus townsendii*). *J. Anim. Ecol.* 50:125–37.

Talamantes, F., and L. Ogren. 1988. The placenta as an endocrine organ: Polypeptides. In *The physiology of reproduction*, ed. E. Kobil and J. D. Neill, 2093–2144. New York: Raven.

Taleisnik, S., L. Caligaris, and J. J. Astrada. 1966. Effect of copulation on the release of pituitary gonadotropins in male and female rats. *Endocrinology* 79:49–54.

Tamarkin, L., C. J. Baird, and O. F. X. Almeida. 1985. Melatonin: A coordinating signal for mammalian reproduction? *Science* 227:714–20.

Tamarkin, L., J. S. Hutchison, and B. D. Goldman. 1976. Regulation of serum gonadotrophins by photoperiod and testicular hormone in the Syrian hamster. *Endocrinology* 99:1528–33.

Tanner, J. M. 1962. *Growth at adolescence.* Oxford: Blackwell Scientific.

Taub, D. M., and F. A. King. 1986. *Current perspectives in primate social dynamics.* New York: Van Nostrand Reinhold.

Taylor, C. R. 1977. Exercise and environmental heat loads: Different mechanisms for solving different problems? *Int. Rev. Physiol.* 15:119–46.

Taylor, K. D., and M. G. Green. 1976. The influence of rainfall on diet and reproduction in four African rodent species. *J. Zool.* (Lond.) 180:367–89.

Taylor, W. P. 1956. *The deer of North America.* Harrisburg, Pa.: Stackpole.

Temme, M. 1981. Reproductive parameters of the Polynesian rat *Rattus exulans* in the northern Marshall Islands. *Z. Angew. Zool.* 68:315–38.

Terman, C. R. 1973. Reproductive inhibition in asymptotic populations of prairie deermice. *J. Reprod. Fert.* 19, suppl., pp. 457–63.

Thomas, D. C. 1982. The relationship between fertility and fat reserves of Peary caribou *Rangifer tarandus* Peary. *Can. J. Zool.* 60:597–602.

Thomas, D. W., and A. G. Marshall. 1984. Reproduction and growth of three species of West African fruit bats. *J. Zool.* (Lond.) 202:265–82.

Thompson, G. E. 1977. Physiological effects of cold exposure. *Int. Rev. Physiol.* 15:29–69.

Thompson, M. K., and E. L. Bradley. 1979. A study of the circadian rhythm and pre-puberty and post-puberty concentrations of serum prolactin in male prairie deermice *Peromyscus maniculatus bairdii*. *Gen. Comp. Endocrinol.* 39:208–14.

Thwaites, C. J. 1967. Embryo mortality in the heat stressed ewe: 1. The influence of breed. *J. Reprod. Fert.* 14:5–14.

Todd, A. W., and L. B. Keith. 1983. Coyote demography during a snowshoe hare decline in Alberta. *J. Wildl. Mgmt.* 47:394–404.

Townsend, C. R., and P. Calow. 1981. *Physiological ecology.* Sunderland, Mass.: Sinauer.

Trethewey, D. C., and B. J. Verts. 1971. Reproduction in eastern cottontail rabbits in western Oregon. *Am. Midl. Nat.* 86:463–76.

Trivers, R. L. 1972. Parental investment and sexual selection. In *Sexual selection and the descent of man*, ed. B. Campbell, 136–79. Chicago: Aldine.

Tsafriri, A. 1988. Local nonsteroidal regulators of ovarian function. In *The physiology of reproduction*, ed. E. Knobil and J. D. Neill, 527–66. New York: Raven.

Tucker, H. A. 1988. Lactation and its hormonal control. In *The physiology of reproduction*, ed. E. Knobil and J. D. Neill, 2235–64. New York: Raven.

Tucker, H. A., and R. P. Wettemann. 1976. Effects of ambient temperature and relative humidity on serum prolactin and growth hormone in heifers. *Proc. Soc. Exp. Biol. Med.* 151:623–26.

Tulley, D., and P. J. Burfening. 1983. Libido and scrotal circumference of rams as affected by season of the year and altered photoperiod. *Theriogenology* 20:435–48.

Tulloch, D. G., and A. Grassia. 1981. A study of reproduction in water buffalo in the Northern Territory of Australia. *Austr. Wildl. Res.* 8:335–48.

Turek, F. W. 1977. The interactions of the photoperiod and testosterone in regulating serum gonadotropin levels in castrated male hamsters. *Endocrinology* 101:1210–15.

Turek, F. W., and C. S. Campbell. 1979. Photoperiodic regulation of neuroendocrine-gonadal activity. *Biol. Reprod.* 20:32–50.

Turek, F. W., S. H. Losee-Olsen, and G. B. Ellis. 1983. Pinealectomy and lesions of the suprachiasmatic nucleus affect the castration response in hamsters exposed to short photoperiods. *Neuroendocrinology* 36:335–39.

Turek, F. W., J. Swann, and D. J. Earnest. 1984. Role of the circadian system in reproductive phenomena. *Rec. Prog. Horm. Res.* 40:143–83.

Turek, F. W., and E. Van Cauter. 1988. Rhythms in reproduction. In *The physiology of reproduction*, ed. E. Knobil and J. D. Neill, 1789–1830. New York: Raven.

Tyndale-Biscoe, C. H. 1984. Mammals: Marsupials. In *Marshall's physiology of reproduction*, ed. G. E. Lamming, 386–454. New York: Churchill Livingstone.

Tyndale-Biscoe, C. H., and M. Renfree. 1987. *Reproductive physiology of marsupials*. Cambridge: Cambridge University Press.

Uchida, H., and Y. Mizuma. 1983. Reproductive efficiency and puberty in mice selected for high levels and low levels of aggressiveness. *Jap. J. Zootech. Sci.* 54:654–60.

Ulberg, L. C., and L. A. Sheean. 1973. Early development of mammalian embryos in elevated ambient temperatures. *J. Reprod. Fert.* 19:155–61.

Underwood, E. J. 1977. *Trace Elements in Human and Animal Nutrition.* New York: Academic Press.

Underwood, E. J., F. L. Shier, and N. Davenport. 1944. Studies in sheep husbandry in western Australia: 5. The breeding season of merino, crossbred and British ewes in the agricultural districts. *J. Dept. Agric. W. Austr.* 21:135–43.

Urbanski, H. F., S. M. Simpson, D. H. Ellis, and B. K. Follett. 1983. Secretion of FSH and luteinizing hormone in castrated golden hamsters during exposure to various photoperiods and to natural day lengths. *J. Endocrinol.* 99:379–86.

Ure, D. C. 1984. Autumn mass dynamics of red-backed voles (*Clethrionomys gapperi*) in Colorado in relation to photoperiod cues and temperature. *Spec. Publ. Carn. Mus. Nat. Hist.* 10:193–200.

Uresk, D. W., and P. L. Sims. 1975. Influence of grazing on crude protein content of blue gramma. *J. Range Mgmt.* 28:370–71.

van Aarde, R. J. 1983. Demographic parameters of the feral cat *Felis catus* population at Marion Island, South Africa. *S. Afr. J. Wildl. Res.* 13:12–16.

———. 1986. Endocrine correlates of the annual reproductive cycle of the porcupine *Hystrix africaeaustralis*. In *Endocrine regulations as adaptive mechanisms to the environment*, ed. I. Assenmacher and J. Boissin, 37–42. Paris: Centre National de la Recherche Scientifique.

van Aarde, R. J., and J. D. Skinner. 1986. Reproductive biology of the male Cape porcupine, *Hystrix africaeaustralis*. *J. Reprod. Fert.* 76:545–52.

van de Graaf, K. M., and R. P. Balda. 1973. Importance of green vegetation for reproduction in the Kangaroo rat *Dipodomys merriami merriami*. *J. Mammal.* 54:509–12.

Van Demark, N. L., and M. J. Free. 1970. Temperature effects. In *The testis*, vol. 3, ed. A. D. Johnson, W. R. Gomes, and N. L. Van Demark, 233–313. London: Academic Press.

Vandenbergh, J. G. 1967. Effect of the presence of a male in the sexual maturation of female mice. *Endocrinology* 81:345–48.

———. 1969a. Endocrine coordination in monkeys: Male sexual responses to the female. *Physiol. Behav.* 4:261–64.

———. 1969b. Male odor accelerates female sexual maturation in mice. *Endocrinology* 84:658–60.

———. 1971. The influence of the social environment on sexual maturation in male mice. *J. Reprod. Fert.* 24:383–90.

———. 1973. Environmental influences on breeding in rhesus monkeys. In *Symposium of the IVth International Congress of Primatology*, vol. 2, *Primate reproductive behavior*, ed. C. Phoenix, 1–19. Basel: Karger.

———. 1976. Acceleration of sexual maturation in female rats by male stimulation. *J. Reprod. Fert.* 46:451–53.

———. 1977. Reproductive coordination of the golden hamster: Female influences on the male. *Horm. Behav.* 9:264–75.

———. 1983. Pheromonal regulation of puberty. In *Pheromones and reproduction in mammals*, ed. J. G. Vandenbergh, 95–112. New York: Acacemic Press.

———. 1986. The suppression of ovarian function. In *Chemical signals in vertebrates*, vol. 4, ed. D. Duvall, D. Muller Schwarze, and R. M. Silverstein, 423–32. New York: Plenum.

Vandenbergh, J. G., and D. Coppola. 1986. The physiology and ecology of puberty modulation by primer pheromones. In *Advances in the study of behavior*, ed. J. S. Rosenblatt, C. Beer, and M. Busnel, 71–107. New York, Academic Press.

Vandenbergh, J. G., L. C. Drickamer, and D. R. Colby. 1972. Social and dietary factors in the sexual maturation of the female mice. *J. Reprod. Fert.* 28:397–405.

Vandenbergh, J. G., J. S. Finlayson, W. J. Dobrogosz, S. S. Dills, and T. A. Kost. 1976. Chromatographic separation of puberty accelerating pheromone from male mouse urine. *Biol. Reprod.* 15:260–65.

Vandenberg, J. G., and S. Vessey. 1968. Seasonal breeding of free-ranging rhesus monkeys and related ecological factors. *J. Reprod. Fert.* 15:71–79.

Van der Lee, S., and L. M. Boot. 1956. Spontaneous pseudopregnancy in mice: 2. *Acta Physiol. Pharmacol. Neerl.* 5:213–14.

Van der Walt, L. A., E. N. Wilmsen, and T. Jenkins. 1978. Unusual sex hormone patterns among desert dwelling hunter-gatherers. *J. Clin. Endocrinol. Metab.* 46:658–63.

Van Horn, R. N. 1975. Primate breeding season: Photoperiodic regulation in captive *Lemur catta*. *Folia Primatol.* 24:203–20.

———. 1980. Seasonal reproduction in primates. In *Seasonal reproduction in higher vertebrates*, ed. R. J. Reiter and B. K. Follet, 155–80, vol. 5 of *Progress in reproductive biology*. New York: Karger.

Van Horn, R. N., and J. A. Resko. 1977. The reproductive cycle of the ring-tailed lemur (*Lemur catta*): Sex steroid levels and sexual receptivity under controlled photoperiods. *Endocrinology* 101:1579–86.

Van Mourik, S., and T. Stelmasiak. 1986. Behavioural endocrinology of the male rusa deer (*Cervus rusa timorensis*) in a temperate zone. In *Endocrine regulations as adaptive mechanisms to the environment*, ed. I. Assenmacher and J. Boissin, 491–96. Paris: Centre National de la Recherche Scientifique.

Van Mourik, S., T. Stelmasiak, and K. H. Outch. 1986. Seasonal variation in plasma testosterone, luteinizing hormone concentrations and LH-RH responsiveness in mature male Rusa deer (*Cervus rusa timorensis*). *Comp. Biochem. Physiol.* 83:347–51.

Van Vugt, D. A. 1985. Opioid regulation of prolactin and luteinizing hormone secretion. In *Handbook of pharmacologic methodologies for the study of the neuroendocrine system*, ed. R. W. Steger and A. Johns, 173–84. Boca Raton, Fla.: CRC.

Van Zegeren, K. 1980. Variation in aggressiveness and the regulation of numbers in house mouse populations. *Neth. J. Zool.* 30:635–770.

Vaughan, M. K., G. M. Vaughan, and R. J. Reiter. 1973. Effect of ovariectomy and constant dark on the weight of reproductive and certain other organs in the female vole, *Microtus montanus*. *J. Reprod. Fert.* 32:9–14.

Vaughan, M. R, and L. B. Keith. 1981. Demographic response of experimental snowshoe hare populations to overwinter food shortage. *J. Wildl. Mgmt.* 45:354–80.

Vaughan, T. A. 1978. *Mammalogy*. Philadelphia: Saunders College Publishing.

Veith, J. L., M. Buck, S. Getzlaf, P. van Dalfsen, and S. Slade. 1983. Exposure to men influences the occurrence of ovulation in women. *Physiol. Behav.* 31:313–15.

Vendreley, E., C. Guerillot, C. Basseville, and C. Delage. 1971. Poids testiculaire et spermatogenese du hamster doré au cours du cycle saisonnier. *Comptes Rendu Soc. Biol.* (Paris) 165:1562–65.

Verme, L. J. 1965. Reproduction studies on penned white-tailed deer. *J. Wildl. Mgmt.* 29:74–79.

Vernikos, J., M. F. Dallman, C. Bonner, A. Katzen, and J. Shinsako. 1982. Pituitary-adrenal function in rats chronically exposed to cold. *Endocrinology* 110:413–20.

Vivas, A. M. 1986. Population biology of *Sigmodon alstoni* (Rodentia: Cricetidae) in the Venezuelan llanos. *Rev. Chil. Hist. Nat.* 59:179–91.

Vivas, A. M., and A. C. Calero. 1985. Algunos aspectos de la ecologia poblacional de los pequenos mamiferos en la estacion biologica de los llanos. *Bol. Socio. Venez. Cien. Nat.* 143:79–99.

Vogel, P. 1972. Beitrage zur fortpflanzungsbiologie der Gattungen *Xorex, Neomys* und *Crocidura* (Soricidae). *V. Nat. Gesell.* (Basel) 82:165–92.

vom Saal, F. S. 1981. Variation in phenotype due to random intrauterine position of male and female fetuses in rodents. *J. Reprod. Fert.* 62:633–50.

———. 1983. The interaction of circulating oestrogens and androgens in regulating mammalian sexual differentation. In *Hormones and behaviour in higher vertebrates,* ed. J. Balthazart, E. Prove, and R. Gilles, 159–77. Berlin: Springer.

vom Saal, F., and F. H. Bronson. 1978. In utero proximity of female mouse fetuses to males: Effect on reproductive performance in later life. *Biol. Reprod.* 19:842–53.

———. 1980. Variation in length of the estrous cycle in mice due to former intrauterine proximity to male fetuses. *Biol. Reprod.* 22(4): 777–80.

vom Saal, F. S., and C. L. Moyer. 1985. Prenatal effect on reproductive capacity during aging in female mice. *Biol. Reprod.* 32:1116–26.

vom Saal, F. S., S. Pryor, and F. H. Bronson. 1981. Effects of prior intrauterine position and housing on oestrous cycle length in adolescent mice. *J. Reprod. Fert.* 62:33–37.

Wade, G. N. 1975. Some effects of ovarian hormones on food intake and body weight in female rats. *J. Comp. Physiol. Psychol.* 88:183–93.

———. 1976. Sex hormones, regulatory behaviors and body weight. In *Advances in the study of behavior,* vol. 6, ed. J. S. Rosenblatt, R. A. Hinde, E. Shaw, and C. G. Beer, 201–79. New York: Academic Press.

Wade, G. N., and J. M. Gray. 1979. Theoretical review: Gonadal effects on food intake and adiposity: A metabolic hypothesis. *Physiol. Behav.* 22:583–93.

Wade, G. N., G. Jennings, and P. Trayhurn. 1986. Energy balance and brown adipose tissue: Thermogenesis during pregnancy in Syrian hamsters. *Am. J. Physiol.* 250:R845–R850.

Wade, P. 1958. Breeding season amongst mammals in the lowland rainforest of north Borneo. *J. Mammal.* 39:429–33.

Wakerley, J. B., G. Clarke, and A. J. S. Summerlee. 1988. Milk-ejection and its control. In *The physiology of reproduction,* ed. E. Knobil and J. D. Neill, 2283–2322. New York: Raven.

Walker, R. F., and L. S. Frawley. 1977. Gonadal function in underfed rats: 2. Effect of estrogen on plasma gonadotropins after pinealectomy or constant light exposure. *Biol. Reprod.* 17:630–34.

Wallen, E. P., and F. W. Turek. 1981. Photoperiodicity in the male albino laboratory rat. *Nature* 289:402–4.

Wallmo, O. C. 1981. *Mule and black-tailed deer of North America.* Lincoln: University of Nebraska Press.

Walter, H. 1971. Ecology of tropical and subtropical vegetation. Edinburgh: Oliver & Boyd.

Walter, M. R., L. Martinet, B. Moret, and C. Thibault. 1968. Regulation photoperiodique de l'activite sexuelle chez le lapin male et femelle. *Arch. Anat. Histol. Embryol.* 51:775–80.

Walters, D. L., W. C. Burrell, and J. N. Wiltbank. 1984. Influence of exogenous steroids, nutrition and calf removal on reproductive performance of anestrous beef cows. *Theriogenology* 21:395–406.

Walton, J. S., J. R. McNeilly, A. S. McNeilly, and F. J. Cunningham. 1977. Changes in concentrations of follicle-stimulating hormone, luteinizing hormone, prolactin and progesterone in the plasma of ewes during the transition from anoestrus to breeding activity. *J. Endocrinol.* 75:127–36.

Ward, I. 1972. Prenatal stress feminizes and demasculinizes the behavior of males. *Science* 175:82–84.

Warren, M. P. 1982. The effects of altered nutritional states, stress and systemic illness on reproduction in women. In *Clinical reproductive endocrinology,* ed. J. L. Vaitukaitis, 177–206. New York: Elsevier Biomedical.

Wasser, S. K., and D. P. Barash. 1983. Reproductive suppression among female mammals: Implications for biomedicine and sexual selection theory. *Q. Rev. Biol.* 58:513–38.

Watson, R. M. 1969. Reproduction of wildebeeste *Connochaetes taurinus albojubatus* Thomas, in the Serengeti region, and its significance to conservation. *J. Reprod. Fert.* 6, suppl., pp. 287–310.

Watts, C. H. S. 1970. Effect of supplementary food on breeding in woodland rodents. *J. Mammal.* 51:169–71.

Webb, J. W., and D. W. Nellis. 1981. Reproductive cycle of white-tailed deer of St. Croix, Virgin Islands. *J. Wildl. Mgmt.* 45:253–58.

Webb, R., G. Baxter, R. D. Preece, R. B. Land, and A. J. Springbett. 1985. Control of gonadotropin release in Scottish blackface and Finnish landrace ewes during seasonal anestrus. *J. Reprod. Fert.* 73:369–78.

Webley, G. E., and E. Johnson. 1983. Reproductive physiology of the grey squirrel *Sciurus carolinensis. Mammal. Rev.* 13:149–54.

Webley, G. E., G. S. Pope, and E. Johnson. 1985. Seasonal changes in the testes and accessory reproductive organs and seasonal and circadian changes in plasma testosterone concentrations in the male grey squirrel. *Gen. Comp. Endocrinol.* 59:15–23.

Webster J. R., and G. K. Barrell. 1985. Advancement of reproductive activity, seasonal reproduction, prolactin secretion and seasonal pelage changes in pubertal red deer hinds (*Cervus elaphus*) subjected to artificially shortened photoperiod or daily melatonin treatments. *J. Reprod. Fert.* 73:255–60.

Wehrenberg, W. B., and I. Dyrenfurth. 1983. Photoperiod and ovulatory menstrual cycles in female macaque monkeys. *J. Reprod. Fert.* 68:119–22.

Weiner, C., N. Schlechter, and I. Zucker. 1984. Photoperiodic influences on testicular development of deermice from two different altitudes. *Biol. Reprod.* 30:507–13.

Weiner, R. I., P. R. Findell, and C. Kordon. 1988. Role of classic and peptide neuromediators in the neuroendocrine regulation of LH and prolactin. In *The physiology of reproduction,* ed. E. Knobil and J. D. Neill, 1235–82. New York: Raven.

Weir, B. J. 1970. The management and breeding of some more hystricomorph rodents. *Lab. Anim.* 4:83–97.

———. 1971. The reproductive organs of the plains viscacha *Lagostomus maximus*. *J. Reprod. Fert.* 25:365–73.

———. 1973. The role of the male in the evocation of oestrus in the cui, *Galea musteloides* (Rodentia:Hystricomorpha). *J. Reprod. Fert.* 19, suppl., pp. 421–32.

Weitlauf, H. M. 1988. Biology of implantation. In *The physiology of reproduction*, ed. E. Knobil and J. D. Neill, 231–62. New York: Raven.

Welsh, T. H., Jr., and B. H. Johnson. 1981. Influence of electro-ejaculation on peripheral blood concentrations of corticosteroids progesterone, luteinizing hormone and testosterone in bulls. *Arch. Androl.* 7:245–50.

Western, D. 1983. Production, reproduction and size in mammals. *Oecologia* (Berl.) 59:269–71.

Weston, J. S., and L. C. Ulberg. 1976. Responses of dairy cows to the behavior of treated herdmates during the post-partum period. *J. Dairy Sci.* 59:1985–90.

Wettemann, R. P., and H. A. Tucker. 1974. Relationship of ambient temperature to serum prolactin in heifers. *Proc. Soc. Exp. Biol. Med.* 146:908–11.

Wheeler, A. G. 1973. Breed and seasonal variation in the incidence of oestrus and ovulation in the sheep. *J. Reprod. Fert.* 35:583–84.

Wheeler, S. H., and D. R. King. 1985. The European rabbit in southwestern Australia: 2. Reproduction. *Austr. Wildl. Res.* 12:197–212.

Whisnant, C. S., T. E. Kiser, F. N. Thompson, and J. B. Hall. 1985. Effect of nutrition on the luteinizing hormone response to calf removal and gonadotropin releasing hormone. *Theriogenology* 24:565–74.

Whitaker, W. L. 1940. Some effects of artificial illumination on reproduction in the white-footed mouse *Peromyscus leucopus noveboracensis*. *J. Exp. Zool.* 83:33–60.

White, M. 1973. The whitetailed deer of the Aransas National Wildlife Refuge. *Tex. J. Sci.* 24:457–89.

Whitford, W. G. 1976. Temporal fluctuations in density and diversity of desert rodent populations. *J. Mammal.* 57:351–69.

Whitsett, J. M., A. D. Lawton, and L. L. Miller. 1984. Photosensitive stages in pubertal development of male deermice (*Peromyscus maniculatus*). *J. Reprod. Fert.* 72:269–76.

Whitsett, J. M., and L. L. Miller. 1985. Reproductive development in male deer mice exposed to aggressive behavior. *Dev. Psychobiol.* 18:287–90.

Whitten, P. L. 1983. Females, flowers and fertility. *Am. J. Phys. Anthro.* 60:269–70.

———. 1984. The relationship of diet to mating seasonality in wild vervet monkeys. *Am. J. Phys. Anthro.* 63:234.

Whitten, W. K. 1956. Modifications of the oestrus cycle of the mouse by external stimuli associated with the male. *J. Endocrinol.* 13:399–404.

———. 1959. Occurrence of anoestrus in mice caged in groups. *J. Endocrinol.* 18:102–7.

Wickler, S. J. 1981. Seasonal changes in enzymes of aerobic heat production in the white-footed mouse. *Am. J. Physiol.* 210:R289–R294.

Widdowson, E. M., W. O. Mavor, and R. A. McCance. 1964. The effect of undernutrition and rehabilitation on the development of the reproductive organs: Rats. *J. Endocrinol.* 29:119–26.

Wiggins, R. C. 1982. Myelin development and nutritional insufficiency. *Brain Res. Rev.* 4:151–75.

Wiggins, R. C., and G. N. Fuller. 1978. Early postnatal starvation causes lasting brain hypomyelination. *J. Neurochem.* 30:1231–37.

Wiggins, R. C., G. Fuller, and S. J. Enna. 1984. Undernutrition and the development of brain neurotransmitter systems. *Life Sci.* 35:2085–94.

Wight, H. M., and C. H. Conaway. 1961. Weather influences on the onset of breeding in Missouri cottontails. *J. Wildl. Mgmt.* 25:87–89.

Wildt, L., G. Marshall, and E. Knobil. 1980. Experimental induction of puberty in the infantile female rhesus monkey. *Science* 207:1373–75.

Wilen, R., and F. Naftolin. 1977. Pubertal food intake, body length, weight and composition in the well fed female rat. *Pediat. Res.* 11:701–3.

———. 1978. Pubertal food intake and body length, weight, and composition in the feed-restricted female rat: Comparison with well-fed animals. *Pediat. Res.* 12:263–67.

Williams, A. H., and I. A. Cumming. 1982. Inverse relationship between concentrations of progesterone and nutrition in ewes. *J. Agric. Sci.* 98:517–22.

Williams, H., and S. Ward. 1988. Melatonin and light treatment of ewes for autumn lambing. *Reprod. Nutr. Dév.* 28:423–30.

Williams, J. P. G., J. M. Tanner, and P. C. R. Hughes. 1974. Catch-up growth in female rats after growth retardation during suckling period: Comparison with males. *Pediat. Res.* 8:157–62.

Williams-Ashman, H. G. 1988. Perspectives in the male sexual physiology of eutherian mammals. In *The physiology of reproduction*, ed. E. Knobil and J. D. Neill, 727–51. New York: Raven.

Wilson, C. A., J. C. Buckingham, and I. D. Morris. 1985. Influence of growth hormone, corticosterone, corticotropin and changes in the environmental temperature on pituitary-ovarian function in the immature rat. *J. Endocrinol.* 104:179–83.

Wilson, C. A., M. B. ter Haar, R. C. Bonney, J. Buckingham, A. F. Dixson, and T. Yeo. 1983. Hormonal changes in the immature rat after administration of pregnant mare serum gonadotrophin: Influence of body weight. *J. Endocrinol.* 99:63–76.

Wilson, D. E. 1979. Reproductive patterns. In *Biology of bats of the New World family Phyllostomatidae*, pt. 3, ed. R. J. Baker, J. K. Jones, Jr., and D. C. Carter, Special Publication no. 10, pp. 1–441. Lubbock, Tex.: Texas Tech University Museum.

Wilson, J. M., and A. H. Meier. 1983. Tryptophan feeding induces sensitivity to short daylengths in photorefractory hamsters. *Neuroendocrinology* 36:59–63.

Wimsatt, W. A. 1960. Some problems of reproduction in relation to hibernation in bats. *Bull. Mus. Comp. Zool. Harv.* 124:249–63.

Wimsatt, W. A., and H. F. Parks. 1966. Ultrastructure of the surviving follicle of hibernation and of the ovum-follicle cell relationship in the Vespertilionid bat *Myotis lucifugus. Symp. Zool. Soc. Lond.* 15:419–54.

Withers, P. C. 1983. Seasonal reproduction by small mammals of the Namib South Africa. *Mammalia* 47:195–204.

Wolff, J. O. 1985. Comparative population ecology of *Peromyscus leucopus* and *Peromyscus maniculatus. Can. J. Zool.* 63:1548–55.

Wood, D. H. 1970. An ecological study of *Antechinus stuartii* (Marsupialia) in a southeast Queensland rain forest. *Austr. J. Zool.* 18:185–207.

Woodside, B., R. Wilson, P. Chee, and M. Leon. 1981. Resource partitioning during reproduction in the Norway rat. *Science* 211:76–77.

Woolley, P. A. 1984. Reproduction in *Antechinomys laniger* ("spenceri" form) (Marsupial:Dasyuridae): Field and laboratory observations. *Austr. Wildl. Res.* 11:481–89.

Wunder, B. A. 1978. Implications of a conceptual model for the allocation of energy resources by small mammals. In *Populations of small mammals under natural conditions*, ed. D. P. Snyder, Special Publications Series of the Pymatuning Laboratory of Ecology, Vol. 15, pp. 68–75. Linesville, Pa.: University of Pittsburgh.

———. 1984. Strategies for, and environmental cueing mechanisms of, seasonal changes in thermoregulatory parameters of small mammals. *Spec. Publ. Carn. Mus. Nat. Hist.* 10:165–72.

Wurtmann, R. J., E. L. Cohen, and J. D. Fernstrom. 1977. Control of brain neurotransmitter synthesis by precursor availability and food consumption. In *Neural regulators and psychiatric disorders*, ed. E. Usiden, D. A. Hamburg, and J. D. Barchasids, 103–21. New York: Oxford University Press.

Wynne-Edwards, K. E., and R. D. Lisk. 1984. Djungarian hamsters fail to conceive in the presence of multiple males. *Anim. Behav.* 32:626–28.

Wysocki, C., N. J. Bean, and G. K. Beauchamp. 1986. The mammalian vomeronasal system: Its role in learning and social behaviors. In *Chemical signals in vertebrates*, vol. 4, ed. D. Duvall, D. Muller Schwarze, and R. M. Silverstein, 471–85. New York: Plenum.

Yabe, T., and Y. Wada. 1983. Food habit and population changes of the roof rat *Rattus rattus* in sugarcane fields on Tokunoshima Island Japan. *Jap. J. Sanit. Zool.* 34:21–24.

Yamauchi, C., S. Fujita, T. Obara, and T. Ueda. 1983. Effects of room temperature on reproduction, body and organ weights, food and water intakes and hematology in mice. *Exp. Anim.* 32:1–12.

Yamazaki, K., G. K. Beauchamp, J. Bard, L. Thomas, and E. A. Boyse. 1982. Chemosensory recognition of phenotypes determined by the Tla and H-2K regions of chromosome 17 of the mouse. *Proc. Natl. Acad. Sci.* 79:7828–31.

Yamazaki, K., G. K. Beauchamp, C. J. Wysocki, J. Bard, L. Thomas, and E. A. Boyse. 1983. Recognition of H-2 types in relation to the blocking of pregnancy in mice. *Science* 221:186–88.

Yamazaki, K., G. K. Yamaguchi, L. Barnowski, J. Bard, E. A. Boyse, and L. Thomas. 1979. Recognition among mice: Evidence from the use of a Y-maze differentially scented by congenic mice of different major histocompatibility types. *J. Exp. Med.* 150:755–60.

Yasukawa, N. J., H. Monder, F. R. Leff, and J. J. Christian. 1985. Role of female behavior in controlling population growth in mice. *Aggr. Behav.* 11:49–64.

Yellon, S. M., E. L. Bittman, M. N. Lehman, D. H. Olster, J. E. Robinson, and F. J. Karsch. 1985. Importance of duration of nocturnal melatonin secretion in determining the reproductive response to inductive photoperiod in the ewe. *Biol. Reprod.* 32:523–29.

Yellon, S. M., and B. D. Goldman. 1984. Photoperiod control of reproductive development in the male Djungarian hamster (*Phodopus sungorus*). *Endocrinology* 114:664–70.

Yellon, S. M., L. Tamarkin, B. L. Pratt, and B. D. Goldman. 1982. Pineal melatonin in the Djungarian hamster: Photoperiodic regulation of circadian rhythm. *Endocrinology* 111:488–92.

Yen, S. S. C. 1986a. The human menstrual cycle. In *Reproductive endocrinology,* ed. S. S. C. Yen and R. B. Jaffe, 200–236. Philadelphia: W. B. Saunders.

———. 1986b. Neuroendocrine control of hypophyseal function: Physiological and clinical implications. In *Reproductive endocrinology,* ed. S. S. C. Yen and R. B. Jaffe, 34–74. Philadelphia: W. B. Saunders.

———. 1986c. Prolactin in human reproduction. In *Reproductive endocrinology,* ed. S. S. C. Yen and R. B. Jaffe, 237–63. Philadelphia: W. B. Saunders.

Yen, S. S. C., and R. B. Jaffe, eds. 1986. *Reproductive endocrinology.* Philadelphia: W. B. Saunders.

Yenikoye, A., and J.-P. Ravault. 1981. Circannual rhythms in the secretion of prolactin in the Peulh ewe. *C.R. Seances Acad. Sci.,* ser. 3, *Sci. Vie* 294:523–26.

Yodyingyaud, U., J. A. Eberhart, and E. T. Keverne. 1982. Effects of rank and novel females on behavior and hormones in male talapoin monkeys *Miopithecus talapoin. Physiol. Behav.* 28:995–1006.

Young, B. A. 1983. Ruminant cold stress: Effect on production. *J. Anim. Sci.* 1601–36.

Zamiri, M. J. 1978. Effects of reduced food intake on reproduction in mice. *Austr. J. Biol. Sci.* 31:629–39.

Zeuner, F. E. 1963. *A history of domesticated animals.* New York: Harper & Row.

Zucker, E., and J. A. Chapman. 1984. Morphological and physiological characteristics of muskrats from three different physiographic regions of Maryland USA. *Z. Saug.* 49:90–104.

Zucker, I. 1983. Motivation, biological clocks and temporal organization of behavior. In *Handbook of behavioral neurobiology,* vol. 6, ed. E. Satinoff and P. Teitelbaum, 3–21. New York: Plenum.

Zucker, I., and M. Boshes. 1982. Circannual body weight rhythms of ground squirrels: Role of gonadal hormones. *Am. J. Physiol.* 243:R546–R551.

Zucker, I., P. G. Johnston, and D. Frost. 1980. Comparative, physiological and biochronometric analyses of rodent seasonal reproductive cycles. *Prog. Reprod. Biol.* 5:102–33.

Zucker, I., and P. Licht. 1983. Circannual and seasonal variations in plasma luteinizing hormone levels of ovariectomized ground squirrels (*Spermophilus lateralis*). *Biol. Reprod.* 28:178–85.

Zuckerman, S. 1953. The breeding season of mammals in captivity. *Proc. Zool. Soc. Lond.* 122:827–950.

Index